Story

Hier findest du lustige und spannende Texte über die *friends* in Greenwich.

Action UK!

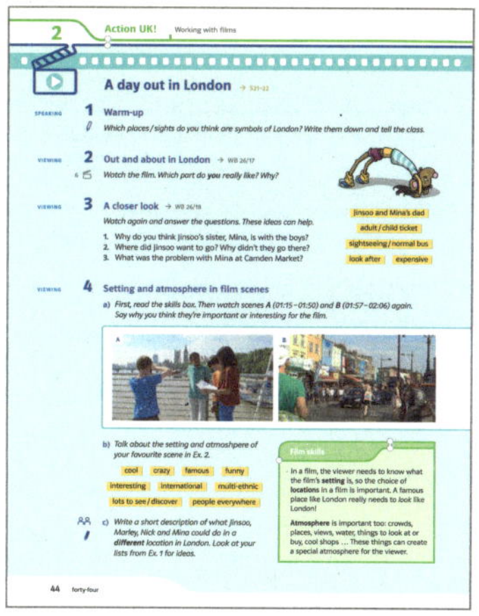

Und hier gibt es tolle Filme aus Greenwich!

Across cultures

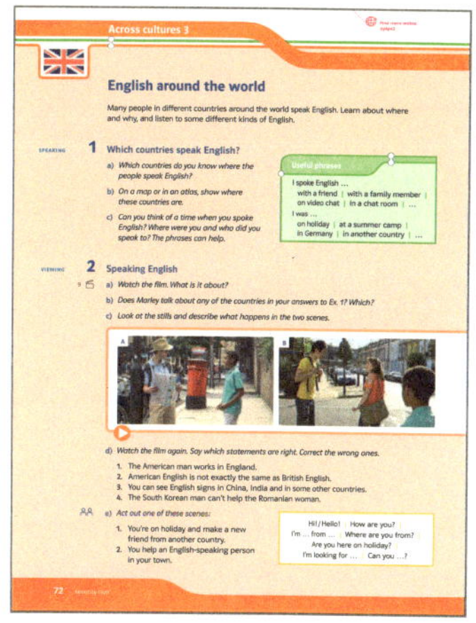

Vergleiche auf diesen Seiten deinen Alltag mit der Alltagskultur und der Geschichte Großbritanniens.

Diff pool

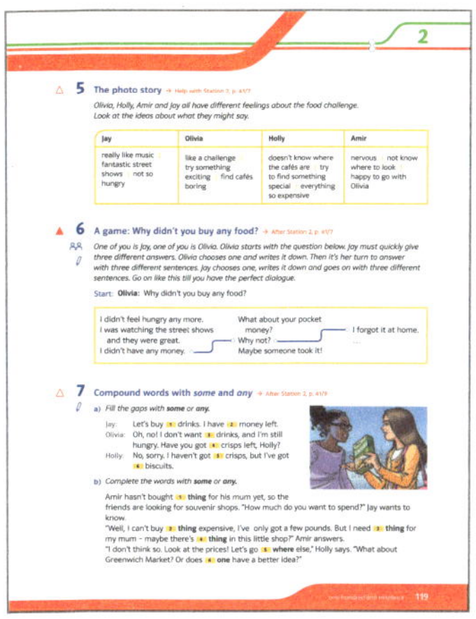

Skills

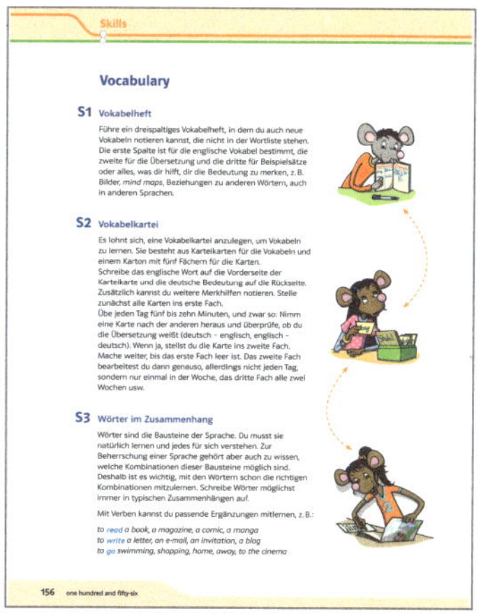

Grammar, Vocabulary

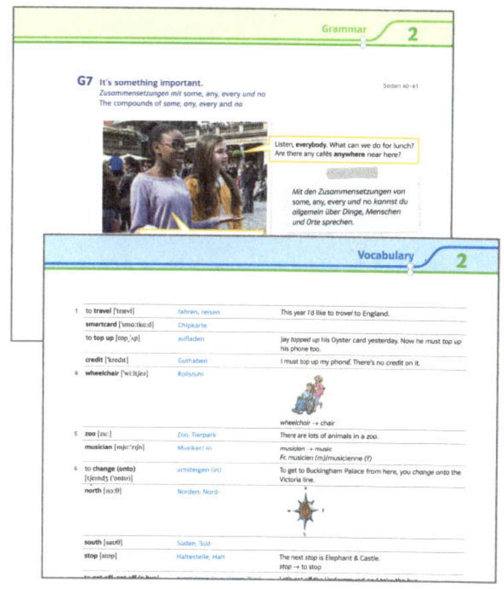

Im hinteren Buchteil stehen dir hilfreiche Anhänge zur Verfügung. *Diff pool, Grammar* und *Vocabulary* kennst du schon aus dem letzten Jahr. Neu ab Green Line 2 ist der *Skills*-Anhang. Hier findest du zu den Lernbereichen *Reading, Writing, Speaking, Listening, Viewing, Mediation* und *Vocabulary* allerlei Lernhilfen und Methodentipps. Die gelben Verweise → S17 bei den Unit-Aufgaben sagen dir, dass es sich lohnt, dort nachzuschlagen!

Symbole

→ △ 132/1	Verweis auf leichtere Aufgaben / Hilfen im Diff pool
→ ▲ 132/2	Verweis auf anspruchsvollere Aufgaben im Diff pool
→ WB 7/4	Verweis auf eine Übung im Workbook
→ G2	Verweis auf die Grammatik im Anhang
→ S2	Verweis auf die Skills im Anhang
	Partnerarbeit
	Gruppenarbeit
	Hier entsteht ein Produkt für dein Portfolio.
	Schreiben (geschlossen / einfach)
	Schreiben (offen / kreativ)
S1/14	Verweis auf die Schüler-CDs im Workbook (Audio)
L1/19	Verweis auf die Lehrer-CDs (Audio)
	Verweis auf die Lehrer-DVD (Film)
	Code auf www.klett.de eingeben und Zusatzmaterial nutzen
2	Übungen, die die Unit task besonders vorbereiten
	Across cultures

Green Line 2 für Klasse 6 an Gymnasien in Baden-Württemberg

Herausgeber: Harald Weisshaar, Bisingen

Autorinnen und Autoren: Marion Horner, Ipswich; Carolyn Jones, Beckenham; Jon Marks, Ventnor; Alison Wooder, Ventnor sowie Jennifer Baer-Engel, Göppingen; Paul Dennis, Lahnstein; Barbara Greive, Dortmund; Cornelia Kaminski, Fulda
unter Mitwirkung von Monique Kunhar, Schwaikheim; Manuela Moll, Eislingen

Beratung: Paul Dennis, Lahnstein; Cornelia Kaminski, Fulda; Nilgül Karabulut, Aachen; Hartmut Klose, Seevetal; Antje Körber, Merseburg; Jörg Nieswand, Berlin; Jörg Schulze, Dresden

Für besondere Unterstützung danken wir herzlich Ms Susan Bolton von der **Thomas Tallis School**, London.

Zusätzliche Informationen in der Lehrerausgabe:

Produktiver Lernwortschatz   Rezeptiver Wortschatz   Neue Grammatik

✿ Natürliche Differenzierung durch die offene Aufgabenform.

△→ ▲→ Help with/Instead of/After ...: Verweis auf unterstützende/alternative/weiterführende Aufgaben im Diff pool des Schülerbuchs für leistungsschwächere bzw. -stärkere Schüler/innen.

HA: Vorschlag zur Hausaufgabe

Transfer: Einbeziehung der Lebenswelt der Schüler/innen

Folie 1: Hier können Sie Folie 1 des Folienordners einsetzen.

WB 4/1: Hier können Sie im Workbook Seite 4, Aufgabe 1 einsetzen.

KV 1: Hier können Sie Kopiervorlage 1 des Lehrerbands einsetzen.

Voc.: Hier sind Verweise auf Wortschatzhilfen im Schülerbuch und Workbook (WB) angegeben.

Lösung: Hier finden Sie Lösungen und Lösungsvorschläge.

1. Auflage

1 5 4 3 2 1 | 2020 19 18 17 16

Redaktion: Michael Mattison; Anette Mohamud; Manuela Moll; Lektorat editoria: Cornelia Schaller, Fellbach sowie für die Lehrerfassung: Gaby Bauer-Negenborn, Weßling
Herstellung: Anita Bauch

Gestaltung: Petra Michel, Essen
Umschlaggestaltung: know idea, Freiburg; Koma Amok, Stuttgart
Illustrationen: Peer Kramer, Düsseldorf; jani lunablau, Barcelona *(Maskottchen und Story)* sowie Christian Dekelver, Weinstadt *(Karten)*
Satz: Satzkiste GmbH, Stuttgart; Mediengestaltung Elke Kurz, Waiblingen
Reproduktion: Schwaben-Repro, Stuttgart
Druck: PASSAVIA Druckservice GmbH & Co. KG, Passau

Printed in Germany
ISBN 978-3-12-834122-4

9 783128 341224

Green Line 2

Lehrerfassung

von
Marion Horner
Carolyn Jones
Jon Marks
Alison Wooder
Jennifer Baer-Engel
Paul Dennis
Barbara Greive
Cornelia Kaminski

herausgegeben von
Harald Weisshaar

Ernst Klett Verlag
Stuttgart · Leipzig

Inhalt

Legende

L	Listening	W	Writing	VOC	Vocabulary		Across cultures
S	Speaking	M	Mediation	SK	Skills	<>	Fakultativ
R	Reading	V	Viewing		Kompetenzaufgabe	R	Revision

Find more online: c736qm

Let's discover TTS!

Folie 7 Reaktivierung von Vorwissen und Wortschatzeinführung

There are quite a few differences between British and German schools – subjects, for example: At Thomas Tallis School, you can also take exams in Dance, Drama, Film studies or Fashion. And there's more than just lessons at British schools. In the afternoons, clubs offer a lot of additional activities like sports, birdwatching, cooking or games like chess. Learn more about TTS and British schools on these pages.

1 A wall painting in the school building

3 Assembly

2 Basketball Club

4 Sign Language Club

5 Dance class

SPEAKING

1 What you can do at TTS

KV 1: Guessing game (sign language)

ösung: a) *1B; 2D; 3A; 4E; 5C*

a) *Look at the <u>quotes</u> in the speech bubbles below. What are they about? Match them to the photos on the left.*

Lou

A We start school with our tutor at 8:30. Or sometimes we go to the <u>hall</u> for Assembly.

B This school is full of <u>art</u>!

C We practise a lot and we sometimes do shows.

D We love <u>competitions</u> against other schools – well, we love winning.

E Everyone is special and everyone <u>belongs</u> here. We all try to help students <u>with special needs</u>.

Transfer

b) *Now talk about what is the same or different at your school.*

c) *Your turn: What pictures can you use to present your school?*

LISTENING

2 This is a <u>fantastic</u> school!

KV 2: Listening (TTS)

L1/1

a) *Listen to Olivia. Who is she talking to? Take notes about the different parts of her presentation and say what each part is about.*

→ S18–20

S18-20 Listening

b) *Choose one of the quotes from A–E. Listen again. What <u>reactions</u> are there from the listeners after the part with that quote?*

Lösung: a) *Olivia is talking to younger students about TTS. Parts of her presentation: B: competitions; D: art; C: special needs; A: Assembly; E: shows*

Tony

LISTENING

3 New friends

L1/2

ösung: a) *Gwen needs livia's and Holly's help. he can't read her new time-able because the words are oo small.*
) Science, Technology, PE

a) *Gwen is a new girl at TTS. She's <u>partially sighted</u>. Listen to her conversation with Holly and Olivia. Why does Gwen need their help?*

Olivia

Holly

Gwen

b) *Listen again. Which subjects do they talk about? How can teachers and other students help Gwen?*

c) *Now that you know a lot about TTS, what do you think: Is it a fantastic school? Say why or why not.*

Transfer

d) *Your turn: Talk about how your school / your class helps students with special needs.*

VOCABULARY

4 School subjects: Gwen's timetable

KV 3: Mediation (Braille)

a) *Look at Gwen's timetable. Compare it with your timetable. The useful phrases can help you.*

Time	Monday	Tuesday	Wednesday	Thursday	Friday
08:30	**Registration**				
08:50	*Technology*	*Science*	*Maths*	*RE*	*English*
09:50	*Technology*	*Science*	*Maths*	*French*	*French*
10:50	**Break**				
11:10	*Maths*	*Art*	*Science*	*English*	*Humanities*
12:10	*English*	*Music*	*Technology*	*Geography*	*Humanities*
13:10	**Lunch**				
14:00	*Dance*	*English*	*PE*	*Maths*	*Dance*
15:00	**Registration in tutor group / Assembly**				
15:10	**Home / Clubs**				

Voc.: Subjects at school, p. 166

Useful phrases

Our school day starts at 7:30 / …
We have … lessons in the afternoon / every day / only on Mondays / Tuesdays / …
There's a break at …
Lunch is from … till …

Gwen and I have the same subjects, but I also have lessons in …
In Maths / History / RE / … we learn / talk about … / we often work on projects.
We have / don't have lots of clubs / activities / … in the afternoon

Transfer

b) *Write your own timetable in English.*

c) *Your turn: Look at the pictures. Say which subjects they show. Then talk about which subjects you like best and why.*

1

2

3

4

5

WRITING

5 The TTS Eco Club → WB 2/1–2

KV 4: Peer evaluation (flyer)
WB 2/1 Vocabulary (crossword puzzle)
WB 2/2 Activity (game)

a) *Holly's favourite club at TTS is the Eco Club. Look at a flyer for that club. Would you like to join it? Say why or why not.*

b) *Read the skills box. Choose **one** of the clubs on the right. Write and design a flyer for it.*

Maths Club | Singing Club | Tallis TV | Football Club | Science Club

c) *Exchange your flyers with another pair of students and peer-edit each other's work.*

Writing skills

When you write a flyer make sure that
- it's easy to read
- it has all the important information about your club:
  the **name** of the club
  what you do
  when you meet (day and time)
  where you meet
  why people should join your club
- you welcome people with a special **welcome message** and a **slogan**!

VIEWING

6 The film star

2

Drama is one of the most interesting classes at TTS. It's fun! But not always, as Laura finds out.

ösung: Laura wants to
in an acting workshop at
hakespeare's Globe Theatre.
er problem is that she
rgets her lines when she is in a room full of people.

Watch the film. Say what Laura wants to win. Explain what her problem is.

VIEWING

7 Good advice?

Folie 10: Writing (thought bubbles)
KV 5: Viewing (advice for an actor)

ösung: a) The teacher:
ou need to practise a bit
ore and try again next
eek. Marley: Believe in
ourself. Jinsoo: You're
ways so confident. (Be
ore confident now.) Polly
IcCane: Don't worry. It /
orgetting your lines
appens all the time. Don't
anic. Take a deep breath.
elax. Act as if it was all
art of the scene and that
ill give you time to
member your lines.

a) *Watch (01:38–04:00) again. What advice do people give Laura? Take notes.*

b) *Talk about the advice for Laura. Here are some ideas:*

A: Polly is a star, so she knows best!
B: Well Marley isn't an actor but *his* advice is great too: "Believe in yourself".

c) *Look at the still (04:35). What is Laura thinking at this moment in the film? Look at the phrases for help.*

d) *Now watch the rest of the film. Explain why Laura thanks Polly.*

Useful phrases

Don't panic! | Don't be nervous! | Just relax! | I'm sure you're good at … | You're always so confident. | Try again. | Take a deep breath. | Believe in yourself!

Find more online: [illegible]

Unit 1

My friends and I

Your classmates – CAUGHT ON CAMERA!

Jay, don't you know that embarrassing outfits always end up in the yearbook? LOL! :)

Dave, Olivia and Luke after a round of boxing. Ouch, those red noses! Oh, wait – it's Red Nose Day, of course! (Nice cake, mmm…)

Folie 1: Bildbeschreibung und Sicherung des Hörverstehens

SPEAKING

1 Talk about the yearbook photos

What can you see? Where are the girls and boys? What do you think they're doing or saying?

LISTENING

2 Caught on camera

L 1/3

a) *Listen to the dialogues. Which photo are the characters talking about? (There is no dialogue for one of the photos.)*

→ S18–20

S18–20 Listening

Lösung: a) *1 C, 2 A, 3 D (There is no dialogue for B.)*

b) *Listen again and then answer the questions.*

1. How does Jay feel about the photo of himself and Holly? 2. Which two characters are on the yearbook team? 3. Who is doing which pages in the yearbook? 4. Why does Holly like the photo of the three boys?

In Unit 1 you learn

… how to talk about special activities in the past and how to give information about places. You learn:

- words about feelings
- the simple past
- words and phrases that describe and compare

The eyes say it all for lovebirds Holly and Jay. (The camera never lies!)

Luke, Dave and Jay are practising for the class trip. Hey guys, we know that you're funny – but now we know that you're silly too!

KV 1: Speaking (feelings)
WB 2/1: Vocabulary (feelings)
WB 2/2: Vocabulary (Thomas Tallis School yearbook)

SPEAKING

3 Feelings → WB 3/1–2

happy | shy | excited | embarrassed | proud

a) *Take turns to act different feelings. Can the others guess your word?*

b) *Look at the photos again. Say how you think the characters feel and why.*

Voc.: Describing a person's character, p. 168

Example: Photo D: I think Dave feels happy because he's having fun with his friends.

→ △ 114/1

c) *Make a mind map for 'feelings'. Add new words to your personal vocabulary.*

114/1 F eelings
△ → Help with …

Across cultures

Yearbooks are an American tradition, but now they are popular in British schools too. Students on a yearbook team work together to make a fun book for their class, with photos of students and reports about activities during the school year. How do you collect the highlights in the school year?

L1/4

I love Red Nose Day

KV 2: Listening (Red Nose Day)

YES, IT'S RED NOSE TIME AGAIN!

RED NOSE DAY
DO SOMETHING FUNNY FOR MONEY

Here at TTS we always do our best for COMIC RELIEF. Two years ago we raised lots of money, but this year let's raise even more! Check the TTS website for more information.

COMIC RELIEF is a great charity. It helps people in need in Africa and also the UK. The comedian Lenny Henry started Comic Relief – that's how it got its name – and on the first Red Nose Day in 1988 people wore red noses, did fun activities to raise money and watched a big comedy show on TV. That was many years ago, but today we still do the same things!

I love Red Nose Day. So when I saw the poster on the school noticeboard last month I felt really excited. My friends and I had lots of crazy ideas about how to raise money. In the end we made and sold cakes with funny faces. After school we went into Greenwich and did our own comedy show in the street. Luke's dog Sherlock was a real star, and lots of people gave us money for the TTS collection. It was great fun! I can't wait till next time.

Olivia Fraser

READING

1 Charity work: Olivia and her friends

→ ▲ 114/2

114/2 Charity work ▲→ After …

Look at what Olivia writes about Red Nose Day. What things sound fun to you?

Across cultures

People in the UK often help **charities**. What charities in Germany do you know about?

LANGUAGE

2 Irregular simple past forms → WB 4/3 → G1

WB 4/3 Listening (Comic Relief)

Lösung: a) *be, was/were; do, did; feel, felt; get, got; give, gave; go, went; have, had; make, made; see, saw; sell, sold; wear, wore*

a) *Look again at Olivia's text and find the past forms of these verbs. Make a list.*

be ✔ do ✔ feel get give go have make see sell wear

Verb	Past form
be do feel	was / were did …

There are no rules for irregular past forms. You must learn them by heart.

Lou

→ △ 114/3

114/3 Irregular simple past forms △→ Instead of …

HA

b) *Put in the correct past forms. (The list of irregular verbs on page 246 can help you.)*

Two years ago the students 1 (do) fun activities and 2 (get) money for Comic Relief. They 3 (bring) the money to school. Then the school 4 (put) all the money together and 5 (give) it to the charity. Red Nose Day 6 (be) a non-uniform day, so everyone 7 (come) to school in different clothes. But they all 8 (wear) something red. Of course they all 9 (have) red noses too. Some students 10 (take) funny photos for the school website.

Lösung: b) 1. *did* 2. *got* 3. *brought* 4. *put* 5. *gave* 6. *was* 7. *came* 8. *wore* 9. *had* 10. *took*

LANGUAGE

3 Find the rule: Regular simple past forms

a) *Look at the example. Find the rule for regular past forms and write it down.*

Example: Lenny Henry **started** Comic Relief in 1988. Last time we **raised** lots of money. In the evening we **watched** the big TV show.

L1/6

→ △ 115/4

15/4 Sounds
→ After ...
14 Speaking (Sprechen üben)

b) *Be careful how you say* ***-ed***. *There are three different sounds. Listen and say:*

1. [d] Two years ago we organis**ed** a great Red Nose Day. I lov**ed** it. We plann**ed** lots of activities.
2. [t] First we help**ed** to raise money. Then we watch**ed** TV. I lik**ed** Lenny Henry's jokes!
3. [ɪd] I want**ed** to look funny so I paint**ed** my face. I need**ed** a red nose too, of course.

LANGUAGE

4 The friends' comedy show

→ WB 4/4–5

WB 4/4 Language (school website)
WB 4/5 Language (Interview)

oc.: Clothes, Word
ank (WB), p. 13

Look at the picture and write 5–6 sentences about the comedy show. Choose from these verbs and use the simple past.

play ✓do
chase watch collect
dance laugh act

Example: The friends did the comedy show after school.

ösung: EH: *Olivia played e saxophone. Jay and ıke acted as clowns. Luke ıased Jay with a big toy ammer. A lot of people atched the comedy show. olly collected money. herlock danced and chased 's tail. The people laughed ecause the comedy show as funny.*

LANGUAGE

5 The star of the show

→ WB 5/6, 6/7

WB 5/6 Language (Red Nose Day)
WB 6/7 Pronunciation (code)

→ △ 115/5

5/5 The star of the show
→ Instead of ...

What does Sherlock tell his dog friends the next day? Write the text again in his words, with the verbs in the simple past. Check if the forms are regular or irregular.

Start: I **did** lots of great tricks in the comedy show yesterday.

Sherlock *does* lots of great tricks in the comedy show. First he *jumps* over a big box. Then he *runs* around and *chases* his tail. After that he *dances* on a skateboard, and when Olivia *starts* to play the sax he also *sings*. The people *love* it. They *laugh* and *clap* and *give* lots of money for Comic Relief. Luke and his friends *try* to do their best too but everyone's eyes *are* on Sherlock. He *feels* happy and proud – he *is* the real star of the show!

Look at G1 on page 144. You must be careful with the spelling of some regular forms.

Lösung: *First I jumped over a big box. Then I ran around and chased my tail. After that I danced on a skateboard, and when Olivia started to play the sax I also sang. The people loved it. They laughed and clapped and gave lots of money to Comic Relief. Luke and his friends tried to do their best too, but everybody's eyes were on me. I felt happy and proud – I was the real star of the show!*

SPEAKING

6 Play a game: Something funny for money

People often pay money when you do funny or hard activities for charity. Take turns to say what you did on Red Nose Day. Roll two dice, for an activity and a comment.

Lou

Example: 2 + 5 I went everywhere in pyjamas. I enjoyed the day.

Activities	Comments
1 turn off my phone for the day	1 have lots of fun
2 go everywhere in pyjamas	2 find that hard
3 swim for 30 minutes	3 feel great
4 eat baby food	4 do my best
5 try not to laugh all day	5 enjoy the day
6 speak in a funny voice	6 raise lots of money

If you like, you can think of new ideas for activities and comments.

WRITING

Transfer → △ 115/6

HA

115/6 A report about a special activity △→ Help with …

7 Your turn: A report about a special activity

KV 3: Peer evaluation (report)

Write a report about an activity that you did with your friends or family. Write 6–8 sentences.

Example: Last year my friends and I helped to tidy a park. We …

Useful phrases

When? Last week / A month ago / In July / …
Who? My friends and I / My dad / …
What? We did a project / show … | We organised a … / made … / helped …
Feelings? It was fun / I felt happy / nervous / proud / …

MEDIATION

8 A flyer in a German classroom

KV 4: Skills (mediation)

→ S17

S17 Mediation

Answer a British student's questions.

1. I know 'groß', so I can see this flyer is about something big. But what is it?
2. Who wants to sell cakes? And why?
3. Is the sale here in the school building?
4. 10th October – that's the date of your sale, right?
5. What's this about Africa?

Lösung: 1. *We're planning a big cake sale.* 2. *We are a German tutor group. We need money for our class trip.* 3. *There's no information about that in the text.* 4. *The date of the cake sale is not in the text. October 10th is the date when we meet to plan it.* 5. *Last year we collected a lot of money for an African school.*

Mediation skills

A **quick answer** helps to keep the conversation going.

Don't worry **if the answer isn't in the text**. Just say there's no information.

GROSSER KUCHENVERKAUF

++ Wichtige Ankündigung! ++

Wir brauchen noch Geld für unsere Klassenfahrt. Deshalb planen wir einen großen Kuchenverkauf. (Erinnert ihr euch? Letztes Jahr haben wir auf diese Weise viel Geld für eine Schule in Afrika gesammelt.) Lasst uns also bald wieder in der Küche fleißig werden und viele leckere Kuchen backen!
Um zu besprechen, wann unser Kuchenverkauf stattfindet und wer was macht, treffen wir uns am 10. Oktober in der ersten Unterrichtsstunde. Merkt euch bitte dieses Datum – und bringt viele Ideen mit!

Folie 2: Bildbeschreibung und Unterstützung des Hörverstehens

L 1/7

How did they know?

Luke: Only ten days till our class trip! I can't wait!
Dave: Sit down and help us, Luke! It's our group's job to think of games to play on the coach.
Luke: Hey, what about puzzle stories?
Holly: I don't know that game. How do you play it?
Dave: I know it! Great idea, Luke. Someone tells a little story with missing information. Then the others ask questions to try and find the solution. Here's a puzzle story for you …

> After an anonymous phone call the police went to an address to arrest a dangerous man. They didn't know what the man looked like. They only knew that his name was John and that he was at that address. When they got to the house they found four people at a table in the kitchen: a taxi driver, a mechanic, a farmer and a postman. The police didn't ask any questions and the other people didn't say anything, but right away the police arrested the postman. How did they know that they had the right person? Why were they so sure?

Luke: Did the police really arrest the right person? — Dave: Yes, they did.
Luke: Were there any photos of the man? — Dave: No, there weren't.
Holly: Did the postman try to run away? — Dave: No, he didn't.
Luke: Did the other people help the police? — Dave: No, they didn't.
Holly: Was it the man's home? — Dave: I don't know. But that isn't important.
Luke: Was the man's name a clue? — Dave: Yes, it was.

→ Solution on p. 19

SPEAKING

9 Talk about games

Do you like guessing games? What ideas have you got for games on a coach trip?

WB 6/8 Language (short answers)

LANGUAGE

10 Ask and answer questions about the puzzle story

→ WB 6/8 → G2–3

1. Did the phone call help the police?
2. Was the man's name Peter?
3. Did the police ask any questions?
4. Was the man dangerous?
5. Were the four people in the kitchen?
6. Were the other people postmen too?

Yes,	he it they	was. were. did.
No,		wasn't. weren't. didn't.

sung: 1. Yes, it did. 2. No, wasn't. The man's name as John. 3. No, they didn't. ey arrested the postman ht away. 4. Yes, he was. Yes, they were. 6. No, they eren't. There was a taxi iver, a mechanic and a rmer.

KV 5: Language (find the rule)

LANGUAGE 11

Find the rule: Differences between present and past → G2–3

*Look at the sentences in the present and the past. What are the differences for **questions** and **negative sentences**? Write down the rule.*

Simple present	Simple past
Do you like the story? What does she say? I don't know the game. He doesn't want to play.	Did you like the story? What did she say? I didn't know the game. He didn't want to play.

LANGUAGE 12

Guess what we did

→ △ 116/7
→ ▲ 116/8

116/7 What they didn't do and what they did
△→ After …
116/8 A perfect day
▲→ After …

Think of a fun activity that you and a friend did on a coach. (It needn't be true.) Your partner guesses what you did.

Example:
Did you tell puzzle stories? – No, we didn't.
Did you count all the red cars? – No, we didn't.
Did you send funny texts? – Yes, we did!

WB 6/9 Language (negating statements)

LANGUAGE 13

Problems on the coach → WB 6/9

Lösung: 1. *I wasn't happy because my best friend didn't sit next to me.* 2. *I helped a girl with her bag but she didn't say thank you.* 3. *It was very loud on the coach so some people didn't hear our puzzle stories.* 4. *The driver was friendly but he didn't speak much English.* 5. *I needed the toilet but the coach didn't stop.* 6. *The coach was slow so we didn't get there till late.*

*Complete the sentences. Use **didn't**.*

Example: I felt hungry but I (not have any food) → … but I didn't have any food.

1. I wasn't happy because my best friend (not sit next to me)
2. I helped a girl with her bag but she (not say thank you)
3. It was very loud on the coach so some people (not hear our puzzle stories)
4. The driver was friendly but he (not speak much English)
5. I needed the toilet but the coach (not stop)
6. The coach was slow so we (not get there till late)

KV 6: Placemat (questions and answers)
WB 7/10 Language (a trip to Oxford)
WB 7/11 Speaking (a special day)

LANGUAGE 14

Make fun questions and answers → WB 7/10–11 → G2

a) *Work in groups of three or four. Think of six fun questions. Start with question words and use the simple past. Write each question on a piece of paper.*

How? Why? What? Where?
Who? laugh? get? see?
be? meet? …?

Examples:
What did you find in your schoolbag?
Why were you in a tree all day?

b) *Swap questions with another group and write funny answers to their questions.*

c) *With the other group, look at all the questions and answers. Choose the three best ideas and read them to the class.*

SPEAKING

15 Revision: Who am I?

→ WB 8/12

WB 8/12 Mediation (a game)

Think of a famous person. It can be a real person (e.g. singer, sports star) or a character from a film or book. Your partner must guess who you are.

Example:

Are you a real person? – No, I'm not.
Can I see you in a film? – Yes, you can.
Is the film a comedy? – No, it isn't.
Do you do dangerous things? – Yes, I do.
Does Daniel Craig act your role? – Yes, he does.
I know! You're James Bond. – Yes, that's right.

You can only ask questions with yes/no answers.
Are you …? Have you got …?
Do/Does …? Is …? …?

LISTENING

16 Luke's dream

Folie 3: Bildbeschreibung und Unterstützung des Hörverstehens

L 1/8

→ S18–20

S18–20 Listening

ösung: a) Picture C is wrong ecause Luke doesn't go by boat. orrect order: D, A, E, F, B. 1. When Luke tried to put his ings in a bag, Sherlock pulled em out again. So he was late. Luke was horrified. He shout-d, but the coach didn't stop. There was a police car near e school, so Luke jumped in e car and asked the police for elp. 4. The police got a phone ll about a man they wanted to rest. 5. Luke found out it was a ain for Greenwich – the wrong ay for him. 6. In the past he as a really fast horse. He won ts of prizes. (But he wasn't ery fast any more because e was too old. And after short time he was dog-ed.) 7. Luke didn't have me to find out the end of e dream. Suddenly it was ven o'clock in the morning ad time to get up.

a) *Listen and find five pictures for Luke's dream. (One picture is wrong.) Put the five pictures in the correct order.*

b) *Listen again and answer the questions.*

1. What was Luke's problem with Sherlock? 2. How did Luke feel when the coach went without him? 3. Who did Luke ask for help first? 4. Why were the police suddenly too busy to help Luke? 5. Why didn't Luke stay on the train? 6. What did Luke find out about the horse in the past? 7. Why didn't Luke find out the end of his dream?

WRITING

17 Your turn: Your puzzle story

Transfer

HA

Write your own short puzzle story (5–6 sentences).
You can use your own idea or maybe you already know a story like this.
Can your friends guess the solution?

Solution to the puzzle story on page 17: There was only one man in the house – the postman. The other people were all women.

G4 Comparison of adjectives

L 1/9

Everyone can enjoy a challenge

Folie 4: Semantisierung des Wortschatzes zur Vorentlastung

Home | About us | Courses | Activities | Events

Ty'n y Berth is an outdoor centre near Snowdonia National Park in Wales. With its mountains, forests and lakes, Wales is great for outdoor activities. We organise adventure courses for school groups. We believe our activities are as important as lessons in the classroom. A course at TYB is not only the most exciting project of the year for students – it also helps them to learn new skills, to work in a team and to be more confident.

Some of the most popular adventures are mountain walking, climbing and gorge scrambling. Younger students do easier routes than older students, but everyone can enjoy a challenge – the hardest challenges are often the favourite activities. There is always something exciting to do, even in the worst weather. That's why at Ty'n y Berth you can see the happiest smiles in Wales!

Voc.: Outdoor activities, p. 171, Landscape, Word bank (WB), p. 12

SPEAKING

18 Talk about the outdoor centre

a) *Close your books. Say what you remember about Wales and the outdoor centre.*

b) *Would you like to go there? What looks fun or interesting to you?*

Transfer

c) *Your turn: Tell the class about a time when you had a challenge.*

Across cultures

Wales is an important part of the UK, but it's also a separate country with its own Celtic culture. Many people there speak two languages, English and Welsh. Ty'n y Berth is a Welsh name. You say it like this: [ti:n‿ə 'bɜ:θ]

LANGUAGE

19 Find the rule: Comparative and superlative forms → G4

Lösung: a)+b) *hard, harder, hardest; big, bigger, biggest; easy, easier, easiest; popular, more popular, most popular; confident, more confident, most confident; bad, worse, worst; young, younger, youngest; old, older, oldest; happy, happier, happiest*

a) *Copy and complete the grid. Look in the text for the missing forms.*

b) *Collect more examples from the text and add them to the grid.*

c) *Write down the rule for comparative and superlative forms of adjectives.*

adjective	comparative	superlative
hard	harder	…
big	…	biggest
easy	…	easiest
popular	more popular	…
confident	…	most confident
bad	worse	…
…	…	…

Lösung: a) *proud, prouder, proudest; good, better, best; interesting, more interesting, most interesting; funny, funnier, funniest; dangerous, more dangerous, most dangerous; quiet, more quiet, most quiet; brave, braver, bravest; excited, more excited, most excited*

LANGUAGE **20**

Practise the new forms

a) *Say the comparative and superlative forms of these adjectives.*

proud | good | interesting | funny | dangerous | quiet | brave | excited

→ △ 116/9

16/9 The new forms
→ After …

b) *What do you think about these things? Compare your ideas.*

Example: A: I think mountain walking is the **most exciting** outdoor activity.
B: Oh, I think climbing is **more exciting than** mountain walking.

exciting outdoor activity | good place for a holiday | interesting hobby | (any more ideas?)

WB 8/13 Listening (phone call)
WB 9/14 Language (e-mail from Wales)
WB 9/15 Language (dog school)

LANGUAGE **21**

Say it in different words → WB 8/13, 9/14–15 → G5

→ △ 117/10

7/10 Say what's different
→ Instead of …

Use a different adjective and a different form.

Example: 1. Wales is **smaller than** England.

ösung: 1. *Wales is smaller than England. 2. The weather today is worse than yesterday. 3. Route B is easier than Route A. 4. The courses aren't as expensive as most people think. 5. I'm not as nervous as I was about new challenges.*

1. Wales isn't as big as England. (small)
2. The weather today isn't as good as yesterday. (bad)
3. Route A is harder than route B. (easy)
4. The courses are cheaper than most people think. (expensive)
5. I'm more confident than I was about new challenges. (nervous)

Be careful with **than** and **as**. When do you use which word?
younger **than** = **not as** old **as**

Tony

KV 7a+b: Language (St Dwynwen's Day)
WB 9/16 Writing (e-mail)

VOCABULARY **22**

Find adjectives to describe what you can see → WB 9/16

Folie 5: Bildbeschreibung (adjectives)

Take turns to describe. Use comparative or superlative forms or '(not) as … as …'

→ △ 117/11
→ ▲ 117/12

7/11 Who's the tallest?
→ After …
7/12 The best thing ever
→ After …

oc.: Comparing things, 171

fast | small | low | big | slow | tall | high

S1/3–7
L1/11–15

It was amazing

This text and the exercises help with the Unit task on pages 26–27.

1 Before you read

→ S5–6, 8

Look only at the words in blue in part A of the text. What do you think the text is about? Collect ideas.

S5–6, 8 Reading (Schnelllesetechniken, wichtige Inhalte herausfiltern, Markierungen und Notizen)

Dave Preston's report for the class yearbook:

A It was a trip to a different planet! We came from a place with busy streets and shops and lots of people, but in this new place there were only mountains and lakes and lots of sheep …

Everyone on the coach was excited when we started our class trip to the Ty'n y Berth Outdoor Centre that Saturday morning. Even our teacher Mr Swindon was excited. "Who wants to go to Wales?" he shouted. "We all do!" we shouted back.

It was a long way from Greenwich, but we played games and ate our sandwiches, and when at last we saw the big sign "Croeso i Gymru" we all clapped. Now the roads were quieter. Everything looked green and the villages and farms had strange Welsh names. Soon we were in the mountains.

B At last the coach stopped in front of an old grey building next to fields and trees. Lots of the buildings in Wales are grey.

A man with a friendly face met us at the door of the building. "Welcome to Ty'n y Berth, everyone!" he said with a smile. "I'm Will, one of the instructors at the centre. And this is your home for the next few days."

Years ago it was a village school. But now it's all different inside. The biggest room is for meals and free time activities, and most of the smaller rooms are bedrooms for people on courses at the centre.

I was in a bedroom with five other boys. Right away there was a problem because Luke and Jay wanted the same bed near the window. "Maybe you can take turns," I said. They thought that was a good solution, and Luke slept in the bed first. For all of us that night it felt a bit strange to be in a new place without our families.

C Most of the time at Ty'n y Berth we were too busy to think of home. Every morning and afternoon there were new and exciting activities to try. Then in the evening we usually played games.

Everyone loved gorge scrambling. It was funny when Olivia, Holly and I tried to help each other to get across a little river. In the end we just helped each other to fall *into* it. The water in mountain rivers is very cold!

We all found some activities harder than others. For me, climbing was the greatest challenge. But our instructor Ceri was great. She gave me lots of tips, and then I felt more confident.

Late one evening there was a surprise. Will gave everyone a torch and we went for a walk in the dark. "Don't talk, just listen," Will said. So we listened and it was amazing because it was so very quiet. In Greenwich there's always noise, even at night. Then we all turned off our torches and that was amazing too. It was much darker than in London so the stars looked much bigger and clearer.

D Too soon it was the last day, but when we went to bed Luke whispered to me, “I’ve got a torch so let’s go for a night walk again. Just you, Jay and me.” We knew it was against the rules, but we wanted one last adventure. We waited till the others were asleep. Then, as quiet as mice, we tiptoed from the bedroom.

It was very dark outside, but with Luke’s torch we found our way across a field and through some trees. Then Luke turned off the torch. Well, I thought he did, and I didn’t know why. “Er, Luke – it’s a cloudy night so we can’t look at the stars, you know. I can’t even see you,” Jay said. “I know,” Luke’s voice answered. “The torch needs a new battery.”

Oh no! Now we had a problem. The night was as black as – well, as black as night. We tried to be cool but we didn’t feel it. Which was the way back to the centre? We had no idea. We started to walk. We just hoped it was the right way. Then suddenly – “Hoo-hoo!” What was that? The strange noise made us nervous. “Hoo-hoo!” It was nearer now. What was it? We started to run, but in the dark it was dangerous. Jay fell over something. “Help! It’s moving! It’s a monster!” he

shouted. We tried to run away together. Something awful hit my face and I shouted too. We were really scared. It was crazy. I don’t know how we got back to the centre again. We were so happy to see that old grey building. We tiptoed to the door and – oh no, the door was locked! What now? We didn’t want trouble, but we needed to get back to our beds. How did we do it? That’s a secret.

E Early the next morning the coach came to take us back to Greenwich. We were sad to say goodbye to Wales, but we’ve all got great memories of our amazing class trip. (And now everyone knows why Luke, Jay and I were tired and slept all the way home!)

WB10/17 Reading (Wales)
WB10/18 Reading (city vs. country life)

READING

2 Questions about the text → WB 10/17–18

a) *Take turns to ask and answer questions about Dave’s report.*

sung: a) 2. *How did every-e get to Ty’n y Berth? – ey got there by coach. Where did the boys and rls eat their meals? – They e their meals in the biggest om of the old village school. Why did Luke and Jay want e same bed? – They wanted e same bed because it was ar the window. 5. What d the students do on the urse? – Every morning and ternoon there were new d exciting activities – like rge scrambling or climbing. c.*

Example: Where did the students go for their class trip? – They went to Wales.

What …?	the students / go for their class trip	Dave / find the hardest challenge
Why …?	everyone / get to Ty’n y Berth	the stars / look so big and clear
Where …?	the girls and boys / eat their meals	the three boys / go for a night walk
How …?	Luke and Jay / want the same bed	Luke’s torch / need?
When …?	the students / do on the course	(*your own idea for questions?*)

b) *Something to think about: What do you think these things were?*

1. the “hoo-hoo” noise (line 97) 2. the monster (line 102) 3. something awful (line 104)

Lösungsvorschlag: b) *1. an owl; 2. a snake or another animal; 3. a part of a tree*

KV 8: Peer evaluation (role play)
WB 10/19 Reading/Writing (options)

SPEAKING **3** **The secret** → WB 10/19

a) *In the report Dave doesn't say how he, Luke and Jay got back to their beds. How do you think they did this? What ideas have you got?*

→ S16 b) *Role play: Work in groups. Think of an ending and write a short scene. Act your scene for the class.*
→ △ 117/13

S16 Speaking (Mündliche Aufgaben und ihre Besonderheiten)
117/13 The secret △→ Help with …

WRITING **4** **How to: Plan a travel report** KV 9: Writing (travel report)

→ S7

S7 Reading (Gliederung als Hilfe)

a) *In one or two sentences say what each of the five parts of the report (A–E) is about.*

Start: Part A is about how the students got from Greenwich to Wales.

b) *Find two or three key phrases in each part that can make good headings for that part.*

Example: Part A: Our class trip – A long way from Greenwich – Croeso i Gymru

S10–13 Writing
→ S10–13

c) *Use your ideas from a) and b) to make Dave's plan for his report. Use a grid to show the five parts and the main ideas in each part.*

Part	Main ideas
A	class trip – from Greenwich to Wales – long way
B	

Lösung: a) *Part B is about the outdoor centre and the boys' bedroom. Part C is about the activities at Ty'n y Berth and a surprise: a walk in the dark under the Welsh stars. Part D is about the last day and the boys' idea to go for another night walk. Part E is about the morning when the coach came and the class trip ended.*
b) *Part B: Welcome to Ty'n y Berth – the rooms – the bed near the window; Part C: exciting activities – challenges – a surprise; Part D: Luke's idea – as black as night – back to the centre; Part E: Goodbye Wales – amazing memories*

Writing skills

Always **make a plan** for a text. A good plan shows how many **parts** the text has got and also the main ideas in each part.

Try to **make your text interesting** for the reader. Think of a special way to start the text. Choose good words and phrases that help the reader to see and feel what you describe.

VOCABULARY **5** **How to: Make a travel report interesting**

→ S13

S13 Writing (Sprachliche Verbesserungen)

a) *Talk about the first sentence of Dave's report. Do you think this is a good way to start a travel report? Why/why not?*

b) *A travel report needs different kinds of words and phrases. Look at the lists below and find more examples in Dave's report. (Some examples can go in more than one list.)*

1. words that explain 'when': that Saturday morning (line 9) – at last (line 22) – …
2. words that describe places: everything looked green (line 18) – busy streets (line 3) – …
3. words that show feelings: excited (line 11) – we all clapped (line 17) – …
4. words that make a text exciting: a different planet! (line 2) – Oh no! (line 91) – …

How to use a dictionary

Think! Do you really need a dictionary? What do you do first when you see a new English word? What do you do if you don't know how to translate a German word into English?

1 Talk about different kinds of dictionaries

ösung: a) *Online: B, C, D, E;*
a book: A, C, E; in an elec-
onic dictionary: B, C, D, E

a) *Match A–E to the right kind of dictionary. (Some sentences are correct for all three kinds.)*

Online … | In a book … | In an electronic dictionary …

A. the words are in a list in alphabetical order.
B. you write in the search box to look up a word.
C. you can see the different meanings of the word.
D. you can hear the word's pronunciation.
E. there are two parts: first words in one language and then words in the other language.

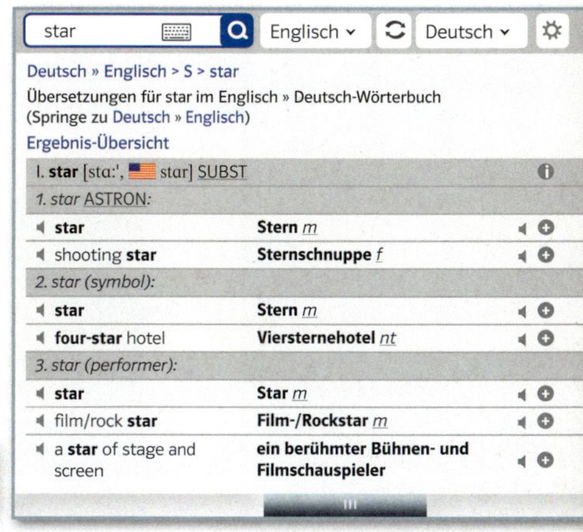

star | Englisch | Deutsch

Deutsch » Englisch > S > star
Übersetzungen für star im Englisch » Deutsch-Wörterbuch
(Springe zu Deutsch » Englisch)
Ergebnis-Übersicht

I. **star** [stɑː', stɑr] SUBST	
1. star ASTRON:	
star	**Stern** *m*
shooting **star**	**Sternschnuppe** *f*
2. star (symbol):	
star	**Stern** *m*
four-star hotel	**Viersternehotel** *nt*
3. star (performer):	
star	**Star** *m*
film/rock **star**	**Film-/Rockstar** *m*
a **star** of stage and screen	**ein berühmter Bühnen- und Filmschauspieler**

b) *What other information do the different dictionaries give?*

c) *Which kind of dictionary do **you** like to use? Explain why.*

WB 11/20 Skills (dictionary translations)
WB 11/21 Skills (alphabetical order)

2 Practise with the alphabet → WB 11/20–21

a) *Revision: Take turns to say the alphabet in English.*

isung: b) *at – busy –*
ome – most – of – the –
ink – time – to – too –
'n y Berth – we – were

b) *Work with the first sentence in part C of Dave's report on page 22. Put all the words in the sentence in alphabetical order. (Be careful with words that start with the same letter – look at the next letters too.) Then check with your partner. Is the order correct?*

KV 10a+b: Skills (electronic dictionary: simple past forms)
KV 11a+b: Skills (electronic dictionary: feelings)
KV 12a+b: Skills (electronic dictionary: describing a character)
WB 11/22 Skills (different meanings)

3 Find the correct meaning → WB 11/22

isung: a) 1. *right:* rechts,
chtig 2. *time:* Zeit, Mal
room: Zimmer, Platz
1. tragen: *wear, carry*
treffen: *meet, hit* 3. Karte:
ap, menu

a) *English → German: When you find more than one meaning for a word, choose the right meaning for the sentence. Look up the words in blue and translate them into German.*

1. Take the second street on the right. That's the right way for the station.
2. I haven't got time to sit and chat today. We can chat when I come next time.
3. This is a very small room. There's room for only one bed.

b) *German → English: Sometimes you need different English words for the same German word. Look up the German words and complete the sentences.*

1. ***tragen***: a) The students … a blue uniform.
   b) They … their books to school in a bag.
2. ***treffen***: a) I often … my friends in the park.
   b) Try to … that tree with your ball.
3. ***Karte***: a) Can you find Wales on the …?
   b) Look at the … for our special lunch.

WB 11/23 Activity (adventure holidays)

Our travel report

For your yearbook, work in groups of four and write a short travel report about a class trip. It can be a real trip – or a fantasy trip! It needn't be as long as Dave's report on pages 22–23, but it's important to make it interesting for your readers.

Step 1

Choose an idea for your trip → WB 12/24 WB 12/24 Collect ideas (matching)

a) *What kind of class trip can your group write about? Do you want to use one of these photos? Or have you got your own great idea? Discuss different ideas and then choose **one** idea for your travel report.*

1

2

3

1. rafting | paddle | current | to capsize
2. science fiction | aliens | planet | spaceship
3. sightseeing | youth hostel | party | trouble

Lou

b) *Work with a placemat to collect ideas for your report. You each think about one of the four topics below. Write down ideas in your part of the placemat.*

1. The place: How did you get there?
2. The people: Who is in the report?
3. Typical activities: What did you do or see during the first part of your trip?
4. A special adventure (e.g. problem, surprise): What happened? What did you do?

c) *Choose which ideas you want to use and write them down in the middle of the placemat.*

For help with questions in the simple past, look back at **Station 2**.

For help with new words, look at the **Skills page**.

For help with placemats look at page 141 in the **Skills section**.

rafting ['rɑ:ftɪŋ] Schlauchbootfahren | **paddle** ['pædl] Paddel | **current** ['kʌrnt] Strömung | **to capsize** [kæp'saɪz] kentern | **to go sightseeing** ['saɪtˌsi:ɪŋ] eine Besichtigungstour machen | **youth hostel** ['ju:θ ˌhɒstl] Jugendherberge

Step 2

WB 12/25 Notes (correct order)

Plan your travel report → WB 12/25

For help with how to write a plan, look at the **Story** again.

a) *Your report has got four parts. Together, write a plan to show the key ideas in each part.*

Part 1: The beginning: Here you describe how you got to the place.
Part 2: The first day(s): Here you describe typical activities for this kind of trip.
Part 3: The special adventure: Say what happened, but don't tell the whole story. This part of the report finishes with a problem or an exciting situation.
Part 4: The ending: Explain how the adventure finished; find a good ending.

b) *Decide who writes which part of the report.*

Step 3

Write your part of the travel report

Do you remember the four kinds of words for travel reports? Look back at the **Story** exercises.

For help with the simple past, look at **Station 1** and **Station 2** again.

Station 3 helps you with adjectives.

a) *Work with the plan from Step 2 and make notes about the information in your part. Don't write sentences – just important words and phrases.*

b) *Read through your notes. Have you got interesting ideas and words?*

c) *Now write your part of the report. Don't forget to use the simple past.* HA

Step 4

WB 13/26 Report (error spotting)

Improve your part of the report → WB 13/26

Work with a partner from your group. Check each other's texts. Help each other to improve the texts.

Look at page 135 in the **Skills section** for tips on how to check texts.

Step 5

WB 13/27 Presentation (travel report)

Finish your travel report → WB 13/27

a) *Put the four parts together and read the whole report. Are you happy with it? If not, discuss it and improve it.*

b) *Now think of the best way to present your report. Use photos or pictures too.*

The new boy
→ S21–22 S21–22 Film skills/Viewing

VIEWING

1 Film scenes → WB 14/28

KV 13a+b: Viewing (Nick's experiment)
WB 14/28 Writing (instructions)

1

a) *Watch (00:00-03:01). Look at the headings for Scene A and B and at the phrases in the box. Match the phrases with the right scene.*

sneaking around | a bad day? | friends again | why lemons? | trouble (between friends)

Scene A: After school **Scene B:** The new boy

Lösung: a) *After school: a bad day?, trouble (between friends), friends again; The new boy: sneaking around, why lemons?*

b) *Jinsoo and Marley want to know why Nick is buying all those things. What do **you** think Nick is up to? What happens next? Talk about your ideas and then watch the last part of the film (03:02-04:45).*

c) *Do you like the film's ending? Explain why / why not. Write two or three sentences.*

Example: I think the ending is nice / funny / surprising / boring / … because …

VIEWING

2 Film and music

Lösung: a) *01:58–02:50 The music asks a question: What is Nick doing? It's slow and a bit scary – even aggressive. 03:13–03:20 The music is happy. The boys have the answer! Nick is buying things for his experiment. 03:54–04:03/ 04:06–04:46 During the experiment the music is cool because it's a cool experiment. At the end of the film the music is loud and fast because Nick is excited about his time machine.*
b) *Mood/feelings: sad, angry, unfriendly, hurt; Music: slow, sad, (perhaps) loud, aggressive (a fight/an argument)*

a) *Before you read the box on the right, watch (01:58-04:45) again and listen to the music in the different scenes. What can you say about the music? Why do you think the filmmakers use music that way?*

b) *Now read the box. Then look at the photo. Which adjectives describe the mood and the feelings in the scene? What kind of music would **you** use for the scene?*

Film skills

Films don't work the same way as texts. A film tells a story with words – *and* with **pictures**, **sounds** and **music** too. So you have the story in a film, and you have different ways to tell that story. These are called the audio-visual effects of a film.

Examples: If you want to show that a person is sad, you can use slow and sad music. For an action scene, you can use loud and fast music.

Mood / Feelings:
excited | sad | tired | happy | angry | unfriendly | hurt | silly | …

Music:
funny | slow | loud | aggressive | sad | fast | sweet | happy | cool | scary | …

WB 14/29 Across cultures (Wales)

→ Solutions p. 248

Can you …

1. talk about activities that you did? — I went to … | We played / sold …
2. find out what happened? — Did you see …? | Why was he …? | How did she …?
3. say how you felt? — I was / felt embarrassed/… | It was exciting / …
4. compare things? — It's bigger than / as big as … | It's the most exciting …

LANGUAGE HA

1 The yearbook team

Look at the list of jobs for the yearbook team. Write down what they did yesterday. Make sentences with the correct past forms.

Start: They talked about … They …

- talk about the 'dreams' page
- put the sports pages together
- look at Jay's ideas for the music pages
- collect ideas for the puzzles page
- take a photo of the yearbook team
- make a list of jobs for next week

LANGUAGE HA

2 Put in the correct past forms

Holly: I **1** (go) swimming in the sea at Southend yesterday.
Dave: Wow! **2** (be) it your mum's idea to go to Southend?
Holly: No, it **3** (not be). Olivia's family **4** (invite) me.
Dave: Lucky you! **5** (you go) on the train?
Holly: Yes, we **6** (do).
Dave: You **7** (be) brave to go in the sea at this time of the year! **8** (be) the water cold?
Holly: Yes, it **9** (be). So we **10** (not stay) in the water for more than a few minutes.

LANGUAGE HA

3 What are the questions?

Olivia calls home from Ty'n y Berth. Her dad wants to know more. What does he ask?

1. Olivia: We *got up* early this morning.
   Dad: When did you …?
2. Olivia: We *went* for a long walk.
   Dad: Where …?
3. Olivia: We *saw* lots of interesting things.
   Dad: What …?
4. Olivia: My classmates *laughed* at me.
   Dad: Why …?

LANGUAGE HA

4 Comparative and superlative forms: Pet profiles for the yearbook

1. Luke's dog Sherlock is the (crazy) animal in England. There's nothing (funny) than when he chases his tail. It's always (fast) than he is!
2. The (cute) pets for Holly are her two guinea pigs. Mr Fluff likes to explore. He thinks a trip in a bag is (interesting) than a game on the floor! Honey isn't as (brave) as Mr Fluff.
3. Cats are the (popular) pets in the class. Dave's cat Sid brings presents for the family. Some presents are (good) than others. The (bad) thing for Dave is a mouse in his bed!

Tony

<Story> ist ein fakultativer Romanauszug. Der neue Wortschatz ist rezeptiv und unter dem Text annotiert.

Folie 6: Vorentlastung des Leseverstehens und Unterstützung der Textbesprechung
KV 1: Language (crossword/mediation); **KV 2:** Reading (famous people); **KV 3:** Reading (Madame Tussauds); **KV 4:** Speaking (a scary story)

S1/8–12
L1/16–20

Middle school: How I got lost[1] in London

Rafe Khatchadorian is not very popular with his classmates, and his best friend Leo only exists in Rafe's imagination. A lot of things go wrong for Rafe, especially on a school trip to London to study Living History (when you visit special museums where they show how people lived in the past). When they go to see a famous London wax museum, he makes some silly mistakes, and his popularity score – a sign of how much the others like him – falls and falls.

The big event of the day was a tour around Madame Fifi's House of Wax. Now, of course we were excited about seeing the main attractions – Will and Kate! David Beckham! Rihanna! – but we were *really* excited about the basement[2]. Because in the basement was Madame Fifi's Temple of Terrors, where you could see beheadings[3], people on spikes and other horrible things. In other words, all the blood[4].

Yeah, yeah, we saw all the famous people. But do you *really* want to stand eye to eye with Tom Cruise? *You do?*

Not me. I wanted stuff from *my* world. So I stayed longest at Henry VIII (he had six wives[5] and beheaded two of them!), Winston Churchill (he said "We shall never surrender"[6] to Adolf Hitler!), Charles Darwin (it's thanks to him we know that we come from monkeys[7]!), Guy Fawkes (he tried to blow up[8] Parliament … Wait: should[9] we like him or not?)

I was sad to leave the upper floors. And also …

"Scared …?" Leo whispered.

"No, of course I'm not scared," I said.

"Frightened?"

"Frightened is the same as scared," I told him. "And no, I'm not frightened."

But, let me tell you a secret: I *was* nervous.

"Is everyone ready?" Gordon, our tour guide, asked.

"Yeah," we all replied.

I remembered my popularity score today (-11) and decided to be brave, so my "Yeah" was the loudest. "YEAH!"

"Right, then, let's go," Gordon said. He opened the door but then stopped. "Does anybody in the group have a weak heart[10]?" he asked.

"No," we replied.

"NO!" came my voice, the loudest.

"And everyone knows about the haunting[11]?"

"YEAH!" I shouted, really enjoying myself.

Everyone looked at me – Gordon too.

"What is your name, young man?" he asked.

1 to get lost [get 'lɒst] verschwinden; verloren gehen | **2 basement** ['beɪsmənt] Keller | **3 beheading** [bɪ'hedɪŋ] Enthauptung | **4 blood** [blʌd] Blut | **5 wives** [waɪvz] Ehefrauen | **6 we shall never surrender** [wi ʃæl ˌnevə sr'endə] wir werden uns nie ergeben | **7 monkey** ['mʌŋki] Affe | **8 to blow up** [bləʊ‿'ʌp] in die Luft sprengen | **9 should** [ʃʊd] sollten | **10 weak heart** [wi:k 'hɑ:t] schwaches Herz | **11 haunting** ['hɔ:ntɪŋ] Spuk

"Rafe," I said in a very small voice.

"And you know about the haunting, do you, Rafe?"

"Yes," I said in an even smaller voice.

"You read about it on the Madame Fifi's website?" he asked, with a strange smile.

"Yes, sir," I replied.

Everyone looked at me. They all really wanted to hear the story about the haunting but thanks to me, they didn't get the chance. Gordon just said: "Excellent. Let's go!" – and my popularity score went down again, to -22.

He opened the door and we saw the stone steps that went down into the dark. Down and down we went. At the bottom we heard a loud noise. One of the girls cried out[12] but Gordon told her it was just a passing[13] London Underground train. (OK, it wasn't "one of the girls" who cried out, it was me. Like I say, it was dark …)

Slowly, we started to see the wax figures.

"Cool," we said when we saw the heads on spikes, the murderers[14], the blood … Really scary stuff. Stuff that had *actually happened*[15].

"Now, Rafe …" Gordon said. "I'm sure you can tell us about the famous Temple of Terrors story?"

NO WAY. I shook my head "no". Gordon smiled. "Well, let me tell you then …"

"Over a hundred years ago, two gentlemen are taking a tour around the famous Madame Fifi's House of Wax. With them is a lady and they both want to impress[16] her.

"Do you know this Temple of Terrors?" the first one says. "They say it's very scary."

"Oh yes, very scary," the second man says.

Eleanor (the lady) says: "Oh, Cedric, it sounds terrible."

Both men see their chance to impress their lady friend.

"But I don't believe it," William says.

"Well, William," Cedric says, "let's go down and find out just how scary it is."

And the two men take the stone steps down into the Temple of Terrors.

"Well," William says. He looks around in the dark at the scary wax figures and feels very nervous. "I'm not frightened at all!"

"Frightened? Not me!" Cedric says, when he suddenly needs to use the bathroom.

"So, let's spend[17] the night here!" William says.

"Good idea!" Cedric says.

And so, because the men badly[18] want to impress Eleanor, they both agree[19] to spend the night …

"They couldn't stay the whole night," Gordon continued. "They soon ran out screaming[20], their eyes wide with terror. And the next day, someone found both men at their homes …"

We looked at Gordon in complete silence. "Dead[21]."

From: *Middle School: How I Got Lost in London* by James Patterson

→ WB 16/1–4

WB 16/1 Reading (multiple choice) WB 16/2 Reading (details) WB 16/3 Vocabulary (writing stories) WB 16/4 Writing (internet message)

12 **to cry out** [kraɪ 'aʊt] aufschreien | 13 **passing** ['pɑ:sɪŋ] vorbeifahrend | 14 **murderer** ['mɜ:drə] Mörder | 15 **stuff that had actually happened** [ˌstʌf ðæt həd ˌæktʃuəli 'hæpnd] Dinge, die tatsächlich passiert sind | 16 **to impress sb** [ɪm'pres] jmdn. beeindrucken | 17 **to spend** [spend] verbringen | 18 **badly** ['bædli] unbedingt | 19 **to agree** [ə'gri:] einwilligen | 20 **screaming** [skri:mɪŋ] schreiend | 21 **dead** [ded] tot

<Revision A> ist fakultativ und dient der Festigung/Wiederholung. Es werden keine neuen Sprachmittel eingeführt.

WB 17/1 Listening (true/false)

LISTENING

1 Mr Preston's scary story

→ WB 17/1

L 1/21

a) *When Mr Preston reads Dave's travel report, he remembers his own class trip to Wales a long time ago. Listen to the story about Mt Snowdon, a castle[1] and ghosts[2] …*

Lösung: a) *1. He saw them after the trip when he looked at the photos. 2. They were a man in trekking clothes and a queen. 3. In the pictures, they are standing near Mr Preston and his classmates, but they weren't there when the students took the pictures. 4. Dave thinks it's a trick.*

1. **When** did Mr Preston see the ghosts?
2. **Who** were they?
3. **What** did the ghosts do – or not do?
4. **What** does Dave think about the story?

b) *In class, compare Dave's trip to Wales in Unit 1 with his dad's trip. Which trip is more interesting to you? Say why. (Think of the different activities, different feelings, …)*

c) *Look at the two 'ghost scences' in the pictures. Choose one of them and write 6–8 sentences about the ghost in your scene. What do you think is his/her story?*

LANGUAGE

2 Olivia's dream

Last night Olivia had a strange dream. Read her e-mail to Holly. What verbs are missing? Sometimes there's more than one possible answer. Use the simple past.

Lösung: *1. had 2. was 3. opened 4. was 5. heard 6. went/ran 7. saw 8. was 9. came 10. opened 11. came/walked 12. said 13. asked 14. came 15. was 16. saw/met*

Holly – I [1] a really strange dream last night …
I [2] at school and [3] the classroom door. But nobody[3] [4] there. Suddenly, I [5] a strange noise outside. So I [6] out to the playground. That's when I [7] something in the air: a UFO! Holly, I [8] sooooo scared! The UFO [9] closer and closer. Then, someone [10] the UFO's door and a green alien [11] out. "Hello Olivia!" he [12]. "But, how do you know my name?!" I [13]. "Oh, it's me. Jay," he said. "I always go to school by UFO." Wasn't that a strange dream? Then, when I [14] to school this morning, I [15] Jay! And: His shirt was GREEN!
xoxo, Olivia

1 **castle** ['kɑːsl] Burg; Schloss | 2 **ghost** [gəʊst] Geist | 3 **nobody** ['nəʊbədi] niemand

WB 17/2 Language (class trip)

SPEAKING

3 At Greenwich Market → WB 17/2

a) *Talk about the scene at Greenwich Market. What is everybody doing? Be creative!*

ɔsungsvorschlag: **a)** *A ɔy is buying some cheese. woman is looking at a ɛllow dress. Two girls are ughing at a man. A black ɔg is sleeping on the floor. man is shouting at a bird tc.*
I think the yellow dress oks better than the white ıirt. The girl is happier ıan the boy because her e cream is bigger than his. ıe boy is angry, but the ıan is angrier than him ecause of the birds.

b) *Use different adjectives to talk about the scene. Here are some ideas:*

funny | good | happy | angry | jealous | tired
bored | boring | interesting | typical | big

Examples: A: The boy's ice cream isn't as big as the girl's.
B: I think the scene with the bird is the funniest! What do you think?

WB 17/3 Writing (report)

VOCABULARY

4 A flyer for Drama Club

a) *Which words can you think of for the gaps? Sometimes there's more than one possible answer.*

b) *Do you think the flyer is a good example for this kind of project? Why/Why not? What can you do differently with this flyer? Find five things.*

ɔsung: **a)** *1. who/that join 3. meet 4. famous/ ıportant 5. need 6. who/ at 7. sing/dance 8. want about 10. clothes 11. make . help 13. information . who*
The brochure isn't a ɔod example because it's o long, there's too much formation, it's difficult read etc. Five things u can do better: think a heading, give only the ıportant information, ld more pictures, design more clearly, think of an teresting slogan etc.

We invite all theatre fans to **1** the TTS Drama Club! We **2** every Wednesday at 3:30 in Room 0.4.04. Our next play[4] is William Shakespeare's Romeo and Juliet – and Shakespeare is of course Britain's most **3** writer[5]! But this isn't just a play: This is a musical of 'R&J', so we **4** LOTS of boys and girls with a talent for acting and singing! And this isn't a historical 'R&J'! No, we **5** to show the London of TODAY! So, forget **6** costumes like in Shakespeare's days. You can wear your own cool **7**! Also, we always need people who[6] can **8** posters, sell tickets or **9** with the sound. For more **10**, just ask Mr Gibbons, the Drama teacher in Years 7 and 9.

4 **play** [pleɪ] Theaterstück | 5 **writer** ['raɪtə] Schriftsteller | 6 **people who ...** [ˌpiːpl 'huː] Leute, die ...

Find more online: 48ww9d

London: A special city

Folie 13: Reaktivierung von Vorwissen und Bildbeschreibung
Folie 14: Ortsangaben und Lokalisierung von Sehenswürdigkeiten (London map)

London is a huge city, and Greenwich is only a small part of it. On these two pages you can learn more about the British capital and find out what makes it so special.

SPEAKING

1 First facts about London → WB 18/1

KV 1: Language (London words)
WB 18/1 Vocabulary (matching)

a) *What can you find out from the photos? The words on the right can help.*

multi-ethnic city | famous / historical sights | green spaces | royal family | river | underground trains | busy streets | festivals

Example: 1. The Thames goes through the centre of London. It's a big, busy river. You can see famous …

Lösung: a) *… sights such as the London Eye and historical sights such as Big Ben. 2. Oxford Street is a very busy street. You can find many people and many shops there. The underground stop on Oxford Street is Oxford Circus. The buses on Oxford Street are famous because you can hop on and hop off. 3. London has got many underground trains. 'The Tube' is another name for the London underground. You can get to many sights by Tube. It's a fast way to get around the city. 4. London is a multi-ethnic city with many festivals; one of the most famous is the Notting Hill Carnival. It takes place in Notting Hill in summer. Many people come to look at the great costumes and to listen to the music of people from different countries. 5. Buckingham Palace is one of the most popular sights in London. It's a huge building. The royal family often stays there and when they do, you can't go inside. So people often look at it from the outside. 6. There are a lot of green spaces in London: Hyde Park, for example. It's a very big park and you can relax there. It has got a boating lake too.*

1 The Thames, Big Ben and the London Eye

2 Oxford Street

3 The Tube

4 The Notting Hill Carnival

5 Buckingham Palace

6 Hyde Park

b) *Match the sentence parts to find out more facts about London.*

1. London was originally a Roman town
2. Today London is the
3. It's the capital city of
4. Over eight million people
5. The students in London's schools speak
6. London has got five

a) England and of the UK.
b) international airports.
c) more than 300 different languages.
d) largest city in Europe.
e) with the name 'Londinium'.
f) live in London.

Lösung: b) *1e); 2d); 3a); 4f); 5c); 6b)*

c) *Take turns to tell your partner as much as you can about London in one minute.*

KV 2: Viewing (royal London)
WB 18/2 Speaking (photos)

VIEWING

2 Royal London → WB 18/2

5

a) *Before you watch: What can you say about Laura's outfit?*

ösung: a) *She's wearing a ecial yellow and dark-red arf, a white T-shirt and a at. She has got a bag too. n the scarf you can see 'illiam and Kate. Her T-irt shows Queen Elizabeth Laura's hat has got the lours red, white and blue n it, and the Union Jack. On e side of the bag it says love London"; on the other de you can see a part of e Union Jack. Fans of the yal family sometimes ear clothes like these.*

b) *Now watch and choose the correct endings.*

1. Laura's clothes
   a) are for a party.
   b) celebrate royal events.
   c) show what the royal family wear.
2. The Changing of the Guards takes place
   a) in front of Buckingham Palace.
   b) at the Tower of London.
   c) in Hyde Park.
3. Prince Albert was
   a) Queen Victoria's brother.
   b) British.
   c) from Germany.
4. The Royals are part of the British identity
   a) for everyone in the UK.
   b) for some people in the UK.
   c) only for older people.

Lösung: b) 1b); 2a); 3c); 4b)

Transfer

c) *Your turn: What do you think about royal families? Explain your opinion.*

WB 18/3 Speaking (famous places)

LISTENING

3 Young Londoners → WB 18/3

L1/23

a) *A class in London is doing a project about their city. While you listen, work in groups of three. Each group takes different notes under one of these headings.*

b) *Share the information from a) with the other groups with the same question.*

What is good in London?	What is not so good?	How is London different?
– exciting things to do	– expensive	– bigger than other cities
– ...	– ...	– ...

WRITING

4 What makes London special?

KV 3: Speaking (mind map)

Talk about what you think makes London a special city. Write your ideas in a mind map.

KV 3: Speaking (mind map)

SPEAKING

5 Your turn: Cities in Germany

Transfer

Talk about German cities. Compare them with London. What is similar and what is different?

Useful phrases

It's also a Roman town / a capital city / ...
It isn't as big / ... as London.
There aren't as many ...
It has / hasn't got famous sights / a river / ...

Find more online: V8kv97

Unit 2

London is amazing!

A Famous sights: the Houses of Parliament and Big Ben

SPEAKING **1** **Talk about places in London**

Folie 14: Zuordnung der Orte (London map)
Folie 15: Bildbeschreibung und Unterstützung des Hörverstehens

Describe the places in the photos. Say what you can see or do there.
Find the places on the map at the back of your book.

LISTENING **2** **A video chat with Amir**

KV 1: Viewing (comprehension)

L1/24
→ S18–20
S18-20 Listening

a) *Jay is having a video chat with Amir, his cousin. Amir lives in Bradford and has plans to see London with Jay. Listen, and say what kind of things each boy is interested in.*

b) *Listen again and take notes about these places.*

Covent Garden | the British Museum | Brick Lane | the London Wall | Shakespeare's Globe

Lösung: a) Amir: Big ben, Horse Guards, British Museum, London Wall (and Tower of London), Shakespeare's Globe; Jay: Big Ben, Horse Guards, Covent Garden, Brick Lane, Shakespeare's Globe

In Unit 2 you learn

… how to discuss plans and how to describe the way people do things. You learn:

- words for things to do and see in London
- the language of plans (*going-to future*)
- word-building with *some, any, every, no*
- words for getting around by public transport

B Brick Lane: multi-ethnic flair and street art

C The wax figures at Madame Tussauds

D Londoners and tourists at Covent Garden

E The Horse Guards at Whitehall

WB 19/1 Vocabulary (London sights)

SPEAKING

Transfer

3 Your turn: Choose your London → WB 19/1

→ △ 118/1

118/1 Choose your London
△ → Help with …

Think about what you already know about London. In groups, take turns to tell each other two things that you would really like to see or do there. Explain why. Use your notes from Ex. 2.

WB 19/2 Vocabulary (report)

VOCABULARY

4 London vocabulary → WB 19/2

Collect useful words and names for your personal vocabulary. Add more words while you work through Unit 2.

L1/25

It's going to be fun

Folie 16: Bildbeschreibung und Unterstützung des Hörverstehens

"It was amazing," Amir tells his aunt. He's staying with the Azads and earlier today Jay took him to the Royal Observatory.

"Good. And what are you two going to do tomorrow?" Mrs Azad asks. "Are you going to see more sights in Greenwich?"

"No, we aren't. We're going to visit the British Museum with Olivia and Holly," Jay tells her. "We met them in Greenwich Park this afternoon, and Olivia is like Amir – she loves museums."

Mrs Azad's face shows that she isn't happy with this plan. But Jay can think fast. "Don't worry," he says. "We aren't going to go alone. Shahid is going to take us." His 18-year-old brother isn't at home at the moment, so Jay must try to persuade him later.

"Oh, is Shahid going to look after you? That's OK then," says Mrs Azad.

"Yes, it's going to be fun. But there's just one thing. The museum is free, but I'm not sure where I'm going to get money for our Oyster cards or for our lunch."

Mrs Azad smiles. "Probably the same place where you *always* get money."

KV 2: Reading/Listening (right/wrong)
WB 20/3 Listening (matching)

READING

1 What do you think? → WB 20/3

Lösung: 1. *She isn't happy if they go to the British Museum alone.* 2. *Jay wants to ask his older brother to come with them.* 3. *Jay is going to get some money from his parents.*

1. What is Mrs Azad's problem with the boys' plan?
2. What is Jay's solution to that problem?
3. Where is Jay going to get money?

Across cultures

The cheapest way to travel by public transport in London is with an **Oyster card**. It's a smartcard and you can top it up with credit. What's the cheapest way to travel where you live?

LANGUAGE

2 Find the rule for *going to* → WB 20/4, 21/5 → G6

WB 20/4 Language (telephone conversation)
WB 21/5 Language (message)

Lösung: a) *time line: tomorrow;*
b) *form of 'to be'+ going to + infinitive*

a) *Find phrases with **going to** in the text. Which part of the time line are they about?*

b) *How do you make **going to** forms? Write the rule and put it in your folder.*

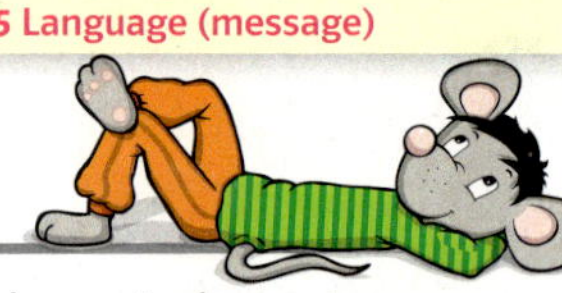

← yesterday ← today → tomorrow →

LANGUAGE

3 Your turn: What are you going to do?

→ △ 118/2
→ S24

118/2 What are they going to do next week?
△ → After ...

S24 Kooperative Lernformen (Milling around)

a) *First, write down three sentences about your weekend. Walk around and ask a few classmates about their plans.*

b) *Take turns to say what you found out about your classmates' plans.*

Transfer

What are you going to do next weekend?

On Sunday I'm going to visit my grandma.

Folie 17: Visuelle Unterstützung zur Festigung der Struktur

LANGUAGE **4**

What's going to happen? → WB 21/6

WB 21/6 Mediation (going-to future)

→ △ 118/3

118/3 What's going to happen?
△ → Help with ...

Write about the people in the picture. Find your own verbs.

Start: 1. The old man and woman **are going to sit down.**
2. The man in the wheelchair **is going to** ...

SPEAKING **5**

Play a game: Guess my plans for tomorrow

→ △ 118/4

118/4 Guess my plans for tomorrow
△ → Help with ...

Think of a place in London but don't say what it is. Your partner must ask questions and guess the activity. Start the questions with "Are you going to ...?"

Example: A: Are you going to listen to music?
B: No, I'm not.
A: Are you going to look at animals?
B: Yes, I am.
A: Are you going to visit London Zoo?
B: Yes, I am. That's right.

look at pictures / ...
watch football / street shows / ...
visit a historical building / ...
listen to street musicians

LISTENING **6**

How to: Get around by Tube → WB 22/7

WB 22/7 Vocabulary (asking the way)

L 1/27
→ S18–20
S18–20 Listening

a) *Work with the map of the Tube and DLR at the back of your book. A tourist is at Elephant & Castle station and wants to get to Buckingham Palace. Listen to the dialogue. Which route do you think is best – the man's or the woman's? Why?*

ösung: a) *The man's route is est. It's shorter. It has only ot 6 stops. The woman's ute has got 11 stops.*

b) *Take turns to describe the routes to the other places above. You can start at Elephant & Castle or go from one sight to another.*

Place / Sight	Station
Buckingham Palace	Victoria
Oxford Street	Oxford Circus
Tower of London	Tower Hill
Transport Museum	Covent Garden
Mudchute Farm	Crossharbour

Useful phrases

You take the ... line to ... | You change onto the ... line. | You go north / south / east / west to ... | It's three stops to ... | You get off at ...

ösung: b) ***From – to:** Elephant & Castle – Victoria; **Lines:** Bakerloo, Circle District. **Change at:** Embankment. **Sight:** Buckingham Palace; **From – to:** ictoria – Oxford Circus. **Linies:** Victoria Line. **Change at:** –. **Sight:** Oxford treet. **From – to:** Oxford Circus – Tower Hill. **Lines:** Central, Circle or District. hange at: Bank/Monument or Liverpool Street. **Sight:** Tower of London. etc.*

Folie 18: Vorentlastung und Sicherung des Hörverstehens/Bildbeschreibung

L 1/28

Good idea!

KV 5: Writing (speech bubbles)
WB22/8 Listening (true/false)

SPEAKING

7 The photo story → WB 22/8

*Imagine you're **one** of the people in the story. What can he / she say about it?*

→ △ 119/5
→ ▲ 119/6

Example: (Jay) I was really hungry. Olivia had a great idea. But then I saw …

119/5 The photo story △→ Help with …
119/6 A game: Why didn't you buy any food? ▲→ After …

LANGUAGE

8 Revision: Comparison of adjectives

*What kind of a food challenge would be the best for **you**? Why? Write about it in 5–6 sentences with different forms of adjectives. The examples can help you.*

Examples: I think the **most important thing** is to find **the best food**!
Healthy food is **better than** … food, but **not as** … **as** …

KV 6: Language (compounds)
KV 7: Speaking (tandem activity)

LANGUAGE

9 Compound words with *some* and *any* → G7

a) *Match the parts.*

ösung: a) 1d); 2a); 3g); 4b);); 6c); 7e)

1. I'm hungry. I need
2. I've only got £1. I can't buy
3. Are there public toilets
4. Let's watch this guy. He's doing
5. I can't see the show – I'm behind
6. We must go now. We haven't got
7. Where's the Tube station? Does

a) anything expensive.
b) some good tricks.
c) any more time.
d) something to eat.
e) anyone know?
f) someone very tall!
g) anywhere here?

9/7 Compound words ith *some* and *any* → After …
0/8 Sherlock, you crazy og! → After …

→ △ 119/7
→ ▲ 120/8

b) *Do you remember the rule for **some** and **any** from last year? Explain it.*

Lösung: b) *We use 'some' in positive statements. We use 'any' in questions and in negative statements.*

WB 23/9 Language (dialogue)
WB 23/10 Language (postcard)
WB 24/11 Writing (postcard)

LANGUAGE

10 Complete the words → WB 23/9–10, 24/11 → G7

some | any | every | no

→ △ 120/9

0/9 Complete the text → Instead of …

Holly: What can we do till we meet Shahid later? Has 1 *body* got a good suggestion?
Jay: It must be 2 *thing* that costs 3 *thing* – we haven't got any money left.
Olivia: Let's just walk around. I'm sure that's fun for 4 *one* new in London like Amir. There are lots of interesting things to see 5 *where* you look. What do you think, Amir?
Amir: Well, if 6 *body* wants to make a different suggestion – yes, I'd like that.
Holly: Is there 7 *where* special you'd like to go or 8 *thing* special you'd like to see?
Amir: Well, 9 *thing* is special for me – it's all amazing. But I'd love to walk near the river.
Jay: Is that OK with 10 *body*? – Great, come on, let's go and find the Thames!

ösung: 1. *anybody* *something* 3. *nothing* *someone* 5. *everywhere* *nobody* 7. *anywhere* *anything* 9. *everything* . *everybody*

KV 4: Language (useful phrases) WB 24/12 Speaking (dialogue)
WB 24/13 Pronunciation (sounds)

SPEAKING

Transfer

11 Your turn: Visitors → WB 24/12–13

a) *With a partner, think of where you can go or what you can do with young visitors where you live. Make a list of 4–5 different ideas.*

b) *Present your 'Top 3' to the class.*

Useful phrases

Pros: good for someone who likes history / … | doesn't cost anything | easy to get there by public transport | something everyone enjoys

Cons: (very) expensive | not everyone is into … | boring | too far away | not good in bad weather

L1/30

They can bite *very* hard

Folie 19: Inhaltliche/Lexikalische Vorentlastung und Bildbeschreibung

If you don't know London well, a bus tour with a guide can be a good idea. You can see and learn much more than if you explore the city alone.

"Now we're going slowly past the Tower of London, one of the city's must-see sights – you can see it clearly on the left. William the Conqueror built the Tower when he became king of England in 1066. In the past it was a castle, a prison and even a royal zoo with big animals like lions and bears! Today it's a must-see sight. Many people come specially to see the Crown Jewels, but the Beefeaters give fantastic tours of the whole Tower – they know its history really well! The Raven Master is a Beefeater too. His job is to look after the ravens carefully and to make sure they stay happily and safely in their home at the Tower. If you visit the Tower, don't go too close to the ravens. They don't always like that – and they can bite *very* hard!"

Across cultures

William the Conqueror and his people came from Normandy in France, so after 1066 many French words became part of the English language. Can you give some examples?

SPEAKING

12 A must-see sight for you too?

Would you like to visit the Tower? Why or why not?

Tony

LISTENING

13 Rocky's audio tour

KV 8: Mediation (audio tour)

L1/31–33

a) *Listen once. Who is Rocky?*
What three topics does he tell you about?

→ S18–20

b) *Listen again. What does Rocky say about* ***food***, ***treasure*** *and* ***ghosts****? Take notes.*

→ S17

c) *Mediation: There's no 'Rocky' audio tour in German, and a young German tourist wants to know what Rocky says because he doesn't speak English. Give the main information in German.*

S18–20 Listening
S17 Mediation

Listening skills

When you listen to information, first just try to understand the gist (main ideas). Then listen again for **more information**. Collect **key words and phrases** that help you to remember.

Lösung: a) *Rocky is one of the ravens that live in the Tower of London. He's a guide at the Tower. He tells us about the tradition of the six ravens at the Tower of London and how they live there today, about the safest place – the Jewel House – with its Crown Jewels, and the two bears that lived in the Tower of London when it was a royal zoo.*

WB 24/14 Vocabulary (bus tour)
WB 25/15 Writing (my hometown)

VOCABULARY

14 Talk about the people in the pictures → WB 24/14, 25/15

→ △120/10

120/10 Act it out
△→ After …

Voc.: Describing people, things and actions, p. 177

a) *What are they doing, and how are they doing it? Match the sentences with the photos.*

Example: 1. He's jumping back **nervously**.

He's jumping back nervously. | She's looking quietly at a tablet PC. | They're clapping their hands loudly. | She's running fast. | He's smiling happily. | She's shouting aggressively.

ösung: EH: 2. *She's running* *st. Maybe she wants to* *et fit. 3. She's shouting* *ggressively. Maybe she's* *ngry. 4. They're clapping* *eir hands loudly. Maybe* *ey're excited. 5. She's look-* *g quietly at a tablet PC.* *aybe she's busy. 6. He's* *niling happily. Maybe he's* *a good mood.*

1 2 3 4 5 6

b) *Discuss what the situation could be.*

Example: 1. He's jumping back nervously. **Maybe he's scared.**

KV 9: Writing (a special place in London)
WB 25/15 Writing (my hometown)
WB 25/16 Mediation (Trafalgar Square)

WRITING

15 Your turn: My special place in London → WB 25/15–16

Transfer

Which sight or special place in London do you find really interesting or cool?
In 6–8 sentences, say what the sight is and where it is. Describe it and say why it's special.

Writing skills

Before you start writing a text, stop and think: Which main points do you want to write about? For example, you can collect your ideas in a mind-map. Or you write down notes under the headings:

Who / What | Where | When | Why

A day out in London → S21–22

S21–22 Film skills/Viewing

SPEAKING

1 Warm-up

Voc.: Out and about in the city, p. 178

Which places/sights do you think are symbols of London? Write them down and tell the class.

KV 10: Viewing/Writing (film stills)
WB 26/17 Vocabulary (odd one out)

VIEWING

2 Out and about in London → WB 26/17

Lou

6

*Watch the film. Which part do **you** really like? Why?*

KV 10: Viewing/Writing (film stills)
WB 26/18 Speaking (Camden Market)

VIEWING

3 A closer look → WB 26/18

Lösung: 1. *Mina said she wanted to take Jinsoo and his friends out in London for the day.* 2. *Jinsoo wanted to go to the London Dungeon, but it was too expensive.* 3. *Mina wanted to try on clothes and it took too long.*

Watch again and answer the questions. These ideas can help.

1. Why do you think Jinsoo's sister, Mina, is with the boys?
2. Where did Jinsoo want to go? Why didn't they go there?
3. What was the problem with Mina at Camden Market?

Jinsoo and Mina's dad | adult / child ticket | sightseeing / normal bus | look after | expensive

VIEWING

4 Setting and atmosphere in film scenes

KV 11: Viewing (London)

a) *First, read the skills box. Then watch scenes **A** (01:15–01:50) and **B** (01:57–02:06) again. Say why you think they're important or interesting for the film.*

Lösung: a) ***Scene A:*** *on Waterloo Bridge with a great view of the Thames and famous London sights.* ***Important:*** *It's clearly London because of the famous sights and the map of the Tube.* ***Scene B:*** *Camden Market in Camden Town.* ***Important:*** *stalls, shops, crowds, many different people.*

A

B

Lösung: b) *The street scene in Camden Town is really cool. There are people everywhere – and there are some crazy people too. There are lots of shops with lots of things to discover. I think Camden Town and Camden Market are really interesting. I'd love to go there.*

b) *Talk about the setting and atmoshpere of your favourite scene in Ex. 2.*

cool | crazy | famous | funny | interesting | international | multi-ethnic | lots to see / discover | people everywhere

c) *Write a short description of what Jinsoo, Marley, Nick and Mina could do in a **different** location in London. Look at your lists from Ex. 1 for ideas.*

Film skills

In a film, the viewer needs to know what the film's **setting** is, so the choice of **locations** in a film is important. A famous place like London really needs to *look* like London!

Atmosphere is important too: crowds, places, views, water, things to look at or buy, cool shops … These things can create a special atmosphere for the viewer.

WB 26/19 Across cultures (shops and markets)

S5, 9 Reading (Schnelllesetechniken, Umgang mit neuen Wörtern)

How to find information on the internet → S5, 9

1 Start with the homepage of a famous attraction's website

Most homepages give basic information and also useful links to other pages. Try to answer these questions with the help of the homepage for the Natural History Museum in London. If the answer is not on the page, which 'quick link' do you think can help?

ısung: 1. The museum is Cromwell Road (London N7 5BD UK). 2. The answer n't on the homepage. The ıick link 'Getting here' ılps. 3. It's open nearly ery day (Monday to ınday from 10:00–17:50), cept for Christmas (24–26 ecember). 4. There's no ıswer on this webpage. e quick link 'Gallery an-ıuncements' helps. 5. No, u needn't pay. The entry free.

1. Where is the museum?
2. How do I get there?
3. Is it open every day?
4. Are there any special displays at the moment?
5. Must I pay to visit the museum?

NATURAL HISTORY MUSEUM

Home	Visit us	Nature online	Education	Support us	Buy online

Cromwell Road London SW7 5BD UK
Open Monday to Sunday from
10:00 – 17:50
except 24 – 26 December.
Last admission 17:30

Entry is free
There is a charge for some exhibitions.

Quick links:
- Getting here
- Book tickets
- Gallery announcements
- Sign up for news
- Dino Directory

2 Skim and scan internet texts → WB 27/20 WB 27/20 Skills (travel information)

ısung: a) The text is about e galleries of the National story Museum and their ur zones: the Blue Zone, e Green Zone, the Red ne and the Orange Zone. is information helps sitors because each zone s got a different topic. This ay you can plan your visit d just go to an interesting llery.
Details about animals the text: Most of the imals are in the Blue ne. Here you can see all fferent kinds of animals, om smallest to largest. The nosaurs' gallery is in the ue Zone too. In the Wildlife rden of the Orange Zone, u can also watch animals ,000 species). You can dis-ver animals in the Darwin ntre as well.

a) *Skim the text on the right for the **gist**. What is it about? How can the information help visitors?*

b) *Now scan the text for **details** about animals. Make notes.*

Try to guess new words. Don't worry about words that aren't important.

Home	**Visit us**	Nature online	Education	Support us	Buy online

The Galleries at the **Natural History Museum** are in four zones. The **Blue Zone** shows you the amazing diversity of life on Earth, from the smallest to the largest animals. This is also where you can find the popular Dinosaurs gallery. In the **Green Zone** you learn about Earth's ecology and how you can help to look after the planet. Visit the **Red Zone** to go back to the beginning of time and find out how and why our planet changes. Here you can see many of the Earth's minerals and treasures. In the **Orange Zone** you can explore nature in the Wildlife Garden – it features over 2,000 species. Also, see science in action in the spectacular Darwin Centre.

Practise with different websites WB 27/21 Activity (website)

Partner A: *Choose a sight in London (an idea from Unit 2 or your own idea).*
Partner B: *Find useful or interesting information about your partner's sight and tell him/her about it.*

Our London tour

For this task, work in small groups. Each group is going to plan and present a different sightseeing tour for a class trip to London. There are three different tour choices:

a tour by bus and boat	a tour by Tube	a tour on foot

Step 1

KV 12: Writing/Note-taking (tour plan)
WB 28/22 Rules

Tour rules → WB 28/22

a) *First, read the rules in class. Then form groups of 4–5 and choose a tour. Try to have **two** groups for each tour.*

b) *The map below can help you to plan your tour and to get a feeling for distances before you use other maps.*

Rules
- *Your tour starts at **Green Park**.*
- *There must be **enough time** (morning till late afternoon) for everything in your plan.*
- *Only **one** stop on your tour costs money. The other sights must be **free**.*
- *You've got sandwiches for **lunch**, so you must plan when and where you can eat them.*

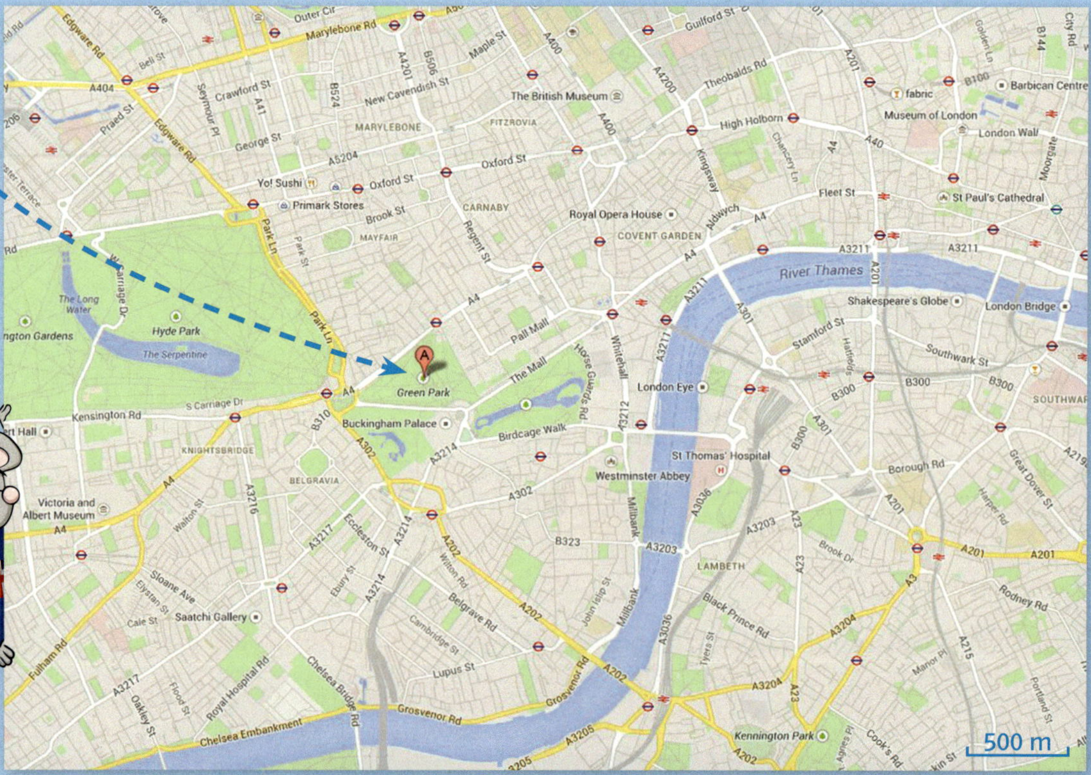

Step 2

KV 4: Language (useful phrases)
WB 28/23 London quiz
WB 29/24 Writing (problems)

Choose the sights on your tour → WB 28/23, 29/24

a) *First think alone for a few minutes about what sights you can visit. Write down your ideas. Which ones would you like to visit in one day? Tick (✔) them.*

b) *Share your ideas. What are your group's favourites? Make your decision about the sights. Look at the map again. Are your plans realistic for the time you have and the distance between activities?*

Start: Good idea – but isn't it a bit far / expensive?
I think we've got enough time / money for …

For help with things to do and see in London, look back at **Across Cultures 2**, at pages 36–44 of **Unit 2** and at your **Workbook**.

For help with how to make and discuss suggestions, look again at **Station 2**.

Step 3

KV 12: Writing/Note-taking (tour plan)

Collect information and write a plan

a) *Collect useful information about each of the sights on your list and work out the best route for your tour. You can look for information on the internet and make notes.*

b) *Use the information to write a plan for the tour (morning → lunch → afternoon). Make sure it's clear where you're going to go and how you're going to get there.*

Step 4

Prepare your presentation

Decide who is going to talk about what. Think what you want to say and make prompt cards. Also prepare some material about your tour. Maybe these ideas can help:

- a poster of the whole tour
- a tour timetable
- a map with your route / sights

Step 5

WB 29/25
Presentation (tour)

Present your tour in class → WB 29/25

a) *Take turns to present your tours.*

Useful phrases

We'd like to tell you about …
First we're going to …
Then … / After that …
We're / You're going to see / visit …
We can get there on foot / by …
It's a fantastic / an amazing …

b) *Take turns to vote for the best tour. Say why you liked that tour best.*

For help with how to find information on the internet, look at the **Skills page** again.

For help with routes on the Tube, look back at **Station 1**.

Look at page 137 in the **Skills section** for tips on how to give a presentation.

S 1/16–20 L 2/1–5

I'm a mudlark

Across cultures

Many London visitors don't know that **the Thames** is a river with two faces – one at high tide, one at low tide. Sometimes, it flows out into the sea like a normal river. But every day at high tide, it flows back towards central London. In the heart of the city there can be a difference of seven metres between high and low tides! At low tide, you can see the muddy banks of the river.

A "Number three is the Wobbly Bridge," Jay told his cousin Amir. The four friends were enjoying their own tour of bridges across the Thames. Now they were walking across their third one, the Millennium Footbridge.

"It isn't wobbly any more. That was just a problem when it was new, but people still use the name," explained Olivia.

Before they got very far, Holly noticed Amir's silver bracelet. "Ooh, that's nice!"

"Yeah, let *me* try it on," Jay said.

"Sure, no problem," Amir said. Jay quickly grabbed his cousin's wrist to take the bracelet off. But he wasn't careful enough, dropped it, and the bracelet rolled off the bridge and down into the Thames!

"Jay!" Amir shouted angrily. "That bracelet really meant something to me. And now it's gone!" They all looked down from the bridge. They were lucky. The tide was out and the bracelet was in the mud between the water and the wall.

"Look, there are steps down to the shore," Olivia said. "Come on, let's go and get it. But hm, should we take off our shoes? It's very muddy."

Stop and think:
What could happen next, and why?

B Down on the shore, they found that the mud was very wet. They weren't wearing the right kind of shoes so they needed to walk carefully. They didn't want to fall.

"Hi. Are you looking for this?"

The voice came from a man under the bridge.

"Oh, we didn't see you! Yes, that's my bracelet. Thanks! I'm so happy to get it back," Amir told him.

"No problem," the man smiled. "I didn't think it was a present for me! Nice to meet you all. My name is Mike."

Olivia looked at the bucket and trowel which Mike had with him. "Excuse me, but can you please tell us what you're doing here?" she asked politely.

"I'm a mudlark," he said.

C The friends didn't know about mudlarks, so Mike explained. "In the 19th century many children or old people tried to make a little money from things that fell into the Thames. You know – from boats and ships."

"And bridges too!" Jay added.

"Yes, from bridges too," Mike laughed. "Anyway, when the tide went out the mudlarks looked on the shore for things to sell. They got their name because they worked in the mud. And at that time, the river was *very* dirty, full of all kinds of pollution. Or worse."

"Worse?" Amir wanted to know.

"Well, dead animals washed up all the time. Human bodies too."

"Yuck!" Holly said. "It's nice to know I've got shoes on my feet!"

"Oh, times are different now – don't worry," Mike explained.

"So you're looking for things to sell?" Holly wanted to know.

"No, no. Mudlarks are different now. We look for history in the mud. Just for fun. There are things in the Thames that go back to Roman times, you know."

"Wow, amazing! Listen to that, Olivia!" said Amir. He knew she loved history too.

"Most things aren't as old as that," Mike told them. "But look at this glass in my bucket. OK, it's broken, so it doesn't look very good any more. But it's over 100 years old! And when I hold it in my hand I like to think of the story behind it. Who drank from it? How did it get here?"

Mike also showed the friends the other things in his bucket: an old green bottle, a piece of an 18th-century clay pipe, and part of a lucky-charm bracelet. The friends had no idea there was treasure like this in the Thames! They all wanted to help Mike to look for more things. "OK, but please stay near me," he said.

D At first the four new mudlarks found it hard to see anything in the mud, but Mike showed them the best places to look and they started to notice things more easily. Olivia found a euro coin, Amir found an old key, and Holly found a shoe. And then she found something awful, with hair on it.

"Ugh, a HEAD!!!" she screamed.

Mike laughed. "Well, a head from across the sea!" he laughed, as he pulled a coconut from the mud. Then he said, "Sorry, guys, time to go now. The tide is coming in fast and – hey, where's your friend?"

Suddenly they saw that Jay wasn't with them. He wasn't far away, but the water between them was already near the wall.

"Jay! Look, you're going to be cut off!" Mike shouted. "Come on – quick! We need to get to the steps!"

Stop and think:
What is Jay's problem?
What could happen next?

E After a few dramatic minutes that felt like *hours*, they all got safely to the top of the steps. The friends said thank you and goodbye to Mike. Then it was time to walk along the south side of the river to the London Eye to meet Shahid.

"Mum isn't going to be very happy when she sees our dirty shoes," Jay said to Amir. "Hey, where are you going? That isn't the way to the London Eye!"

Jay, Olivia and Holly watched as Amir ran quickly back onto the bridge and threw something into the river.

"But – that's his bracelet!" Holly said. Jay was surprised too. "The crazy idiot! Why did he do that?"

Olivia just smiled. She understood.

KV 13a: Reading (sentence completion)
WB 30/26 Reading (matching)

SPEAKING

1 Your reaction → WB 30/26

Voc.: Water words, p. 181

Talk about what you found interesting about the story: the people, the history, the things in the river?

KV 13b Reading (sentence completion)
WB 30/27 Reading (questions)

READING

2 Understanding the text → WB 30/27

a) *Explain the difference between mudlarks in the 19th century and modern mudlarks.*

b) *Why do you think Amir threw his bracelet back into the Thames?*

WRITING

3 One story, three different perspectives

Lösung: a) *Key words: the bracelet, mud, the tide was out, mudlark, bucket and trowel, history, the tide is coming in fast, Thames*

a) *Work in groups of three. In your group, each of you (A, B and C) writes about the main ideas of the story in three different ways:*

A. *Find 6–8* ***key words / phrases*** *from the text. Write down why they're important.*
B. *Tell the* ***main ideas*** *of the story in 6–8 sentences.*
C. *In 6–8 sentences, talk about* ***your reaction*** *to the story.*

b) *Now tell each other your ideas. What ideas are the same or different?*

WRITING

4 What's the story behind it? → WB 30/28

WB 30/28 Writing/Speaking (options)

→ ▲ 120/11
→ S10–13

120/11 A treasure in the Thames
▲ → Instead of …

S10–13 Writing

Voc.: Environment, Word bank (WB), p. 15

Choose ***one*** *thing from Mike's bucket and create a little story about its history. Who did it belong to? How long ago? How did it get into the Thames? Write at least six sentences.*

Useful phrases

The … belonged to a girl / sailor / tourist / …
He / She lived in the 18th / … century.
He / She visited London last year / …
It was for wine / a treasure box / …
It was his / her favourite …
He / She threw it into the river because …
They / … didn't want it any more because …
It broke (into pieces) when …
One day it fell into the river while …

KV 14: Viewing (Thames)
KV 15: Writing (dialogue)

Example:

The wine glass

The wine glass belonged to a family over a hundred years ago. They lived in a house next to the Thames. One day …

7 Mehr zum Thema Thames

→ Solutions p. 248

Can you …

1. talk about your plans? — I'm / We're going to visit London.
2. use compound words with *some* and *any*? — I need something to eat. | Has anybody got anything nice?
3. understand and give directions for travelling by public transport? — You take the … line to … | It's three stops to … | You get off at …

LANGUAGE
HA

1 What are they going to do tomorrow?

Use the clues in the pictures and make sentences about their plans.

Start: 1. The Frasers are going to have …

1 The Frasers

2 Luke and Sherlock

3 Mr and Mrs Azad

4 Holly

5 Amir

6 Shahid

LANGUAGE
HA

2 What do these sellers at Camden Market say?

A: Does **1** want to buy a cool hat? What about you, young man? I'm sure it's just the right thing for **2** cool like you!
B: Come on, **3** ! If you want **4** good to eat, this is the place to get it!
C: A book about London in German? I'm sure I've got one **5** . Yes, here you are. Look, **6** is in German.
D: Great souvenirs! You can't find cheaper ones **7** in London – **8** costs more than £1!

everything | anybody | something | someone | anywhere | somewhere | nothing | everybody

SPEAKING
HA

3 Public transport

*A British visitor to Stuttgart doesn't know how to get around. Tell him how to get from **Bad Cannstatt** to the **Fernsehturm** by public transport.*

1. Fahrt — Empfehlen | Kalendereintrag | Drucken | Kaufen/Tarif

S-Bahn S2 Richtung Filderstadt
^ Früher — heute
ab 16:21 — 16:22 — Bad Cannstatt Gleis 2 #) — Karte
an 16:25 — 16:26 — Stuttgart Hauptbahnhof (tief) Gleis 101 — Karte
Fachmesse
Bad Cannstatt: Aufzug außer Betrieb

Fußweg (ca. 2 Minuten)

Stadtbahn U7 Richtung Ostfildern
ab 16:31 — Hauptbf (A.-Klett-Pl.) Gleis 4 — Karte
an 16:41 — Ruhbank (Fernsehturm) — Karte
˅ Später
Heumaden: Stadtbahnersatzverkehr zwischen Heumaden und Ostfildern Nellingen

Fußweg (ca. 11 Minuten) 6m
Ruhbank (Fernsehturm) — Karte
Stuttgart, Fernsehturm — Karte

2. Fahrt

<Story> ist ein fakultativer Romanauszug. Der neue Wortschatz ist rezeptiv und unter dem Text annotiert.

Folie 20: Vorentlastung und Bildbeschreibung zur Unterstützung des Leseverstehens
KV 1: Reading (gapped text)
KV 2: Reading (story characters)

S 1/21–24
L 2/6–9

The copper[1] treasure

Jamie, Ten Tons and Davies are young mudlarks who live in London in the 1850s. One day, they climb aboard a big ship in the River Thames and start to look for things which they can take away and sell for food; they're all hungry. With them is Patty, a woman who doesn't like Ten Tons very much. This is when they find a real treasure … the copper treasure.

We were moving carefully across the decks and looking for bits and pieces. But there wasn't much so we followed Patty down and started to look for spoons[2] and knives[3] and stuff in the cabins.

I could hear Ten Tons two cabins away. He was talking and shouting to himself as usual. Then I saw Patty at the end of the corridor. She was doing well. You could hear the sound of metal things under her skirts[4]. She looked annoyed[5] when she heard Ten Tons, but I didn't say anything. Yes, Ten Tons was a crazy man, but he was *our* crazy man.

I was crazy too – why was I stealing like this? Davies and Ten Tons didn't have parents – they needed to do this to live. But I had a mother and father and a home. I didn't need to do this. The others laughed each time I looked to check that everything was OK. But it was a good thing I checked so often: I looked up again and … and I saw the dock. It was floating past[6].

I thought … what? There was a man with some cows on the river bank … we were on the other side of the river now! He pointed at us and shouted. The ship started to circle and I suddenly understood … Oh no! The anchor[7] was broken and we were floating away[8] from the bank.

"Davies, Tens!" I screamed. "We're moving!"

Ten Tons was up on deck right away. "My God, I've stolen[9] a whole ship this time!" he shouted. Like a captain, he started to march up and down the decks and to give orders[10] to no one. It was so funny! He was very short and he was going up and down the deck like a crazy little engine[11].

Davies came up too. He looked over the side.

"We should[12] get …" he started to say.

Then everything moved. We floated sideways across the river and hit a tugboat[13]. Our ship went up and down and we all fell to the deck floor.

1 **copper** [kɒpə] Kupfer | 2 **spoon** [spu:n] Löffel | 3 **knife** [naɪf] Messer | 4 **skirt** [skɜ:t] Rock | 5 **annoyed** [ə'nɔɪd] verärgert | 6 **to float past** [fləʊt 'pɑ:st] vorbeitreiben | 7 **anchor** ['æŋkə] Anker | 8 **to float away** [fləʊt ə'weɪ] wegtreiben, abtreiben | 9 **I've stolen** [aɪv 'stəʊlən] ich habe gestohlen | 10 **order** ['ɔ:də] Befehl | 11 **engine** ['endʒɪn] Lokomotive; Motor | 12 **should** [ʃʊd] sollten | 13 **tugboat** ['tʌgbəʊt] Schlepper *(Schiff)*

Davies almost[14] fell into the river. I saw Ten Tons – he was sliding along on his bum[15] and shouting 'Whhhhhooooah!' I held on to the rail[16]. And then we heard a strange sound, like music. I looked along the deck and saw …

The copper! What a sight! It was rolling along the deck and opening itself up into a shining red sheet. It was like a magician[17] who was slowly opening his cape. The ship moved again and the deck turned to one side. The copper was moving faster and faster … and then it crashed into the rail. The rails broke and the copper hung for a moment, right on the edge[18] of the deck. Then there was another movement. It caught[19] the sun[20], flashed[21] red-golden light[22] at me, went over the edge … and dropped.

I watched it go down. It hummed[23] as it fell. It flashed again in the evening sun and sent a bright[24] red light across the river. Then it hit the water. It was so bright it looked red hot[25]. I was waiting for it to hiss[26]. There was a huge splash in the water … and it was gone. Half a ton or more of new copper, down under the water and lost forever[27].

From: *The Copper Treasure* by Melvin Burgess

→ WB 32/1–3

14 almost ['ɔ:lməʊst] fast | **15 bum** [bʌm] Hintern | **16 rail** [reɪl] Reling | **17 magician** [mə'dʒɪʃn] Zauberer | **18 edge** [edʒ] Rand | **19 to catch** [kætʃ] einfangen | **20 sun** [sʌn] Sonne | **21 to flash** [flæʃ] blitzen | **22 light** [laɪt] Licht | **23 to hum** [hʌm] summen | **24 bright** [braɪt] leuchtend | **25 red hot** [red 'hɒt] glühend heiß | **26 to hiss** [hɪs] zischen | **27 lost forever** [lɒst fə'revə] für immer verloren

WB 32/1 Reading (multiple choice)
WB 32/2 Reading (true/false)
WB 32/3 Vocabulary (verbs)

Find more online: c27n8p

Unit 3

Sport is good for you!

B Marathon

A Camel racing

C BMX

D Rugby

LISTENING

1 On the radio

KV 1: Language (world of sports)

L 2/10

→ S18–20

S18–20 Listening

Gwen is preparing for the TTS sports and health project week. She's listening to sports programmes on the radio. Which sports? Three of them are in the photos; which ones?

runner race lose catch match run kick net throw team pass win time racquet court hit score stadium ball pitch goal point

SPEAKING

2 Talk about sports

Folie 21: Vokabular reaktivieren und Bildbeschreibung
KV 2: Speaking (my favourite sports)

→ S4

S4 Vocabulary (Methoden)

a) *Use the word cloud from Ex. 1 to describe the sports in the photos. Where and why are these sports popular?*

Transfer → △ 121/1

121/1 Talk about sports
△→ Help with ...

b) *Your turn: Talk about your favourite sports.*

Vocabulary skills

You can use **word clouds** to show how often a word is in a text. The more often a word is in the text, the bigger it is. You can make word clouds on your computer.

In Unit 3 you learn

… how to talk about sports, about your experiences in the past, and about things which have just happened and are still important now. You learn:

- words for sports
- words for health and accidents
- the language of news reports
- the present perfect

E Wheelchair basketball

LISTENING

3 TTS sport and health projects

L 2/11

sung: a) *Gwen: skiing.*
e likes winter sports.
via: rugby. She likes team
orts.
football, netball, swim-
ng, running, cycling,
ating

a) *Say which sports Olivia and Gwen are going to use for their projects and why?*

b) *What other sports do they talk about? Make a list.*

c) *Why is sport good for your health?*

Across cultures

The **number one sport** in Britain is football, rugby is number two. Other popular team sports in Britain are cricket and hockey. What team sports are popular in Germany and what do you know about them?

OCABULARY

4 Sports words → WB 33/1–2

KV 3: Language (sports words)
WB 33/1 Vocabulary (matching)
WB 33/2 Vocabulary (crossword puzzle)

What sports are you interested in? Make a grid with words and phrases. (Use a dictionary for help.) Use these four headings:

Sport | Place | Equipment | Team / Individual sport

L 2/12

Have you ever run in a marathon?

"Have you ever seen the London Marathon?" Gwen asked.

"Of course we have!" Holly said. "It starts right here in Greenwich Park."

"I want to run in it," Luke said. "But I've checked: You can't until you're 18."

"But haven't you heard of the *mini* marathon?" Gwen asked.

"No, I haven't," Jay said. "What's that?"

"It's for 11- to 17-year-olds," Gwen explained. "It's just the last part of the race, and it's before the *real* marathon."

"Are you going to run in it?" Olivia asked Gwen. "I know you like running."

"It isn't that easy," Gwen said. "There are teams for different parts of London, and there are trials to find the fastest runners."

"Where are the trials?" Dave asked.

"For the Greenwich team, here in the park, next Saturday," Gwen said.

"Let's do it!" Olivia said. "Who's in?"

"Me," said Gwen. "It was my idea, remember?"

"I'm in too!" Luke said.

Nobody said a word. Then Jay said, "No thanks, I'm out. I've never enjoyed running much. It isn't cool. And Dave has never run in a race. Right, Dave?"

"I've run in races before, but not in a big one like that," Dave said.

Holly said, "I've only ever run in short races too, and I'm not very good at running. But I've got an idea: Why don't you run for charity? People often do charity runs to raise money."

"That's great," Olivia said. "We can ask our parents, teachers and friends to give money. So it's Gwen, Luke and me."

"Er … just one thing," Gwen said. "Can we run together? You know, my eyes …"

"Of course," Olivia said.

"Yeah," Luke said, "we'll be Team Thomas Tallis! The fastest, coolest team in Greenwich. No, in *London*! Look out, here we come!"

READING

1 Are you going to run in it?

a) *Would you like to run in a marathon? Why / Why not?*

b) *Answer these questions:*

1. Say who likes / doesn't like running.
2. What's Holly's idea?
3. Who isn't going to run in the trials for the mini marathon?

Lösung: b) 1. *Olivia, Gwen and Luke like running. Jay doesn't like running.* 2. *Holly's idea is that the friends could run for charity.* 3. *Jay, Dave and Holly are not going to run in the trials for the mini marathon.*

Across cultures

The **London Marathon** is one of the world's biggest races, with over 35,000 runners. It starts in Greenwich Park and finishes at Buckingham Palace. Have you ever watched a marathon? What running events are there in your area?

Folie 22: Visuelle Unterstützung zur Erarbeitung der neuen Struktur
WB 34/3 Listening (correct answers)
WB 34/4 Language (conversation)

LANGUAGE

2 Find the rule → WB 34/3–4 → G8

ösung: a) ***Irregular verbs:*** *e, seen; hear, heard; n, run;* ***Regular verbs*** *(infinitive + ed): check, checked; enjoy, enjoyed.*

a) *There are examples of a new tense in the text, the present perfect. Look at these sentences and the verb forms in the box. What is different between verbs like **see** and verbs like **check**?*

I have run in a race before.
Have you ever watched a marathon?

Infinitive	– Past participle
see	– seen
check	– checked
hear	– heard
enjoy	– enjoyed
run	– run

There's a list of irregular verbs on page 246.

b) *Now make two sentences like this about Dave.*

He … … . | … he ever … ?

c) *Write down how you make and answer questions in the present perfect.*

WB 35/5 Writing (message)

LANGUAGE

3 Say who has done what → WB 35/5

→ ▲ 121/2

121/2 Have you really done that? ▲ → After …

sung: *1. been 2. has been heard 4. have watched run 6. has played prepared 8. given*

… you ever 1 (be) to London? – No, I …, but my sister 2 (be) there.
… you 3 (hear) of the London Marathon? – Yes, I …, I 4 (watch) it three times.
… your parents ever 5 (run) in a marathon? – No, they …, but my dad 6 (play) in an international tennis match.
… your little brother ever 7 (prepare) a meal? – Yes, he … He always helps in the kitchen.
… your grandma ever 8 (give) you extra pocket money? – No, she …

WB 35/6 Pronunciation (past participles)

SPEAKING

4 Your turn: Have you ever …? → WB 35/6

Transfer

→ S24

S24 Kooperative Lernformen (Milling around)

a) *Write at least three questions for your classmates with **Have you ever …?** The words on the right can help.*

finished | done | written | fallen
found | broken | asked for | run | been

homework | arm / leg | race
money | book | another country

Examples:
Have you ever seen …?
Have you ever been to …?
Have you ever eaten …?

b) *Ask some of your classmates the questions you wrote.*

c) *Write down what you've found out and tell the class.*

Example: Nicolas and Maria have been to Austria, but Tom and Lara haven't.

L 2/15

Have you been to the doctor's yet?

KV 5: Listening/Language (dialogue)

Voc.: Parts of the body, p. 183; Body parts, Word bank (WB), p. 14

Gwen: Hi Olivia. Are you still at home?

Olivia: Hi Gwen. Yes, I'm at home. I haven't left for school yet.

Gwen: Good. I've just had an idea. Let's train for the marathon trials. Do you want to go for a run in the park after school today?

Olivia: Great idea, but I've hurt my foot! I think I've twisted my ankle.

Gwen: Oh no! Have you been to the doctor's yet?

Olivia: No, I haven't. I hope it isn't serious. But it hurts when I walk, and I can't run on Saturday with pain like this.

Gwen: But you've already prepared for the trials!

Olivia: I know, it's so unfair! I've done everything I can! I've bought new running shoes, I've stopped eating chocolate, I've found information on the internet about the *best* way to run, I've –

Gwen: Listen, don't worry. I can train with Luke today, and maybe you can join us tomorrow.

Olivia: OK. Have you already asked Luke?

Gwen: No, not yet. I can ask him at school today. See you there.

Olivia: Yeah, see you later. Bye!

READING

5 Questions on the text

1. Why does Gwen call Olivia?
2. What's Olivia's problem?
3. What has Olivia done to prepare for the marathon trials?

Lösung: 1. *Gwen calls Olivia because she wants to train with her for the marathon trials.* 2. *Olivia's problem is her foot. It hurts when she walks.* 3. *Olivia has done a lot: She's bought new running shoes, she's stopped eating chocolate, and she's found information on the internet about the best way to run.*

LANGUAGE

6 The checklist → G8

KV 4: Language (signal words)

Ask and answer questions about what the friends have done or haven't done.

Example: **Has** Gwen **called** Olivia **yet**? – Yes, she **has**.

Things to do	Who?	Done?
1. call Olivia	Gwen	✔
2. make a poster for the charity run	Holly	✘
3. run three miles	Luke	✔
4. read a book about running	Olivia	✔
5. write a chant to cheer the runners	Jay	✘
6. find a good place to watch the marathon	Dave	✘
7. tell their parents about the marathon	Gwen, Luke, Olivia	✔

Lösung: 2. *Has Holly made a poster for the charity run yet? – No, she hasn't.* 3. *Has Luke run three miles yet? – Yes, he has.* 4. *Has Olivia read a book about running yet? – Yes, she has.* 5. *Has Jay written a chant to cheer the runners yet? – No, he hasn't.* 6. *Has Dave found a good place to watch the marathon yet? – No, he hasn't.* 7. *Have Gwen, Luke and Olivia told their parents about the marathon yet? – Yes, they have.*

LANGUAGE

→ △ 121/3
→ ▲ 122/4

121/3 Great runners
△ → After …
122/4 Write a profile about Brandon
▲ → After …

-sung: EH: 2. *Mr Azad -as just finished preparing -nner. 3. Luke has just -me back from a walk with -erlock. 4. Jamie has just -llen off his bike. 5. Amber -s just bought a new dress. Olivia has just tidied her -sk. 7. Shahid has just writ- -n a text message. 8. Lucy -s just gone to bed.*

7 What has just happened?

KV 4: Language (signal words)
KV 6: Language/Speaking (present perfect)

Example: Mrs Elliot has just cleaned the windows.

Mrs Elliot – clean ✓

Mr Azad – finish

Luke – come back

Jamie – fall off

Amber – buy

Olivia – tidy

Shahid – write

Lucy – go to

-OCABULARY

→ S9

S9 Reading (Umgang mit neuen Wörtern)

Voc.: Health, p. 184

8 At the doctor's

WB 36/7 Listening (doctor's notes)
WB 36/8 Language (phone call)
WB 36/9 Writing (message)

Read Olivia's dialogue with the doctor. Practise your own dialogues with the ideas in the box.

Doctor: So, what's the problem today?
Olivia: I've had an accident and hurt my foot.
Doctor: Can you walk on it?
Olivia: No, I can't.
Doctor: Let me have a look. – Oh yes, you've twisted your ankle.
Olivia: Is it serious, Doctor?
Doctor: No, it isn't. But you need to walk very carefully for a couple of days.

Useful phrases

I've hurt my hand / foot / arm / head / shoulder. | I've got a headache / backache / stomachache. | I feel bad / sick and I can't … | I've got a cold / a cough / a fever. | You need to … | You shouldn't … | You can take pills / …

Olivia: Oh no, so I can't run in the marathon trials on Saturday …
Doctor: No, you really shouldn't. Here's a prescription for an ointment. You can put it on your ankle to stop the pain.

MEDIATION

→ △ 122/5
→ S17

122/5 Children and accidents
△ → Help with …

S17 Mediation

9 Children and accidents

WB 37/10 Mediation (dialogue)
WB 37/11 Speaking (role play)

Pia has found a German survey on the internet and thinks that Olivia could use it for her project. What does the introduction say about German children's health? Tell a partner in English.

Obwohl sie zum größten Teil vermeidbar wären, zählen Unfallverletzungen zu den häufigsten gesundheitlichen Beeinträchtigungen von Kindern und Jugendlichen. Pro Jahr erleiden etwa 15 Prozent der Kinder und Jugendlichen mindestens eine behandlungsbedürftige Unfallverletzung; Jungen sind öfter betroffen als Mädchen. Kleinkinder verletzen sich am häufigsten zu Hause. Ältere Kinder und Jugendliche erleiden Unfälle insbesondere beim Sport und in der Freizeit sowie in der Schule.

A picnic in the park

→ S21–22 S21–22 Film skills/Viewing

VIEWING

1 Understanding the story so far

KV 7: Viewing (film stills)

8 *Watch (00:00–03:55). Then match the sentences / the sentence parts below.*

Lösung: *1f); 2e); 3a); 4b); 5d); 6c)*

1. Marley's ankle hurts.
2. Laura is going to stay with her grandad in Kent
3. Marley wants to watch the football match
4. Marley thinks it's unfair
5. Jinsoo's mum has made 'kimbap'[1].
6. At first, Jinsoo doesn't like the idea

a) but his dad needs his help in the attic.
b) that everyone is going to watch football and he can't.
c) that Alicia is going to come to Kent too.
d) It's typical Korean snack food.
e) and invites her friends to visit her.
f) He thinks he has twisted it.

SPEAKING

2 How's your ankle?

Lösung: a) *Marley fakes an injury so he can watch the Arsenal football game, and his father must clear out the attic alone.*

a) *Watch the rest of the film. What does Marley do? The phrases can help you.*

b) *What does Marley's father say at the end? Do you think he's right? Say why / why not. Think about it from Marley's point of view and from Mr Thompson's too. Look at the box again.*

Useful phrases

to fake an injury / a headache / …
to teach somebody a lesson
It's fair / unfair because …
I think / don't think his father is right …
Marley deserves it / doesn't deserve it …

Transfer

c) *Your turn: Have you ever faked anything? Did you get away with it? Tell the class.*

KV 8: Language (picnic food)
WB 38/12 Vocabulary (picnic in the park)

VOCABULARY

3 The picnic

→ WB 38/12

a) *The friends are having different food for their picnic. Look at the photo and the food words and say what looks good.*

Transfer

b) *Your turn: In class, talk about **your** 'perfect picnic'. What food from your country / your area / other countries could you have?*

1 kimbap ['kɪmbæp] *koreanischer Snack aus Seegras, Reis, Rindfleisch, Käse und Ei* | **2 cress** [kres] Kresse | **3 Scotch egg** [skɒtʃ 'eg] *hart gekochtes Ei in Wurstbrät* | **4 quiche** [kiːʃ] Quiche | **5 pasta salad** [ˌpæstə 'sæləd] Nudelsalat | **6 tuna** ['tjuːnə] Thunfisch

WB 38/13 Across cultures (picnic rules)

How to understand news reports and take notes

→ S18–20

S18–20 Listening

For the task on pages 62–63, you need to know what the parts of a radio report are and what language is typical for a radio report. This page can help you.

WB 39/14 Skills (radio report)

1 A mountain rescue → WB 39/14

L 2/17

ösung: a) *Time:* earlier this orning. *Place:* nearby Scafell ke, area of the Lake District ational Park. *People:* group teenage hikers from Bristol; aaron (girl with broken g); Danny Sampson, friend Sharon; mountain rescue ople; Annie Price, rescue rvice; Sean Abbott, reporter; ndy, newsreader. *Event:* enage hikers walking along ountain path; path fell away der the feet of 17-year-old rl; fell 50 metres, broke leg; ends called mountain rescue rvice; hospital.

a) *Listen to a radio report about an accident in the mountains. Take notes in a grid.*

Time	Place	People	Event

b) *Use your notes and answer the questions.*

1. What was the accident?
2. Why did it happen?
3. What did the mountain rescue team do?
4. Why was the rescue difficult?
5. How serious was the accident?
6. How is the way the news presenter and the reporter speak different to the way the witnesses speak?

KV 9a: Language (radio report)
KV 9b: Writing (your radio report)
WB 39/15 Activity (interviews)

2 The language of a radio report → WB 39/15

Read the boxes. Then listen to the report again. Note down which phrases from the bigger box you can hear in the report.
*Also, note down **other** interesting or typical phrases for the news presenter, the reporter, the witness.*
Why do you think they are typical?

Vocabulary skills

The situations are different, but the **language** of radio reports is often the same:

- **News presenters** and **reporters** stay more formal and use a language of facts.
- An **eyewitness** has just seen something dramatic, strange or maybe scary; the language he / she uses often shows more feelings.

Useful phrases

News presenter at radio station:
Hello / Good morning to all our listeners out there. | We've just received news of … | Now we're going to hear from our reporter at the scene: Can you describe the … / Can you tell us about the … | Stay with us for more …

Reporter at the scene:
Where were you when …? | What have you seen? | Has anyone else …? | What else can you tell us?

Eyewitness at the scene:
I couldn't believe my eyes! | This is strange / dramatic / exciting / … | I've never seen anything like it!

The aliens have landed!

Folie 23: Semantisierung des Wortschatzes und Bildbeschreibung

Imagine that aliens have landed on Earth – in Greenwich Park! In this Unit task, you and your group write your own radio report about this strange event. For the report, there are five roles: **three witnesses**; a **reporter** (he interviews the witnesses); the **radio news presenter**. Your job is to write – and record – a fun report. Your report should be 3–4 minutes long. Be as creative as possible!

Step 1

WB 40/16 Gapped text (the Martians)

The situation → WB 40/16

In groups of five, look at the scenes above. Talk about what you think is happening / has happened in each scene. Look closely at the words in the box. You need them to talk about the pictures.

Martian | Mars | space | spaceship | UFO | light | sky | star | customer | stomachache | human | to land | to invade | to come in peace | to make friends | to get sick on (too much) chocolate | strange-looking | bright | friendly

Examples:

A: In this scene, you can see that the aliens have landed.
B: What's happening at the hospital? Have the aliens eaten too much chocolate?
C: Look at the park scene: It looks like the aliens want to make friends!

Martian ['mɑːʃn] Marsmensch | **space** [speɪs] Weltraum | **spaceship** ['speɪsʃɪp] Raumschiff | **light** [laɪt] Licht | **sky** [skaɪ] Himmel | **customer** ['kʌstəmə] Kunde / Kundin | **human** ['hjuːmən] Mensch | **to invade** [ɪn'veɪd] eindringen | **in peace** [ɪn 'piːs] in Frieden | **to make friends** [meɪk 'frendz] Freundschaft schließen | **to get sick on sth** [get 'sɪk ɒn] sich an etw. den Magen verderben | **strange-looking** ['streɪndʒ ˌlʊkɪŋ] seltsam aussehend | **bright** [braɪt] hell

Step 2

KV 10a: Making notes (role play)
WB 40/17 Matching

Choose roles and form expert groups → WB 40/17

a) *In your group, each of you chooses one of the five roles.*

b) *Form expert groups: All students with the same role work together. In your new group, talk about what kind of things* ***your character*** *should/could say in a radio report. Make notes – and be creative!*

Examples:

A: *(doctor group)* As a doctor, I want to tell the reporter how the aliens are feeling. The people should know that they got sick on chocolate. They don't speak English, but we know they're feeling better; they're smiling now!

B: *(reporter group)* A reporter should ask how the man in his garden felt when he first saw the UFOs. I'm sure it was a big shock! – Oh, and a reporter should ask how the aliens *paid* for their chocolate at the shop!

For typical phrases for reporters and witnesses, have another look at the **Skills page** you've just done.

Step 3

KV 10b: Writing (part of the radio report)
WB 41/18 Listening (radio report)

Plan and write your report → WB 41/18

a) *Go back to your home group. Each of you is now an expert for one of the roles. Talk about how you all want to put the report together. Think about these points first:*

How should it start? | How should it end: Does the news presenter tell the listeners to listen for more information later? Is the Martians' visit to Earth over? | Which order are the interviews in? | How serious (or silly) should the presenter and the reporter be? | Remember that the presenter needs to say something after every reporter interview.

b) *Now write your report, interview by interview. Each person writes some of it.*

c) *Peer-editing: Trade your part with somebody else and check each other's texts.*

d) *One of you now reads it to the rest of the group. Listen carefully. Does it sound like a radio report? Does it sound interesting enough? Make changes for a better text.*

Step 4

WB 41/19Listening (reports)

Practise and record your report → WB 41/19

a) *Practice your report a few times, and record yourselves with a smartphone. Does it sound right? Remember: Don't read from the page!*

b) *Now record your final report.*

c) *Play it for the class. Tell the groups what you liked about* ***their*** *reports.*

S 1/29–33
L 2/19–23

Hey, don't call *me* silly!

Folie 24: Inhaltliche Vorentlastung und bildgestützte Nacherzählung

A In Greenwich, it's almost time for the mini marathon to start …

Gwen: It's too bad Olivia can't join us.

Luke: But she can cheer us on with the others and help us to do well today.

Gwen: Yes, for us *and* for 'See with your Heart'. It means a lot to me, as a partially sighted person.

Luke: Your charity means something to *all* of us, Gwen. – But anyway, remember: You mustn't let go of my hand!

Gwen: Luke, that's *my* line: *I'm* the one who can't see well, remember?

Luke: Oh, sorry. I'm just nervous. Do you think I've trained enough?

Gwen: Well, I have! I did lots of extra training. But I can't speak for *you*.

Luke: Great, that really helps.

Gwen: Don't think so much, silly. Just run. And not too fast too soon!

Luke: Hey, don't call *me* silly – look at *them* in their crazy animal costumes. Can you see them?

Gwen: Er, not very well. But there are always people in fancy dress at events like these. They're running for charity too.

Luke: Oh yes: a pet charity, I'm sure; they've got cat and dog costumes. But how can they *run* in them?!

Gwen: No idea. – But hey, look! There are Holly and Olivia! But hm, where are Dave and Jay?

B A few minutes into the race …

Gwen:
This feels GREAT! My big day, after all that training … Now is the moment – MY moment! I can show them how good I am. Just breathe … run … enjoy it! … But what about Luke? Can he keep up? He didn't do any extra training like me. And *he's* worried about *me*? … Oh, those silly runners in the animal costumes in front of us – they aren't really taking this seriously. … What are they doing? Jumping from right to left and getting in the way. Clowns! … I hope they don't get in *our* way.

C Ten minutes later …

Gwen:
Ouch! What's that?! Oh, my stomach; it *really* hurts. … Oh no, I mustn't stop! I'm running for the charity – *and* for Luke! … I don't want to be the new girl with the funny glasses; I want to be the new girl with fast legs! Oh, but my stomach… Come on, just run! … RUN!

D Not far from the finish line …

Gwen:
I think that stupid cramp is gone. YES! And Luke is still doing fine too. … We're still running fast: I think our time is going to be *really* good. … I want to see our photos on the TTS website! "Gwen Parker, the new running star". Sounds great! – OH NO!!!!!!!!! What's happening?!?! Oh no, I don't want to fall!

E Just after the race …

Luke: Gwen, we did it, WE DID IT!

Gwen: Yes, we did! And it feels GREAT!

Luke: Well, *now* it feels great. But during the race I had a bad cramp. You started too fast for me!

Gwen: *You* had a cramp? Oh, now I feel better.

Luke: I had a cramp and now *you* feel better? I don't understand.

Gwen: Well, I had a cramp too – but I didn't want to tell you; I didn't want to stop the race.

Luke: And I didn't want to tell *you* and hear, "You didn't train enough!"

Gwen: Well, we *both* finished, yippee! And 'See with your Heart' gets some money too!

Luke: Well, they almost *didn't*: That stupid dog and that stupid cat almost ruined everything for us! I couldn't believe my eyes when they pulled out a smartphone and took a selfie. That one boy fell because of them, and we almost fell too!

Gwen: They took a *selfie*? In the middle of the race? Oh, I knew those two were trouble!

Olivia: *(suddenly)* Yes, that's what the race officials thought too so they finally took the dog and the cat out of the race. – Look who I've found!

Luke: Dave and Jay?!?!

Gwen: YOU were the dog and the cat?!?! Aaaargh!!!

Dave: Don't be angry, please! We're really sorry. We only wanted to surprise you.

Jay: Yes, we trained in secret, and ran for the pets' charity!

Gwen: But somebody *fell* because of you two. Luke and I almost fell! I'm sure that boy trained hard. Have you ever thought of that?

Jay: Well, er …

Dave: We said sorry, Gwen.

Gwen: Well, don't tell *me*. Have you told the boy yet?

Dave: Er, no.

Gwen: Well, *tell* him. *(smiling now)* So we can finally forgive you.

Luke: But I'm not sure 'sorry' is enough. How about a present for him?

Olivia: That sounds good. I'm sure we all have nice present ideas.

Gwen: Yes boys, you must do something nice for him. But you can do something nice for me and Luke too. – Luke, where's your phone? Picture time!

Luke: Oh yes – those silly costumes, those faces in the next TTS yearbook! Say CHEESE!

READING

1 Working with the text → WB 42/20

WB 42/20 Reading (comprehension)

Lösung: a) 1. A and E are dialogues; B, C and D are thoughts of a character in the story (interior monologues). (The texts in A and E show what people say; in B, C and D they show what someone thinks.) etc.

a) *Look at the text and talk about these questions.*

1. What different kinds of text are there in parts A–E?
2. Why do people run in a marathon? Find reasons in the text and say who gives them.
3. What can cause problems in a marathon race?
4. What do we learn about Gwen and Luke's hopes and fears?
5. What can you say about their relationship?

→ △ 122/6 **b)** *Use the text and the pictures to retell what happened.*

122/6 The London Mini Marathon △→ Help with …

READING

2 What do you think?

a) *Find adjectives to describe Gwen, Luke, Jay and Dave and their actions.*

→ △ 123/7 **b)** *Find positive and negative things in the story that they did. Use words from a) to discuss what you think about their actions. Here are some ideas:*

123/7 What's the person like? △→ Help with …

*Lösung: a) **Gwen:** brave, confident, helpful, ambitious, clever, fast; **Luke:** helpful, nice, responsible, lazy, brave, ambitious, fast; **Jay and Dave:** crazy, silly, stupid, selfish, helpful, good.*

Positive	Negative
On the one hand it was **good** that … I think Gwen was **brave** … …	On the other hand it was really **stupid** … But it was also **dangerous** … …

Voc.: Positive and negative words, p.187

VOCABULARY

3 Looking at spoken language

KV 11: Language (freeze frame)

→ △ 123/8
→ ▲ 123/9

Read the dialogues and Gwen's thoughts out loud. How do Gwen and Luke talk to each other? What language do they use to express their feelings? Which words and phrases would you like to use again? Collect them in a mind map.

123/8 Useful phrases from the story △→ Help with …

WRITING

4 Another story → WB 42/21

WB 42/21 Writing (options)

→ S10–13
S10–13 Writing

*Write about what **isn't** in the story. Choose one of these two topics. You can write a story, a dialogue or a comic. Use your vocabulary from Ex. 2.*

- Just for fun: The race from Jay and Dave's point of view.
- Can you forgive us: Jay and Dave talk to the boy who fell because of them.

→ Solutions p. 248

Can you ...

1. talk about experiences in your life / in somebody else's life? — Have you ever played rugby?
2. talk about things which have (just) happened? — I've hurt my foot!
3. use *just*, *already* and *yet*? — I haven't had my dinner yet.

LANGUAGE

HA

1 Match the sentence halves.

1. I think you've broken
2. We've been to
3. I've never eaten
4. Jay has just written
5. Holly hasn't finished
6. I've already asked

a) a new chant.
b) in an Indian restaurant.
c) your ankle.
d) Olivia to help me with my project.
e) Buckingham Palace three times.
f) her homework yet.

LANGUAGE

2 Make dialogues about Luke and Dave

Example: Dave: write | your health report? → Have you already written your report?
Luke: no | have | no time | yet → No, I haven't. I haven't had time yet.

HA

1. Luke: find | information on the internet yet?
   Dave: yes | already | use information in report
2. Luke: Jay | draw | mangas for his report?
   Dave: yes | create | great new characters
3. Dave: see | two new manga comics yet?
   Luke: yes | already | finish one of them
4. Luke: see | Olivia today?
   Dave: no | but I | just | send text
5. Dave: Holly | write about guinea pigs?
   Luke: hope not! | write about guinea pigs | many times before
6. Dave: go | to the park with Sherlock yet?
   Luke: no | but Irina | just | go for a walk with him

VOCABULARY

HA

3 Which word is right?

I love football. I think it's the best **1** in the world! I **2** every **3** of my favourite team, the Wellsey. Do you want to **4** my new poster of the best player ever, Adriano Donaldo? He scores lots of goals with his head because he's very **5**. He even **6** the **7** score of three head goals in one match. My dream is to **8** a football star like him.

highest | match | become | tall | watch | got | see | game

<Story> ist ein fakultativer Romanauszug. Der neue Wortschatz ist rezeptiv und unter dem Text annotiert.

Folie 25: Inhaltliche Vorentlastung und bildgesteuerte Nacherzählung
KV 1: Reading (bullies)
KV 2: Reading/Writing (summary/chat)
KV 3: Speaking (useful phrases)

S 2/1–4
L 2/24–27

The summer[1] table

August was born[2] with a genetic defect and has 'facial issues[3]'. To other people, the highly intelligent boy looks like a monster. Everyone stares at him so he doesn't go to school; his mum teaches him at home. When he is about 10, his parents finally decide to send him to school. On his first day, Auggie has a really hard time. The other children stare at him or ignore him completely. At lunchtime, Auggie feels really bad – his friend Jack Will isn't there, and because of[4] his face, August has problems eating, too. When a girl, Summer, sits down at his table, he is very surprised.

"Hey, is somebody sitting here?"

I looked up, and a girl I never saw before was standing across from my table with a lunch tray[5] full of food. She had long wavy brown hair, and wore a brown T-shirt with a purple peace sign[6] on it.

"Uh, no," I said.

She put her lunch tray on the table, dropped her rucksack on the floor, and sat down across from me. She started to eat the pasta with cheese sauce on her plate.

"Ugh," she said when she took the first bite. "Why didn't I bring a sandwich like you did?"

"Yeah," I said.

"My name is Summer, by the way. What's yours?"

"August."

"Cool," she said.

"Summer!"

Another girl who was carrying[7] a tray came over to the table. "Why are you sitting here? Come back to the table."

"There were too many people," Summer answered her. "Come sit here. There's more room."

The other girl looked confused[8] for a second. I recognized[9] her. She was sitting at another table with some friends a few minutes ago: They were looking at me and she had her hand over her mouth and was whispering. I guess Summer was one of the girls at that table too.

"Don't worry," the girl said and went away.

Summer looked at me, smiled, and took another bite of her pasta.

"Hey, our names match," she said, as she ate.

I guess she noticed that[10] I didn't know what she meant.

"Summer? August?" she said and smiled, her eyes open wide, as she waited for me to understand.

"Oh, yeah," I said after a second.

"We can make this the 'summer only'

1 summer ['sʌmə] Sommer | **2 to be born** [bi 'bɔ:n] geboren werden | **3 facial issues** [ˌfeɪʃl 'ɪʃu:z] Gesichtsprobleme | **4 because of** [bɪ'kɒz‿əv] wegen | **5 tray** [treɪ] Tablett | **6 peace sign** ['pi:s saɪn] Friedenszeichen | **7 to carry** ['kæri] tragen | **8 confused** [kən'fju:zd] verwirrt | **9 to recognize** ['rekəgnaɪz] wiedererkennen | **10 that** [ðæt] dass

lunch table," she said. "Only kids with summer names can sit here. Let's see, is there anyone here named June or July?"

"There's a Maya," I said.

"Technically, May is spring[11]," Summer answered, "but if she wants to sit here, we can make an exception[12]." She said it as if[13] she already had a plan. "There's Julian. That's like the name Julia, which comes from July."

I didn't say anything.

"There's a kid named Reid in my English class," I said.

"Yeah, I know Reid, but how is Reid a summer name?" she asked.

"I don't know," I said. "I just imagine … it's like a reed of grass[14] in summer."

"Yeah, OK," she answered and pulled out her notebook[15]. "And Ms.[16] Petosa could[17] sit here, too. That sounds like the word 'petal[18]', which is a summer thing too, I think."

"She's my tutor," I said.

"I have her for Maths," she answered and made a face[19].

She started to write the list of names on a page of her notebook.

"So, who else?" she said.

When we finished lunch, we had a whole list of names of kids and teachers who could sit at our table if they wanted. Most of the names weren't really summer names, but they were names that had some kind of connection to summer. I even found a way to put Jack Will's name on the list – I suggested that we could put his name into a sentence about summer, like "Jack will go to the beach[20]," and Summer agreed that that was fine.

"But if someone doesn't have a summer name and wants to sit with us," she said very seriously, "they can still sit here if they're nice, OK?"

"OK," I agreed. "Even if it's a winter name."

"Cool," she answered and gave me a thumbs-up.

Summer looked like her name. She had a tan[21], and her eyes were green like the leaves of a tree.

'The Summer Table' from *WONDER* by R. J. Palacio

WB 44/1 Reading (main idea) WB 44/2 Reading (details)
WB 44/3 Vocabulary (names) WB 44/4 Writing (next part)

11 **spring** [sprɪŋ] Frühling | **12** **exception** [ɪk'sepʃn] Ausnahme | **13** **as if** [əz‿'ɪf] als ob | **14** **reed of grass** [ˌriːd‿əv 'grɑːs] Schilf | **15** **notebook** ['nəʊtbʊk] Notizbuch | **16** **Ms.** [mɪz] Frau *(Anrede)* | **17** **could** [kʊd] könnte | **18** **petal** ['petl] Blütenblatt | **19** **to make a face** [meɪk‿ə 'feɪs] das Gesicht verziehen | **20** **beach** [biːtʃ] Strand | **21** **tan** [tæn] sonnengebräunte Haut

<Revision B> ist fakultativ und dient der Festigung/Wiederholung. Es werden keine neuen Sprachmittel eingeführt.

VOCABULARY

1 On tour on a London pedicab[1]

a) *Choose the right word.*

Lösung: a) 1. *different* 2. *quickly* 3. *exciting* 4. *easily* 5. *famous* 6. *friendly* 7. *important* 8. *interesting* 9. *slowly* 10. *carefully* 11. *fresh* 12. *hard* 13. *amazing* 14. *well* 15. *cheaply* 16. *cool*

amazing | quickly | fresh | well | cool | interesting | slowly | cheap | different | easily | important | carefully

The London pedicabs

Do you want to go on a 1 kind of sightseeing tour? Then hop on[2] 2 and enjoy London's sights and attractions from the backseat[3] of a pedicab. Pedicabs are an exciting and environmentally friendly[4] way to travel around the city 3 . Enjoy all the famous sights and get off anywhere you like. Our friendly drivers speak three languages and know all the 4 facts and 5 stories about London. And, of course, they always drive 6 and 7 !

You can start your tour at different places, for example at Covent Garden, with its shops, cafés and restaurants with 8 food from all over the world. You want to take a photo or buy something to drink? – No problem. Our drivers work hard to make your tour an 9 experience. Have a look at Buckingham Palace and see the Changing of the Guard. Stop in front of the Houses of Parliament and listen to the sound of Big Ben. You want to know where you can eat 10 and buy 11 food? Or where you can buy 12 clothes? Just ask our drivers!

Tours:
- Mini tour: 1 hour | £50 | 1–2 persons
- Shopping tour: 1 hour | £30 | 1–2 persons

b) *Would you like to see London in a pedicab? Say why/why not.*

c) *Where else could the pedicab tour go? Continue the text.*

LISTENING

2 A radio report: Shopping for souvenirs

→ WB 45/1 WB 45/1 Language (pictures)

L 2/28

a) *Listen to the radio report and say where the reporter is and what the report is about.*

Lösung: a) *The reporter is in Covent Garden. The report is about souvenirs of London.*

b) *Listen again. Copy the grid and fill in the missing information.*

Lösung: b)

	Mr Smith	Amir	American tourist
souvenir	"I love London" T-shirt	book with ghost stories and horror stories about London	teddy bear with Beefeater costume
for	his daughter	himself	a friend in America
price	£20	£24.99	£19.99
problem	They didn't have size S. He hopes size M isn't too big.	It's quite expensive and he needs to find something for his mum too.	She'd like to buy more souvenirs, but her suitcase is too full.

c) *What do you think is the best souvenir? What souvenir would you bring? Say why.*

1 **pedicab** ['pedɪkæb] Fahrradtaxi, Fahrradrikscha | 2 **to hop on** [hɒp‿'ɒn] (schnell) einsteigen | 3 **backseat** ['bæksi:t] Rücksitz | 4 **environmentally friendly** [ɪnˌvaɪrənˌmentli 'frendli] umweltfreundlich

VOCABULARY

3 A sports quiz → WB 45/2 WB 45/2 Language (conversation)

a) *Work with a partner. What sport do you both like? Make notes: where people play, what equipment they need, how many players there are in a team, etc. (For new words, use a dictionary.) Don't show each other your notes!*

b) *Write 5–6 quiz questions with the information in your notes.*

Example: Which of these football teams has never won the World Cup?
A. England B. Poland C. Italy

c) *Test your partner with your quiz! Who knows the most about the same sport?*

READING

4 Are they crazy?

ösung: a) *The text is about the Ben Nevis race. Every year in early September runners run up Ben Nevis and back down again.*
1344 metres: height of Ben Nevis; 125,000: people climb Ben Nevis every year; 9.9 miles: distance to the top and back down again; 1984: Kenny Stuart broke the record; 1 hour, 25 minutes and 34 seconds: Kenny Stuart's time; 600: the number of runners; September 27, 1895: date when William Swan was the first person to run up and down the mountain; 2 hours and 41 minutes: William Swan's time in 1895.
Safety rules: Only 600 runners can run the race; they must have a lot of experience; they must wear waterproofs, a hat, gloves and a whistle.
The history of the race: On September 27, 1895, William Swan was the first person to run up and down Ben Nevis. He started at Fort William.

a) *Skim the text for the gist. Say what it is about in 2–3 sentences.*

BEN NEVIS

You've probably heard of Ben Nevis in Scotland[5]. With its 1344 metres it is the highest mountain in Great Britain. Each year 125,000 people climb this mountain. It usually takes a few hours to get to the peak[6]. But if you go up on the first Saturday in September, you can see people who[7] run up or down the mountain. You think they're crazy? Well, they probably are …
They take part in the Ben Nevis race. It takes place every year in early September. The race starts and finishes in Fort William. The runners do not only run up the mountain but also back down again – that's a distance of 9.9 miles with a height[8] difference of 1,340 metres. And some runners are really fast. In 1984 Kenny Stuart ran up and down the mountain in 1 hour, 25 minutes and 34 seconds – that's still the record[9] today.
To run up and down the mountain you must be really fit. Only runners with a lot of experience can take part in the race. For safety reasons[10] the number of runners is limited to[11] 600. The weather can change quickly in the mountains, so the runners must wear waterproofs[12], a hat, gloves and a whistle[13].
But who had this crazy idea anyway? People say that it was William Swan. On September 27, 1895 he ran from Fort William to the top of the mountain in 2 hours and 41 minutes. He probably didn't know what he started …

b) *Scan the text. What numbers are there in the text and what do they mean? What does it tell you about 1. safety rules 2. the history of the race? Take notes.*

5 **Scotland** ['skɒtlənd] Schottland | 6 **peak** [pi:k] Gipfel, Bergspitze | 7 **people who …** [ˌpi:pl 'hu:] Leute, die … | 8 **height** [haɪt] Höhe | 9 **record** ['rekɔ:d] Rekord | 10 **safety reasons** ['seɪfti ˌri:zns] Sicherheitsgründe | 11 **limited to** ['lɪmɪtɪd tə] begrenzt auf | 12 **waterproofs** ['wɔ:təpru:fs] Regenkleidung | 13 **whistle** ['wɪsl] Trillerpfeife

Find more online: xy4p42

Folie 26: Bewusstmachung der Rolle des Englischen als lingua franca und Bildbeschreibung

English around the world

Many people in different countries around the world speak English. Learn about where and why, and listen to some different kinds of English.

SPEAKING

1 Which countries speak English?

a) *Which countries do you know where the people speak English?*

b) *On a map or in an atlas, show where these countries are.*

c) *Can you think of a time when you spoke English? Where were you and who did you speak to? The phrases can help.*

Useful phrases

I spoke English …
with a friend | with a family member | on video chat | in a chat room | …
I was …
on holiday | at a summer camp | in Germany | in another country | …

VIEWING

2 Speaking English

KV 1a: Speaking (role play)
KV 1b: Evaluation/Feedback (role play)

9

a) *Watch the film. What is it about?*

b) *Does Marley talk about any of the countries in your answers to Ex. 1? Which?*

c) *Look at the stills and describe what happens in the two scenes.*

A

B

d) *Watch the film again. Say which statements are right. Correct the wrong ones.*

1. The American man works in England.
2. American English is not exactly the same as British English.
3. You can see English signs in China, India and in some other countries.
4. The South Korean man can't help the Romanian woman.

e) *Act out one of these scenes:*

1. You're on holiday and make a new friend from another country.
2. You help an English-speaking person in your town.

Hi! / Hello! | How are you? |
I'm … from … | Where are you from? |
Are you here on holiday? |
I'm looking for … | Can you …?

Lösung: a) *The film is about the use of English in different countries. It shows that the English people speak in different countries is not exactly the same. The British and the Americans use some different words, for example. English also helps people from two different countries to talk to each other.*
b) *United States of America, Australia, New Zealand, Canada, India, Rwanda*
c) A: *A young man is looking at a map. Marley asks him where he's from. The young man is a tourist from America.* **B:** *A young woman asks Marley where she can find a supermarket. Marley isn't sure. A young Asian man hears this and offers to show the woman where the supermarket is.*
d) 1. *wrong: He is on holiday.* 2. *right* 3. *right* 4. *wrong: He can show her where the supermarket is.*

WB 46/1 Speaking (quiz)

READING

3 How English became a world language → WB 46/1

a) *Before you read: Why do you think so many people in the world speak English?*

b) *Read the text. Make a list of the reasons why so many people speak English today. Only take notes! Then use your notes to explain to your partner why English is so important today.*

sung: b) first reason om about 1600 for many ars): British sailors/mer- ants crossed sea; started lonies; British Empire ew; examples of British lonies: Australia, India, uth Africa; second reason fter World War II): USA = perpower; started to influ- ce world: rock'n'roll music, llywood films; later: new chnology from America C, internet, e-mail) = com- unication in English with ery part of the world

More than 400 million people in the world today speak English as their first language, and more than 600 million speak it as a second or official language. The first important reason for this is that from about 1600, British sailors and merchants crossed the sea and started colonies. This went on for many years and the British Empire became huge. For example, Australia was a British colony; India and South Africa too. Today, the British king or queen is still head of state in many countries, e. g. Australia.

There's a second important reason why so many people speak English. After World War II, the USA became a superpower and started to influence the world in many new ways. American rock 'n' roll music and Hollywood films became popular almost everywhere. And later, new technology from America (the PC, the internet, the e-mail) made it possible to communicate in every last corner of the world. In English, of course!

KV 2: Language (BE and AE)
WB 46/2 Reading (signs)

LISTENING

4 Where are we from? → WB 46/2

L 2/29

a) *Listen to four people from different English-speaking regions or countries. Which place is each person from? Which ones did you find easy or difficult to understand? Why?*

b) *Listen again. In which place can you hear these words and expressions? Can you remember what they mean?*

sung: a) Speaker 1: Scot- nd; Speaker 2: Australia; eaker 3: USA; Speaker 4: land Scotland: lad and las- s, wee, loch; Australia: nnies, G'day; USA: cookie, ndy, movie; Ireland: I'm and, What's the craic?

Lou

cookie | sunnies | wee | loch | lads and lasses | I'm grand | G'day | candy | movie | What's the craic? |

OCABULARY

Transfer

5 Your turn: English in your language

Collect words in German that are similar to or the same as words in English. Put the words into these categories. (Maybe you can think of more categories too.)

Clothes | Technology | Food | Sport | ...

Find more online: tn37p7

Unit 4

Stay in touch

Folie 27: Inhaltlich/Sprachliche Vorentlastung und Aufbau einer Leseerwartung

SPEAKING

1 Media and TTS students: A survey

Read what TTS students say about different media in A–E. Which of the activities have you done this week?

VOCABULARY

2 Media collocations

→ △ 123/1

Match these verbs and nouns to make phrases to talk about media.

→ S3

Example: I like to change my profile and post new photos. What about you?

123/1 Media collocations △ → Instead of ...

S3 Vocabulary (Wörter im Zusammenhang)

change | post | receive | send | read | talk to | reply to | play | join | check | chat | take part in | write | text | have	profile | photo | text message | forum | social network | video game | video chat | magazine | discussion | each other | friend

Voc.: Media collocations, p. 189; Media, Word bank (WB), p. 16

Lösung: siehe S. 189 (Voc)

In Unit 4 you learn

… how to talk and write about communication in your life. You learn:

- media vocabulary and phrases
- the language of giving and getting advice
- modals
- writing skills for letters and replies

KV 1: Vocabulary (survey)
WB 47/1 Vocabulary (media)
WB 47/2 Vocabulary (statements)
WB 47/3 Vocabulary (messages)

LISTENING

3 More about the survey → WB 47/1-3

L 2/30–34

sung: a) *smartphone/ ɔbile; special interest ·ums; online magazines/ ·int magazines; video ·mes; social networks*

a) *Which media do the TTS students use? Listen and make a list.*

b) *Listen again and take notes. What do the students say about the media?*

Useful phrases

Smartphones / Social networks / … are great because they're fun / practical / easy to use / …
… are great for meeting … / for staying in touch with … / for sharing information about …

Which media?	What's positive?	What's not so positive?
smartphone / mobile	texts / easy to stay in touch	texts from parents!
special interest forums	…	…

Transfer

c) *Your turn: Talk about how you use the different media.*

L 2/35

Dear Ruby

Holly and Olivia have found an interesting problem in the 'agony aunt' pages of their favourite magazine.

Across cultures

In Britain, the advice pages of teen magazines are often very popular. People write to an **agony aunt** for help with their problems. What kind of agony aunts are there in your country?

JUST ASK RUBY!

Dear Ruby,

I'm writing to you because I don't know what to do. Last week I had a big fight with one of my best friends. Before the fight, we spent all our free time together. But now she has made friends with another girl and they're having a lot of fun. I know this because she posts photos of the two of them on the social network site we use. She acts like she's having a much better time without me! Whenever I see these photos, it really hurts my feelings.

Can you please help? I would really like to hear your advice.

Lauren

Dear Lauren,

I'm sorry you're feeling so upset. I understand how hard it is to share a friend; it was the same with me when I was young. As a first step, my advice is to be self-critical: Are you overreacting? Maybe the situation isn't as serious as you think.

The next step is to talk to your friend in a friendly way and tell her how you feel. Why don't you invite her to your house after school? Or have you tried texting her? Things usually get better as soon as you talk.

Another tip: Please stop looking at your social network site until you've talked to her. The photos only make you feel worse!

I hope you two can be friends again very soon.

Ruby

WB 48/4 Listening (matching)

READING

1 Understanding the problem → WB 48/4

→ ▲ 124/2

124/2 Ruby's answer
▲ → After ...

Answer these questions about Lauren's letter and Ruby's reply.

1. Why is Lauren writing to Ruby?
2. How does Lauren know about her friend's new friend?
3. When does Lauren feel really bad?
4. Compare how her friend acted before the fight and after (in Lauren's opinion).

Lösung: *1. Lauren had a big fight with one of her best friends. Now they don't talk any more. Her friend made friends with another girl. 2. Lauren has seen that her friend has posted photos of her and her new friend on a social network site. 3. She feels really bad when she looks at these photos. 4. Her friend spent all her time with Lauren before the fight. Now she acts like she's having a much better time with her new friend (without Lauren).*

WB 48/5 Language (media day)
WB 48/6 Pronunciation (sounds)

LANGUAGE

2 Using linking words → WB 48/5–6 → G9

→ △ 124/3

→ S13

.4/3 Using linking words: ny and his phone → After … 3 Writing (Sprachliche rbesserungen)

sung: 1. *until/before Whenever/As soon as Before/Whenever; As on as/After 4. because/ ter 5. like/because because*

Read what different teens say about how they use different social media websites. Put these words in the gaps. There's sometimes more than one correct answer.

after | before | as soon as | until | whenever | like | because

1. I'm careful. I never give my phone number ___ I've met a new friend face-to-face.
2. ___ somebody starts asking too many personal questions, I just block them.
3. ___ you post photos of yourself online, remember: ___ you post them, they're probably on the internet forever!
4. I'm angry with my cousin ___ she posted that awful photo of me at the lake.
5. My friend doesn't even know some of the people on her friends list! It's ___ she doesn't care about real friends, she just wants a long list of 'friends'.
6. I don't get much attention online ___ I don't post pictures of myself very often!

WRITING

3 Your turn: Media in your life

Transfer

Write 5–6 sentences about yourself like the ones you see in Ex. 2. Think about these ideas:

- How much information about yourself do you share online? Why? How often?
- Do you and your friends use media differently? How?

VOCABULARY

4 The right vocabulary for advice → WB 49/7

WB 49/7 Writing (dialogue)

sung: a) *Asking for vice: I'm writing to you cause I don't know what do. Can you please help? would like to hear your vice. Giving advice: … y advice is to be self-tical. The next step is to . Why don't you invite her your house . Or have you ed texting r? Please op looking . Showing derstanding: You're ving a hard time, aren't u? I'm sorry you're feeling upset. I know how hard is to share … I hope you n be friends …*

a) *In the letters on page 76, you see some phrases with 'advice vocabulary' in green. In a grid like this one, match the phrases to the three categories.*

Asking for advice	Giving advice	Showing understanding

→ S3

b) *Here are some important advice phrases. Think of them as 'building blocks' for your own sentences about advice. Write a sentence with each phrase. You can write about the same problem as on page 76, or about something different.*

S3 Vocabulary (Wörter im Zusammenhang)

Useful phrases

My advice is to be self-critical / to see it from the other side / to find a compromise.

Why don't you talk to your friend / invite your friend over / text your friend / …

The next step is to talk to / write to / …

It's always a good idea to talk / try / …

I'm sorry you're feel**ing** sad / **you're** hav**ing** trouble with …

I understand how hard / difficult it is to …

Have you tried talk**ing** to him / text**ing** her?

Stop look**ing** at … / think**ing** about / worry**ing** about / …

MEDIATION

WB 49/8 Speaking (discussion)

5 Learn how to mediate in a fight

→ WB 49/8

→ S17

S17 Mediation

Pia saw a fight between two of her classmates. She decides to join a special club at her school where students learn how to mediate in a fight. She wants to tell Olivia what she found out on the school website, but she doesn't know all the words in English. Help her to describe in her own words what the club is about.

Lösung: EH: *In this club you learn how you can help when your classmates or friends have a fight. You learn how to look for a solution together and how to solve the problem with words. People in this club get special training.*

Mediation skills

If you don't know a word in English, try to **describe it in other words** that you already know.

Example:

"*Zeuge* – He or she saw what happened in an accident or in a fight, for example."

Streitschlichter-AG
Mach dich und andere stark!

In unserer AG lernst du, wie du bei einem Streit zwischen Mitschülern oder Freunden vermitteln kannst. Als Streitschlichter hilfst du den Streitparteien, gemeinsam nach einer Lösung zu suchen. Es geht darum, Konflikte durch Reden – und nicht durch Gewalt! – zu lösen.
Lass dich zum Streitschlichter ausbilden und trage zu einem freundlichen Miteinander an unserer Schule und in deinem Freundeskreis bei!

149/5 You can hear the difference, can't you?
▲→ After ...

LISTENING

6 < A song: Friends > Aura Dione

KV 2: Listening/Writing (friendship)

L 3/1

→ S9

S9 Reading (Umgang mit neuen Wörtern)

Free, free to be myself
Free to need some time
Free to need some help
So I'm reaching baby, out
When I'm lonely in the crowd
When the silence[1] gets too loud
I'll be crashing[2] on some couch

And even if I never forget you baby
Tonight I'm gonna let your memory[3] baby
go, oh it's sad I know

But at least[4] I got my friends
Share a raincoat in the wind
They got my back[5] until the end
If I never fall in love again
Well at least I got my friends
Like a lifeboat in the dark
Saving me from the sharks[6]
Even though I got a broken heart
At least I got my friends, got my friends

Text: Aura Dione, Antonina Armato, Tim James, David Jost

Lösung: a) *"Free, free to be myself": wants to be free again; "Free to need some help": needs help because his/her love with another person is over; "lonely", "silence", "crashing": feels lonely, sad and tired; "And even if I never forget you baby": cannot forget his/her love*
b) Symbols of friendship: *"share a raincoat" – help, not lonely; „they got my back until the end" – help as long as you need it; "like a lifeboat" – help in a dangerous situation*

a) *Which words / lines tell you what kind of a situation the main character is in?*

→ △ 124/4

124/4 Symbols of friendship
△→ Help with ...

b) *Your turn: What things are symbols of friendship in the song, and for* ***you****? Why?*

Transfer

1 silence ['saɪləns] Stille | **2 to crash** [kræʃ] schlafen *(ugs.)* | **3 memory** ['memri] Erinnerung | **4 at least** [ət 'li:st] wenigstens | **5 They got my back** [ðeɪ ˌgɒt maɪ 'bæk] Sie halten mir den Rücken frei; sie passen auf mich auf *(ugs.)* | **6 shark** [ʃɑ:k] Hai

Folie 28 Wortschatzvorentlastung und Unterstützung des Hörverstehens

L 3/2

Forum? What forum?

Luke: Dad, can I go over to Jay's house? Er, what on earth are you doing? There's water everywhere!

Dad: Really? Where?

Luke: Very funny. What's happened?

Dad: There's a problem with one of the pipes. I must fix it before your mum comes home and goes crazy!

Luke: Dad, do you know what you're doing?

Dad: Of course! It's just taking longer than I thought.

Luke: You could look at a forum for help.

Dad: Forum? What forum? You mean on the internet? So I can't fix my own washing machine – is that what you think? I don't need the internet. And *you* don't have to look everything up on the internet either!

Luke: But you're wasting so much time! I cannot believe you don't just look online – there's step-by-step advice for everything!

Dad: Well, when I was young, there was no such thing as the internet. But I still learned to do things my way, step-by-step.

Luke: Your way? Hm …

Dad: I've done this a million times before. You should watch me and learn! – Er, what are you doing with my tablet?

Luke: Well, I can use it, right? Anyway, let's see … hm … Oh yes, look: I've found a great website. Hey, over 1,000 people have given it five stars!

Dad: You shouldn't believe everything you read online, Luke!

Luke: OK, but … Hey, Dad, what are you doing?! You mustn't remove that pipe! Just listen, please. You see that knob on the right?

Dad: Yes, I think I can reach it.

Luke: You have to turn it off, then you …

15 minutes later …

Luke: Yes! It's working! These forums are great! No, please, you needn't say "thanks". Advice is free!

Dad: Fantastic! I fixed it.

Luke: Only because I'm a genius!

Dad: With a very big head. Now, may I have my tablet back, please?

READING

7 Luke knows best?

*…sung: a) **Luke:** wants to …k for help at a forum; …nts to follow the step-by-…p advice; finds a great …bsite; reads out the advice …his father. **His dad:** has a …od look at everything first; …nts to do it step-by-step; …s experience; doesn't …lieve what's in the forum.*

a) *Luke and his dad have different ideas about how to solve the problem. What are they?*

b) *Have you ever had conversations like this one with family or friends? Tell the class.*

G10 Modals
G11 The modals *should, shouldn't* and *could*

LANGUAGE

8 Revision: Modals → G10

Lösung: 1. e) 2. a) 3. f) 4. b) 5. d) 6. c)

Match the sentence parts.

1. Here are the instructions. If you want, you
2. That pipe isn't the problem. You
3. Look at the mess in the kitchen. We
4. If Mum says yes, you
5. Is that the right knob? I
6. I've found advice on the internet, so you

a) mustn't remove it.
b) may use her tablet.
c) needn't read the instructions.
d) can't see anything.
e) can look at them for help.
f) must clean it up.

LANGUAGE

9 *Must, needn't* and *have to* → WB 50/9 → G10

WB 50/9 Language (dialogue)

Lösung: a) *l. 7: I must fix it before your mum comes home and goes crazy. l. 14–18: And you don't have to look up everything on the internet either! l. 38: You mustn't remove that pipe! l. 42: You have to turn it off, then you … ll. 45–46: No, please, you needn't say "thanks".* b) vgl. Tabelle

a) *Find examples of the forms **must, mustn't, needn't** and **have to/ don't have to** in the text.*

b) *Match the new forms (positive and negative) to the correct German meaning.*

	Modal
müssen / brauchen	must/have to
nicht müssen / nicht brauchen	needn't/don't have to
nicht dürfen	mustn't

LANGUAGE

10 Fill in: *must, mustn't, needn't, have to/don't have to* → WB 50/10 → G10

WB 50/10 Language (rules)

→ △ 124/5
→ ▲ 125/6

124/5 I've finally got my own smartphone
△ → After …
125/6 VIC – very important chats!
▲ → After …

At our school, we have tablet classes, so we 1 bring our tablet to school every day. I think I 2 ask for a new one soon because my tablet is broken. We're lucky that we 3 pay for the tablets ourselves – they're very expensive. I think tablet classes are really cool because we 4 carry so many books to school any more, and we can look up information on the internet. But we 5 follow rules, too: We 6 use the tablets for private communication and we 7 leave our mobiles in our bags!

Lösung: 1. *must / have to* 2. *must / have to* 3. *needn't / don't have to* 4. *needn't / don't have to* 5. *must / have to* 6. *mustn't* 7. *must / have to*

LANGUAGE

11 *Should, shouldn't* and *could* for advice → WB 51/11–12 → G11

WB 51/11 Mediation (internet)
WB 51/12 Writing (message)

→ ▲ 125/7
→ △ 125/8

125/7 Giving and taking advice
▲ → After …
125/8 You could do that, but I think you should …
△ → After …

*Tony is having a very bad day. Look at his problems, then write sentences with advice for him. Use **should, shouldn't** or **could**. The ideas on the right can help.*

Example: Oh no, that was my dinner for Lou!
– Maybe you **could** take her to a restaurant.

1. I forgot Lou's birthday yesterday!
2. I've got a new neighbour.
3. I've left my money at home.
4. I want to do something nice for Dad.
5. I want to buy a new phone but haven't got enough money.
6. Someone has taken my bike!

ask a friend | buy flowers | go to the police | take her to a restaurant ✓ | say hello | take him to a football game | help your parents at home for pocket money

Lösung: 1. *Too bad, I forgot Lou's birthday yesterday! – You should/could buy her some flowers today.* 2. *How nice, I've got a new neighbour. – You could/should say hello to him/her.* 3. *Oh, no, I've left my money at home. – You could ask a friend.* 4. *I want something nice for Dad. – Well, you should/could take him to a football game then.* 5. *I want to buy a new phone but I haven't got enough money. – You could/should help your parents at home for pocket money.* 6. *Oh no, someone has taken my bike! – You should go to the police.*

12 Are you media mad?

→ ▲ 126/9
126/9 Media mad
▲→ After ...

Take the test and find out how media mad you are!
Do you agree with your results? Why/why not?

Yes No

You sometimes use the internet, but not often.

You spend a few hours online every day.

You spend much more time online than with other hobbies.

You don't have many apps on your phone.

You check your messages all the time!

You like meeting your friends face-to-face. Texting or e-mailing isn't so important to you.

You have video chats with friends and family who you don't see very often.

Your parents think you spend too much time online or in front of the TV.

Do you ever post photos of yourself online?

Have you ever bought anything online?

You like 'real' shopping in shops better than online shopping.

You download all your music and listen to it on your phone.

You check for messages just two or three times a day.

You like looking at photos of your friends online and you always comment.

You post lots of photos of yourself online so everyone can see.

You love new apps for your phone.

You always compare prices online before you go shopping.

You don't care about video games. Boring!

– You're media mad! You love technology and media and have a lot of fun with it. Too much? Remember that sometimes it's good to go out and do other things with your friends. Try to stay away from your phone or laptop a few hours every day!

! You're clever with media! You know media can help you a lot, e.g. to talk to your friends. You like to be outside and have fun in other ways. But look for *new* ways to use the media too! There are *lots* of things to discover.

? You don't use media very much! You like to be outside, talk to your friends face-to-face, and go to real shops. But maybe your 'media mad' friends could tell you about how much fun media can be and how media can help you. Think about it!

Where's Maisie? → S21–22 S21–22 Film skills/Viewing

VIEWING

1 Little dog, big trouble → WB 52/13 WB 52/13 Vocabulary (feelings)

a) *Have you ever lost a pet? How did you feel? Tell the class about it.*

10 **b)** *Watch the film and then talk about the roles of Laura, Nathan and Polly in the story.*

Examples: A: I think Nathan is awful. He's too busy with girls and then …
B: Laura has great friends! They all help …

c) *Now imagine you are Laura. She wants to tell Alicia about what happened with Maisie.*

Start like this: Alicia, I can't believe what Nathan did! He lost Maisie! He was …

SPEAKING

2 Media in the film scenes → WB 52/14–15

KV 3: Viewing (media)
WB 52/14 Writing (message)
WB 52/15 Across cultures (newspapers)

Watch the film again. How many different kinds of media can you see in the film? Say how they helped the friends to find Maisie.

Lösung: *mobile telephone calls, text messages, messages on online social networks, video chat on a smartphone, print media ('missing' posters), online news*

Tony

SPEAKING

3 Close-ups

Folie 29: Bildbeschreibung der Standbilder/Nahaufnahmen
KV 4: Viewing (close-ups)

a) *First, read the skills box.*

Film skills

In Unit 1 you learned how music can help to show / describe feelings or atmosphere. Another way to do this in films is with **close-ups**: very close shots of a character's face. In this example, the girl isn't sure: Should she give Nathan her phone number, or not?

With the camera so close, you can 'read' the question in her face!

A

B

b) *Look at scenes A and B from the film. What do the two close-ups tell us? The ideas on the right can help you.*

can't believe it | is happy again | loves her dog | wants to look cute / cool for Polly | thinks he's so cool | likes himself a lot | …

Lösung: b) EH: ***Laura:*** *Laura can't believe it. She's got her Maisie back again. / Laura is so happy because Polly found Maisie in the park. / Laura really loves her dog – and she likes Polly too. / …*
Nathan: *Nathan is Laura's big brother and he wants to look cool for Polly. / Nathan thinks he's so cool and he offers to buy Polly a drink. / Nathan likes himself a lot, and he thinks Polly likes him too. / …*

How to write a letter and a reply

→ S10–13 S10–13 Writing

When you write a letter – to an agony aunt, for example – your letter should have different parts. This page shows you how to put a letter and a reply together.

1 The parts of a letter

KV 5: Writing (letter and reply)

a) *Read this letter to an agony aunt, and then read the reply. The box on the right shows you which parts of the letters there are. You need to know this for Ex. 2.*

Dear Ruby,

I'm writing to you because I just don't know what to do. I'm 13, and a new friend has invited me to go on holiday with his family this summer, to Spain. They always go to really cool places, and we just go camping. We never have much money. Before I met my friend, camping was fun. But it doesn't sound fun now. My parents say: "No, you can't go." That isn't fair! I feel like I'm missing a lot of fun. I'm angry with my parents. What do you think, Ruby?
Thanks for your help!

Yours, Ben

Begin with a greeting.

The main idea(s): In an advice letter, the main idea is the problem.

Ask for advice.

Say 'Thank you'.

Your name (often with 'Yours')

Dear Ben,

Yes, I understand that a cool holiday in Spain sounds like fun. But my advice is to ask yourself this: Is your friend really a good friend? Do you care about each other? Why don't you ask him to come with your family on a camping trip. If he's a good friend, you can have fun together anywhere, right? It needn't be on a beach in Spain.
I hope this advice helps!

Ruby

Begin with a greeting.

The main idea(s): A reply should show understanding / feelings.

Give advice.

Finish your letter.

Name

Look back at the phrases box on page 77 for the language of advice.

b) *Say what you think about Ben's problem and Ruby's advice.*

KV 6: Evaluation (letter and reply)

2 Write your own letter and reply

→ WB 53/16–18 WB 53/16 Skills (advice) WB 53/17 Skills (letter to agony aunt) WB 53/18 Activity (problems)

a) *Your partner writes a short letter to an agony aunt, and you write another short letter about a* ***different*** *problem. Choose one of the ideas below, or an idea of your own:*

- "My friends say I'm weird because I don't like their music."
- "My two best friends are good at everything and I'm not."

b) *When you're both finished, exchange letters and write a reply to each other with advice.*

Advice letters and replies: Our collection

In this task, you get the chance to talk more about advice for young people's problems. Later, after the different groups have collected and discussed advice for different problems, you're going to write letters and replies for a class advice collection.

Step 1

WB 54/19 Making notes (topics)

Choose a topic → WB 54/19

In groups of 4 or 6, choose one of the problems in the list below. Make sure there is at least one group for each question:

A. I want a pet, but my parents say "no".
B. My friends say, "You share too much information about yourself on the internet".
C. My parents never buy cool clothes for me. I look stupid!
D. I never have enough pocket money.
E. I can only watch TV or play video games for an hour on weekday evenings. It isn't enough!

Step 2

WB 54/20 Making notes (problems)

Pair work: What do you think? → WB 54/20

Before you talk to your group about advice for your problem, work ***with a partner*** *in your group for a few minutes. Make notes while you talk about these questions:*

- What places / people could the person go to for help?
- What advice could you give?

Look back at the **Stations** and the **Skills page** for help with advice.

Example:
A: As soon as I have a problem, I ask somebody in my family, or maybe a friend at the club I go to / on my football team / …
B: I've never written to an agony aunt, but a friend sometimes writes posts in advice forums.
A: And about the problem: Well, the person should … because it's always a good idea to …

Step 3

WB 55/21 Writing (letter to agony aunt)

Write an 'agony aunt' letter

→ WB 55/21

a) *Back in your group, discuss the different pairs' ideas about your group's problem. Use your notes from Step 2.*

b) *Now write one letter to an agony aunt about your group's problem. Then put your letter into a class box.*

You know how to write letters. Just look at the **Skills page** again.

Step 4

WB 55/22 Writing (reply)

Exchange questions

→ WB 55/22

Pick one of the letters from the box. As a group, discuss the problem and write a reply. Everyone in the group should help to check the letter:

- Is the form of the letter correct?
- Is the language for the advice correct?
- Is the advice helpful? How / Why?

Step 5

Present the problem and advice

→ WB 55/23 WB 55/23 Reading conference

What problem did you choose from the class box and what advice did you write? Tell the class. (Speak freely; don't just read from the page!)

The rest of the class should think about these things during the discussion:

- What do you think of the advice?
- Why is it helpful / not so helpful?

Step 6

Organise your letters and replies

Lösung: Mögliche Kategorien: *Family/Parents: A, C, D, E; Media: B, E; Friends: B, C*

As a class, talk about which topics the different problems fit into. Then organise your letters and replies by those topics. Think of how you can make nice pages with pictures, comics, etc.

Lou

Folie 30: Semantisierung des Wortschatzes und Bildbeschreibung zur Unterstützung des Hör-/Leseverstehens

S 2/7–12 L 3/3–8

It's a disaster!

A Dave's dad, Frank, stopped his car in front of his house. It was raining very hard – he wasn't able to see the house from his car but he was able to see that all the lights were on. The storm was getting worse every minute, with lots of thunder and lightning. He waited for a while and then quickly got out of the car, ran for the house and opened the front door. As he went inside, he nearly fell over all the bags and shoes. "I see Dave's friends are here again!" he thought. He shouted "Hello everyone!" But there wasn't a sound. "Hello-o-o?!" he called again. Nothing. "That's strange," he thought.

Stop and think:
Why do you think the house is so quiet?

He looked in the kitchen – nobody was there. Next, he looked in the living room and saw Gwen, Holly and Olivia. "Hi girls!" he said, but they didn't notice him because they were watching a *loud* music video on Olivia's laptop. Then he saw Jay in the corner.

"How are you, Jay?" he asked, but Jay was busy with text messages and music on his tablet PC. Frank went upstairs. As soon as he opened the door to Dave's bedroom, he saw Dave and Luke. They were sitting on the bed wearing headphones and playing a video game – they didn't notice Frank. "Well, they all look *very* happy to see me, I must say!" he said to himself, as he went back downstairs.

B Jay took off his headphones and tapped the girls' shoulders. "I was thinking," he said. "We should talk about that party we want to have soon."

"Yeah, I was thinking about that too," Olivia answered. "We can have it at my house. My dad and Claire say it's OK. Look, I've already written the invitation."

"Great! Let's post a message with the invitation and tell everyone to go to Olivia's house on –"

"No!" Olivia shouted. "We can't just post the invitation like *that*! A lot of people we don't know could see it and come to my house. No, we can only invite people face-to-face. People we *know*."

"Olivia, it's much quicker by internet," Jay said. "Come on, let's just do it! It's fun! He then grabbed Olivia's laptop.

"Jay, what are you doing?!" Olivia cried.

"I'm going to post it, what do you think?" They all started fighting for the laptop. At first they were laughing and joking, but then the girls saw that Jay was *serious*! They were horrified and tried to push him away from the laptop, but Jay was quicker. "Party on Friday 22nd at my house, 52 Begbie Road. Come and have fun!" it said in the invitation text. But just as Jay was pressing 'post', there was a very loud "BANG!" and everything went black.

C Suddenly, the house became very loud and all the friends started shouting at the same time: "What's happened?" – "I can't see!" – "My computer has crashed!" – "Oh no, we're offline too!" – "I can't find my phone!" – "Help! I don't like the dark!"

Frank shouted, "Calm down, it's only a power cut! Wait a moment while I find some candles."

"Did you really send that message?" whispered Holly. "I don't know, I think so!" Jay said.

"To Olivia's friends?" Holly asked.

"No. To *everyone*! But I'm not sure …" He was really starting to worry now, but he didn't want to tell the girls. Five minutes later, they were all sitting round the kitchen table in candlelight.

"Dad, what do we need candles for?" asked Dave. "Look, our phones have all got torches!"

"Sometimes, the old ways are better!" smiled Frank. "The only problem we have right now," Frank went on, "is that we can't cook – and I'm *really* hungry!"

"How is that a problem?" asked Luke. "Who needs to cook when there are pizza apps?" Dave and Luke started to show Mr Preston fantastic apps for his phone. Mr Preston was impressed! But nobody noticed that Jay wasn't speaking. "What have I done?" he thought to himself. "I was just showing off and I went a bit crazy for a moment. Please tell me the power cut stopped the message." Then he said, "Luke, Dave: Can I borrow a phone? I need to check something and I left mine in the other room." But they were busy with Mr Preston and his new pizza app.

D Frank was still talking about the old days. "When I was young, we *talked* to each other, we didn't text all the time."

"Oh no, he *loves* this topic!" Dave said and, as he spoke, there was a loud CLICK, and all the lights were back on.

The girls ran to the living room and waited nervously to get back online.

"Come on, come on!" Holly said. And suddenly they were online again. They went on to their social network site and … "Fantastic!" shouted Olivia. "The power cut stopped the message! But let's teach Jay a lesson." Gwen and Holly smiled at each other.

E Jay walked slowly back into the living room.

"You're in *big* trouble now!" Olivia said.

"How many messages are there?" he whispered. His face was white. He felt sick. "More than 50!" Holly said. "Listen to these: 'You don't know us but we *love* parties – see you there!', or 'Party? Cool! I love meeting new people!'"

Now Jay felt *really* sick. "It's a disaster!" he said. Holly and Olivia were trying very hard not to laugh.

"What's so funny?" Jay asked.

"Don't worry. The power cut stopped your message. Nobody got it," Olivia said.

"But you're lucky, Jay Azad!" Holly added. "And you *really* should leave the party invitations to us next time!"

"That," said Jay, "is no problem at all!"

KV 7: Reading (feelings and thoughts)
WB 56/24 Reading (questions)
WB 56/25 Reading/Writing/Speaking (options)

Tony

READING

1 Understanding the story → WB 56/24–25

a) *Do you think 'It's a disaster!' is a good title for the story? Say why or why not. What ideas for a different story title do you have?*

b) *There are two main characters in this story: One is Frank, and the other is Jay. Which sentences in the text show that they both feel left out at some point in the story?*

Example: He shouted "Hello everyone!" But there wasn't a sound. (Frank, lines 12–13)

126/10 Writing a dialogue
△→ Help with …

→ △ 126/10
→ S16

S16 Speaking (Mündliche Aufgaben und ihre Besonderheiten)

c) *Do one of these role plays:*
- *One of you is Frank, the other is Dave's mum. She asks him what happened.*
  Or:
- *One of you is Jay, the other is Olivia. They talk about what happened and about their feelings. Use ideas from the text.*

WRITING

2 Writing about pros and cons

→ S8

S8 Reading (Textbearbeitung mit Markierungen und Notizen)

a) *What can people today do with modern technology and what did people do or use when Frank was very young? Make a grid with examples from the text. Then think of more examples and add them to your grid.*

New world	*Old world*
– watch a video	*– use candles*
– send text messages	*…*
…	

→ S13

S13 Writing (Sprachliche Verbesserungen)

b) *What are the pros and cons of modern technology? First read the skills box. Then write about the two worlds. The phrases box can help you too.*

Lösung: a) ***New world:*** *watch a video, send text messages, post messages, use the internet, use apps, …;* ***Old world:*** *use candles, write notes or letters, write invitation cards, invite people face-to-face, use a normal phone, read brochures or books etc. …*

Writing skills

Use these words / phrases to link ideas and give information:

When things happen (time):
When my parents were young…, then …, now …, today …, before …, after …, as …, when …

Where things happen (place):
in the house, on my phone/PC, everywhere

Why things happen (reasons):
… because …

What else happens:
and …, or …, but …

How things happen:
easily, carefully, dangerously, more quickly, in a friendly way, without thinking, by internet, face-to-face

Useful phrases

Today we've got … | We can … | It's great that … because … | (Not) everything was …, I think … is better than … | But … can be dangerous. We should …

Unsocial Networking

→ Solutions p. 248

Can you ...

1. talk about media in your life? — I use ... to send / receive / post / chat / play / read / look up / take part in ...
2. link ideas? — I do it when / after / before / because ...
3. talk about rules and instructions? — You must ... / have to ... / needn't ... / mustn't ...
4. give advice to somebody? — Why don't you ...? You should ... You could ... Have you tried ...ing ...?

VOCABULARY

1 How do people use media?

Match the sentence parts and make sentences.

Example: When my grandma wants to chat with her sister, she calls her on the telephone.

HA

1. my dad / want / relax
2. I / want / know / words of a song I've heard
3. my mum / work away from home
4. I / want / tell all my friends how great my holiday is
5. my sister / want / know about the coolest new clothes

a) post / it on my social network profile
b) send / me text messages
c) read / girls' magazines
d) look / it up on the internet
e) watch / football on TV

SPEAKING

2 What can you say to give these people advice?

HA

1. Your brother hurts his foot and doesn't know if it's broken.
2. Your friend missed his favourite TV show.
3. Your sister doesn't know how to fix her bike.
4. Your friend tells you that someone posted really embarrassing photos of her on the internet.
5. Your friend's parents are angry with her: She can't use her smartphone for a week.

LANGUAGE

3 How do you say it in German?

HA

1. My brother's mobile is really old, I think he must buy a new one.
2. He's lucky because he doesn't have to pay for it himself – it's his birthday in two months.
3. I'm even luckier because I needn't wait that long. I can have my dad's new smartphone!
4. But I mustn't tell my brother anything – he can be very jealous!

<Story> ist ein fakultativer Romanauszug. Der neue Wortschatz ist rezeptiv und unter dem Text annotiert.

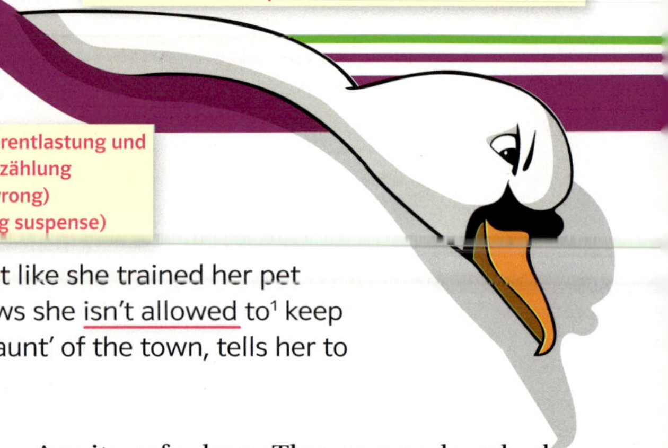

S 2/13–17
L 3/9–13

Ten-tonne truck

Folie 31: Inhaltliche Vorentlastung und bildgesteuerte Nacherzählung
KV 1: Reading (right/wrong)
KV 2: Reading (creating suspense)

Zoe finds a rat in her room. She wants to train it like she trained her pet hamster (who could break-dance), but she knows she isn't allowed to[1] keep any pets. Raj, a shopkeeper[2] who is the 'agony aunt' of the town, tells her to set Armitage the rat free[3] in the park.

"What am I going to do with him, Raj? I'm not allowed to keep him at home; he's the reason why I was suspended[4] from school. My stepmother hated my hamster, she is *never* going to let me keep a rat."

Raj thought for a moment. "Maybe you should set him free," he finally said.

"Free?" Zoe said, with a tear[5] in her eye.

"Yes. Rats shouldn't be pets …"

"But this little one is so cute …"

"Maybe, but he's going to grow[6]. He can't spend his whole life in your pocket."

"But I love him, Raj, I really do."

"I'm sure you do, Miss Zoe," Raj said. "And if you love him, you should set him free."

So this was goodbye. Zoe knew deep down she would[7] never be able to keep Armitage for long. There were a hundred reasons, but the most important one was: HE WAS A RAT.

Children don't have rats as pets. They have cats and dogs and hamsters and mice and rabbits and tortoises. Some kids even have ponies, but never rats. Rats live underground, not in little girls' bedrooms.

Zoe walked sadly out of Raj's shop. It was true that sometimes he tried to sell his customers[8] a half-eaten chocolate bar, but all the kids in town knew that when they needed advice, he was the best.

And so she had to say goodbye to Armitage. Zoe took the long way back to her flat, through the park. She thought this was the perfect place to set little Armitage free. There were always bits of bread for the ducks – Armitage could[9] eat these. He could drink from the pond and take a bath in it. And maybe there was a squirrel or two he could make friends with.

The little girl carried[10] the little rat in her hand. It was the middle of the afternoon and there were just a few old ladies and their dogs in the park. Armitage wrapped his tail around her thumb – maybe he knew that something was wrong …

Zoe walked as slowly as possible. Finally, she reached the middle of the park. She was looking for a nice quiet place. Then she bent down[11] to the ground slowly and opened her hand. But Armitage didn't move. He just stayed in her hand. It was breaking Zoe's heart …

1 to be allowed to do sth [bi ə'laʊd tə] dürfen | **2 shopkeeper** [ʃɒp'ki:pə] Ladenbesitzer | **3 to set sb/sth free** [set 'fri:] jmdn./etw. freilassen | **4 to be suspended** [bi sə'spendɪd] (vorübergehend) der Schule verwiesen werden | **5 tear** [tɪə] Träne | **6 to grow** [grəʊ] wachsen | **7 would** [wʊd] würde | **8 customer** ['kʌstəmə] Kunde | **9 could** [kʊd] könnte | **10 to carry** ['kæri] tragen | **11 to bend down** [bend 'daʊn] sich bücken

Zoe shook[12] her hand a little, but Armitage only held on tighter[13] to her fingers. She was fighting back tears when she picked the rat up gently[14] and put him carefully on the grass. Once again Armitage didn't move. He just looked up at her sadly. Zoe kissed him gently on his little pink nose.

"Goodbye, little friend," she whispered. "I'm going to miss[15] you."

A tear dropped from her eye.

The little rat turned his little head to one side, like a friend who was trying to understand her. This just made it harder for Zoe.

Finally, Zoe took a big breath and stood up. "Don't look back!" she told herself. But after a few steps she had to look one last time at the place she left him. To Zoe's surprise, Armitage wasn't there.

"He has already run away to the safety of the bushes," she thought. She looked at the grass, but it was long and he was short, and the grass didn't move. Zoe turned round[16] and sadly started to walk home.

She left the park and crossed[17] the road. For a moment, there was no noise of cars, and in the silence, Zoe heard a small 'eek'. She turned round quickly, and in the middle of the road was Armitage.

He was following her!

"Armitage!" she shouted excitedly. He didn't want to be free; he wanted to be with her! She was so happy. Now she didn't have to imagine all kinds of terrible scenes any more: A hungry swan[18] couldn't eat him for dinner, and a ten-tonne truck couldn't run him over[19].

At that moment, she heard a loud thundering noise. Something came along the road towards Armitage, who was still moving slowly to get to Zoe. It was a ten-tonne truck!

Zoe wasn't able to move, she just watched the truck which was speeding[20] closer and closer towards Armitage. How could the driver see a baby rat in the road?

From: *Ratburger* by David Walliams → WB 58/1–4

WB 58/1 Reading (correct order)
WB 58/2 Reading (matching)
WB 58/3 Vocabulary (word friendships)
WB 58/4 Vocabulary/Speaking (pets)

12 to shake [ʃeɪk] schütteln | **13 tight** [taɪt] fest | **14 gently** ['dʒentli] sanft | **15 to miss sb/sth** [mɪs] jmdn./etw. vermissen | **16 to turn round** [tɜːn raʊnd] (sich) umdrehen; wenden | **17 to cross** [krɒs] überqueren | **18 swan** [swɒn] Schwan | **19 to run sth over** [rʌn‿'əʊvə] etw. überfahren | **20 to speed** [spiːd] rasen

Find more online:

Unit 5

Goodbye Greenwich

A A beach in Cornwall, in the south-west of England

B A medieval 'living history' show at Caerphilly Castle in Wales

Folie 32: Reaktivierung von Vorwissen, Orientierung auf Landkarte
Folie 33: Vorentlastung des Wortschatzes und Bildbeschreibung

SPEAKING **1**

Parts of the British Isles

→ △ 126/1

126/1 Talking about places
△ → Help with ...

Look at the pictures and find the places on the map at the back of your book. Which part of the British Isles do they belong to? Which part of them looks most interesting to you and why?

Lösung: A: *England* B: *Wales* C: *Ireland* D: *Scotland*

Voc.: Parts of the British Isles, p. 195; The United Kingdom, Word bank (WB), p. 17

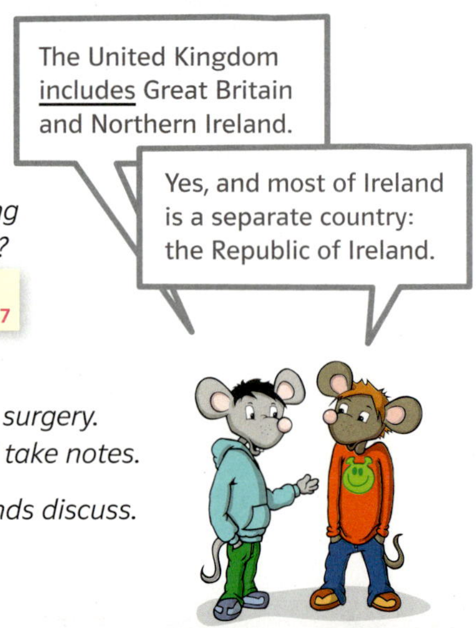

LISTENING **2**

Come on Dave, don't be so negative!

L 3/14

a) *Dave is talking about his parents' plans and his mum's vet surgery. What is the problem from Dave's point of view? Listen and take notes.*

b) *Now talk about the different places that Dave and his friends discuss. Make a grid for your answers with these headings:*

→ S18–20

S18–20 Listening

Place | Landscape | Things to do | Other information

In Unit 5 you learn
… how to talk about places in the British Isles.
You learn:
- to describe places
- to talk about plans for a journey
- to talk about the future with *will*
- to report what people have just said

C Pony trekking in Ireland

D The Edinburgh Festival in the Scottish capital

WB 59/1 Vocabulary (Cornwall)
WB 59/2 Vocabulary (Scotland)

'OCABULARY

3 Places → WB 59/1–2

…c.: Places and …at you can do …ere, p. 196; …ndscape, …rd bank …B), p. 12

a) *Collect vocabulary in different categories like landscapes, sights, things to do.*

b) *Each of you does the following: Take four cards and write* ***one*** *of your words / phrases from a) on each card. Shuffle all the cards and pick four. Choose a place in the British Isles and take turns to talk about it, with the words on your cards.*

Transfer

c) *Your turn: Find information about a German region (e.g. the North Sea). Write a short text and present it.*

…sung: a) ***Landscapes:*** *high mountain, field, forest, sandy/rocky beach, wide river, deep lake, island;* …hts: *city, village, harbour;* ***Things to do:*** *visit a castle, go hiking/climbing/mountain biking/* …ind)surfing/pony trekking*

Useful phrases

high mountain | field | forest | sandy / rocky beach | wide river | deep lake | island | city | village | harbour | visit a castle | go hiking / climbing / mountain biking / (wind) surfing / pony trekking

Across cultures

Did you know that palm trees grow in the south-west of England? Some call it the **English Riviera**. Are there any surprising facts about the region where you live?

Folie 34: Unterstützung des Hörverstehens und Möglichkeit zum Perspektivwechsel

L3/15

Moving to the middle of nowhere

Dave's parents have found a beautiful house near St Agnes, in the Cornish countryside. Dave is very sad to leave.

Dave: Oh no, why do we have to move to the middle of nowhere? London is just fine. And I'll miss you so much!

Olivia: But the house looks fantastic! And your mum never wanted to live in the city. She'll be happy there with her new surgery and all the farm animals and pets to work with, won't she?

Dave: Yes, but will I be happy? Has anyone ever asked *me*? If I want to see farm animals, I can go to Mudchute Farm.

Luke: What about your dad? Will he find work there?

Dave: Well, he travels a lot anyway. He'll stay in London with Aunt Frances when he has to work there. I think it'll be OK for *him*. But me?

Holly: Oh Dave, I'll miss you too! I'm so sorry you won't be able to go to the park with us any longer.

Jay: And we won't be able to play video games together.

Gwen: Come on now, it's not the end of the world. There are games you can play online. Oh, and we'll text you and have lots of video chats together.

Olivia: And we'll come to visit you! Cornwall is a great place. Most British people go there for a holiday. I've been there with my mum.

Dave: That's nice for people on holiday – but *I'll* be in a new school, and there'll be nobody I know. It'll be horrible. And I'm sure Sid will hate it too.

Jay: Don't worry, you'll make lots of new friends. But what about Olivia's idea? We could go to Cornwall to visit you.

Holly: All of us together, in Cornwall? Wow! I'll ask my mum.

Luke: Well, maybe. I'll think about it. But we'll have to find the money first, won't we?

Gwen: I'm sure we'll find a way to get there.

Olivia: Will it be OK for us to stay with Dave?

Luke: I'm sure it will. His parents are cool.

Dave: That's a wonderful idea. It'll be great to see you all there.

WB 60/3 Pronunciation (sounds)

READING

1 Questions about the future

→ WB 60/3

Lösung: 1. … with her new surgery. 2. … or they'll have video chats together. And they'll come to visit him. 3. … for the money first. They'll have to decide on a date. They'll have to find out how to get there.

1. What does Dave say about the Prestons' future in Cornwall?
2. What do his friends say to make him feel better?
3. What will the friends need to do before they go to Cornwall? Think about these things: parents, dates, transport, money.

Examples:

1. He'll miss his friends. His mum will be happy …
2. They'll miss him too. They'll text him …
3. They'll have to ask their parents …

LANGUAGE

sung: *Prediction: Will I happy? Will he find work ere? I think it'll be OK for m. We won't be able to ay video games any longer. ontaneous reaction/deci- on: We'll come and visit you.*

2 Rules for the *will* future → WB 60/4 → G12

WB 60/4 Listening (correct answers)

*Find 4–5 sentences with **will** or **won't** in the text. Say if they're predictions about the future or spontaneous reactions / decisions. You see some examples on the right.*

Prediction	Spontaneous reaction / decision
I'll miss you. She'll be happy there.	I'll ask my mum. We'll text you.

LANGUAGE

3 How will we get there?

KV 1: Language (Dave's future)

→ 127/2
→ 127/3

7/2 Frequently asked estions
→ After …
7/3 Mediation: a German station
→ After …

sung: a) *will be – won't – I'll/I will check – will e – it'll/it will be – won't – I'll/I will talk Will we – we'll/we will – It'll/It will be – won't ke – won't have – will I get*

Luke goes to a travel agent's to ask about the journey to St Agnes.

a) *Complete dialogue A with forms of the* ***will future*** *and read it with a partner.*

b) *Now do the same with dialogue B.*

Train + bus: London Paddington to St Agnes
Time: 6 – 7 hours
Prices: £50 – £70
Children under 12 must travel with an adult.

Coach + bus: London Victoria to St Agnes
Time: 8 hours
Prices: £65 – £75
Children under 14 must travel with an adult.

A

Luke: My friends and I want to go to Cornwall, but we're worried that tickets (be) expensive.

Assistant: Don't worry. It (not be) too expensive. But it depends on the date. Give me your dates and I (check) for you.

(a few minutes later)

Yes, on those dates, train tickets per person are £5 cheaper than by coach. – Oh, but now I see better prices for the next day. Between £10 and £15 cheaper by train.

Luke: £15 cheaper per person? Cool! My friends (like) that.

Assistant: Well, I can't promise £15, but it (be) a better price than a day earlier. – Oh, and children under 12 need to travel with a person who is 16 or older.

Luke: Oh, that (not be) a problem. – Anyway, I (talk) to my friends and come back.

B

Olivia: (we go) by train or by coach?

Luke: I think we (go) by train. It (be) cheaper and (not take) so long.

Gwen: And we (not have) to find an adult to go with us.

Holly: There's just one problem: Where (I get) the money?

LISTENING

4 Preparing for the trip → WB 60/5

WB 60/5 Language (website)

L 3/18

sung: a) *Holly wants to it Dave together with r friends, but she hasn't t enough money for the kets. She could ask her her, sell some of her ngs or take on a small . In the end, Amber can p her.*

Listen to the dialogue and answer the questions.

a) *What's Holly's problem? What can she do and who can help her?*

b) *What will these people do? Say one sentence about each person: Dave, Granny Rose, Luke, the girls, the boys, Luke's grandparents, Holly, Amber.*

Dave will go to Cornwall soon. Granny Rose will go with the friends. Luke will visit Dave too because his ndparents will help him. The girls will stay in one room together. The boys will stay in Dave's room. Luke's ndparents will help Luke. Holly will have a great time in Cornwall. Amber will give Holly the money.

Folie 35: Festigung und Anwendung des neuen Wortschatzes (Ticketbuchung)
WB 61/6 Language (train tickets)

VOCABULARY

5 How to: Book train tickets on the internet → WB 61/6

127/4 Buying train tickets on the internet
△→ After …

→ △ 127/4
→ S9

S9 Reading (Umgang mit neuen Wörtern)

Voc.: Travel words, p. 198; Transport, Word bank (WB), p. 17

Luke wants to book tickets for the five friends and Granny Rose online. They want to leave next Sunday morning and return a week later.

a) *Help him to fill in the form (1). He clicks on "Buy train tickets". Then he chooses a connection and clicks on it. A new window shows details for this connection (2).*

Useful phrases

One-way / single ticket | return ticket | fee | to depart | to arrive | to change at … | outward journey | inward journey | price / fare | platform

1

Find train times and tickets

From
To
Out 09/08/2015 Today Tomorrow
Leave after 08 30
One way
Return Same day Next day
Leave after 09 00
Open Return
Adults 1 Children 0
Railcards
Buy train tickets
Booking and credit card fees

2

Journey Summary Outward Journey (9 Aug 2015)

Depart		Arrive		Travel by	Duration
09:32	Greenwich	09:43	London Bridge	Train	00h 11 Calling Points
09:53	London Bridge	10:23	London Paddington	Tube	00h 30
10:43	London Paddington	16:46	Redruth	Train	06h 03 Calling Points
17:12	Redruth	17:46	St Agnes	Bus	00h 34

Text me these details Add to calendar

Lösung: a) *From Greenwich to St Agnes – Return: Sunday – one adult, five children*
b) *1. to depart 2. to change at … 3. return ticket 4. outward journey 5. price/fare 6. to arrive 7. one-way/single ticket 8. inward journey 9. fee*

b) *Match words and phrases from the phrases box with these definitions.*

1. to leave
2. to leave one train and get on another
3. a ticket to go to a place and back
4. going away to a place
5. this tells you what a ticket costs
6. to get to a place
7. a ticket to go to a place
8. going back to your starting place
9. extra money you have to pay

You often hear *will* future in weather forecasts.

Folie 36: Festigung und Anwendung des neuen Wortschatzes (Wetter)

KV 2: Language/Writing (weather)
WB 61/7 Writing (weather forecast)

MEDIATION

6 The weather forecast → WB 61/7

→ △ 128/5
→ S17

S17 Mediation

128/5 What will the weather be like?
△→ Help with …

Voc.: Weather words, p. 198; Weather, Word bank (WB), p. 17

A British tourist wants to do a 5-hour mountain climbing tour. He shows you this weather forecast for tomorrow and asks you if he can go on his tour. What is your advice?

Wettervorhersage Oberallgäu: Während es heute bei Höchsttemperaturen über 30 Grad noch sehr heiß mit viel Sonne ist, zieht morgen eine Schlechtwetterfront von Südwesten herein. Es ist mit starken Unwettern und Hagel zu rechnen, vor allem Samstagnachmittag und -abend. Im Bergland besteht Gefahr durch orkanartige Windböen mit Geschwindigkeiten bis zu 105 km/h. Durch starke Niederschläge kann es zu Überflutungen kommen.

Lösung: EH: *Tomorrow there will be heavy rain and it'll be very stormy. There will also be hail, especially in the afternoon and evening. The tourist shouldn't do the tour.*

How to get information
→ S10–13 S10–13 Writing

For the Unit task you'll need information about different parts of the British Isles: England (e.g. Cornwall, or maybe London), Scotland, Wales and Ireland (Northern Ireland or the Republic of Ireland).

1 Where to get information

If you want to collect pictures and facts about interesting places, you can write to a tourist board and ask for free material. What else can you do?

WB 62/8 Skills (contact form)
WB 62/9 Skills (e-mail)
WB 62/10 Activity (options)

2 Asking for information
→ WB 62/8–10

Make four groups, one for each of the regions on pages 92–93.
Some organisations have interesting material. Find their e-mail addresses and write a polite e-mail to ask for the material. Some of them don't give you their e-mail addresses but ask you to fill in an internet contact form. Make sure you don't write to the same organisation about the same material more than once!

Writing skills

Before you send off your e-mail or contact form, **remember**:
- Don't forget your greetings.
- Who are you?
- What do you want to do?
- What do you need?
- How do you ask for it politely?
- What information about yourselves do you need to give?

Dear Sir or Madam,

We are students of a German grammar school. We would like to do a project about the British Isles and need information about Scotland for it.
Could you please send us some free material about interesting places in Scotland, Scottish history and things to do in Scotland?
Here is our address:
…-Gymnasium
Class …
…straße (XX)
D-(XXXXX) …

Thank you very much for your help.

Best wishes,
The students of Class (…)

3 Working with the material

When you have enough material, go through it together in your group.
Make notes of interesting ideas for a presentation, and look for the best photos.

G13 Indirect speech with the reporting verb in the present

L 3/19–20

Dave says he can't wait for us to go there

Dave has been in Cornwall for two days and sends an e-mail to Luke.

Hi Luke! Greetings from sunny Cornwall! It's very hot here today and I've just come back from the beach. Maybe this place is not that bad after all … But I really hope that you aren't having too much fun without me! I miss you all a lot – I even miss my old school! Anyway, I can't wait for you to come here. There's lots to see – the beaches, for example. The coastline is almost 300 miles long. You must bring your swimming things! Look at these photos. This is my favourite beach – I can see it from my bedroom window. I'll send you some more photos soon.

There's lots to do too – all kinds of water sports and other outdoor activities like adventure sports and pony trekking. It feels so different from Greenwich. The landscape here is very wild and dramatic. And there's lots of ancient history – Bodmin Moor with its prehistoric monuments and all the old tin mines and Celtic place names … So, you won't get bored. See you on Sunday!
Love, Dave

KV 3a: Pre-viewing (mind map/pictures)
KV 3b: While-viewing (right/wrong)

A few minutes later Luke gets a call from Olivia.

Olivia: Hi Luke. Have you heard from Dave?
Luke: Yes – he sent me an e-mail a few minutes ago. He writes that it's very hot there today. He's just come back from the beach!
Olivia: Lucky Dave! Is he missing us?
Luke: Oh yes. He says he hopes that we aren't having too much fun without him. And he can't wait for us to go there.
Olivia: Did he send some photos?
Luke: Yes, wait, I'll send you one from my mobile. That's his favourite beach – he can see it from his bedroom window. Isn't it amazing?
Olivia: Wow! I want to go swimming there.
Luke: Well, he tells us that we must take our swimming things. So I'm sure we'll spend some time on the beach.
Olivia: Great! What else does he say?
Luke: Well, he says that the landscape in Cornwall is very wild and dramatic and that there's lots of ancient history too. You'll like that, right?
Olivia: Definitely! I can't wait to go.
Luke: Me neither. Dave promises we won't get bored.

11
Mehr zum Thema Cornwall

READING 7

WB 63/11 Listening (conversation)

Dave and Cornwall → WB 63/11

Lösung: a) EH: *Dave says that maybe Cornwall is not that bad after all and that his new life feels so different from his life in Greenwich.*

a) *How does Dave feel about his new life in Cornwall compared to his old life in Greenwich?*

b) *What does Dave tell his friend about Cornwall? Talk about:*

1. activities you can do there 2. the landscape 3. the history

b) 1. *activities you can do there: swimming, outdoor activities (adventure sports, pony trekking) 2. the landscape: wild and dramatic, beaches, long coastline 3. the history: prehistoric monuments (Bodmin Moor), old tin mines, Celtic history*

LANGUAGE

8 Find the rule: From direct to indirect speech → G13

ung: 3. He says he can't it for us to go there. 4. says that's his favourite ach. He can see it from window. 5. He writes t we must take our mming things. 6. He s that the landscape in nwall is very wild.

Copy the grid and put in the sentences from Dave's e-mail in direct speech. Then add the sentences from Luke's and Olivia's conversation in indirect speech. Underline the words that change and find the rule.

Direct speech	Indirect speech
1. Dave: It's very hot **here** today. 2. **I** hope that **you** aren't having too much fun without **me**!	Dave writes that it's very hot **there** today. He says **he** hopes that **we** aren't having too much fun without **him**!

3. I can't wait for you to come here. **4.** This is my favourite beach. I can see it from my window. **5.** You must bring your swimming things! **6.** The landscape here is very wild.

LANGUAGE

9 An e-mail from Olivia → WB 63/12 → G13

WB 63/12 Language (e-mail)

→ △ 128/6
→ ▲ 129/7

'6 I'm coming soon
› After …
'7 Where do you want ravel?
› After …

Olivia sends Dave an e-mail with a selfie. Dave tells his mum what she says.

Start like this: Olivia says it's really wet …

Hi Dave! It's really wet here today. This is me in Greenwich Park in the rain! So we're really excited that we're going to Cornwall soon. Maybe you could even teach us how to surf?! Oh, and we **must** visit all the historical sights near you – I love history and the Celts! And I want to bring typical Cornish food home for my mum. So you mustn't forget the shopping tour! 🙂 Bye for now. Olivia.

Lösung: *Olivia says it was really hot there today. That's her in Greenwich Park in the rain. She writes that they're really excited that they're coming here soon. She asks me if I could even teach them how to surf! She says that we / they must visit all the historical sights near us – she loves history and the Celts. She says she wants to take typical Cornish food home for her mum. She writes that we mustn't forget the shopping tour.*

SPEAKING

10 Languages in Britain

Look at the photo. Which of the Cornish words can you understand?

Across cultures

Everybody in the British Isles speaks English. But Cornwall, Ireland, Scotland, Wales and the Isle of Man still have their own **Celtic languages**. What languages do people in your class speak besides German? Do people speak in a local dialect or with an accent?

Listening (Typische verstehenssituationen)

LISTENING

11 Announcements

KV 4: Listening (right/wrong)

L 3/22–25

→ S20

Listen to the dialogues and find out this information for each scene. Take notes:

1. where Mr Preston is **2.** where Mr Preston wants to go **3.** what sight they talk about **4.** what the announcement is about.

ng: EH 1. *Wales, station; London; Cardiff; train to London is arriving; 2. Scotland, ticket office; London (King's Cross); burgh Castle; passengers must keep their bags with them at all times; 3. Cornwall, on a train; Redruth; Eden Project; next station is Redruth, train terminates there, passengers have to get off the train; 4. Ireland, airport; London throw), Greenwich; Dublin, Jeanie Johnston; flight to Heathrow will depart at 19.30 instead of 18.20*

WB 64/13 Speaking (holiday ideas)
WB 64/14 Writing (holiday plans)
WB 64/15 Mediation (tourist information)

SPEAKING

12 Role play: At the travel agent's → WB 64/13–15

→ S16

S16 Speaking (Mündliche Aufgaben und ihre Besonderheiten)

One of you is an assistant at a travel agent's. The other chooses one of these roles:
A: *A father who wants to travel with his wife and young children;* **B:** *A teenager who wants to travel with her mum; or* **C:** *a young couple who is interested in sports. They all want to go to Cornwall. Use the useful phrases to make dialogues. (You can also look back at Ex. 3 on p. 95.)*

Useful phrases

Assistant:
Hello, what can I do for you?
How long would you like to stay?
Do you want to go by car, by train or by coach? Do you need a ticket?
Would you like to book a room / a flat / a house?
If you want to …, you can …

Customer:
I'd like to travel to … with …
Over the weekend / two weeks / …
We love … / We're into …
How long does it take?
We need … tickets.
How much is it?
Oh, I think that's too expensive.
Yes, that's fine. Thank you.

READING

13 British history: A poem about the Romans

KV 5: Writing (poem)

→ ▲ 129/8

129/8 A poem about your home town ▲ → After …

Lösung: a) EH: *The poem says that the Romans built many things, such as aqueducts, roads and bridges. They gave water and food to the people and ruled the country.*
b) *Great Britain is an island. It is in the North Sea. It's got green fields and mountains. It's where I'd like to be. The biggest city is London. It's got a lot to show. There's always something happening. It's where I'd like to go.*

a) *Explain what the poem says about the Romans and what they did in Britain.*

The Romans in Britain
(A history in 40 words)
by Judith Nicholls

The Romans gave us aqueducts
fine buildings and straight[1] roads,
where all those Roman legionaries
marched with heavy loads[2].

They gave us central heating[3],
good laws[4], a peaceful[5] home …
Then after just four centuries
they shuffled back to Rome.

Useful phrases

to build (a bridge, a road, a town) |
to supply somebody (with water, food) |
to rule (a country)

b) *Think of how you could complete this little poem about Britain.*

Great Britain is an island.
It is in the North …
It's got green fields and mountains.
It's where I'd like to …

The biggest city is …
It's got a lot to show.
There's always something happening.
It's where I'd like to…

1 straight [streɪt] gerade | **2 heavy load** [ˌhevi ˈləʊd] schwere Last | **3 central heating** [ˌsentrl ˈhiːtɪŋ] Zentralheizung | **4 law** [lɔː] *hier:* Gesetz | **5 peaceful** [ˈpiːsfl] friedlich

The caves

→ S21–22 S21–22 Film skills/Viewing

SPEAKING

1 Things to do in the country

Talk about which of these activities are interesting for you.

1. feeding animals
2. milking cows
3. exploring a cave
4. swimming in a lake
5. playing in an adventure playground
6. reading ghost stories
7. walking
8. geocaching

VIEWING

2 Themes

→ WB 65/16

KV 6: Viewing (film stills)
WB 65/16 Vocabulary (matching)

12

Watch the film. Then say which themes below play a role in the film. Explain why / why not. Which of them are more important / the most important?

sung: doesn't play a role: not really important: 1, 6, Important: 2, 4, 8; ery important: 5

1. food
2. city and country life
3. school
4. children and adults
5. stories
6. sports
7. love
8. ghosts

VIEWING

3 Suspense: What's going to happen?

KV 7: Viewing (suspense)

Watch the film again, find examples of the ideas below and take notes. They can help you to talk about elements that create suspense in a story.

Story: What about ...
- Laura's grandpa?
- ghosts?
- getting lost?
- phones, maps and torches?

Acting: What about ...
- people's faces?

Audiovisual effects: What about ...
- darkness?
- strange sounds, a voice in the caves?
- dramatic music?

Film skills

Elements that create suspense:
- clues in the story about what could happen
- acting
- music
- light
- sounds

WRITING

4 Laura and her grandpa

→ S15

S15 Speaking (Gesprochene Sprache)

Write a sequel to the last scene in the film:
Laura and her grandpa talk about what has really happened and why.
Act it and film it.

WB 65/17 Across cultures (Celtic languages)

Our big British Isles quiz

You're going to work in four groups. You're going to make question cards for a quiz about the British Isles (Wales, England, etc.). You can use information in this book and from other sources. When you're finished, you'll be able to play a quiz game.

Step 1

WB 66/18 Information (ranking)
WB 66/19 Places in Britain

Get organised

→ WB 66/18–19

Make four groups of 4–6, one for a different part of the British Isles. In your group, agree on 16 interesting sights or places in your region. Each of you makes 2–4 question cards so you have one for each sight in the end.

For ideas, look at **this unit** and **the other units** in the book. Use information material from **books**, the **internet** and **tourist boards**.

Step 2

Prepare your cards

Make cards like the one below (front and back). But don't finish them until you've done Step 3.

Tower of London

(A question about the sight / place / thing)
Which of these animals never lived at the Tower?

(Three answers, two of which are wrong)
a) a polar bear that loved to fish
b) a raven that was able to talk
c) a zebra that liked beer

(The right answer)

Step 3

WB 67/20 Example cards (multiple choice)

Test your cards → WB 67/20

a) *Show the picture of the sight / place / thing on the front of your card. Read the question and the three answers. The others guess which answer is right. Correct them if they're wrong. You can give tips to help them.*

b) *Are the questions, answers and tips OK? If a quiz question is too difficult, make changes or give more tips.*

c) *Now make your cards.*

Useful phrases

Ideas for tips:
In this place you can …
It's famous for …
One of the attractions here is …
If you want to …, you will … here.
If you're interested in history, you should …
It's in the north / east / south / west.
… built it.

Step 4

WB 67/21 Speaking (questions)

Play the quiz game in your groups → WB 67/21

- *Shuffle the 16 cards for your group and place them on a table face down.*
- *Each group draws four cards from each group.*
- *In each group, shuffle all the cards again.*
- *Every player draws the same number of cards. One player starts and uses a card for the person next to him / her. If the person gets the answer right, he / she can keep the card.*
- *When you've used all the cards once, the person with the most cards wins!*

Step 5

Your 'British Isles Top 5'

a) *Copy an outline of the map of Britain at the back of this book.*

b) *Mark your 'Top 5' sights / places on the map. Write information about them next to each one.*

c) *Gallery walk: Look at the other posters and try to guess the sights / places.*

a polar bear that … [əˌpəʊlə beə ˈðæt] ein Eisbär, der … | **to fish** [fɪʃ] Fische fangen | **zebra** [ˈzebrə] | **beer** [bɪə] Bier

S 2/21–25
L 3/26–30

Things will get better

A Come in, come in!" Mrs Preston said from the hall of the big old house by the sea. "I'll make some tea."

"We can't have tea, Mum," Dave said. "There's no electricity, remember?"

"Oh, yes," she answered. "Well, a glass of water then?"

"Er … OK, yes please, Mrs Preston," Olivia said.

"Hi," Dave said to his friends and his granny. "Thanks for coming. Good journey?"

"Yeah, the journey was fine, thanks," Luke answered. "But *you* don't look fine. What's the matter? Is everything OK?"

"No, not really," Dave said. "We've been here a week, and there's no electricity yet. Dad is in London, the cat has run away, I haven't got any friends and I really miss my old life in Greenwich. It's awful here. I hate it."

"Oh, Dave!" Granny Rose said. "Don't be sad. You've only been here a week. Things will get better. You know they will."

B "Here are your glasses of water," Mrs Preston said. Then she looked at one of the glasses. "Oh dear," she said "Why is this water brown? I think we've got a problem with the water now too."

"Let's go out," Dave said to his friends. "We'll go up to the coastal path, to the old mine. Is that OK, Mum?"

"Yes, that's fine," Dave's mum answered. "See you later. I'll call a plumber."

"But it's Sunday", Granny Rose said. "It'll be *really* expensive."

C The friends stood on a hill by an old building. It had a tall chimney, but no roof. There was a strong wind from the sea, and it brought lots of big black clouds.

"This old building looks a bit scary," Holly whispered.

"Don't be silly. It's just one of many old mine buildings in this area. Tin was really important here," Olivia said. "Going right back to Celtic times. Tin from Cornwall went all over the world. But now there's almost no tin left."

"Looks like a great place for geocaching!" Luke said excitedly as he grabbed his smartphone. "Let's see if there's a cache somewhere near here. – Yes, there must be a difficult puzzle cache."

"Really?" Dave asked, "Let's solve the puzzle and get to that cache!"

Suddenly a deep voice behind them boomed, "Hey you, what are you doing here?! Keep away from MY treasure!"

The friends were scared. They turned around and saw a big man with a serious face and a kind of skirt and trousers. He had wild hair and looked dangerous, not only because of the long spear in his hand.

"I'm sorry, we – we didn't want to steal anything from you. We didn't know the cache was yours," Dave said. He was really scared.

Suddenly the sun came out again and the man's face looked much friendlier.

"Hello!" he said to Dave. "It was only a joke. Have you just moved into number 7?"

"Er, yes," Dave said. "And are you a Celtic warrior?"

"I'm Bob," the man said. "Your new neighbour."

"Ah," Dave said. "Are you on your way to a fancy dress party?"

The others just looked at Bob's strange clothes and said nothing.

"Oh, don't worry!" Bob laughed. "I don't always wear these clothes. I'm in the local history society. We do shows about the history of Cornwall. These are clothes from Celtic times."

"Right," Dave said. "Nice to meet you."

"I just came up to say hello," Bob said. "Tea at my house anyone?"

D "This is my wife, Helen," Bob said.

The friends were in the kitchen of Bob's house. "And these are my children, Jago and Tamara." The boy and girl were both about 13. "Good old Cornish names."

"Hello Dave. I'm Jago," the boy said.

"We're twins," the girl said. "Do you like computers, Dave?"

"Not now, Tamara," Bob said. "I'm sure Dave doesn't want to hear about your new computer games."

Then Olivia saw a big bag of tools on the kitchen floor.

"What do you do, Mr … er …?

"Call me Bob. I'm a plumber. And Helen here's an electrician. We do the plumbing and electrics for half the village. Well, the *whole* village, really."

Then Bob's bag of tools moved. A cat came out of it.

"Oh, there he is! This cat moved in here last week." Bob said.

"Sid!" Dave shouted. "There you are!"

E An hour later, there were thirteen people and a cat in Dave's garden. The friends, Bob and his family, Granny Rose and Dave's parents were all at a big table in the garden. There was tea and a cake.

"We were on the train before you," Granny Rose said to Dave's dad. "I didn't know that you wanted to come today."

"Change of plan at work," Dave's dad said. "I can be here all this week."

"Thanks again for fixing the water," Dave's mum said to Bob. "Are you sure I can't pay you for …"

"No, no," Bob said. "It was a five-minute job, and we're neighbours. But I'll have another piece of Rose's cake, if that's OK."

"And I'll have a look at your electrics tomorrow morning," Helen added.

Dave turned to Luke. "I think it'll be OK here after all," he said.

KV 8: Writing (visit in Cornwall)
WB 68/22 Reading (correct order)

READING

1 Understanding the text → WB 68/22

→ S5–7
S5–7 Reading

a) *Find headings for parts A–E of the story.*

b) *Answer these questions.*

Voc.: More jobs, p. 202

1. What problems do the Prestons have in their new home?
2. What do the friends think of Bob at first? What do we learn about him?
3. Think of what Granny Rose said at the end of part A. At the end of the story, was she right? Explain.

SPEAKING

2 Help for Dave

Talk about what everyone can do to make Dave happier in his new home.

Example: Tamara and Jago can play computer games with him.

KV 9a+b: Creative writing (diary entry/postcard)
WB 68/23 Writing/Speaking/Reading (options)

WRITING

3 Creative writing → WB 68/23

→ S10–13
S10–13 Writing

a) *Write a diary entry for one of the characters about what happened on their first day in Cornwall and what he / she felt.*

b) *Write a postcard from one of Dave's friends to his / her parents at home.*

Lösung: b) EH: ***Holly:*** *Dear Mum and Amber, We've arrived in St Agnes. Our journey was good. The Prestons still have a few problems with their house, but their neighbours Bob and Helen are very nice and they'll help them. They have got two children too. That's great for Dave! We had tea and a cake in the garden. Love, Holly*

Writing skills

A **diary entry** is a very personal text. Usually nobody else reads it. It's like writing to a close friend. Put the date at the top and start writing about what happened, what was important and how you feel about it. You can also write about your hopes and plans for the future.

Dear Mum and Dad,

How are you? We arrived in St Agnes yesterday. There is a beautiful harbour with nice sailboats, and we're camping really close to the sea. The weather is great, and we've spent a lot of time at the beach.

See you soon,

Megan

→ Solutions p. 249

Can you ...

1. say what will happen in the future? – Tomorrow there will be ...
2. talk about places and regions? – It's in ... | It has got ... | There are ... | You can ... there.
3. talk about travelling? – We can go by ... | It takes ... | We'll have to change
4. report what people have just said? – He says that ... / They tell us that ...

LANGUAGE

HA

1 Tomorrow's weather forecast

Complete the weather forecast with the correct forms of the verbs in the box.

Tomorrow 1 a nice day. There 2 a lot of sun. There 3 too many clouds. In the morning, it 4 cool, but it 5 nicer in the afternoon. It 6 a fine day for outdoor activities. You can be sure it 7 . But in the evening there 8 more wind, and at night the weather 9 . Clouds 10 and at about 12 o'clock it 11 to rain.

be (5x) | not be | change | get | move in | not rain | start

LANGUAGE

HA

2 What will happen?

Use the ideas to say what will happen.

Example: 1. I really like surfing. – Oh, then you'll love Cornwall!

2. I have to work late today. – No problem. ...
3. I didn't do my homework. – Too bad! ...
4. Hurry up! The train leaves in an hour. – Don't worry, it's not far to the station. ...
5. Let's book the train tickets now. Tomorrow ...

they be more expensive | you love Cornwall ✓ | we not be late | we cook dinner for you | Mum say you can't play on your computer

LANGUAGE

HA

3 What people say

Luke has just called his family from Cornwall. Read what they say. What does Luke tell his friends?

Start like this: Jamie says he ...

1. Jamie: I know about the Celts from the Asterix stories. They're my favourite comics.
2. Irina: You must bring some Celtic souvenirs! I love everything Celtic.
3. Mr Elliot: Sherlock is really missing you! He must go with you next time.
4. Mrs Elliot: The whole family will go to Cornwall next year. I'm going to make a list of places to visit when you're back home.

<Story> ist eine fakultative Sage. Der neue Wortschatz ist rezeptiv und unter dem Text annotiert.

Folie 37: Vorentlastung des Wortschatzes und Bildbeschreibung
KV 1: Reading (legend) KV 2a+b: Mediation (German legends)

S 2/26–29
L 3/31–34

A harp[1] on the water – a Welsh legend

Most countries have their legends – stories handed down from generation to generation. These stories talk of kings and queens, of fights between good and bad, rich and poor. Maybe you know the legend of Robin Hood, or of King Arthur? This one from Wales is about what happened to a very cruel[2] king.

Long long ago, at the beginning of time on this island, there was a very cruel king who lived in a stone palace where the lake of Bala is now. People said about him: "He kills[3] who he can," and it was true – he killed many.

One day, not long after he became king, and while he was still a young man, he was walking in his garden and thinking about cruelty when he suddenly heard a voice. It sounded like something between a silver bell and a bird's cry[4] and it said: "Vengeance[5] will come. Vengeance will come." Then he heard a second voice, farther away than the first. It asked: "When will it come? When will it come?" Then the first voice replied: "In the third generation. The third generation." At this he laughed loudly and shouted through the garden: "If it doesn't come before that, why should I care?"

And he planned to be crueller than ever.

Years later, the king's three sons[6] were born[7] and they were even crueller than he was. One day he was again walking in the garden when he heard the same voices. They were crying the same words: "Vengeance will come. When will it come? In the third generation, the third generation." Again he laughed loudly. "I laugh in the face of vengeance," he shouted. And he hurried back into the palace to teach his sons more cruelty.

Years passed[8], until the day when the whole palace was celebrating the birth of a son to the king's son and heir[9]. The king sent his guards out into the country. They had to tell everyone who loved the king (and their own lives too) to hurry to the palace to celebrate. One guard had to find a harp player with white hair who lived high up in the hills; he should play music for all the people who came to eat and dance in the palace that night.

The harp player didn't want to come, but he had to. When he saw the silver candlesticks, the golden cups and the beautiful dresses of the ladies, it felt like a strange dream and he couldn't say a word. He wasn't in the mood to play as he watched the faces of the king and his sons

1 **harp** [hɑːp] Harfe | 2 **cruel** [ˈkruːəl] grausam | 3 **to kill** [kɪl] töten | 4 **cry** [kraɪ] Ruf, Schrei | 5 **vengeance** [ˈvendʒəns] Rache | 6 **son** [sʌn] Sohn | 7 **to be born** [bi ˈbɔːn] geboren werden | 8 **to pass** [pɑːs] vorübergehen | 9 **heir** [eə] Thronfolger

with their hard smiles and ice-cold eyes. But the king said: “Play!”, and so he had to play.

At midnight[10] there was a break between the eating and dancing. The harp player was left alone, with nothing to eat and drink, in a quiet corner. Suddenly he heard a clear voice which said: “Vengeance will come. Vengeance will come.” He turned to the window, and in the light of the moon[11] he could see a small brown bird which was flying[12] around in the garden. It seemed[13] to invite him to follow!

He was very tired, but he stood up and left the palace. The bird flew in front of him and showed him the path[14] he should take. At the palace wall he stopped for a moment, but “Vengeance, vengeance!” the brown bird cried. Now it seemed as easy to go on as to go back. So they went on and on, until the harp player could see the hill in front of them.

When they reached[15] the top of the hill at last, he was so tired that he had to sit down. For the first time the bird was silent[16]. The moon moved behind a black cloud. In the dark the harp player couldn’t see his hand in front of him and the noise of water below told him that it was dangerous to move.

He suddenly thought that he was crazy to follow the voice of a bird, and he remembered sadly that his harp was back at the palace. “I must go back before the dancing starts!” he shouted. But when he thought of those cruel faces he was so horrified that he couldn’t move. He was so tired and it was so dark … He fell asleep quickly.

In the morning, he got up and rubbed[17] the sleep from his eyes. Then he rubbed them again and again because when he looked towards the palace, there was no palace there! He saw only a huge, calm lake where before there were walls and towers[18]. And his harp was swimming on the water towards him.

‘A Harp on the Water’ from *Welsh Legends and Folktales* by Gwyn Jones

→ WB 70/1–3

10 midnight [ˈmɪdnaɪt] Mitternacht | **11 moon** [muːn] Mond | **12 to fly** [flaɪ] fliegen | **13 to seem** [siːm] scheinen | **14 path** [pɑːθ] Pfad | **15 to reach** [riːtʃ] erreichen | **16 silent** [ˈsaɪlənt] still | **17 to rub** [rʌb] reiben | **18 tower** [taʊə] Turm

WB 70/1 Vocabulary (puzzle) **WB 70/2 Reading (details)**
WB 70/3 Writing (summary)

<Revision C> ist fakultativ und dient der Festigung/Wiederholung. Es werden keine neuen Sprachmittel eingeführt.

VOCABULARY

1 Offline for a month

a) *Sally is a 14-year old blogger from London. Last month she was offline for four weeks. Read about her experience. Fill in the gaps. Put the verbs in the right tense.*

to spend | to send | face-to-face | to post | to download | to stay in touch | to watch | offline | social networks | to see | challenge | phone | media mad | to get

Lösung: a) 1. *media mad* 2. *spend* 3. *offline* 4. *stay in touch* 5. *social networks* 6. *sent* 7. *phone* 8. *posted* 9. *see* 10. *watched* 11. *downloaded* 12. *got* 13. *face-to-face* 14. *challenge*

SALLY'S BLOG

MY MONTH OFFLINE – A REAL CHALLENGE!

I'm [1]! I use the computer and the internet *very* often. I've got a smartphone, a tablet and a laptop – yes, I [2] a lot of time online. "When I was young we didn't have all those things," my Aunt Elizabeth told me one day. "I bet you can't live for a week [3]." "Ha," I said. "Of course I can. I can even do it for a month! You'll see!"

Well, that's how it started. I wasn't able to[1] [4] with my friends on my phone or on [5] for four weeks. When my friends met in town they [6] me texts but I wasn't able to read them because I didn't have my [7] anymore. They [8] photos I wasn't able to [9], and when they [10] videos or [11] new music and then talked about how great it all was, I didn't know what they were talking about. And once, my friend Anne forgot that I was offline. At school, she asked me angrily, "Why didn't you come to my party?!" "*What* party?" I replied. "My birthday party!" Anne answered. Oops, I never [12] her invitation! So that wasn't so great.

But I also discovered that I had more time for other things when I was offline. I read more books, I did more sports and I talked to people [13] more often. But now I'm happy to be online again and tell you about this experience. Try it. It's a real [14]!

b) *Would you be able to stay offline for a month? Say why / why not.*

MEDIATION

2 A new computer game

Your little brother has a new computer game, but the instructions are in English and he doesn't understand everything. Explain the main ideas of the game to him.

Welcome to **Jungle World**, where Jolly Joe and his monkey friends swing from tree to tree and try to grab as much fruit as they can! But they have to be careful – the jungle is a dangerous place full of wild animals who want the fruit *and* you! Choose which monkey you want to be and give him / her a name. Then start your adventure through the jungle. With [S-P-A-C-E] your monkey jumps. Press [←] [→] if you want to move left or right and press [↑] [↓] to go up or down. Try to grab as much fruit as you can – the more you get, the more points you get! You find different kinds of small fruit in the trees – but watch out: There are snakes in the trees too! The fruit on the ground is bigger, but be careful there too: Before you can grab some fruit, a tiger or lion could grab *you*! Enjoy **Jungle World**.

1 **I wasn't able to …** [ˌaɪ wɒznt‿ˈeɪbl‿tə] ich konnte nicht …

WRITING

3 A postcard from ...

Have a look at the material you collected for the Task in Unit 5. Imagine you've been to one of the places. Write a postcard to your friend / your grandma / .... Tell them ...

- what you did
- what the weather was like
- anything special about the place where you are (landscape, sights, events, etc.)
- anything strange / interesting / exciting that happened to you
- any special food you ate

LISTENING

4 Travelling around the world: Announcements

L 3/35

a) *Listen to five announcements and say where the people are. Which words helped you to find out about where they are?*

b) *Listen again. Who is the announcement important for? What is the most important information for these people?*

Transfer

c) *Your turn: Write your own announcement and read it to your partner. Your partner has to guess where you are.*

Lösung: a) 1. *at a train station (delayed; platform; tickets);* 2. *in an airport terminal (boarding call; British Airlines; gate; captain; aircraft);* 3. *on a ferry (captain; on board; ferry; cruise; knots);* 4. *on the Tube (station; Bond Street; change; Jubilee Line; Central Line train; mind the gap; train; platform);* 5. *in a train station (information desk; entrance hall; train station)*

WRITING

5 The world 50 years from now

*In a short text, make predictions about the future. What will life be like 50 (or 100, 200) years from now? Use the **will** future in your text, and think of these ideas:*

how people will live / travel | what people will eat / drink | what school / nature / technology will be like | how people will communicate with each other

forest skyscrapers to live in

robots for cleaning the house

Find more online: x2u7bm

British stories and legends

Every country has special places where famous historical people lived or important events happened. When we don't know all the facts, we like to hear strange and wonderful stories about them. But how much is really true?

SPEAKING

1 Warm-up

What famous historical people do you know about in your country or in Britain?

READING

2 Typical ingredients of legends

Folie 38: Wortschatzvorentlastung und Bildbeschreibung

a) *Read the text. Which ingredients do you like in a story or legend? Why?*

Lösung: a) Typical ingredients of legends: stories about people in history; usually not completely true; often show the difference between right and wrong; colourful characters, e.g. kings, queens, wizards; good and bad characters: heroes and villains; heroes usually win fights; heroes: brave knights or normal people who do brave things; villains: criminals or powerful people; more modern legends from popular books, e.g. Sherlock Holmes

Legends are stories about people in history – but usually they aren't completely true. Often, writers have taken historical events and changed them a bit to make the stories more exciting, or maybe to show the difference between right and wrong. Legends have colourful characters like brave kings and cruel queens, or magical characters like wizards. Heroes ('good guys') and villains ('bad guys') have dangerous fights – of course, the good guy usually wins! Popular heroes are often brave knights, but sometimes they're just normal men and they do brave things to help other people. Villains can be dangerous criminals or very powerful people. They use their power in a bad way. And finally, there are more modern legends from popular books, like Sherlock Holmes. He was a private detective and solved mysterious crimes. He never lived at all, but people all over the world love to think he did!

b) *Look at the stills of Jinsoo and Marley. They're playing the roles of three famous British legends. What do you think the stories are about? What do you know about them?*

Useful phrases

Nouns: king | queen | wizard | hero / heroine | villain | knight | robber | outlaw

Adjectives: colourful | magical | brave | cruel | dangerous | powerful | mysterious

Phrases: to have a fight | to hide in the forest | to use your power | to solve a crime

VIEWING

3 Stories and legends (1) KV 1: Activity (card game)

13 🎬 **a)** *Watch the film and take notes about the three legends.*

ösung: b) *1a), d), g); 2c), f),); 3b), e)*

b) *Match the sentence parts. Find the correct statements for each character.*

1. Sherlock Holmes was a private detective.
2. Robin Hood was a famous outlaw.
3. King Arthur was a powerful king.

a) Dr Watson was his assistant.
b) Many people think Tintagel was his castle.
c) He lived in Sherwood Forest, near Nottingham.
d) He lived in Baker Street in London.
e) His knights sat at the Round Table.
f) He loved Maid Marian.
g) He solved many mysterious crimes.
h) He stole from the rich and gave to the poor.

KV 2: Role play (useful phrases)
WB 71/1 Vocabulary (crossword puzzle)
WB 71/2 Speaking (characters)

VIEWING

4 Stories and legends (2) → WB 71/1–2

ösung: a) ***Sherlock olmes:** typical outfit: cape d cap, magnifying glass; **obin Hood:** green hat with feather, green top, bow d arrow; **King Arthur:** own*

a) *Watch the film again. Which characters have which props?*

b) *Your turn: Read the skills box. Then find out about another character from a legend or story, maybe a woman like the Celtic queen Boudicca (she fought against the Romans), Vivien, the Lady[6] of the Lake (she gave King Arthur his sword[7] Excalibur) or Miss Marple (a detective in Agatha Christie's crime stories). Which costume, props or set could you give that character in a film? Why?*

bell | castle | bow and arrow[1] | gloves | cape[2] | crown[3] | lucky charm | magnifying glass[4] | cap[5]

Film skills

A film uses more than pictures, sounds and words to tell a story. It also uses **costumes**, **props** and a **set**. The characters wear **costumes** and they carry or use **props**. We can also see where they live – this is called the **set**.

Example:
If you want to show that a woman is a queen, she can wear a crown and beautiful clothes and live in a castle.

c) *Role play: In groups of three, each of you chooses to be one of the characters. Your characters meet. Talk to each other about*

1. where you live
2. what you do
3. what you wear and carry
4. what's good and bad about your life.

Example:
A: Hi there. I'm Robin, I help the poor.
B: And I'm Miss Marple. I love to solve mysterious crimes.
C: …

1 **bow and arrow** [ˌbəʊ ən ˈærəʊ] Pfeil und Bogen | 2 **cape** [keɪp] Umhang | 3 **crown** [kraʊn] Krone | 4 **magnifying glass** [ˈmægnɪfaɪŋ ˌglɑːs] Lupe | 5 **cap** [kæp] Kappe; Mütze | 6 **lady** [ˈleɪdi] Herrin; Dame | 7 **sword** [sɔːd] Schwert

Legende

Diese Symbole und Erklärungen zeigen dir, wie du mit den Hilfen, Aufgaben und Aktivitäten auf den *Diff pool*-Seiten arbeiten kannst.

△ Hilfe zur Unit-Aufgabe | oder eine leichtere Variante der Unit-Aufgabe | oder eine zusätzliche Aufgabe

▲ eine zusätzliche Herausforderung

Unit 1

△ 1 Feelings → Help with Check-in, p. 13/3

How can you feel in these situations? Match the feelings with the sentences. There's often more than one answer.

Lösung: EH 1. *I feel nervous because there's a test in English tomorrow. 2. I feel excited because my team won a football match. 3. I feel bad because I forgot my homework again. 4. I feel good because I know all the answers in class today. 5. I feel shy because I'm the new student. etc.*

1. There's a test in English tomorrow.
2. Your team won a football match.
3. You forgot your homework – again.
4. You know all the answers in class today.
5. You're the new student.
6. You're alone, and you don't know what to do.
7. You're at the park and are playing with your friends.
8. You meet your favourite star.
9. You can't find your lucky charm.
10. You have chocolate on your white jeans and everyone can see it.

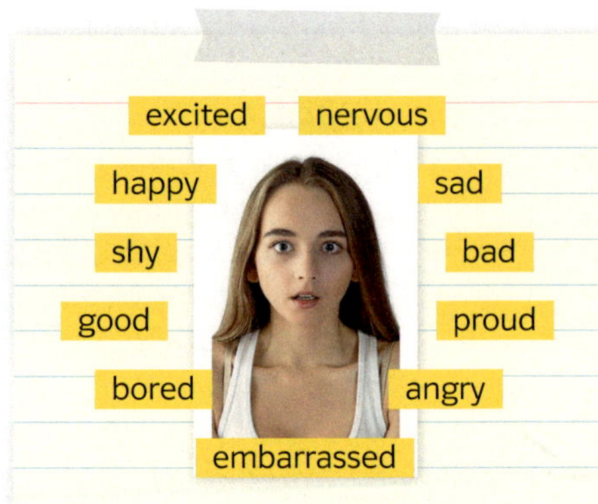

▲ 2 Charity work → After Station 1, p. 14/1

Do you know any children in charity projects? What can ***you*** *do to raise money? Write down some ideas and prepare a short talk for the class.*

△ 3 Irregular simple past forms → Instead of Station 1, p. 14/2 b)

Put in the correct past forms. Use the verbs below.

Lösung: *1. did 2. got 3. brought 4. put 5. gave 6. was 7. came 8. wore 9. had 10. took*

Two years ago the students **1** (do) fun activities and **2** (get) money for Comic Relief. They **3** (bring) the money to school. Then the school **4** (put) all the money together and **5** (give) it to the charity. Red Nose Day **6** (be) a non-uniform day, so everyone **7** (come) to school in different clothes. But they all **8** (wear) something red. Of course they all **9** (have) red noses too. Some students **10** (take) funny photos for the school website.

got | brought | gave | was | took | wore | had | put | did | came

△ 4 Sounds → After Station 1, p. 15/3

How do you say these simple past forms? Put them in the right box, then read them to your partner. Can you hear the difference?

ösung: 1. played, turned; . stopped, danced, chased, ıughed, watched, looked, ımped; 3. acted, collected, ʋanted, started

played | stopped | acted | danced | collected | chased
laughed | watched | wanted | started | looked | turned | jumped

[d]	[t]	[ɪd]
played	stopped	acted

△ 5 The star of the show → Instead of Station 1, p. 15/5

What does Sherlock tell his dog friends the next day? Write the text again in his words, and use the verbs in the simple past below.

ösung: First I jumped ver a big box. Then I ran round and chased my tail. fter that I danced on a kateboard, and when Olivia arted to play the sax I also ıng. The people loved it. ıey laughed and clapped ıd gave lots of money to ɔmic Relief. Luke and his iends tried to do their best o, but everybody's eyes ere on me. I felt happy ıd proud – I was the real ar of the show!

Start: I **did** lots of great tricks in the comedy show yesterday.

1. Sherlock does lots of great tricks in the comedy show. **2.** First he jumps over a big box. **3.** Then he runs around and chases his tail. **4.** After that he dances on a skateboard, and when Olivia starts to play the sax he also sings. **5.** The people love it. **6.** They laugh and clap and give lots of money to Comic Relief. **7.** Luke and his friends try to do their best too, but everyone's eyes are on Sherlock. **8.** He feels so happy and proud – he is the real star of the show!

was | did ✔ | ran | danced | sang | chased | loved | started
tried | laughed | gave | were | clapped | jumped | felt

△ 6 A report about a special activity → Help with Station 1, p. 16/7

What did these people do to raise money for charity? The words below can help you.

ösung: 1. These people sold d things on a flea market. These people made cakes ıd biscuits and had a ke sale. 3. These people n for charity. They found onsors. They paid money r metre. 4. These people ganised a talent show. ey sold tickets and drinks the break.

sell old things | flea market

make cakes and biscuits | cake sale

run for charity | find sponsors | pay money per metre

organise talent show | sell tickets | sell drinks

△ 7 What they didn't do and what they did → After Station 2, p. 18/12

Tony was tired last week, but Lou wasn't – so they didn't do things together. What didn't they do? What did they do? Take turns!

Lösung: **1. A.** *Tony didn't go swimming in the boating lake with Lou, he watched TV.* **B.** *Lou didn't watch TV, she went swimming in the boating lake.* **2. A.** *Tony didn't play tennis with a friend, he slept on the sofa.* **B.** *Lou didn't sleep on the sofa, she played tennis with a friend.* **3. A.** *Tony didn't buy cheese at Greenwich Market, he listened to music.* **B.** *Lou didn't listen to music, she bought cheese at Greenwich Market.* **4. A.** *Tony didn't prepare dinner for his friends, he played a computer game.* **B.** *Lou didn't play a computer game, she prepared dinner for her friends.*

Example:
You: Tony didn't go skating with Lou, he read a book.
Your partner: Lou didn't read a book, she went skating in the park.

Lou	Tony
go skating in the park	read a book
swim in the boating lake	watch TV
play tennis with a friend	sleep on the sofa
buy cheese at Greenwich Market	listen to music
prepare dinner for her friends	play a computer game

▲ 8 A perfect day → After Station 2, p. 18/12

Think of something you did on a perfect day. (It needn't be true). Now your partner must find out what it was. He / She can ask questions like these:

Did you do something funny / exciting? Did you do it at home / in the park? Did you do it with friends / parents / alone? Were you nervous / excited / happy?

Think of more questions. Take notes, and then tell your classmates what your partner did on his / her perfect day!

△ 9 The new forms → After Station 3, p. 21/20 b)

Tony and Lou are fighting! What do they say?

Lösung: *1. bigger 2. big 3. nicer 4. more popular 5. funnier 6. funny 7. worse 8. faster 9. taller 10. more intelligent 11. faster*

Tony: I'm 1 (big) than you, Lou!
Lou: OK, I'm not as 2 (big) as you, but I am 3 (nice).
Tony: Maybe. But I'm 4 (popular) than you!
Lou: Oh no, you aren't. That's because I'm 5 (funny) than you.
Tony: You aren't as 6 (funny) as I am. Your jokes are 7 (bad) than my jokes! And I'm 8 (fast) than you.
Lou: That's because you're 9 (tall). But I'm 10 (intelligent). I can use my skates – and then I'm 11 (fast) than you!

△ 10 Say what's different → Instead of Station 3, p. 21/21

Make sentences with comparisons.

sung: 1. *Wales is smaller* *an England. 2. The* *ather today is worse* *an yesterday. 3. Route B is* *sier than Route A. 4. The* *urses aren't as expensive* *most people think. 5.* *not as nervous as I was* *out new challenges.*

Example: 1. Wales is **smaller than** England.

1. Wales is ▬ ▬ (small) England.
2. The weather today is ▬ ▬ (bad) yesterday.
3. Route B is ▬ ▬ (easy) route A.
4. The courses aren't ▬ ▬ ▬ (expensive) most people think.
5. I'm not ▬ ▬ ▬ (nervous) I was about new challenges.

△ 11 Who's the tallest? → After Station 3, p. 21/22

Find out about your classmates! Choose one of the ideas in the box, find two partners and stand next to each other! Who is taller than you? Who has got the most interesting hobby? When you have got a group, shout "Stop!" and present your group to the class. Find the next group.

tall / short | young / old | boring / interesting hobby | big / small family | long / short way to school | young / old parents | silly / nice brother / sister

▲ 12 The best thing ever → After Station 3, p. 21/22

Choose two of these things and write a short text about them. Use ***than*** *and* ***as … as*** *too. You can start like this: The tastiest meal I ever had was … It was tastier than…*

tasty meal[1] | good film | nice teacher | funny book | exciting holiday | bad joke

△ 13 The secret → Help with Story, p. 24/3 b)

You can use these ideas and phrases to write your scene.

1. Look! I think that window … / … help me up?
2. Hey, here's another … / Do you think it's …? / Shshsh, quiet! / Don't … noise!
3. There's a light[2] …! / I think it's … window! / Let's throw …
4. Who's there? / Oh, it's you! / I heard …
5. We can use this to … / I can climb up, and then I can open …

1 **tasty meal** ['teɪsti 'miːl] leckeres Essen; leckere Mahlzeit | 2 **light** [laɪt] Licht

Unit 2

△ 1 Choose your London → Help with Check-in, p. 37/3

Here are some useful phrases that can help you to discuss where you want to go.

Useful phrases

I'd like to visit … It's free. | I think … is the best place. Let's go there!
We must see …, it's fantastic. | Can we go to …? I hear it's really great.
I'm sure it's fun to …, so I really want to …

△ 2 What are they going to do next week? → After Station 1, p. 38/3

Monday	Tuesday	Wednesday	Thursday	Friday
Amir and Jay – go to the cinema	*Amir – go shopping with Aunt Yasmin, buy a London T-shirt*	*Amir – meet Jay's friends in the afternoon*	*Amir and Shahid – visit Cutty Sark*	*Amir and Jay – have a sleepover at Luke's house*

Lösung: *… to go to the cinema. On Tuesday, Aunt Yasmin is going to go shopping with me – she's going to buy a London T-shirt for me. On Wednesday, I'm going to meet Jay's friends in the afternoon. And on Thursday, Shahid and I are going to visit the Cutty Sark. On Friday, Jay and I are going to have a sleepover at Luke's house.*

Amir tells his mum about these plans in an e-mail – what does he write?

Start like this: Dear Mum, I can't call you very often next week because I have so many plans! On Monday, Jay and I are going to go … On Tuesday, Aunt Yasmin is going to …

△ 3 What's going to happen? → Help with Station 1, p. 39/4

These words can help you to write about the people in the picture on p. 53:

open the door | clean the street | take the bus | buy an ice cream
give some money | go to the cinema | play the saxophone

Start: 1. The old man and woman are going to sit down. 2. The man is going to …

△ 4 Guess my plans for tomorrow → Help with Station 1, p. 39/5

What can you do where? These ideas can help you to guess your partner's plans. Match the activities with the right places first.

Lösung: *1e); 2d); 3b); 4a); 5c)*

1. London Dungeon
2. London Eye
3. Royal Observatory
4. Shakespeare's Globe
5. Brick Lane

a) learn about the theatre, watch a Shakespeare play
b) stand on the time line, watch the time ball fall down
c) buy great clothes, see street art
d) get a great view of London
e) hear horror stories, see ghosts

△ 5 The photo story → Help with Station 2, p. 41/7

Olivia, Holly, Amir and Jay all have different feelings about the food challenge. Look at the ideas about what they might say.

Jay	Olivia	Holly	Amir
really like music | fantastic street shows | not so hungry	like a challenge | try something exciting | find cafés boring	doesn't know where the cafés are | try to find something special | everything so expensive	nervous | not know where to look | happy to go with Olivia

▲ 6 A game: Why didn't you buy any food? → After Station 2, p. 41/7

One of you is Jay, one of you is Olivia. Olivia starts with the question below. Jay must quickly give three different answers. Olivia chooses one and writes it down. Then it's her turn to answer with three different sentences. Jay chooses one, writes it down and goes on with three different sentences. Go on like this till you have the perfect dialogue.

Start: **Olivia:** Why didn't you buy any food?

I didn't feel hungry any more.
I was watching the street shows and they were great.
I didn't have any money. →

What about your pocket money?
Why not? →
Maybe someone took it!

I forgot it at home.
…

△ 7 Compound words with *some* and *any* → After Station 2, p. 41/9

ung: a) 1. some 2. some
ny 4. any 5. any 6. some
. any 2. any 3. some
ome 5. some 6. any

a) *Fill the gaps with **some** or **any**.*

Jay: Let's buy **1** drinks. I have **2** money left.
Olivia: Oh, no! I don't want **3** drinks, and I'm still hungry. Have you got **4** crisps left, Holly?
Holly: No, sorry. I haven't got **5** crisps, but I've got **6** biscuits.

b) *Complete the words with **some** or **any**.*

Amir hasn't bought **1** **thing** for his mum yet, so the friends are looking for souvenir shops. "How much do you want to spend?" Jay wants to know.
"Well, I can't buy **2** **thing** expensive, I've only got a few pounds. But I need **3** **thing** for my mum – maybe there's **4** **thing** in this little shop?" Amir answers.
"I don't think so. Look at the prices! Let's go **5** **where** else," Holly says. "What about Greenwich Market? Or does **6** **one** have a better idea?"

▲ 8 Sherlock, you crazy dog! → After Station 2, p. 41/9

Luke's mum is away at the weekend. She wrote a note for the family – but Sherlock found it and now it's in pieces! Match the parts and write a new note in the right order.

Lösung: 1. Hi everyone, I hope you can manage without me! 2. I wanted to get to the station, so I didn't do everything before I left. 3. You needn't buy anything for dinner. 4. There's something in the fridge for you, please check. 5. I don't want to find any food on the sofa when I come back. 6. Everybody should clean up a bit. 7. Can someone please clean the windows? 8. Remember: someone must take Sherlock for a walk tomorrow morning. 9. Lots of love for everybody, Mum.

1. You needn't buy
2. Remember: someone must
3. I wanted to get to the station, so
4. There's something
5. Lots of love for
6. Can someone please
7. I don't want to find
8. Everybody should
9. Hi everyone, I hope

a) clean the windows?
b) in the fridge for you, please check.
c) anything for dinner.
d) clean up a bit.
e) any food on the sofa when I come back.
f) you can manage without me!
g) I didn't do everything before I left.
h) take Sherlock for a walk tomorrow morning.
i) everybody, Mum.

△ 9 Complete the text → Instead of Station 2, p. 41/10

Fill the gaps with these words. Use each word only once.

Lösung: 1. anybody 2. something 3. nothing 4. someone 5. everywhere 6. nobody 7. anywhere 8. anything 9. everything 10. everybody

nothing | everywhere | anybody | someone | something | everybody | everything | nobody | anywhere | anything

Holly: What can we do till we meet Shahid later? Has **1** got a good suggestion?
Jay: It must be **2** that costs **3** – we haven't got any money left.
Olivia: Let's just walk around. I'm sure that's fun for **4** new in London like Amir. There are lots of interesting things to see **5** you look. What do you think, Amir?

Amir: Well, if **6** wants to make a different suggestion – yes, I'd like that.
Holly: Is there **7** special you'd like to go or **8** special you'd like to see?
Amir: Well, **9** is special for me – it's all amazing. But I'd love to walk near the river.
Jay: Is that OK with **10**? – Great, come on, let's go and find the Thames!

△ 10 Act it out! → After Station 3, p. 43/14

Write these activities on cards. One of you chooses an activity and acts it without words. The others guess what you're doing, and how.

smile happily | dance slowly | talk quietly | look around nervously | walk carefully | write fast | sing loudly | shout aggressively

▲ 11 A treasure in the Thames → Instead of Story, p. 50/4

Think of one thing that the friends find in the Thames: a gold coin, an old ring, a statue, an oil lamp … Tell the story of how they find it, what they do with it, etc.

Unit 3

△ **1** ## Talk about sports → Help with Check-In, p. 54/2b)

*Two students made these word clouds. What are their favourite sports? And what sports are **you** interested in? You can use the words to talk about it.*

sung: red cloud: tennis, do, skating; green cloud: rate, gymnastics, dancing ip hop, ballet)

▲ **2** ## Have you really done that? → After Station 1, p. 57/3

*Work with a partner. Each of you writes down six very strange or exciting activities. **One** of them must be an activity that you have really done. Exchange your activities and find out which one **your** partner has done.*

eat worms – take a llama to the park – go water-skiing with my granny – play with a tarantula[1] – sleep in a haunted house[2]

△ **3** ## Great runners → After Station 1, p. 59/7

Lisa and Mark help to organise the London Marathon; they need great runners. Put the verbs into the present perfect.

sung: 1. have you written e-mail to 2. haven't got have found 4. Have they n 5. have never heard have run 7. has won 8. sn't won 9. Have you ecked 10. have copied haven't had 12. have ked

Lisa: We need some great runners this year. Mark, **1** (you write an e-mail to) last year's winners?
Mark: Yes, I have. But I **2** (get) answers from everyone yet. What about the German twins[3], Klara and Lena – I **3** (find) some info about them on the internet.
Lisa: **4** (they win) anything yet? I **5** (never hear) of them.
Mark: They **6** (run) in a few important races. Klara **7** (win) one big marathon, the Frankfurt City Marathon. Lena **8** (win) yet, but she was 'Best European' in the Hamburg Marathon. They always run together.
Lisa: **9** (you check) if they have a website?
Mark: Of course I have. Here, I **10** (copy) their address for you. Let's write them an e-mail. We **11** (not have) famous twins in the Marathon yet.
Lisa: No, it's a good idea to ask them. But wait till I **12** (look) at their website first!

1 **tarantula** [təˈræntjələ] Vogelspinne | 2 **haunted house** [ˌhɔːntɪd ˈhaʊs] Geisterhaus | 3 **twins** [twɪnz] Zwillinge

▲ 4 Write a profile about Brandon → After Station 2, p. 59/7

For a magazine, write a short profile about a rich[1] and famous young actor, Brandon Fairchild. What has he ***already / just / never done****, or* ***not yet done****? What is he* ***going to do*** *in the future? Use the ideas below, but also add some of your own ideas. Be creative! (Use a dictionary for help with new words.)*

already ✔	buy a cool house in Hollywood
never ✘	have a famous girlfriend
just ✔	get award[2] for 'Coolest Actor'
not yet ✘	find a new house in London
future plans ✔	buy his own ship / win an Oscar

△ 5 Children and accidents → Help with Station 2, p. 59/9

These words can help you to tell your partner in English about the German survey.

young people | often | get hurt[3] | have accidents | per cent[4] | every year | injury[5] | see a doctor | small children

Remember, your partner only needs to understand **the main ideas**. You needn't try to translate everything word for word!

Lou

△ 6 The London Mini Marathon → Help with Story, p. 66/1b)

These words and phrases for the three pictures can help you to retell the story.

When the race started, Gwen was sure … | Olivia wasn't there, so … | Gwen was a bit worried about … | She told Luke, "Don't …" | Luke saw two people in …

Ten minutes later, Gwen felt … | She told herself … | Then there was a problem with the … | They got … | But Luke and Gwen …

Suddenly, … pulled out a phone and … chaos … | Another runner … | But Gwen and Luke finished … | Olivia found out that the dog and cat were …

1 **rich** [rɪtʃ] reich | 2 **award** [əˈwɔːd] Auszeichnung; Preis | 3 **to get hurt** [ˌgetˈhɜːt] sich verletzen | 4 **per cent** [pəˈsent] Prozent | 5 **injury** [ˈɪndʒəri] Verletzung

△ 7 What's the person like? → Help with Story, p. 66/2

*Which of these words can you use if you want to say something **positive** about someone? Which ones are **negative**? Make two lists. Some of the words can help you to describe the children and their actions.*

brave | unfriendly | stupid | fast | polite | crazy | clever | careful | helpful | funny | silly | interesting | great | good | boring | confident | friendly | popular | awful | nice

△ 8 Useful phrases from the story → Help with Story, p. 66/3

Complete the phrases; you know them from the story. This can help with your mind map.

sung: 1. *means a lot*
too bad 3. *don't call*
feels so 5. *nervous*

1. "My charity does a lot of really important work, so it really ___ to me."
2. "Olivia can't join us. That's ___!"
3. "You're silly, not me! So ___ me silly."
4. "This ___ great! After all that training, this is the moment, *my* moment!"
5. "There are so many people here, and it's my first marathon! I'm ___! You too?"

▲ 9 A game: Frozen image[6]! → After Story, p. 66/3

Get together in groups of four or five. Choose a scene from the story and practise a frozen image of that scene. (Practise in another room so your classmates can't see you.) Back in the classroom, the others then shout "One… two… freeze[7]!" and your group does its frozen image. Your classmates must guess the scene and explain how they guessed.

Unit 4

△ 1 Media collocations → Instead of Check-in, p. 74/2

a) *Write down all the media collocations in the text.*

ung: Vgl. Übersicht
89.

Tony loves the world of media! He checks his text messages all the time. He loves texting his friends. He sends and receives text messages during lessons too. (Bad boy!) And Tony has joined a popular social network: He's on Mousebook, of course. He regularly posts photos and changes his profile. It's important for Tony to stay in touch with his friends, so he often talks to them on video chat. At weekends, he often plays video games or takes part in discussions. It's easy to forget the time when you're online! Lou isn't so happy about this: Tony doesn't always reply to her text messages quickly enough, and she has to check his profile on Mousebook to see what he's doing!

b) *You can use some of the verbs with more than one noun, e.g., you can **change** your **profile** and you can **check** your **profile** too. How many different media collocations of nouns and verbs can you find?*

6 **frozen image** [ˌfrəʊzn‿ˈɪmɪdʒ] erstarrtes Bild | 7 **to freeze** [friːz] erstarren

▲ 2 Ruby's answer → After Station 1, p. 76/1

Work with a partner. What different bits of advice does Ruby have for Lauren? Write them down on little pieces of paper. Then put the pieces of paper face down on the table. Take turns to pick one up and talk about it. Do you think it's good advice? Why / Why not?

△ 3 Using linking words: Tony and his phone → After Station 1, p. 77/2

Read what Tony's friend Robby says about Tony. Use these words to make one sentence out of the two. There's sometimes more than one way!

Lösung: 1. *We often saw each other before he got a new smartphone for his birthday.* 2. *Tony can't leave his smartphone alone for a minute because he's really into texting.* 3. *When I wanted to go to the cinema with him, he said "yes".* 4. *At the cinema, someone said, "You must turn off your phone because the film is starting."* 5. *When/After Tony heard that, he was shocked.* 6. *Whenever/As soon as a phone rings at the cinema, it makes other people angry.*

after | before | as soon as | whenever | because | when

Example: Tony plays video games too often. He doesn't call me. → **Whenever** Tony plays video games, he doesn't call me.

1. He got a new smartphone for his birthday. We often saw each other before that.
2. Tony can't leave his phone alone for one minute. He's really into texting.
3. I wanted to go to the cinema with him yesterday. He said "yes".
4. At the cinema, someone said, "You must turn off your phone. The film is starting."
5. Tony heard that. He was shocked.
6. Sometimes a phone rings at the cinema. It always makes the other people angry.

△ 4 Symbols of friendship → Help with Station 1, p. 78/6 b)

Here are some phrases and ideas for talking about symbols of friendship.

Useful phrases

A symbol can be **something you do**, like … when you wear the same clothes / colours | when you have a secret together | when you talk about / help each other with problems | …

A symbol can be **a thing**, like … a photo together | a mascot keyring[1] / a mascot toy | special words for things | favourite stickers | …

△ 5 I've finally got my own smartphone → After Station 2, p. 80/10

*Make sentences with **must, mustn't, needn't, have to** or **don't have to**.*

Lösung: 1. *don't have to* 2. *have to* 3. *have to* 4. *don't have to/needn't* 5. *mustn't* 6. *must*

1. Now that I've got my own phone I ___ ask my mum to use hers.
2. But the bad thing now is that I ___ pay for all my calls myself.
3. My parents are strict[2], so at 9:00 p.m. I ___ leave my phone with them for the night.
4. But I ___ give it to them at the weekend.
5. If it costs too much I'll get in trouble[3] so I ___ spend a lot of time on the internet.
6. Excuse me, I ___ go now – my best friend is waiting in the chatroom for me!

1 **mascot keyring** [ˌmæskət ˈkiːrɪŋ] Maskottchen-Schlüsselanhänger | 2 **strict** [strɪkt] streng | 3 **to get into trouble** [get ˌɪntə ˈtrʌbl] Ärger bekommen |

▲ 6 VIC – very important chats! → After Station 2, p. 80/10

Complete the sentences. Use a verb from the box and ***must / mustn't, have to / don't have to*** *or* ***needn't****.*

tell | remember | study | text | go

1. This is a big secret. You …
2. It's 9:00 p.m. so I …
3. Last week I forgot to return[4] the books. This week I …
4. "Have you finished your studies?" – "Yes, I know everything for the test. I …"
5. We're going to the cinema tonight, so you …

Lösung: EH: *1. This is a big secret. You mustn't tell anybody! 2. It's 9:00 p.m. so I must go to bed. 3. Last week I forgot to return the books. This week I have to / must remember to return them. 4. "Have you finished your studies?" – "Yes, I know everything for the test. I don't have to / needn't study anymore. 5. We're going to the cinema tonight, so you needn't text me.*

▲ 7 Giving and taking advice → After Station 2, p. 80/11

On cards, write down situations where ***you*** *might need advice. (The ideas on the right can help you.) Put them face down on the table, between you and your partner. Take turns to choose a card, read the situation to your partner, and say what advice you have for him / her.*

not good at school | trouble with teacher | fight with friend | not enough pocket money | small room | …

△ 8 You could do that, but I think you should … → After Station 2, p. 80/11

Read these situations and decide what advice you want to give. Do you need ***could*** *or* ***should****? (Remember, there's a difference! Check G11 for help.)*

ösung: 1. *You could use ine. 2. You should buy a ew one. 3. You shouldn't ost private photos. . I could check it. 5. You hould/could try both. . You could/should tell her ou're sorry. 7. You could rite something interesting/ xciting.*

1. Oh no. I left my smartphone at home! (use mine)
2. This phone doesn't work at all. (buy a new one)
3. Do you like this photo? I want to post it. (not post private photos)
4. My computer has been so slow! (let me check it)
5. Hmm, 'World of Heroes' or 'Super Talents' – which game is better? (try both)
6. Susan is still angry because I sent her that text. (tell her you're sorry)
7. I think my profile is boring. (write something interesting / exciting)

4 **to return** [rɪˈtɜːn] zurückgeben

▲ 9 Media mad → After Station 2, p. 81/12

When you read a flow chart, always start at the top and work down, step by step. First read the text in the middle box in the first line, and then decide if you must follow the red (= no) or green (= yes) flash. Are you surprised abour your results?

Work with a partner. Choose a box for your partner (e.g. 'five / four' is the box with "You don't care about video games"). Your partner must find the box and comment on it. Then it's his / her turn.

Example: A: Two / two. "You check your messages all the time!"
B: I don't know. When I'm bored I often check them. But when I'm with my friends, I don't do that. What about you?

△ 10 Writing a dialogue → Help with Story, p. 88/1c)

Here are some ideas to help you write your dialogue.

Mrs Preston: When did you get … | Didn't you ask them what… | What happened when … | That sounds like a lot of fun, but …
Mr Preston: When I got home … | I was angry because… | I found some candles and thought … | The kids used their smartphones to …

Jay: I thought about the party we wanted to have and … | It takes so long to write … | I'm sorry, it was stupid to … | I was so worried when…
Olivia: Don't you know how dangerous it is to … ? | Why didn't you wait for … ? | We were really lucky that … | I think next time you should … | But it's OK, don't worry …

Unit 5

△ 1 Talking about places → Help with Check-In, p. 92/1

Lösung: 1. *Lou should go to Wales. She can visit old castles there and learn something about the past.* 2. *Sandy should go to Ireland. She can do pony trekking there.* 3. *Andrew should go to Edinburgh. He can visit the Edinburgh Festival.* 4. *Ellen should go to Cornwall. She can go to the beach and swim in the sea.*

Where should these people go on holiday?

Start like this: Lou should go to Wales. She can visit …

1. Lou likes stories about the past and she likes to visit old castles.
2. Sandy loves horses and she likes to be outside every day.
3. Andrew is interested in music and traditions. He loves watching shows and listening to traditional songs.
4. Ellen is a good swimmer and loves the sea. She thinks it's great to walk along the beach and look for treasures.

△ 2 Frequently asked questions → After Station 1, p. 95/3

Work with a partner and fill in the gaps. Take turns to ask and answer the questions.

ösung: 1. *Will it* 2. *will you* *Will you* 4. *will you* 5. *will* u 6. *Will you* 7. *Will you* *will you*

1. ___ rain today?
2. What ___ do ten years from now?
3. ___ meet friends after school?
4. Where ___ spend your holidays?
5. When ___ do your homework?
6. ___ watch a scary film with me?
7. ___ buy me some ice cream?
8. Where ___ live when you're 30?

▲ 3 Mediation: At a German station → After Station 1, p. 95/3

An English boy is trying to buy a ticket at a German station. He's talking to a man, but the man doesn't speak English. Can you help the boy? Try to use the ***will*** *future where you can.*

Boy: Excuse me, I need to take the next train to Cologne. Will it wait a few more minutes?
Man: *Entschuldigung, ich spreche kein Englisch.*
You: *Dieser Junge muss …*
Man: *Ach so. Nein, der Zug wartet nicht. Aber ich bin sicher, der nächste Zug wird ihm besser gefallen. Es ist ein Express-Zug.*
You: Sorry, the train … But the man is sure …
Boy: Express train? Won't … expensive?
You: …
Man: *Warte kurz, ich schaue nach.*
You: …
Man: *Nein, es wird sogar günstiger! Und er wird früher in Köln ankommen als der frühere Zug!*
You: No, he says it'll … And, he says …
Boy: Cool! I … earlier and I … more money for my visit in Cologne! – Yes, I think I … buy that ticket.
You: Great, but I must go now or my train … leave without me!

△ 4 Buying train tickets on the internet → After Station 1, p. 96/5

Fill in the new travel words.

price | inward | arrive | one-way | return | change | fee | depart | outward

sung: 1. *return* 2. *price* *ne-way* 4. *inward* *utward* 6. *arrive* *epart* 8. *change* 9. *fee*

First, Luke forgets to click on [1], but he doesn't only need the [2] for a [3] ticket. So he has to fill in the dates for the [4] journey and then the [5] journey. He clicks on [6], but then he remembers that he doesn't know how long the journey takes. So he chooses the time he wants to [7]. He learns that for St Agnes you have to [8] at London Bridge and Paddington. Then he wants to know how much the booking[1] [9] is.

1 **booking** ['bʊkɪŋ] Reservierung

△ 5 What will the weather be like? → Help with Station 1, p. 96/6

Here are weather pictures and words to help you with exercise 6 on page 96.

Start like this: Today the weather is still … | But tomorrow it'll be… | Temperatures[1] will … | There will be …

Lösung: *Today the weather is still sunny. The temperatures are up to 30 degrees and there isn't any wind. But tomorrow it'll be partly cloudy. It'll still be warm and there won't be too much wind. The next day there will be a storm with thunder and lots of wind. The temperatures will fall to 17 degrees.*

lots of sun

temperatures up to 30 degrees[2]

no wind

partly cloudy

not too much wind

warm | 24 degrees

storm | thunder

lots of wind

temperatures fall to 17 degrees

△ 6 I'm coming soon → After Station 2, p. 99/9

Change the bold words to put the sentences in indirect speech. Use the words below.

write | say | tell | promise | hope

Lösung: *2. She writes that she's so excited to see me again. 3. She tells that she wants to see where I go to school and meet my friends. 4. She promises to take some special food. Her mother gave it to her. 5. But it's not for her – it's all for me!!! 6. She promises that my brother can have a little bit of it. 7. She hopes that me and my family are excited to see her too. 8. She says that next year I can visit them!*

1. **I**'ll be **there** soon!
2. **I**'m so excited to see **you** again.
3. **I** want to see where **you** go to school and meet **your** friends.
4. **I**'ll **bring** some special food. **My** mother gave it to **me**.
5. But it's not for **me** – it's all for **you**!!!
6. **I** promise **your** brother can have a little bit of it ;-)
7. **I** hope that **you** and **your** family are excited to see **me**, too.
8. Next year **you** can visit **us**! Love, Jenna

Examples: 1. She says that **she**'ll be **here** soon.
2. She writes that …

1 temperature ['temprətʃə] Temperatur | **2 degree** [dɪ'griː] Grad

▲ 7 Where do you want to travel? → After Station 2, p. 99/9

Lösung: He says he wants to travel to London. He thinks that he can go there by train. He says he'll take his friend with him. But he can't take his dog with him. When he's there he wants to visit Covent Garden with his friend.

Work with a partner. Partner A talks about travelling for 20 seconds and Partner B takes notes. Then Partner B reports what Partner A thinks, hopes etc. Take turns.

Start like this: I want to travel to …
I think I can go there …
I'll take my …
But I can't take my …
When I'm there I want to … with …

▲ 8 A poem about your home town → After Station 2, 100/13

Write a poem about your town or area. The word groups below rhyme[3]; they can help you with your poem. Maybe you can think of more words in English that rhyme?

city | be | sea | me | free | village | language | manage | image | live | give | active

like | bike | hike | site | bright | night | right | light | run | fun | sun | one

3 **to rhyme** [raɪm] sich reimen

Vocabulary

S1 Vokabelheft

Führe ein dreispaltiges Vokabelheft, in dem du auch neue Vokabeln notieren kannst, die nicht in der Wortliste stehen. Die erste Spalte ist für die englische Vokabel bestimmt, die zweite für die Übersetzung und die dritte für Beispielsätze oder alles, was dir hilft, dir die Bedeutung zu merken, z. B. Bilder, *mind maps*, Beziehungen zu anderen Wörtern, auch in anderen Sprachen.

S2 Vokabelkartei

Es lohnt sich, eine Vokabelkartei anzulegen, um Vokabeln zu lernen. Sie besteht aus Karteikarten für die Vokabeln und einem Karton mit fünf Fächern für die Karten.
Schreibe das englische Wort auf die Vorderseite der Karteikarte und die deutsche Bedeutung auf die Rückseite. Zusätzlich kannst du weitere Merkhilfen notieren. Stelle zunächst alle Karten ins erste Fach.
Übe jeden Tag fünf bis zehn Minuten, und zwar so: Nimm eine Karte nach der anderen heraus und überprüfe, ob du die Übersetzung weißt (deutsch – englisch, englisch – deutsch). Wenn ja, stellst du die Karte ins zweite Fach. Mache weiter, bis das erste Fach leer ist. Das zweite Fach bearbeitest du dann genauso, allerdings nicht jeden Tag, sondern nur einmal in der Woche, das dritte Fach alle zwei Wochen usw.

S3 Wörter im Zusammenhang

Wörter sind die Bausteine der Sprache. Du musst sie natürlich lernen und jedes für sich verstehen. Zur Beherrschung einer Sprache gehört aber auch zu wissen, welche Kombinationen dieser Bausteine möglich sind. Deshalb ist es wichtig, mit den Wörtern schon die richtigen Kombinationen mitzulernen. Schreibe Wörter möglichst immer in typischen Zusammenhängen auf.

Mit Verben kannst du passende Ergänzungen mitlernen, z. B.:

to ***read*** *a book, a magazine, a comic, a manga*
to ***write*** *a letter, an e-mail, an invitation, a blog*
to ***go*** *swimming, shopping, home, away, to the cinema*

Du solltest auch wissen, wann bestimmte grammatische Formen auf bestimmte Wörter folgen. Schreibe dir passende Beispiele zusammen mit der Vokabel auf, z. B.:

I ***would like to*** *swim,* ***to*** *read,* ***to*** *go shopping*
I ***like*** *swimm**ing**, read**ing**, go**ing** shopping*

Welche die richtigen Präpositionen sind, muss man in jeder Sprache auswendig lernen. Notiere auch dafür Beispiele und lerne sie, z.B.:

The party is ***on Friday****,* ***at seven****,* ***at the weekend****.*
My house is ***in Dover Street****. We're* ***on the road to London****.*
London is ***on the Thames****.*

S4 Methoden

Du hast schon mehrere Methoden gelernt, wie du dir Vokabeln besser einprägen kannst:

- Klebezettel mit englischen Wörtern an die entsprechenden Gegenstände in deinem Zimmer kleben
- Wörter als Bildwörter oder mit passenden Bildern aufmalen
- Wörter zusammen mit anderen, die zu einem Thema gehören, in *mind maps* anordnen
- Wörter pantomimisch darstellen und gegenseitig erraten lassen
- Wörter aussprechen, zusammen mit ihrer Übersetzung und vielleicht einem Beispielsatz aufnehmen und immer wieder anhören
- Wörter mit ähnlichen Wörtern in anderen Sprachen notieren
- Wörter, die miteinander in Beziehung stehen, zusammen notieren, z. B. verwandte Wörter, Gegensatzpaare, zusammengehörige Paare

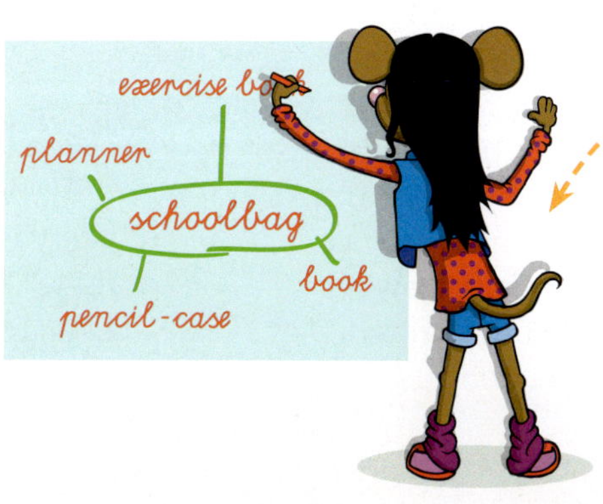

Reading

S5 Schnelllesetechniken

Normalerweise denkst du während des Lesens nicht darüber nach, wie du dabei vorgehst. Wenn du aber eine Aufgabe zu einem Text bekommst oder eine bestimmte Information suchst, liest du bewusster und gezielter. Diese Techniken helfen dir, wenn die Zeit begrenzt ist.

Skimming („den Rahm abschöpfen")	**Scanning („maschinell durchsuchen")**
Wenn du danach gefragt wirst, worum es in einem Text geht, sollst du ihn nicht einfach nacherzählen, sondern nur das Wichtigste *(gist)* zusammenfassen. Dazu kannst du den ganzen Text überfliegen und darauf achten, ob bestimmte Wörter *(key words)* oder Personen häufiger vorkommen. Auch die Überschrift oder Bilder können dir helfen einzuschätzen, was wichtig ist und was nicht. Diese Art des Schnelllesens nennt man *skimming*.	Wenn du nach bestimmten Einzelheiten *(details)* in einem Text gefragt wirst, musst du ihn überfliegen und die Stellen mit der wichtigen Information finden. Dazu suchst du gezielt nach passenden Stichwörtern *(key words)*. Sie zeigen an, welche Teile du genauer lesen solltest, um die gesuchte Information zu bekommen. Diese Art des Überfliegens nennt man auch *scanning*.

S6 Wichtige Inhalte von Texten herausfinden

Wenn du einen Text liest, solltest du danach immer folgende Fragen beantworten können:

Who ...?
Wer ist beteiligt?

What ...?
Was geschieht?

When ...?
Wann?

Where ...?
Wo?

Dazu kannst du Schnelllesetechniken anwenden, Markierungen im Text machen und dir Fragen und Anmerkungen notieren (S8). Wenn du den Text noch genauer liest, kannst du weitere Fragen beantworten, z. B. Warum geschieht etwas? Wenn es eine Geschichte ist, wer erzählt sie? Für wen wurde der Text geschrieben (Adressat)?

S7 Gliederung als Hilfe

Um einen Text besser zu verstehen, kann es dir helfen, ihn in mehrere Abschnitte zu gliedern. Orientiere dich dabei z. B. an Absätzen und inhaltlichen Punkten, die du dir markiert hast. Überlege anschließend, was in den einzelnen Teilen jeweils das Wichtigste ist und formuliere passende Überschriften. Dies erleichtert es dir, Zusammenfassungen von Texten zu geben oder *Mediation*-Aufgaben zu lösen.

A Henry hopes to play the lead
B Henry is disappointed
C Henry sees the positive side of things

S8 Textbearbeitung mit Markierungen und Notizen

Im geliehenen Buch darfst du das zwar nicht, aber auf Kopien oder in Arbeitsheften solltest du dir angewöhnen, wichtige Stellen in Texten zu markieren und Randnotizen zu machen (z. B. Fragen oder Anmerkungen). Verwende am besten verschiedene Farben: Markiere z. B. wichtige inhaltliche Punkte grün und Informationen zu den Personen blau. Wörter, die du nachschlagen musst, solltest du auch hervorheben. Unterstreiche sie beispielsweise und notiere die richtige Übersetzung am Rand. So fällt dir das erneute Lesen leichter.

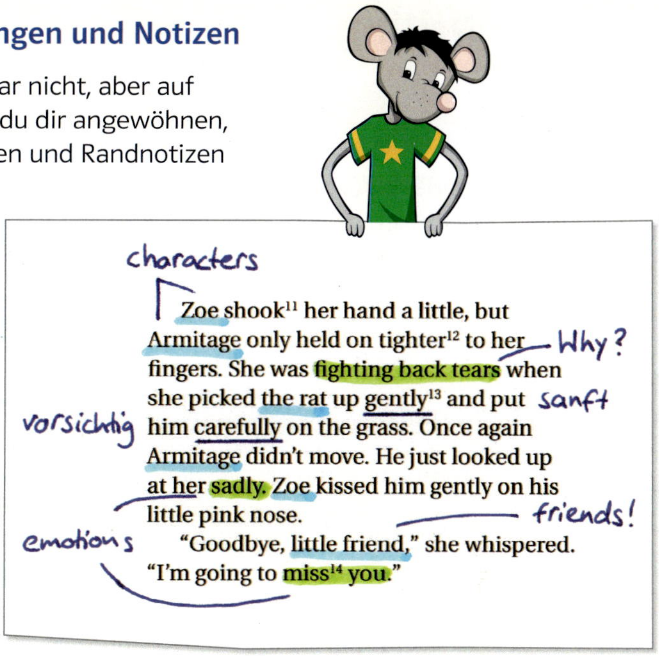

Zoe shook[11] her hand a little, but Armitage only held on tighter[12] to her fingers. She was fighting back tears when she picked the rat up gently[13] and put him carefully on the grass. Once again Armitage didn't move. He just looked up at her sadly. Zoe kissed him gently on his little pink nose.

"Goodbye, little friend," she whispered. "I'm going to miss[14] you."

S9 Umgang mit neuen Wörtern

Viele Wörter kannst du schon verstehen, obwohl du sie noch nicht gelernt hast.

1. **Ähnlichkeit mit Wörtern, die du schon kennst**
   Oft haben verwandte Wörter den gleichen Stamm, aber andere Vorsilben oder Endungen. Wenn du z. B. *happy* schon kennst, wirst du *unhappy* sicher auch verstehen. Englische Wörter haben oft keine Endungen, aber es gibt sie in verschiedenen Wortarten. Wenn du also das Wort *guide* als Nomen kennst, kannst du dir bestimmt denken, was das Verb *to guide* oder die Zusammensetzung *travel guide bedeutet*.

2. **Ähnlichkeit mit Wörtern, die du aus einer anderen Sprache kennst**
   Viele englische Wörter gibt es genauso oder ähnlich auch im Deutschen, z. B. *computer, hobby* oder *pony*. Manchmal hilft dir auch ein Wort, das du aus einer anderen Sprache kennst (Französisch, Latein, …) ein englisches Wort zu verstehen, z. B. weil es ähnlich geschrieben wird oder ähnlich klingt.

3. **Verstehen der Wörter im Zusammenhang**
   Manchmal kannst du dir anhand eines Bildes oder einer Überschrift denken, was ein Wort in einem Text bedeutet. Und wenn du alle Wörter in einem Satz verstehst außer einem, kann dieses oft nur eine bestimmte Bedeutung haben. Was bedeutet z. B. *return* in diesem Satz?
   My dog ran away, and I was really happy when he ***returned*** *after three days.*

Und wenn du doch im Wörterbuch nachschlagen musst, helfen dir die Tipps auf S. 25.

Writing

S10 Planung deines Textes

Überlege, für wen dein Text bestimmt ist (Adressat) und welchen Zweck er erfüllen soll. Vor dem Schreiben machst du dir am besten einen Plan: Notiere in Stichwörtern, was in der Einleitung, dem Hauptteil und dem Schluss deines Textes stehen soll. So vergisst du nichts Wichtiges und findest auch leichter eine schöne Einleitung und einen guten Schluss.

S11 Textsorten und ihre Besonderheiten

Du kennst schon einige wichtige Textsorten und ihre Haupteigenschaften:

E-mail, letter, postcard, invitation	Achte auf die richtige Anrede für den Adressaten, z. B. *Dear …*, Grußformeln am Schluss, z. B. *Yours/Love/Best wishes*, und beachte die Höflichkeitsregeln. Denke bei einem Brief an die Angabe der Empfänger- und Absenderadresse und an das Datum.
Story	Wenn du eine Geschichte vervollständigen sollst, muss dein Teil zum vorgegebenen Text passen. Vermeide also inhaltliche Widersprüche. Außerdem sollten die Erzählperspektive und die Erzählzeit nicht wechseln. Meistens sind Geschichten im *past tense* geschrieben. Gestalte deine Geschichten sprachlich abwechslungsreich und schmücke sie aus.
Dialogue	Wenn du einen Dialog, z. B. für eine Filmszene, schreibst, denke daran, dass du echte mündliche Sprache verwendest, also z. B. *short forms*, verstärkende Ausdrücke usw.
Report	Bei einem Bericht ist die Vollständigkeit und Verständlichkeit der sachlichen Informationen das Wichtigste. Er wird im *past tense* geschrieben.
Prompt cards	Wenn du dich auf eine Präsentation vorbereitest, notiere auf Karteikarten nur Stichwörter, die dich an die einzelnen Punkte des Vortrags erinnern. Schreibe z. B. wichtige Namen, Ereignisse, Orte und Daten unter die Überschriften *Who, What, Where, When*.
Flyer	Ein Flyer sollte gut lesbar sein (Schriftart- und größe) und alle wichtigen Informationen enthalten: *Who?, What?, When?, Where?, Why?* Formuliere außerdem einen ansprechenden Slogan.
Diary entry	Ein Tagebucheintrag erzählt und kommentiert vergangene und erwartete Ereignisse aus der ganz persönlichen Sicht einer Person und ist normalerweise nicht für andere Leser bestimmt.

S12 Überarbeitung deines Textes

Wenn du einen Entwurf erstellt hast, liest du ihn am besten noch einmal gründlich durch. Meistens entdeckst du so noch einige Fehler und kannst holprige Formulierungen verbessern. Nimm dabei eine Checkliste zur Hilfe (siehe rechts), damit du nichts Wichtiges vergisst. Es ist auch eine gute Übung, die Texte mit einem Partner zu tauschen.

Checkliste

Rechtschreibung:
- Wörter richtig geschrieben?
- Am Satzanfang groß?
- Getrennt oder zusammen?

Grammatik:
- Richtige Zeitformen?
- Richtige Formenbildung?

Inhalt:
- Alle wesentlichen Punkte enthalten?
- Keine inhaltlichen Fehler?
- Zusammenhänge erkennbar und logisch?

S13 Sprachliche Verbesserungen

Je größer dein Wortschatz wird, desto mehr Möglichkeiten eröffnen sich dir beim Schreiben von Texten.
Einzelne Sätze kannst du genauer und interessanter gestalten, indem du z. B. Nomen durch Adjektive oder durch weitere Nomen näher beschreibst. Verben kannst du durch adverbiale Bestimmungen ergänzen. Vergleiche die unterschiedliche Information in den beiden folgenden Sätzen:

A *I went to the shop.*

B *I went to the big pet shop in Greenwich with my sister last Saturday.*

Deinen gesamten Text kannst du flüssiger gestalten, indem du die Sätze miteinander verknüpfst. So werden logische Zusammenhänge klarer und der Text liest sich leichter. Vergleiche die beiden folgenden Textausschnitte. Der erste wirkt durch die unverbundenen Hauptsätze abgehackt. Der zweite enthält auch Satzgefüge aus Haupt- und Nebensätzen, die mit Hilfe von Bindewörtern *(linking words)* logische Zusammenhänge herstellen. Außerdem geben die vielen Adjektive und Adverbien genauere Informationen und machen den Text interessanter.

A *I went to the shop. I wanted a guinea pig. We looked at all the guinea pigs. I didn't like them. We wanted to leave.*
A girl came in with a box. She brought back a guinea pig.
It was cute! I bought it. I'm happy.

B *I went to the big pet shop in Greenwich with my sister last Saturday* ***because*** *I wanted to buy a nice guinea pig.*
We looked at all the guinea pigs, ***but*** *I didn't like them.*
Just when *I wanted to leave, a girl came in with a box.*
She brought back a ***really*** *cute guinea pig.*
So *I bought it* ***and*** *I'm very happy now.*

Speaking

S14 Sprechen üben

Sprechen lernt man nur durch Sprechen. Du solltest dir angewöhnen, im Englischunterricht immer englisch zu sprechen, ob mit deiner Lehrerin/deinem Lehrer oder in der Partner- und Gruppenarbeit. Um Sprechen zu üben, solltest du allerdings viel mehr sprechen als nur im Unterricht. Vielleicht üben deine Freunde, Eltern oder Geschwister mit dir?

Eine Voraussetzung für das richtige Sprechen ist natürlich, dass du übst, die englischen Wörter richtig auszusprechen. Beim Lernen mit dem Buch kann dir die Lautschrift dabei helfen. Sage sie dir immer wieder laut vor. Einfacher und einprägsamer ist es natürlich, die Vokabeln richtig ausgesprochen anzuhören und nachzusprechen. Hilfsmittel dafür sind Audio-CDs mit den Schülerbuchtexten, Lernsoftware oder Online-Wörterbücher, in denen du jedes Wort anklicken und anhören kannst.

They **th**ought of **th**e **th**ree **th**ousand **th**ankful **th**ieves.

Why **w**ork **w**ith **v**ocabulary **w**hen you can **v**isit a **w**onderful **v**illage **w**orld?

Übe schwierig auszusprechende Laute, die anders sind als im Deutschen, z. B. das stimmhafte oder stimmlose *th* oder das *w* im Kontrast zum *v* oder ein stimmhaftes *d* oder *g* am Wortende. Dazu kannst du (lustige) Sätze erfinden, sie dir immer wieder vorsprechen und dabei das Tempo steigern, bis die Aussprache zuverlässig klappt.

She wante**d** her ba**g** back and sai**d** what a nice hat she ha**d**.

Wenn du ganze Texte hörst, bekommst du ein Gefühl dafür, wie die Wörter im Textzusammenhang ausgesprochen werden. Die Aussprache unterscheidet sich manchmal stark von der Aussprache der Einzelwörter. Aufeinander treffende Laute werden z. B. häufig miteinander verbunden.

This is the end of the story. They know over **a** hundred different stories.

Du hast auch schon gehört, wie die Betonung die Aussprache beeinflussen kann, wenn jemand besonders starke Gefühle ausdrücken will. Das kannst du auch üben.

It's **so** unfair! Why doesn't anyone **ever** ask **me** what I'm feeling?

S15 Gesprochene Sprache

Auch beim Sprechen kommt es auf die Situation und deinen Gesprächspartner an, wie du dich ausdrückst. Denke z. B. auch an Höflichkeitsregeln.
In der gesprochenen Sprache ist es normal, dass Pausen, unvollständige Sätze, Wiederholungen oder Füllwörter vorkommen:

- Während bei Gleichaltrigen ein *Hi!* als Begrüßung ausreicht, ist Lehrpersonen oder fremden Erwachsenen gegenüber ein *Good morning! / Good morning …* eher angemessen.
- Statt *I want …* sagst du höflicher *I would like …* oder *Could I please have …?*
- Entscheidungsfragen beantwortest du mit Kurzantworten, nicht einfach mit *Yes* oder *No: Yes, I do. No, I'm not.*

***Well, I – I** really don't know. It's – **er**, maybe you want to …?*

Es ist wichtig, einem Dialogpartner immer das Gefühl zu geben, dass er einbezogen wird. Dazu dienen *feedback phrases* und Nachfragen.

*Then we went to the city farm, Mudchute, **you know**. And there was this cute little pig – **you saw it too, right? Guess what Linda did when she saw it!***

S16 Mündliche Aufgaben und ihre Besonderheiten

Es ist viel wichtiger, dass du regelmäßig länger zusammenhängend sprichst, als dass jedes Wort perfekt ausgesprochen und die Grammatik absolut korrekt ist. Wie wäre es, wenn jeder in deiner Klasse in einer Englischstunde eine Minute lang Englisch über ein selbst gewähltes Thema spricht? Hier findest du ein paar Tipps für bestimmte mündliche Aufgaben:

Interview	Sei höflich, aber scheue dich nicht nachzufragen, wenn du etwas nicht sofort verstehst. Achte bei der Fragestellung auf die richtige Zeitform und das richtige Hilfsverb. Antworte auch in der passenden Zeitform.
Asking/ Showing the way	Auch hier ist Höflichkeit wichtig und ganz bestimmte Vokabeln wie *go down X Street, go straight on, go past/turn left/right into Y Lane, it's on the left / right / opposite Z.*
Role play	Versetze dich in deine Rolle und versuche nachzufühlen, was die Person weiß und was sie denkt und fühlt. Verwende typische Merkmale der gesprochenen Sprache und unterstütze deine Worte mit Mimik und Gestik.
Presentation	Bereite deine Präsentation gut vor. Recherchiere die Fakten gründlich. Überlege, was dir wichtig ist und was du sagen möchtest. Besorge Material, das du zeigen willst, und bereite es so auf, dass es gut aussieht und verständlich ist. Mache dir einen Ablaufplan. Schreibe dir Notizen auf *prompt cards*. Versuche frei zu sprechen und nicht abzulesen. Übe deine Präsentation vorher und stoppe die Zeit, die du brauchst.

Mediation

S17 Bearbeitung von Mediationsaufgaben

Mediation ist die Übertragung wichtiger Informationen aus einem gesprochenen oder geschriebenen Text in eine andere Sprache, z.B. aus dem Englischen ins Deutsche oder umgekehrt. Das machst du, wenn du einen Text für jemanden zusammenfassen sollst, der die Sprache des Ausgangstexts nicht versteht. Gelegentlich kann es auch sein, dass du dolmetschen musst, also zwischen Gesprächspartnern vermittelst, die nicht dieselbe Sprache sprechen. Ganz wichtig: Es geht bei der *Mediation* niemals um eine wörtliche Übersetzung *(translation)*!

Lies dir die *Mediation*-Aufgabe gut durch und beachte besonders folgende Dinge:

Adressat:
Für wen ist die Information bestimmt?
--> Je nachdem, wer die Person ist und wie viel sie schon weiß, sprichst du sie unterschiedlich an.

Zweck:
Wozu benötigt die Person die Information?
--> Du musst nur die Informationen wiedergeben, die für den Adressaten in der jeweiligen Situation wichtig sind. Alles andere kannst du weglassen. Es kann aber auch vorkommen, dass du Dinge zusätzlich erklären musst.

Beispiel: Dein Ausgangstext ist die Infobroschüre eines Museums, die alle Öffnungszeiten und Eintrittspreise enthält. Wenn dein Gegenüber dich fragt, ob das Museum heute geöffnet ist, musst du nicht unbedingt sagen, wann es sonst noch geöffnet oder geschlossen ist. Will die Person den Eintrittspreis wissen, kommt es auf ihr Alter an und darauf, ob sie allein oder mit einer Gruppe unterwegs ist.

Einen schriftlichen Ausgangstext kannst du in Ruhe durchlesen und die wichtigen Informationen auswählen. Dabei helfen dir alle Techniken, die auf S. 132/133 unter *Reading* beschrieben sind. Formuliere die entsprechenden Inhalte so, dass der Adressat sie gut verstehen kann.
Bei einer Dolmetscheraufgabe wird eine echte mündliche Gesprächssituation simuliert. Deshalb musst du schneller reagieren, um möglichst viel von dem sinngemäß wiederzugeben, was die Gesprächspartner zueinander sagen.

Wenn dir ein Wort in der Zielsprache nicht einfällt, umschreibe es mit anderen Worten *(paraphrasing)*. Beachte bei der schriftlichen und mündlichen Bearbeitung von *Mediation*-Aufgaben außerdem die Tipps unter *Writing* und *Speaking* (siehe S. 134–137)

Listening

S18 Hörverstehen üben

Grundsätzlich ist es zur Übung immer sinnvoll, viele echte englische Texte anzuhören, z. B. Nachrichten oder Kindersendungen in Radio und Fernsehen oder Hörbücher. Dabei ist es nicht schlimm, wenn du nicht jedes Wort verstehst. Dir wird außerdem auffallen, wie unterschiedlich die Aussprache des Englischen je nach Herkunft des Sprechers sein kann.

S19 Techniken des Hörverstehens

Analog zum Lesen gibt es auch beim Hörverstehen unterschiedliche Techniken. Beim *Listening for gist* geht es darum, das Wichtigste in einem Hörtext zu erkennen und zusammenzufassen. Beim *Listening for detail* hingegen sollst du einem Hörtext bestimmte Einzelheiten entnehmen.

Listening for gist	Listening for detail
Welche Wörter und Themen kommen mehrmals vor und spielen deshalb vermutlich eine wichtige Rolle? Höre besonders auf diese und fasse die wichtigsten Inhalte des Textes zusammen.	Nach welchen bestimmten Einzelheiten im Text wirst du gefragt? Höre besonders auf Wörter, die du in der Antwort erwartest, und die Informationen dazu.

Auch beim Hörverstehen hilft eine Tabelle wie beim Leseverstehen. Du kannst darin während des Hörens deine Notizen machen.

Who ...?	What ...?	When ...?	Where ...?

S20 Typische Hörverstehenssituationen

Manchmal hilft dir beim Hörverstehen auch die Kenntnis von typischen Textsorten und Situationen. Wenn du die Textsorte des Hörtextes kennst, überlege dir, worauf es beim Telefonieren, beim Dolmetschen, bei Präsentationen, Durchsagen, Radio- oder Fernsehsendungen ankommt und welche Themen jeweils zu erwarten sind. Gelegentlich geben dir auch Bilder Hinweise zur entsprechenden Situation: Wenn z. B. bestimmte Personen oder Orte dargestellt sind, kannst du leichter einschätzen, worum es in dem Hörtext geht. Achte beim Hören auf Geräusche sowie Stimme und Tonfall des Sprechers. In echten Gesprächssituationen oder Filmen können dir auch Gestik und Mimik das Verständnis erleichtern.

Film skills/Viewing

S21 Inhalt und Gliederung

Ein Film ist auch eine Art Text. Deshalb lassen sich viele ähnliche Fragen dazu stellen:

- Worum geht es?
- Wird eine Geschichte erzählt?
- Welche Personen spielen mit?
- Welches sind die Hauptpersonen?
- Was passiert in welcher Reihenfolge?
- Wann und wo passiert es?
- Welche Gliederung und welche Themen sind zu erkennen?
- Aus wessen Sicht wird die Geschichte erzählt?
- Wer hat den Film gemacht, für welches Publikum und wozu?

Das Anschauen und Verstehen eines Films verlangt dir jedoch nicht nur das Verständnis der Sprache ab, sondern du musst auch auf viele weitere Dinge achten.

S22 Wichtige filmische Aspekte

Wie stellen die Schauspieler den Charakter der Personen dar, die sie verkörpern? Wie drücken sie Gefühle aus?

--➤ Achte vor allem auf Sprache, Mimik und Gestik. Aber auch Kleidung oder Frisuren können eine Rolle spielen.

Wie werden Handlungsort und -zeit dargestellt *(setting)*?

--➤ Achte auf Landschaften, Gebäude und Innenräume, Kleidung und Gegenstände.

Wie wird eine bestimmte Atmosphäre geschaffen *(atmosphere)*?

--➤ Achte auf Licht, Farben, Musik, Geräusche.

Wie unterstützt die Musik den Inhalt des Films?

--➤ Beachte, wann welche Musik ertönt und wann sie wechselt.

Wie helfen bestimmte Kameraeinstellungen den Inhalt deutlicher darzustellen *(shot)*?

--➤ Achte z. B. auf Nahaufnahmen *(close-ups)*.

Wie wird Spannung erzeugt *(suspense)*?

--➤ Achte auf Vorandeutungen, Musik, Licht, Geräusche und natürlich die Gestik und Mimik der Schauspieler.

Mit der Zeit wirst du weitere filmische Mittel kennen lernen, die bestimmte Wirkungen auf den Zuschauer erzeugen.

Kooperative Lernformen

Hier findest du die Erklärung für einige ausgewählte Methoden der kooperativen Arbeit.

S23 Think – Pair – Share

1. *Think:* Du sammelst still mögliche Lösungen zu der Aufgabe. Du kannst deine Ideen in Stichpunkten notieren.
2. *Pair:* Zusammen mit deinem Partner besprichst du leise deine gesammelten Ideen.
3. *Share:* Im Klassengespräch meldet ihr euch und teilt euren Mitschülern die Ergebnisse eurer Partnergespräche mit.

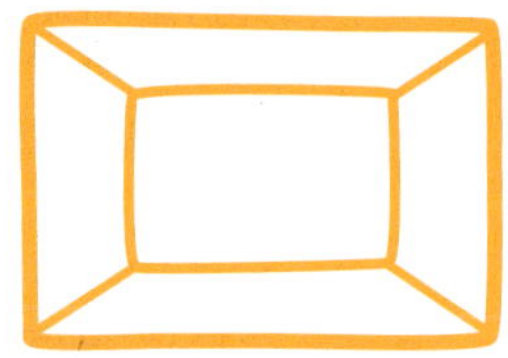

Variante: *Placemat* in Vierergruppen

S24 Milling around (Marktplatz)

Du gehst durch das Klassenzimmer, erfragst von deinen Mitschülern bestimmte Informationen und gibst auch selbst Auskunft. Versuche mit möglichst vielen Mitschülern zu sprechen und verschiedene Informationen zu sammeln. Ihr könnt auch ein Signal vereinbaren, zu dem ihr eure Gesprächspartner wechselt.

S25 Inside outside circle (Kugellager)

1. Bildet zwei Stuhlkreise, einen inneren und einen äußeren.
2. Setzt euch in den Stuhlkreisen so hin, dass immer ein Schüler des äußeren und des inneren Stuhlkreises sich gegenüber sitzen.
3. Stellt euch gegenseitig eure Fragen und beantwortet diese.
4. Rutscht im inneren oder äußeren Kreis nach dem Ende der Gesprächsrunde einen Platz weiter und beginnt ein Gespräch mit einem neuen Mitschüler.

S26 Bus stop (Lerntempoduett)

Sobald du deine Aufgabe fertig bearbeitet hast, gehst du zu einem vereinbarten Treffpunkt, dem *bus stop*. Dort wartest du auf den nächsten Mitschüler, der fertig ist, und zusammen besprecht und vergleicht ihr eure Lösungen. Anschließend verlasst ihr den *bus stop* und bearbeitet die nächste Aufgabe.

S27 Gallery walk (Museumsgang)

1. *Group work:* In der Gruppe erarbeitet ihr ein Thema und haltet euer Ergebnis, z. B. auf einem Poster, fest.
2. *Gallery walk:* Es werden neue Gruppen gebildet. In jeder Gruppe ist ein Schüler jeder Ausgangsgruppe. Jede Gruppe betrachtet die verschiedenen Ergebnisse der Gruppenarbeiten. Jeder präsentiert nun in der neuen Gruppe das Ergebnis seiner Ausgangsgruppe.

Grammar

Liebe Schülerin, lieber Schüler,
jede Sprache besteht aus bestimmten Bausteinen und funktioniert nach bestimmten Regeln. Die Bausteine sind z.B. einzelne Wörter (Vokabeln). Die Regeln für ihre Zusammensetzung nennt man Grammatik. Diese musst du außer den Vokabeln lernen, damit du dich verständigen kannst und damit es nicht zu Missverständnissen kommt.

Jedes Grammatikkapitel (**G**) behandelt Themen, die auf bestimmten Seiten vorne in den *Units* vorkommen (z.B. Seiten 14–15). Erklärungen, Bilder und Tabellen helfen dir, …
- die Grammatik zu verstehen,
- beim Nachholen, wenn du ein paar Stunden gefehlt hast,
- bei den Hausaufgaben,
- beim Wiederholen,
- bei der Vorbereitung auf Tests und Klassenarbeiten

Regeln sind mit einem blauen Punkt (●) gekennzeichnet.
Ein Ausrufezeichen (**!**) bedeutet, dass du hier besonders aufpassen musst. Mit kleinen Aufgaben (**Test yourself**) kannst du überprüfen, ob du alles verstanden hast.
Die Lösungen findest du ab Seite 250.

Hier ist eine Liste aller grammatischen Begriffe aus diesem Buch in alphabetischer Reihenfolge zum Nachschlagen. Links findest du den englischen Begriff, in der Mitte ein Beispiel und rechts den deutschen Ausdruck.

Grammatical terms

English term		Example	*Deutsche Bezeichnung*
adjective comparison of adjectives comparisons with adjectives	G4, G5 G4 G5	exciting, easy, young After the adventure course I was **more confident**. Wales is**n't as big as** England or Scotland, but it's **bigger than** Northern Ireland.	*Adjektiv* *Steigerung der Adjektive* *Vergleiche mit Adjektiven*
compounds of some, any, every and no	G7	Listen, **everybody**. What can we do for lunch? Are there any cafés **anywhere** near here?	*Zusammensetzungen mit* some, any, every *und* no
going-to future	G6	Jay and Amir **are going to visit** the British Museum.	*Futur mit* going to
indirect speech	G13	He **says** that the landscape in Cornwall **is** very wild.	*indirekte Rede*

English term		Example	*Deutsche Bezeichnung*
modal auxiliary, modal	G10 G11	can, can't, must, needn't, mustn't, have to should(n't), could	*Modalverb, modales Hilfsverb*
past participle	G8	Gwen and Luke have already **prepared** for the trials. Olivia has **hurt** her foot.	*Partizip Perfekt*
present perfect simple	G8	**Have** you ever **seen** the London Marathon?	*einfache Form des Perfekts*
simple past irregular verb regular verb negating statements questions	G1–G3 G1 G1 G2 G3	Lenny Henry **started** Comic Relief in 1985. came, had, met, wore answered, played, watched The man **didn't break** any shop windows. Did the police arrest the man? What did he take from the shop?	*einfache Form der Vergangenheit* *unregelmäßiges Verb* *regelmäßiges Verb* *Aussagesätze verneinen* *Fragen*
subordinate clauses of comparison, time, reason	G9	The girl wrote to an agony aunt **because** she had a problem. **Before** we had an argument, we spent all our free time together.	*Nebensätze des Vergleichs (Komparativsätze), der Zeit (Temporalsätze), des Grundes (Kausalsätze)*
will future	G12	I'**ll miss** you so much!	*Futur mit* will

Unit 1

G1 Two years ago we raised lots of money.

Seiten 14–16

Die einfache Form der Vergangenheit

The simple past

Lenny Henry **started** Comic Relief in 1985 to help people in Africa. On the first Red Nose Day in 1988 people **wore** red noses, **did** fun activities to raise money and **watched** a big comedy show on TV. That **was** many years ago, but today people still do the same things.

Das simple past *verwendest du, um über eine Handlung oder ein Ereignis zu sprechen, das in der Vergangenheit liegt und abgeschlossen ist. Du findest es oft in Berichten und Geschichten.*

- *Bei der Bildung des* simple past *unterscheidest du zwischen regelmäßigen und unregelmäßigen Verben. Anders als bei den Gegenwartsformen sind sie in allen Personen gleich.*
- *Das* simple past *von* ***regelmäßigen Verben*** *bildest du aus der* ***Grundform des Verbs + -ed****. Doch bevor du* -ed *anhängst, musst du folgende Besonderheiten bei der Schreibweise beachten:*

normal	*stummes -e*	*einfacher Konsonant*	*y nach Konsonant*
play – play**ed**	like – lik**ed**	plan – plan**ned**	try – tri**ed**

- *Beachte, dass* -ed *auf drei verschiedene Weisen ausgesprochen wird. Sprich …*

[d] *nach Vokalen gefolgt von stimmhaften Konsonanten:*	love – lov**ed**, organise – organis**ed**
[t] *nach stimmlosen Konsonanten:*	help – help**ed**, like – lik**ed**
[ɪd] *nach* [t] *oder* [d]:	need – need**ed**, paint – paint**ed**

- *Bei unregelmäßigen Verben musst du die Formen des* simple past *auswendig lernen.*

come – came [keɪm]
do – did [dɪd]
go – went [went]
get – got [gɒt]
give – gave [geɪv]

have – had [hæd]
make – made [meɪd]
put – put [pʊt]
see – saw [sɔː]
take – took [tʊk]

! *Das Verb* be *hat im* simple past *zwei Formen:*
I / He / She / It **was** … [wɒz]
We / You / They **were** … [wɜː]
Die verneinten Formen lauten **wasn't** *und* **weren't**.

Auf Seite 246 findest du weitere unregelmäßige Verben. Im Dictionary *erkennst du sie am* *.

- *Im Englischen verwendest du das* simple past, *um eine abgeschlossene Handlung der Vergangenheit wiederzugeben. Im Deutschen kannst du dafür das Präteritum (z.B. er spielte, er ging) oder aber das Perfekt (z.B. er hat gespielt, er ist gegangen) verwenden. Vergleiche:*

Zeitangaben wie yesterday, last week / month / year, in 1985 *oder* two years ago *können dir den Gebrauch des* simple past *signalisieren.*

Letztes Jahr **haben** wir viel Geld **gesammelt**. – Last year we **raised** lots of money.

Test yourself *Complete the e-mail. Use the verbs in the simple past.*

Dear Olivia,
Thank you for your e-mail and the photos. I like them a lot.
You (want) to know about our charity event. Well, last month we (organise) an event in the park and we (plan) lots of activities. First there (be) games for students, parents and teachers. After that we (sell) cakes. In the afternoon the students in Year 7 (do) some really cool tricks. And then it (be) the turn of the students in Year 8. They (create) a comedy show. The girls (want) to look funny so they (paint) their faces and (wear) some funny costumes too. In the evening the school band (sing) in the park – lots of people (come) to listen. Michael (be) the real star of their show. He (do) some cool moves!
We (raise) 400 euros in just one day!
Write soon.
Pia

G2 How did they know?

Seiten 17–19

Fragen in der einfachen Form der Vergangenheit
Questions in the simple past

Policeman:	**Where were** you last Saturday evening?
Man:	Last Saturday evening? Let me think … Oh yes. On Saturday evening I was at the cinema.
Policeman:	**What** time **did** the film **finish**?
Man:	At about 10 p.m.
Policeman:	**Did** you **go** home right away?
Man:	Well, … **no, I didn't**. I walked along Trafalgar Road before I went home.
Policeman:	Um, … Trafalgar Road?

Bei Fragen unterscheidest du zwischen Entscheidungsfragen und Ergänzungsfragen. ***Entscheidungsfragen*** *beantwortest du im Deutschen mit* ***„ja" oder „nein"***. ***Ergänzungsfragen enthalten ein Fragewort*** (what, who, where, when, why, how).

- *Du kennst schon die Fragebildung im simple present:*

(Fragewort)	do / does	*Subjekt*	*Vollverb*	*restlicher Satz*	*Antwort*
	Do	**you**	**go**	shopping at the market?	– Yes, I **do**.
When	**do**	**you**	**go**	shopping at the market?	– I usually go there in the mornings.
	Does	**Olivia**	**go**	shopping on Sundays?	– No, she **doesn't**.
Why	**does**	**Olivia**	**go**	shopping on Saturdays?	– Because she's got time then.

- *Im* **simple past** *hat das Hilfsverb* do *nur eine Form, nämlich* **did**. *Nach dem Subjekt folgt die* ***Grundform des Vollverbs****, weil das Hilfsverb bereits die Vergangenheit ausdrückt.*

(Fragewort)	did	*Subjekt*	*Vollverb*	*restlicher Satz*	*Antwort*
	Did	the police	**arrest**	the man?	– Yes, they **did**.
	Did	the man	**take**	any money?	– No, he **didn't**.
What	**did**	he	**take**	from the shop?	– He took some T-shirts, sports shoes and a bike.

- *Enthält die Frage eine Form von* be, *verwendest du im* simple past *bei* I / he / she / it **was** *und bei* we / you / they **were**.

(Fragewort)	was / were	*Subjekt*	*restlicher Satz*	*Antwort*
	Was	the man	in Trafalgar Road last Saturday?	– Yes, he **was**.
	Were	there	any photos of him in Trafalgar Road?	– No, there **weren't**.
Where	**were**	you	yesterday evening?	– I was at the cinema.
Who	**was**		with you?	– My friend was with me.

! *Wenn* who *oder* what *Subjekt des Fragesatzes sind, darfst du das Hilfsverb* did *nicht verwenden. Die Fragebildung funktioniert dann genauso wie im Deutschen:*

Who phoned the police? – *Wer rief die Polizei an?*
What happened on 4th September? – *Was geschah am 4. September?*

Du brauchst ein ,not' in deiner Frage? Kein Problem! Es schließt sich direkt an das Hilfsverb bzw. die Form von be *an:* Why did**n't** you go home after the film?, Why were**n't** you at home?

Test yourself *Work in pairs. After somebody broke into a sports shop in Trafalgar Road, the police got a tip from an anonymous caller. What kind of questions did the police ask the caller? Write down four questions and give them to your partner to answer.*

Example: Policeman: What did the man look like?
Caller: He had brown hair and big ears.

G3 The police didn't know what the man looked like.

Seiten 17–19

Aussagesätze in der einfachen Form der Vergangenheit verneinen

Negating statements in the simple past

Yesterday evening a man broke into a sports shop in Trafalgar Road. He came in through the door, so he **didn't break** any shop windows. He took ten pairs of expensive sports shoes, some T-shirts and a bike. He **didn't take** any money or computers. Luckily, there **weren't** any people in the shop.

Mit didn't, wasn't / weren't *kannst du sagen, dass jemand etwas nicht gemacht hat oder etwas nicht geschehen ist.*

- *Aussagesätze im* simple present *kennst du schon. Du verneinst sie, indem du ein Hilfsverb einsetzt und es verneinst:*
  I / You / We / They **don't** like dogs.
  He / She / It **doesn't** like dogs.

- *Im* **simple past** *hat das verneinte Hilfsverb* do *nur eine Form, nämlich* **didn't**. *Danach folgt die* **Grundform des Vollverbs**, *weil das Hilfsverb bereits die Vergangenheit ausdrückt.*

+	−
The man **took** a bike.	The man **didn't take** any money.
The shoes **looked** nice.	The shoes **didn't look** cheap.
He **did** judo on Friday.	He **didn't do** any other sport.

- *Ist im Satz eine Form von* be *vorhanden, verwendest du bei* I / he / she / it **wasn't** *und bei* we / you / they **weren't**.

+	−
The man **was** young.	The man **wasn't** old.
There **were** people in the street.	There **weren't** any people in the shop.

- *Sätze mit modalen Hilfsverben* (can, can't, must, mustn't, needn't) *kannst du noch nicht in der Vergangenheit verwenden. Das lernst du erst später.*

Test yourself *Complete the article. Use the verbs in the simple past.*

8th September

Man arrested

Greenwich. On 4th September a young man (break into) a sports shop in Trafalgar Road. Yesterday the police (arrest) him. They (not know) what he (look) like at first. But then they (get) an anonymous phone call. The caller (not give) them much information, but she (give) them an address in Greenwich. When the police (get to) the house, two women (be) there but the man (not be). So they (wait) till he (come) home and then they (arrest) him – he (not try) to run away. The police (find) the sports shoes and the T-shirts in the loft, but they (not find) the bike.

G4 An adventure course helps students to be more confident.

Seiten 20–21

Steigerung der Adjektive

Comparison of adjectives

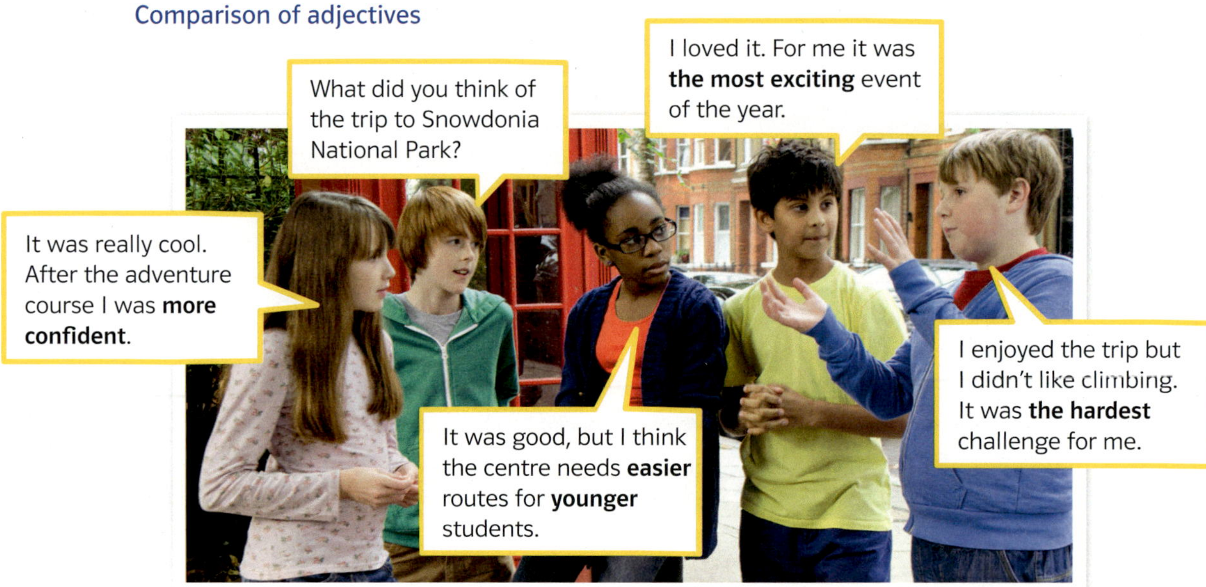

Du verwendest Adjektive und ihre Steigerungsformen, um Lebewesen und Sachen näher zu beschreiben und um sie miteinander zu vergleichen.

- *Es gibt zwei Möglichkeiten Adjektive zu steigern. Welche du benötigst, hängt von der Anzahl der Silben ab, die die Grundform des Adjektivs (Positiv) hat.*
- ***Einsilbige Adjektive** und **zweisilbige Adjektive**, die **auf -y** enden, steigerst du, indem du **-er** (1. Steigerung / Komparativ) bzw. **-est** (2. Steigerung / Superlativ) an die Grundform des Adjektivs anhängst.*

- *Fast alle anderen* ***zweisilbigen Adjektive*** *sowie* ***alle Adjektive mit mehr als zwei Silben*** *steigerst du, indem du* **more** *(1. Steigerung / Komparativ) bzw.* **most** *(2. Steigerung / Superlativ)* ***vor*** *die* ***Grundform*** *des Adjektivs setzt.*

	Grundform	1. Steigerung	2. Steigerung	Besonderheiten
	einsilbige Adjektive			
Endungen -er, -est	hard	hard**er**	the hard**est**	–
	big	bi**gger**	the bi**ggest**	*Endkonsonant wird nach kurzem Vokal verdoppelt*
	nic**e**	nic**er**	the nic**est**	*stummes -e am Ende des Adjektivs fällt weg*
	zweisilbige Adjektive auf -y			
	eas**y**	eas**ier**	the eas**iest**	y *wird zu* i*, wenn das Adjektiv auf Konsonant + -y endet (außer:* shy*)*
	funn**y**	funn**ier**	the funn**iest**	
	andere zweisilbige Adjektive sowie mehrsilbige Adjektive			
more, most	awful	**more** awful	the **most** awful	–
	interesting	**more** interesting	the **most** interesting	–

! *Beachte, dass* ***zweisilbige Adjektive****, die* ***auf -le, -ow oder -er*** *enden, mit* -er / -est *gesteigert werden:*
simp**le** *(einfach)* – simpl**er** – the simpl**est** *(e am Ende des Adjektivs fällt weg)*
narr**ow** *(eng, schmal)* – narrow**er** – the narrow**est**
clev**er** *(klug, schlau)* – clever**er** – the clever**est**

! *Einige wenige Adjektive werden unregelmäßig gesteigert. Diese musst du auswendig lernen:*
bad – worse – the worst
good – better – the best

Test yourself **a)** *Copy the grid into your exercise book and fill it in.*

Grundform	1. Steigerung	2. Steigerung
big		
		the worst
	happier	
important		

b) *Write sentences and describe the pictures.*

tall

Luke is tall.
Holly is … .
But Olivia is the … of the three.

expensive

The red car is … .
The blue … .
But … .

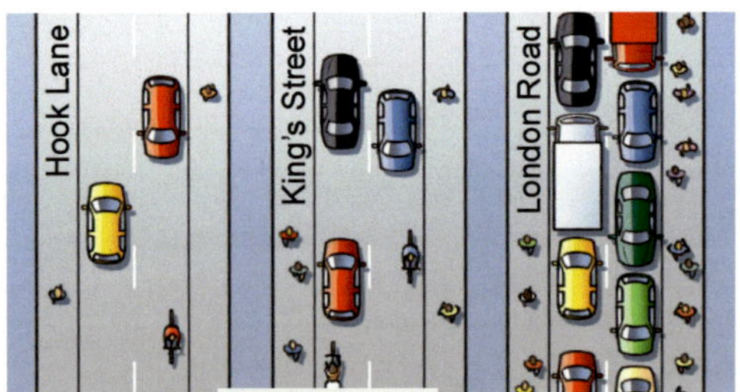

busy road

Hook Lane is … .
King's Street is … .
But London Road … .

good idea

Luke has got a … .
Holly's idea is … .
But Dave has got … .

G5 Outdoor activities are as important as lessons in the classroom.

Seiten 20–21

Gleich oder verschieden: Vergleiche mit Adjektiven
The same or different: Making comparisons with adjectives

DID YOU KNOW …?

1. Wales is part of the UK. It is**n't as big as** England or Scotland, but it's **bigger than** Northern Ireland.
2. Mount Snowdon (1,085 m) is the highest mountain in Wales. But it is**n't higher than** Ben Nevis (1,343 m) in Scotland.
3. The River Severn (362 km) is the longest river in the UK. It is **as long as** the River Neckar in Germany.

Vergleiche mit Adjektiven benutzt du, um Lebewesen oder Sachen miteinander zu vergleichen.

- *Wenn die Lebewesen oder Sachen in Bezug auf eine Eigenschaft* ***gleich*** *sind, benutzt du* **as + *Grundform* + as***:*

The River Severn is **as long as** the River Neckar. … *genauso/so lang wie …*

- *Wenn die Lebewesen oder Sachen in Bezug auf eine Eigenschaft* **verschieden** *sind, benutzt du entweder* **not as** + ***Grundform*** + **as** *oder* ***1. Steigerung*** + **than**:

  Wales is**n't as big as** England. — *… nicht so groß wie …*

  Wales is **bigger than** Northern Ireland. — *… größer als …*

  Is climbing **more dangerous than** gorge scrambling? — *… gefährlicher als …*

! *Verwechsle nicht* **than** *(als) und* **then** *(dann)!*

Test yourself *Write sentences and compare the rivers, cities, mountains and regions.*

big small short high long

Rhine: 1,233 km
Spree: 400 km
Oder: 854 km

Düsseldorf: 590,000
Stuttgart: 590,000
Cologne: 1 million

Brocken: 1,141 m
Feldberg: 1,493 m
Großer Arber: 1,455 m

the Saarland: 2,570 km²
Hesse: 21,100 km²
Saxony: 18,415 km²

Unit 2

G6 It's going to be fun.

Das Futur mit going to

The going-to future

Seiten 38–39

Mit dem going-to future *drückst du feststehende Pläne und Absichten für die nahe Zukunft aus. Du verwendest es auch, wenn es bereits jetzt deutliche Anzeichen dafür gibt, wie die Zukunft werden wird:* A visit to London **is going to be** fun.

- *Das* going-to future *bildest du aus einer* ***Form von be (am/is/are) + going to + Grundform des Verbs****:*

Aussage:	The boys **are going to visit** the British Museum with Olivia and Holly.
Verneinung:	Jay **isn't going to go** alone.
Ergänzungsfrage:	What **are** you **going to do** tomorrow, Amir?
Entscheidungsfrage mit Kurzantwort:	**Are** you **going to see** more sights in Greenwich? – Yes, I **am**. / No, I'**m not**.

! *Um etwas Zukünftiges auszudrücken, kannst du im Deutschen neben dem Futur oft auch das Präsens verwenden. Im Englischen geht das nicht.*
Vergleiche:
We'**re going to visit** London next week.
Wir ***werden*** *nächste Woche London* ***besuchen****.*
Wir ***besuchen*** *nächste Woche London.*

Wörter wie tomorrow *und* next week *können dir den Gebrauch des* going-to future *anzeigen.*

Test yourself *What are/aren't the people going to do tomorrow? Look at the pictures and write sentences.*

Jay

Amir

Olivia and Holly

Shahid

Mrs Azad

Mr Azad

G7 It's something important.

Zusammensetzungen mit some, any, every *und* no
The compounds of *some, any, every* and *no*

Seiten 40–41

Listen, **everybody**. What can we do for lunch? Are there any cafés **anywhere** near here?

Follow me, there's a great place **somewhere** around the corner here.

Mit den Zusammensetzungen von some, any, every *und* no *kannst du allgemein über Dinge, Menschen und Orte sprechen.*

- *Das kennst du schon:*
  Some *benutzt du in positiven Aussagen:* Jay has got **some** money.
  oder in höflichen Bitten, Angeboten oder Vorschlägen, wenn du eine positive Antwort erwartest: Can you give me **some** money, please? – Yes, sure.

  Any *benutzt du in Fragen und zur Verneinung:*
  Are there **any** cheap cafés near here? – No, there are**n't any** cheap cafés near here.

- *Für* some *und* any *gibt es Zusammensetzungen mit* -body/-one *(„jemand"),* -thing *(„etwas") und* -where *(„irgendwo"). Du verwendest sie auf die gleiche Weise wie* some *und* any.

Somebody *und* someone *bzw.* anybody *und* anyone *sind bedeutungsgleich.*

Zusammensetzungen mit some	
somebody / someone:	I can't see the show – **someone** tall is standing in front of me.
something:	I'm hungry. I need **something** to eat.
somewhere:	I know a good café. It's **somewhere** near Covent Garden.
Zusammensetzungen mit any	
anybody / anyone:	Did you ask **anyone**?
anything:	He hasn't got **anything**!
anywhere:	Are there any cheap cafés **anywhere**?

- *Auch von* no *und* every *gibt es Zusammensetzungen mit* -body/-one, -thing *und* -where. *Sie drücken jeweils das Gegenteil aus:*

Zusammensetzungen mit every	⟷	*Zusammensetzungen mit* no
Everybody likes London.		Olivia bets **nobody** can beat her.
jeder, alle		*niemand, keiner*
Everything is OK.		The British Museum costs **nothing**.
alles		*nichts*
There are people **everywhere**.		There's **nowhere** to sit.
überall		*nirgends, nirgendwo*

! *Beachte den Unterschied zwischen* everybody/-one *und* anybody/-one*:*
Everybody in my class likes London. *(ausnahmslos) Jeder …*
Anybody can visit Tate Britain. It's free. *Jeder (x-beliebige) …*
Mit anybody/-one *ist keine bestimmte Person gemeint, sondern jeder x-beliebige. In dieser Bedeutung kann es auch in positiven Aussagesätzen verwendet werden.*

! Everybody/-one *und* anybody/-one *sind Singularformen. Die dazugehörigen Pronomen und Possessivbegleiter stehen aber meist im Plural:*
Everybody pays for **their** own Oyster card.
Anybody at the Tube station can tell you where you can buy an Oyster card if you ask **them**.

Test yourself *Complete the dialogue.*

Amir: Listen, (*alle*). I want to buy a little present for my aunt to say 'thank you'. Is there a good shop (*irgendwo*)?
Olivia: What are you thinking of?
Amir: Well, it must be (*etwas*) special, but it mustn't be (*nichts*) expensive.
Jay: (*Alles*) is expensive in London!
Holly: That's not true! I know a good shop where (*nichts*) costs more than £10.
Amir: OK. Let's go there and see if we can find (*etwas*) for her.

Unit 3

G8 Have you ever run in a marathon?

Seiten 56–59

Die einfache Form des Perfekts

The present perfect simple

Mit dem present perfect simple *verbindest du die Vergangenheit mit der Gegenwart.*

- *Mit dem* present perfect simple *kannst du verschiedene Situationen beschreiben:*

a) *Mit* Have you ever … *fragst du, ob jemand etwas schon ein- oder mehrmals gemacht hat.*

Have you ever …? *In den Antworten auf die Frage findest du oft eines dieser Signalwörter:* **never, before, only ever, … times.**	**Has** Jay **ever run** in a marathon? – No, he **hasn't**. He **has never run** one mile.
	Have Dave and Holly **ever run** in big races? – No, Dave **hasn't run** in big races **before**. And Holly **has only ever run** in short races.
	Have the Elliots **ever watched** the London Marathon? – Yes, they **have**. They**'ve watched** it **three times**.

b) *Mit dem* present perfect simple *kannst du sagen, dass eine Handlung bereits, gerade erst oder noch nicht abgeschlossen wurde:*

already *(schon, bereits)*	Olivia **has already prepared** for the trials.
just *(gerade erst, eben)*	Gwen **has just had** an idea.
not yet *(noch nicht)*	The girls **haven't left** for school **yet**.

Die Signalwörter never, only ever, already *und* just *stehen direkt nach dem Hilfsverb.*

c) *Außerdem kannst du ausdrücken, dass eine Handlung irgendwann in der Vergangenheit stattfand und das Ergebnis dieser Handlung bis in die Gegenwart spürbar bzw. sichtbar ist:*

I'**ve hurt** my foot. It hurts when I walk.
Olivia **has bought** new running shoes. They're still clean.

- *Du bildest das* present perfect simple *aus einer Form von* **have (have/has)** *und dem* **past participle**.

Das past participle *von regelmäßigen Verben entspricht ihrer Form im* simple past (→G1). *Die Formen von unregelmäßigen Verben musst du lernen. Du findest sie in der 3. Spalte auf den Seiten 244–245.*

Aussage:	I'**ve run** in races before, but not in a big race like a marathon.
Verneinung:	Jay **hasn't run** one mile.
Ergänzungsfrage:	Who **has heard** of the mini marathon?
Entscheidungsfrage mit Kurzantwort:	**Has** Dave ever **run** in race? – Yes, he **has.** / No, he **hasn't**.

❗ *Beachte die Unterschiede zum Deutschen:*

a) *Das* present perfect simple *bildest du immer mit* have / has + past participle. *Vergleiche:*
I'**ve hurt** my foot. = Ich **habe** mir den Fuß **verletzt.**
I **haven't left** yet. = Ich **bin** noch nicht **losgegangen**.

b) *Auch in Sätzen, die das* present perfect simple *beinhalten, gilt im Englischen die Regel* ***S – V – O****. Das* ***Objekt*** *steht also nach der Verbform.*
Olivia **has hurt** **her foot**.
Olivia **hat** sich **den Fuß** **verletzt**.

Test yourself a) *You and your classmates are talking about Sports Day. Make questions and write them in your exercise book.*

Have you …	(prepare) (buy) already (start) ever (hurt) (find)	eating healthy food? a name for your team yet? your foot? for Sports Day yet? new sports shoes yet?

b) *Work in small groups. Ask and answer the questions from a).*

Example:
Sabrina: Have you prepared for Sports Day yet?
Martin: Yes, I have. I've already run around the park three times.

Unit 4

G9 I'm writing to you because I need your advice.

Seiten 76–77

Nebensätze der Zeit, des Grundes und des Vergleichs
Subordinate clauses of time, reason and comparison

Du kannst Nebensätze verwenden, wenn du deiner Hauptaussage zusätzliche Informationen hinzufügen möchtest. Mit den aus Haupt- und Nebensatz entstehenden Satzgefügen stellst du logische Verbindungen her. Sie sind stilistisch eleganter als hintereinander gereihte Hauptsätze.

a) *Nebensätze der Zeit (= Temporalsätze):*

after *(nachdem)*	**After** I spoke to my friend, I felt much better.
as soon as *(sobald)*	Things often get better **as soon as** you talk to somebody about it.
before *(bevor, ehe, vor)*	**Before** they had an argument, Lauren spent a lot of her free time with her friend.
until *(bis)*	Never give your address **until** you've really met your new friend face-to-face.
when *(wenn)*	Ask your parents, older sister or brother **when** you need advice.
whenever *(jedes Mal, wenn)*	**Whenever** you want to put photos of other people online, ask them first.

b) *Nebensätze des Grundes (= Kausalsätze):*

because *(weil)*	Lauren wrote to an agony aunt **because** she had a problem.

c) *Nebensätze des Vergleichs (= Komparativsätze):*

like *(als ob)*	My friend acts **like** she's having a much better time without me.

❗ *Beachte, dass die Satzstellung im Deutschen anders ist als im Englischen. Im Englischen bleibt die Reihenfolge* ***Subjekt*** *–* ***Verbform*** *–* ***Objekt*** *sowohl im Haupt- als auch Nebensatz immer erhalten. Vergleiche:*
After **I** **spoke** to my friend, **I** **felt** much better.
Nachdem **ich** mit meinem Freund **gesprochen hatte**, **fühlte** **ich** mich besser.

❗ *Wenn du dir die Beispiele in a) – c) einmal genauer anschaust, wirst du feststellen, dass Nebensätze sowohl nach dem Hauptsatz als auch vor dem Hauptsatz stehen können. Steht der* ***Hauptsatz vor*** *dem* ***Nebensatz****, setzt du* ***kein Komma****, weil die Konjunktion die Sätze trennt. Steht der* ***Nebensatz vor*** *dem* ***Hauptsatz****, trennst du beide durch* ***ein Komma****.*

Test yourself *Read the posts of some* TeenLife *readers. Complete the sentences with the correct linking word. Add commas where you need them.*

Joe: I like your magazine … it's always got interesting news on my favourite stars in it.
Ginny: I buy *TeenLife* … I get my pocket money from my parents. I love it!
Michael: The concert photos are fantastic. When I look at them it's … I'm there.
Lisa: … I read Ruby's advice I think she really understands our problems.
Sheila: … I tried the make-up in last week's magazine. I'm not going to buy *TeenLife* again! It looked awful on my face.

G10 I must fix it before your mum comes home.

Modalverben
Modals

Seite 79–80

Luke: You could look at a forum for help.
Dad: You mean on the internet? So I **can't fix** my own washing machine – is that what you think? I don't need the internet. And *you* **don't have to** look everything up either!

Mit **can** *oder* **may** *kannst du eine* ***Erlaubnis*** *einholen oder erteilen.*
Mit **can't** *oder* **mustn't** *drückst du ein* ***Verbot*** *aus.*
Mit **can** *bzw.* **can't** *sagst du, dass jemand* ***(nicht) in der Lage*** *ist etwas zu tun.*
Mit **must, (not) have to** *und* **needn't** *drückst du* ***eine*** *oder* ***keine Notwendigkeit*** *aus.*

Erlaubnis:	**Can** I go over to Jay's house? **May** I have my tablet back, please?	*Kann ich …* *Darf ich …*
Verbot:	You **mustn't** remove that pipe. He **can't** use his dad's tools.	*… darfst nicht* *… kann/darf nicht*
(Un)fähigkeit:	I **can** reach the knob. I **can't** fix the washing machine.	*… kann; … bin in der Lage* *… kann nicht;* *… bin nicht in der Lage*
(keine) Notwendigkeit:	I **must** fix the pipe. You **needn't** say "thanks". You **have to** turn the knob off. Luke **doesn't have to** look everything up on the internet.	*… muss* *… musst nicht; … brauchst nicht* *… musst* *… muss nicht; … braucht nicht*

- *Die Modalverben* **can**, **can't**, **may**, **must**, **mustn't** *und* **needn't** *sind in allen Personen gleich. Nur bei* **have to** *musst du in der 3. Person Singular* **has to** *bzw.* **doesn't have to** *verwenden.*

May ist höflicher als can und wird meist in Fragen und den Antworten darauf verwendet.

! *Nicht verwechseln:*
Must *benutzt du, um zu sagen, dass etwas aus Sicht des Sprechers notwendig ist.* **Have to** *verwendest du, wenn jemand anderes dem Sprecher eine Verpflichtung auferlegt hat oder es um Regeln und Gesetze geht:*
Mr Elliot: I **must** fix the pipe.
Mr Elliot: You **don't have to** look everything up on the internet, Luke.

! *Nicht verwechseln:*
You must … = *Du musst …*
You mustn't … = *Du darfst nicht …*
You needn't … = *Du musst nicht … / Du brauchst nicht …*

! *Beachte den Unterschied in der Wortstellung:*
He **can't** **use** his dad's tools.
Er ***darf*** *das Werkzeug seines Vaters* ***nicht*** ***benutzen***.

Test yourself *You want to take part in a computer course. Write what students can, can't, must, needn't mustn't or (don't) have to do.*

arrive early | bring own computer | pay before the course starts | wear a uniform | do fun things with computers | eat in computer room | keep computer room clean | …

G11 You could look at a forum for help.

Seite 79–80

Die Modalverben should, shouldn't *und* could
The modals *should, shouldn't* and *could*

Have you got a problem? Well, you **could** look at a forum for help. But you **shouldn't** believe everything you read online.

- *Die Modalverben* should, shouldn't *und* could *funktionieren wie die Modalverben, die du schon kennst: Du verwendest sie im* simple present, *sie sind in allen Personen gleich und nach ihnen folgt immer ein Vollverb in der Grundform. Vergleiche:*

Mr Elliot **could look** for help on the internet.	*Herr Elliot* ***könnte*** *im Internet nach Hilfe* ***suchen****.*
They **should ask** their parents for advice.	*Sie* ***sollten*** *ihre Eltern um Rat* ***fragen****.*
You **shouldn't try** to fix everything yourself.	*Du* ***solltest nicht versuchen****, alles selbst zu reparieren.*

Test yourself *What should, could or shouldn't they do? Give advice.*

1. Olivia: In netball I pushed a girl. She fell and hurt her hand.
2. Jay: I've ruined Dave's book.
3. Holly: Mr Fluff often explores under my bed. It's difficult to get him out when he needs to go to bed.
4. Dave: Last weekend I pulled out some flowers in Granny's garden. I thought they were weeds[1].

1 **weeds** [wiːdz] Unkraut

Unit 5

G12 I'll miss you so much!

Seiten 94–96

Das Futur mit will

Will future

Du verwendest das Futur mit will *für spontane Entscheidungen, Versprechen, Hoffnungen und Vorhersagen, die die Zukunft betreffen.*

- *Mit dem* will future …

a) *drückst du spontane Entscheidungen oder Versprechen aus.*

I'**ll text** you.
Holly and I **will visit** you in Cornwall.

b) *machst du Vorhersagen über zukünftige Ereignisse. (Der Sprecher kann diese nicht beeinflussen.)*

Gwen:	We'**ll miss** you, Dave.
Assistant:	The trip to St Agnes **will take** about seven hours.

Diese Wörter können dir den Gebrauch des will future *anzeigen:* tomorrow, next week/month/year, in a year, probably, perhaps, maybe.

c) *sagst du, was jemand über ein zukünftiges Ereignis denkt, hofft oder vermutet. Diese Sätze beginnen häufig mit* I hope, I think *oder* I'm sure.

Jay:	I think you'**ll make** lots of new friends quickly.
Dave:	I'm sure Sid **will hate** his new home.

- *Das* will future *bildest du für alle Personen aus dem Hilfsverb* **will (not) + *Grundform des Verbs.*** *Die Kurzform lautet* 'll *bzw. bei verneinten Sätzen* won't.

Aussage:	Dave hopes that his friends **will visit** him in St Agnes.
Verneinung:	Aunt Frances **won't come** to Cornwall with them.
Ergänzungsfrage:	What do you think Dave's new school **will be** like?
Entscheidungsfrage mit Kurzantwort:	**Will** your dad **find** work there? – Yes, he **will.** / No, he **won't.**

❗ *Mit dem* going-to *und dem* will future *kennst du zwei Zeitformen der Zukunft. Möchtest du über Zukünftiges sprechen, musst du abwägen:*
Für feststehende ***Pläne*** *oder* ***Absichten*** → going-to future (→G6):
The Prestons **are going to move** to Cornwall in summer.
Für ***spontane Entscheidungen*** → will future:
"I need to put all my things into boxes." – "Don't worry. I**'ll help** you."
Für ***Vermutungen, Hoffnungen*** *oder* ***Vorhersagen*** → will future:
I think Dave **will be** OK in Cornwall.

❗ *Verwechsle nicht „Ich will …"* (= I want to …) *und "I will …"* (= Ich werde …).

Test yourself *What do the friends say when Dave isn't with them? Complete the sentences.*

1. Olivia: I hope Dave … his new school. (love)
2. Holly: I'm sure the Prestons … Granny Rose and Aunt Frances in London soon. (visit)
3. Luke: I don't think the new home … a problem for Sid. He … new cat friends quickly. He … ! (be / make / not get bored)
4. Gwen: I hope Dave … us. (not forget)

G13 He says the landscape in Cornwall is very wild.

Seite 98–99

Die indirekte Rede mit Einführungssatz im Präsens
Indirect speech with the reporting verb in the present

Mit der indirekten Rede berichtest du, was jemand sagt oder vor kurzem gesagt hat.

Direkte Rede	*Indirekte Rede*
"It'**s** very hot in Cornwall."	Dave **says that** it'**s** very hot in Cornwall.
"I'**ve** just **got** back from the beach."	He **tells me that** he'**s** just **got** back from the beach.

- *Die indirekte Rede leitest du durch einen Einleitungssatz mit* say, write, tell sb *oder* promise *ein. Darauf folgt ein Nebensatz, der mit oder ohne* that *eingeleitet werden kann.*
- *Steht das Verb im Einleitungssatz im* simple present, *wird die Zeitform aus der direkten Rede in den Nebensatz der indirekten Rede übernommen.*

! *Anders als im Deutschen steht nach* that *kein Komma.*

- *Pronomen, Zeit- und Ortsangaben ändern sich in der indirekten Rede:*
  "**I** hope **you** aren't having too much fun without **me**."
  → He says **he** hopes **we** aren't having too much fun without **him**.
  "There's a lot of ancient history **here**."
  → He says that there's a lot of ancient history **there**.
  "**You** should look at **these** photos."
  → He tells us that **we** should look at **those** photos.
  "**This** is my favourite beach. **I** can **see** it from **my** window."
  → He writes that **that**'s his favourite beach. **He** can see it from **his** window.
- *Auch einige Verben ändern sich in der indirekten Rede:*
  "I can't wait for you to **come** here."
  → He says that he can't wait for us to **go** there.
  "You must **bring** your swimming things!"
  → He tells us that we must **take** our swimming things.

Test yourself *Look at the pictures and report the statements.*

Vocabulary

Im ***Vocabulary*** findest du alle wichtigen englischen Wörter und Redewendungen aus *Green Line* 2. Sie stehen in der Reihenfolge, in der sie im Buch vorkommen. Diese Wörter solltest du lernen und anwenden können. Mager gedruckte Einträge musst du **nicht** auswendig lernen. Sie helfen dir, Texte zu verstehen. Weitere nützliche Wörter und Begriffe (z. B. Arbeitsanweisungen), die du **nicht** auswendig lernen musst, findest du ab S. 243.
Das *Vocabulary* ist in drei Spalten aufgeteilt:

- Links stehen die englischen Wörter und Sätze. Die Lautschrift in Klammern zeigt dir, wie du das Wort oder den Satz aussprichst.
- In der Mitte steht die deutsche Übersetzung.
- Rechts findest du Beispielsätze, Erklärungen, Bilder oder Hinweise auf Besonderheiten.

An manchen Stellen im Buch stehen neue Wörter in Fußnoten. Sie helfen dir, die Texte zu verstehen, du musst sie aber nicht lernen.

Auf das *Vocabulary* folgt das ***Dictionary (English – German, German – English)***. Falls du ein Wort vergessen hast, kannst du in diesen alphabetischen Wortlisten nachsehen.

Englische Begriffe wie *e-mail*, *cool* oder *cornflakes*, die du auch im Deutschen verwendest, stehen nicht im *Vocabulary*. Du kannst ihre Aussprache und Übersetzung aber im *Dictionary* nachschlagen. Das gleiche gilt für Wörter, die auf Englisch und Deutsch fast gleich geschrieben und ausgesprochen werden, wie z. B. *park* oder *partner*.

Abkürzungen und Zeichen

pl	Mehrzahl (Plural)	↔	ist das Gegenteil von
sg	Einzahl (Singular)	→	ist verwandt mit
ugs	umgangssprachlich	=	entspricht
5	In dieser Übung kommen die Wörter vor.	*Fr./Lat.*	verwandte Wörter in anderen Fremdsprachen
!	Achtung!		

Englische Laute

Mitlaute (Konsonanten)

[b]	**b**ed	[p]	**p**icture
[d]	**d**ay	[r]	**r**ed
[ð]	**th**e	[s]	**s**ix
[f]	**f**amily	[ʃ]	**sh**e
[g]	**g**o	[t]	**t**en
[ŋ]	morni**ng**	[tʃ]	**ch**air
[h]	**h**ouse	[v]	**v**ideo
[j]	**y**ou	[w]	**w**e, **o**ne
[k]	**c**an, mil**k**	[z]	ea**s**y
[l]	**l**etter	[ʒ]	revi**s**ion
[m]	**m**an	[dʒ]	pa**g**e
[n]	**n**o	[θ]	**th**ank you

Selbstlaute (Vokale)

[ɑː]	c**a**r	[i]	happ**y**
[æ]	**a**pple	[iː]	t**ea**cher
[e]	p**e**n	[ɒ]	d**o**g
[ə]	**a**gain	[ɔː]	b**a**ll
[ɜː]	g**ir**l	[ʊ]	b**oo**k
[ʌ]	b**u**t	[u]	Jan**u**ary
[ɪ]	**i**t	[uː]	t**oo**, t**wo**

Doppellaute

[aɪ]	**I**, m**y**
[aʊ]	n**ow**, m**ou**se
[eɪ]	n**a**me, th**ey**
[eə]	th**ere**, p**air**
[ɪə]	h**ere**, id**ea**
[əʊ]	hell**o**
[ɔɪ]	b**oy**
[ʊə]	s**ure**

[ː]	der vorangehende Laut ist lang, z. B. *you* [juː]	[ˈ]	die folgende Silbe trägt den Hauptakzent
[‿]	der Bindebogen zeigt, dass zwei Wörter in der Aussprache verbunden werden	[ˌ]	die folgende Silbe trägt den Nebenakzent

Across cultures 1 Let's discover TTS!

to **discover** [dɪ'skʌvə]	entdecken	The students *discover* Thomas Tallis School.
subject ['sʌbdʒɪkt]	Schulfach	What *subjects* do you like?
exam [ɪg'zæm]	Examen; Prüfung	An *exam* is an important test ***Fr.*** examen *(m)*
dance [dɑ:ns] *(no pl)*	Tanz	*dance* → to dance
drama ['drɑ:mə]	Theater; Drama	 In *Drama* class, you can learn how to be an actor.
studies *(pl)* ['stʌdiz]	Studium; Lernen; Arbeit für die Schule	My favourite subject is Film *Studies*. ***Lat.*** studēre
fashion ['fæʃn]	Mode	In *Fashion* lessons you learn about clothes.
to **offer** ['ɒfə]	(an)bieten	Can I *offer* you something to drink? ***Fr.*** offrir
additional [ə'dɪʃnl]	zusätzlich	
birdwatching ['bɜ:dˌwɒtʃɪŋ]	Vogelbeobachtung	*Birdwatching* is an additional activity at TTS.
bird [bɜ:d]	Vogel	
chess [tʃes]	Schach	
painting ['peɪntɪŋ]	Malerei; Gemälde	*painting* → to paint 
assembly [ə'sembli]	Versammlung; Morgenappell	
sign [saɪn]	Zeichen; Schild	In Wales the *signs* are in Welsh. ***Lat.*** signum *(nt)*
class [klɑ:s]	*hier:* Unterricht	In *class*, sometimes you work on your own, sometimes with your classmates.
1 **hall** [hɔ:l]	Halle; Saal	In the *hall*, the students meet for Assembly.
art [ɑ:t]	Kunst	Not every painting is *art*! ***Lat.*** ars *(f)*
competition [ˌkɒmpə'tɪʃn]	Wettbewerb; Turnier	There's a painting *competition* at our school this year. ***Fr.*** compétition *(f)*
to **belong (to)** [bɪ'lɒŋ (tə)]	gehören (zu)	
with special needs [wɪð ˌspeʃl 'ni:dz]	behindert	Students *with special needs* belong to TTS too.

2	**fantastic** [fæn'tæstɪk]	fantastisch; großartig	*fantastic* great *Fr.* fantastique
	reaction [ri'ækʃn]	Reaktion	
	Maths [mæθs]	Mathematik; Mathe	*Fr.* maths *(f)* (pl)
	Science [saɪəns]	Naturwissenschaften	*Lat.* scientia *(f)*
	Technology [tek'nɒlədʒi]	Technik; Computerunterricht	
3	**partially sighted** [ˌpɑːʃəli 'saɪtɪd]	sehbehindert	Gwen is a new girl at TTS. She's *partially sighted*.
4	**registration** [ˌredʒɪs'treɪʃn]	Anwesenheitskontrolle	*Registration* is before lessons.
	break [breɪk]	Pause	After the first two lessons we always have *break*.
	PE *(= Physical Education)* [ˌpiː'iː; ˌfɪzɪkl‿edʒʊ'keɪʃn]	Sportunterricht	In *PE* you do lots of sport.
	RE *(= Religious Education)* [ˌɑːr'iː; rɪˌlɪdʒəs‿edʒʊ'keɪʃn]	Religion *(Schulfach)*	
	French [frenʃ]	französisch; Französisch	
	Geography [dʒi'ɒgrəfi]	Geografie; Erdkunde	What do you know about the *geography* of Southern Germany?
	Humanities *(pl)* [hjuː'mænətiz]	Sozialwissenschaften	*Lat.* humanitas *(f)*
	History ['hɪstri]	Geschichte	*Lat.* historia *(f)*

Subjects at school

English	Englisch	**Music**	Musik
German	Deutsch	**Humanities**	Sozialwissenschaften
French	Französisch	**Technology**	Technik
Maths	Mathe	**Science**	Naturwissenschaften
PE	Sport	**RE**	Religion
Art	Kunst	**Geography**	Erdkunde

Make you own fantasy timetable and compare it with your partner's.

5	**Eco** [ɪkəʊ]	Öko-	
	to **join** [dʒɔɪn]	beitreten; sich anschließen; verbinden	Let's *join* the Computer Club!
	to **design** [dɪ'zaɪn]	entwerfen; gestalten	*to design* → design
	should [ʃʊd]	sollte; solltest; sollten; solltet	
	to **welcome** ['welkəm]	willkommen heißen	Let's go and *welcome* our new classmates.
	wildlife ['waɪldlaɪf]	Tierwelt *(in freier Wildbahn)*	The Eco Club did a *wildlife* project.
	to **protect** [prə'tekt]	schützen	
	nature ['neɪtʃə]	Natur	It's important to protect *nature*.
	to **save** [seɪv]	sparen	I want to buy a new smartphone. I need to *save* money for it.

	energy ['enədʒi]	Energie; Kraft	*Fr.* énergie *(f)*
	pollution [pə'lu:ʃn]	Verschmutzung	*Pollution* makes a river dirty.
	to **make a difference** [ˌmeɪk‿ə‿'dɪfrns]	etw. verändern	*to make a difference* → to change sth.
6	**as** [æz; əz]	wie	My favourite music is not the same *as* yours. We don't like the same music.
7	**advice** [əd'vaɪs]	Rat; Ratschlag	What *advice* can you give me?
	actor ['æktə]	Schauspieler	*actor* → to act *Lat.* actor *(m)*
	moment ['məʊmənt]	Moment; Augenblick	! Achtung Betonung.
	to **panic** ['pænɪk]	panisch werden	Don't *panic*! *Fr.* paniquer
	to **relax** [rɪ'læks]	sich entspannen; sich ausruhen; sich beruhigen	Just *relax*!
	confident ['kɒnfɪdnt]	selbstsicher; selbstbewusst	*Lat.* confidens
	Take a deep breath. [ˌteɪk‿ə ˌdi:p 'breθ]	Atme(t) tief ein.	
	to **thank** [θæŋk]	danken	*to thank* → Thank you.

Unit 1 My friends and I

Check-in

past [pɑ:st]	Vergangenheit	'Today' is now, 'yesterday' is the *past*.
feeling ['fi:lɪŋ]	Gefühl	*feeling* → to feel
phrases that … [ˌfreɪzɪz 'ðæt]	Redewendungen, die …	
caught on camera [ˌkɔ:t‿ɒn 'kæmrə]	ertappt; mit der Kamera festgehalten	
embarrassing [ɪm'bærəsɪŋ]	peinlich	In the photo Jay is wearing an *embarrassing* outfit.
to **end up** [ˌend‿'ʌp]	enden; landen	
yearbook ['jɪəbʊk]	Jahrbuch	A book with information about events and students at the school.
round of boxing [ˌraʊnd‿əv 'bɒksɪŋ]	Boxrunde	
nose [nəʊz]	Nase	They look funny with their red *noses*.
eye [aɪ]	Auge	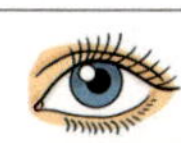
lovebirds *(pl)* ['lʌvˌbɜ:dz]	Turteltauben	

to **lie** [laɪ]	lügen	The camera never *lies*!
trip [trɪp]	Trip; Reise; Ausflug; Fahrt	Let's go on a fun *trip* at the weekend!
guy [gaɪ]	Typ; Kerl; *(Pl.)* Leute	Our new classmate is a really cool *guy*.
2 **himself** [hɪm'self]	(er) selbst; sich (selbst)	You mustn't help him. He wants to do everything *himself*.
3 **shy** [ʃaɪ]	schüchtern	I don't like parties because I'm *shy*.
embarrassed [ɪm'bærəst]	verlegen	*embarrassed* → embarrassing *Fr.* embarrassé/-e
proud (of) ['praʊd‿əv]	stolz (auf)	Jay is *proud of* himself because he is good at singing.
American [ə'merɪkən]	Amerikanisch; amerikanisch; aus Amerika; Amerikaner/-in	Yearbooks are an *American* tradition.
report [rɪ'pɔ:t]	Bericht; Meldung	Who can write the *report* about the class trip?
during *(+ noun)* ['djʊərɪŋ]	während *(+ Nomen)*	Don't eat *during* lessons.
highlight ['haɪlaɪt]	Highlight; Höhepunkt	

Describing a person's character

He**'s** a very **shy** person. It isn't easy for him to give presentations.	schüchtern
She's good at lots of things so she**'s** always **confident** that she can do almost anything.	zuversichtlich; selbstbewusst
He**'s** so **brave**. He's never scared.	tapfer; mutig
She**'s** a **nice / friendly / unfriendly / funny** person.	nett / freundlich / unfreundlich / lustig
He**'s lucky** because he**'s happy**.	Glück haben / glücklich sein

Describe a person to your partner. Who is it?

Station 1: I love Red Nose Day

(the) best [best]	(der/die/das) Beste	I always try to do *my best* when there's a class test.
ago [ə'gəʊ]	vor *(zeitlich)*	! *Ago* steht meistens am Satzende: I did my homework two days *ago*.
to **raise money** [ˌreɪz 'mʌni]	Geld sammeln	Charities *raise money*.
in need [ɪn 'ni:d]	bedürftig; in Not	*in need* → to need
also ['ɔ:lsəʊ]	auch	I like football and I *also* like basketball. = I like football and I like basketball too.
that's how [ðæts 'haʊ]	so	Look at Luke. *That's how* you play football – he's good!
noticeboard ['nəʊtɪsbɔ:d]	schwarzes Brett	Olivia saw a Red Nose Day poster on the school *noticeboard*.
month [mʌnθ]	Monat	day – week – *month* – year
in the end [ˌɪn ðiˌ'end]	schließlich; zum Schluss	
real [rɪəl]	echt; richtig; wirklich	Not everything you see on TV is *real*. *real* → really

	collection [kəˈlekʃn]	Kollektion; Sammlung	*collection* → to collect *Fr.* collection *(f)*
	I can't wait till next time. [aɪ kɑ:nt ˌweɪt tɪl nekst ˈtaɪm]	Ich kann es bis zum nächsten Mal kaum erwarten.	
2	**non-** [nɒn]	nicht-	Red Nose Day is a *non*-uniform day.
5	**the next day** [ðə ˌnekst ˈdeɪ]	am nächsten Tag	What did Luke tell his friends *the next day*?
	yesterday [ˈjestədeɪ]	gestern	*yesterday* – today – tomorrow
6	**pyjamas** *(pl)* [pɪˈdʒɑ:məz]	Schlafanzug; Pyjama	Do you wear *pyjamas* in bed? 
	to **enjoy** [ɪnˈdʒɔɪ]	genießen; sich freuen an	The party was great. I really *enjoyed* it.
	comment [ˈkɒment]	Kommentar	This is a serious problem, so I don't need your funny *comments*!
	to **turn off** [ˌtɜ:n‿ˈɒf]	abschalten; ausschalten	Please *turn off* the TV. It's time to go to bed.
	hard [hɑ:d]	hart; schwer; schwierig	I find German *hard*.
	for ... [fɔ:; fə]	... lang	Sherlock can swim *for* 30 minutes.
	to **think of** [ˈθɪŋk‿əv]	(sich) ausdenken; sich etwas einfallen lassen	Can you *think of* other things to do at the weekend?
7	an activity that ... [ən‿ækˌtɪvəti ˈðæt]	eine Aktivität, die ...	
	nervous [ˈnɜ:vəs]	nervös; aufgeregt	I felt *nervous* before the class test. *Fr.* nerveux/nerveuse
8	**sale** [seɪl]	Verkauf	*sale* → to sell
	to **keep going** [ˌki:p ˈgəʊɪŋ]	aufrechterhalten	A quick answer *keeps* the conversation *going*.

Station 2: How did they know?

coach [kəʊtʃ]	Reisebus	A big bus (for holidays or long trips). 
someone [ˈsʌmwʌn]	jemand	*someone* = somebody
missing [ˈmɪsɪŋ]	fehlend; verschwunden	What's the *missing* word? "I really ... you."
solution [səˈlu:ʃn]	Lösung	Let's find a *solution* for your problem. *Fr.* solution *(f)*
anonymous [əˈnɒnɪməs]	anonym	
police [pəˈli:s]	Polizei	! The *police* are looking for a dangerous man. *Fr.* police *(f)*
to **arrest** [əˈrest]	festnehmen; verhaften	The police *arrested* two men. *Fr.* arrêter
what the man looked like [ˌwɒt ðə mæn ˈlʊkt laɪk]	wie der Mann aussah	I didn't see the man. I don't know *what he looks like*.

	taxi ['tæksi]	Taxi	
	driver ['draɪvə]	Fahrer/-in	! My uncle is a taxi *driver*. = Mein Onkel ist Taxifahrer.
	mechanic [mə'kænɪk]	Mechaniker/-in; Kfz-Mechaniker/-in	
	farmer ['fɑ:mə]	Farmer/-in; Landwirt/-in	*farmer* → farm
	postman ['pəʊstmən]	Briefträger	
	clue [klu:]	Hinweis; Spur	The man's name is the *clue*.
13	**friendly** ['frendli]	freundlich; nett	I always try to be *friendly* to everyone. *friendly* → friend
14	**all day** [ɔ:l 'deɪ]	den ganzen Tag	What did you do *all day* on Saturday?
15	**singer** ['sɪŋə]	Sänger/-in	Jay thinks he's a *singer*. *singer* → to sing
16	**dream** [dri:m]	Traum	In my *dream* I was James Bond.

Station 3: Everyone can enjoy a challenge

challenge ['tʃælɪndʒ]	Herausforderung	
course [kɔ:s]	Kurs	They organise sports *courses* for school groups. ***Lat.*** cursus *(m)*
mountain ['maʊntɪn]	Berg	
forest ['fɒrɪst]	Wald	There are lots of trees in a *forest*. ***Fr.*** forêt *(f)*
adventure [əd'ventʃə]	Abenteuer	*Adventure* stories tell about exciting events.
walking ['wɔ:kɪŋ]	Wandern	! Wenn man *-ing* an ein Verb anhängt, wird es zum Hauptwort (Nomen): walk – *walking*, climb – climbing
climbing ['klaɪmɪŋ]	Klettern	! Achtung Aussprache.
gorge scrambling ['gɔ:dʒ ˌskræmblɪŋ]	Schluchtenklettern	
route [ru:t]	Strecke; Route	***Fr.*** route *(f)*
than [ðæn]	als *(bei Vergleichen)*	Her English is better *than* her French.
the worst [ðə 'wɜ:st]	der/die/das schlimmste; der/die/das schlechteste	*the worst* ↔ the best
that's why [ðæts 'waɪ]	deshalb	I went to bed late last night. *That's why* I'm tired.

Outdoor activities

to **play** football / tennis	Fußball / Tennis spielen
to **go** skating / swimming / climbing / gorge scrambling	inlineskaten / schwimmen / schluchtenklettern gehen
to **ride** your bike / a horse	Fahrrad fahren / reiten
to **run**	laufen; rennen
to **go for a walk** in a park / in a forest / in the mountains	im Park / im Wald / in den Bergen spazieren gehen
to **climb** a mountain	einen Berg besteigen
to **do** gorge scrambling / mountain climbing	schluchtenklettern / bergsteigen

Tell your partner what you'd like to do in your holidays.

18	**separate** ['seprət]	separat; getrennt; verschieden	Wales is a *separate* country. *Lat.* separatus/-a/-um
	Celtic ['keltɪk; 'seltɪk]	keltisch	*Fr.* celtique
	Welsh [welʃ]	walisisch; Walisisch; Waliser/-in	*Welsh* people are from Wales. Some of them still speak *Welsh*.
22	**low** [ləʊ]	niedrig	
	tall [tɔːl]	groß; hoch	Olivia is *taller* than Lucy.
	high [haɪ]	hoch; groß	*high* ↔ low

Comparing things

Tony: My house is **big**.
Lou: My sister's house is **bigger**.
Tony: I think my house is **the biggest**.

Lou: Your joke is **good**. But my joke is **better**.
Tony: No, my joke is **the best**.

Lou: Football is **exciting**, but tennis is **more exciting**, and inline skating is **the most exciting** sport.

Compare the things in your schoolbag with a partner's things.

Story: It was amazing

amazing [ə'meɪzɪŋ]	unglaublich; toll; erstaunlich	That's an *amazing* story!
planet ['plænɪt]	Planet	
sheep, sheep *(pl)* [ʃi:p]	Schaf	
road [rəʊd]	Straße	I live in King's *Road*.
soon [su:n]	bald	in a short time from now; a short time later
field [fi:ld]	Feld; Spielfeld; Wiese; Weide; Acker	On farms there are *fields*.
Welcome! ['welkəm]	Willkommen!	*Welcome* to Wales!
instructor [ɪn'strʌktə]	Lehrer/-in; Betreuer/-in	An *instructor* shows you how to do things. ***Lat.*** instructor *(m)*
few [fju:]	wenige	! He's got a *few* friends. = … ein paar Freunde. He's got *few* friends. = … wenige Freunde.
meal [mi:l]	Mahlzeit; Essen	Lunch is a *meal*.
a bit [ə 'bɪt]	ein bisschen; ein wenig	
cold [kəʊld]	kalt	The nights in Wales were a bit *cold*.
torch [tɔ:tʃ]	Fackel; Taschenlampe	
to **go for a walk** [ˌgəʊ fər‿ə 'wɔ:k]	spazieren gehen	It's nice today. Let's *go for a walk*.
the dark [ðə 'dɑ:k]	Dunkelheit	in *the dark* = im Dunkeln
noise [nɔɪz]	Lärm; Geräusch	What's all the *noise*? I can't sleep!
dark [dɑ:k]	dunkel	*dark* → the dark
night walk ['naɪt wɔ:k]	Nachtwanderung	
against [ə'genst]	gegen	It was *against* the rules.
to **be asleep** [ˌbi ə'sli:p]	schlafen	*to be asleep* = to sleep
to **tiptoe** ['tɪptəʊ]	auf Zehenspitzen gehen	They *tiptoed* back to their rooms.
cloudy ['klaʊdi]	bedeckt; bewölkt	On a *cloudy* night you can't see the stars.
battery ['bætri]	Batterie; Akku	*Fr.* batterie *(f)*
no idea [ˌnəʊ‿aɪ'dɪə]	keine Ahnung	Which is the right way? – I have *no idea*!
locked [lɒkt]	abgeschlossen	*locked* ↔ open
trouble ['trʌbl]	Ärger; Probleme; Schwierigkeiten	We didn't want *trouble* with our teacher.
secret ['si:krət]	Geheimnis	Don't tell the others, it's a *secret*. *Fr.* secret *(m)*

	memory ['memri]	Erinnerung; Gedächtnis	We all have great *memories* of our school trip. ***Lat.*** memoria *(f)*
4	**travel report** [ˌtrævl rɪ'pɔ:t]	Reisebericht	Do you like Dave's *travel report* about the class trip?
	words that … [wɜ:dz 'ðæt]	Wörter, die …	

Skills: How to use a dictionary

1	**electronic** [ˌelek'trɒnɪk]	elektronisch	Do you use an *electronic* dictionary?
	search [sɜ:tʃ]	Suche; Such-	Write the word in the *search* box.
	meaning ['mi:nɪŋ]	Bedeutung; Sinn	What's the *meaning* of 'to describe'?

Unit task: Our travel report

	spaceship ['speɪsʃɪp]	Raumschiff	In science fiction stories there are often *spaceships*.
	topic ['tɒpɪk]	Thema	This story is connected with the *topic* of my presentation.
	beginning [bɪ'gɪnɪŋ]	Anfang; Beginn	*beginning* ↔ end

Action UK! The new boy

1	to **sneak around** [ˌsni:k‿ə'raʊnd]	herumschleichen	
	lemon ['lemən]	Zitrone	
	surprising [sə'praɪzɪŋ]	überraschend	*surprising* → surprise
2	**filmmaker** ['fɪlmˌmeɪkə]	Filmemacher/-in	A *filmmaker* makes films.
	mood [mu:d]	Stimmung; Laune	Can you describe the *mood* in that scene?
	unfriendly [ʌn'frendli]	unfreundlich	*unfriendly* ↔ friendly
	hurt [hɜ:t]	verletzt	He made some really unfriendly comments and now I feel *hurt*.
	aggressive [ə'gresɪv]	aggressiv	! Achtung Aussprache. ***Fr.*** agressif/agressive
	scary ['skeəri]	unheimlich; gruselig; beängstigend	*scary* → to be scared

Across cultures 2 London: A special city

	huge [hju:dʒ]	riesig; riesengroß; gewaltig	Berlin is a big city. London is a *huge* city.
	capital ['kæpɪtl]	Hauptstadt	London is the *capital* of England. ***Lat.*** capitalis
1	**fact** [fækt]	Fakt; Tatsache	***Lat.*** factum *(nt)*
	multi-ethnic [ˌmʌlti'eθnɪk]	Vielvölker-; international	London is a *multi-ethnic* city.

	sight [saɪt]	Sehenswürdigkeit; Anblick	A *sight* is an interesting thing to see in a city.
	space [speɪs]	Raum; Fläche; Platz; Ort	Please leave some *space* for my picture on the wall.
	underground ['ʌndəgraʊnd]	U-Bahn	Let's go by *underground*.
	the **Tube** [ðə 'tju:b]	die Londoner U-Bahn	Another name for the London underground is *the Tube*.
	carnival ['kɑ:nɪvl]	Karneval	What costume do you want to wear at the *carnival*?
	originally [ə'rɪdʒnli]	ursprünglich	Luke's mother is *originally* from Poland.
	Roman ['rəʊmən]	Römer/-in; römisch	London was originally a *Roman* town. ***Lat.*** Romanus/-a/-um
	airport ['eəpɔ:t]	Flughafen	London has got five *airports*. ***Fr.*** aéroport *(m)*
	million ['mɪljən]	Million	1,000,000
	large [lɑ:dʒ]	groß; riesig	London is the *largest* city in Europe.
	bell [bel]	Glocke	
2	**guard** [gɑ:d]	Wache; Wächter/-in	There are always *guards* in front of Buckingham Palace.
	queen [kwi:n]	Königin	Elizabeth II is the *Queen* of England.
	identity [aɪ'dentəti]	Identität	***Fr.*** identité *(f)*

Unit 2 London is amazing!

Check-in

	to **get around** [ˌget‿ə'raʊnd]	*hier:* sich fortbewegen	What's the best way to *get around* London? – By Tube.
	public transport *(no pl)* [ˌpʌblɪk 'trænspɔ:t]	öffentliche Verkehrsmittel	*public transport* = the Underground, buses, trains
	flair [fleə]	Flair; Atmosphäre	Brick Lane has a multi-ethnic *flair*.
	wax figure ['wæks ˌfɪgə]	Wachsfigur	At Madame Tussauds you can see *wax figures* of famous people.
2	to **be interested in** [bi‿'ɪntrəstɪd‿ɪn]	interessiert sein an; sich interessieren für	*Are* you *interested in* history?
3	things that … [θɪŋz 'ðæt]	Dinge, die …	

Station 1: It's going to be fun

to **stay with** ['steɪ wɪð]	wohnen bei	Amir is *staying with* the Azads.
this afternoon [ðɪs 'ɑ:ftənu:n]	heute Nachmittag	yesterday afternoon – *this afternoon* – tomorrow afternoon
18-year-old [ˌeɪti:n 'jɪər‿əʊld]	18-jährig	My sister is 18. I've got an *18-year-old* sister.
to **persuade** [pə'sweɪd]	überreden	Jay wants to *persuade* his brother to come with them. ***Lat.*** persuadēre
probably ['prɒbəbli]	möglicherweise; wahrscheinlich	

1	to **travel** ['trævl]	fahren; reisen	This year I'd like to *travel* to England.
	smartcard ['smɑ:tkɑ:d]	Chipkarte	
	to **top up** [tɒp‿'ʌp]	aufladen	Jay *topped up* his Oyster card yesterday. Now he must *top up* his phone too.
	credit ['kredɪt]	Guthaben	I must top up my phone. There's no *credit* on it.
4	**wheelchair** ['wi:ltʃeə]	Rollstuhl	 *wheelchair* → chair
5	**zoo** [zu:]	Zoo; Tierpark	There are lots of animals in a *zoo*.
	musician [mju:'zɪʃn]	Musiker/-in	*musician* → music *Fr.* musicien *(m)*/musicienne *(f)*
6	to **change (onto)** [tʃeɪndʒ ('ɒntʊ)]	umsteigen (in)	To get to Buckingham Palace from here, you *change onto* the Victoria line.
	north [nɔ:θ]	Norden; Nord-	
	south [saʊθ]	Süden; Süd-	
	stop [stɒp]	Haltestelle; Halt	The next *stop* is Elephant & Castle. *stop* → to stop
	to **get off, got off (a bus/ train)** [ˌget‿'ɒf; ˌgɒt‿'ɒf]	aussteigen (aus einem Bus/ Zug)	Let's *get off* the Underground and take the bus.

Station 2: Good idea!

to **deal, dealt (with)** [di:l; delt (wɪð)]	sich befassen (mit); umgehen (mit)	We've got a problem so let's *deal with* it.
a while [ə 'waɪl]	eine Weile	*a while* = a little time
to **mean, meant** [mi:n; ment]	meinen; bedeuten	You think the new boy is strange? What do you *mean*? I think he's nice.
girlfriend ['gɜ:lfrend]	Freundin *(in einer Paarbeziehung)*	Shahid has a *girlfriend*.
souvenir [ˌsu:vn'ɪə]	Souvenir; Andenken	I'd like to buy a *souvenir* of London.
anywhere ['eniweə]	irgendwo; überall (egal, wo)	Are there any souvenir shops *anywhere*?
everybody ['evribɒdi]	jeder; alle	all the people
... where to go. [ˌweə tə 'gəʊ]	... wohin ich gehen kann.	I don't know *where to go*.
to **follow** ['fɒləʊ]	folgen; hinterhergehen; befolgen	The bird is *following* the man. 

	corner ['kɔ:nə]	Ecke	Most rooms have four *corners*.
	I bet [aɪ 'bet]	ich wette	
	to **beat, beat** [bi:t; bi:t]	schlagen; besiegen	I bet nobody can *beat* Arsenal this year!
	nobody ['nəʊbədi]	niemand	*nobody* ↔ somebody
	one *(sg)*/**ones** *(pl)* [wʌn/wʌnz]	eine/-r/-s	Wenn du im Englischen ein Nomen nicht wiederholen möchtest, kannst du es durch *one*/*ones* ersetzen: This sandwich is big, that *one* is bigger.
11	**pro** [prəʊ]	Argument dafür	*Lat.* pro
	good for someone who … [ˌgʊd‿fə ˌsʌmwʌn 'hu:]	gut für jemanden, der …	
	con [kɒn]	Argument dagegen	*Lat.* contra
	far [fɑ:]	weit	Is Big Ben *far* from Buckingham Palace?

Station 3: They can bite very hard

to **bite, bit** [baɪt; bɪt]	beißen	Does your dog *bite*? It looks a bit scary!
tour [tʊə]	Tour; Fahrt; Rundgang	
guide [gaɪd]	Führer/-in; Reiseführer	A *guide* gives you information (e.g. about a city or a museum). *Fr.* guide *(m) (f)*
to **build, built** [bɪld; bɪlt]	bauen	We *built* a new house last year.
to **become, became** [bɪ'kʌm, bɪ'keɪm]	werden	William the Conqueror *became* king of England in 1066.
castle ['kɑ:sl]	Schloss; Burg	! Das „t“ in *castle* wird nicht gesprochen.
prison ['prɪzn]	Gefängnis	*Fr.* prison *(f)*
lion [laɪən]	Löwe	 *Fr.* lion *(m)*
bear [beə]	Bär	
crown jewels [ˌkraʊn 'dʒu:əlz]	Kronjuwelen	The Tower is a museum where you can see the *Crown Jewels*.
Beefeater ['bi:fˌi:tə]	königlicher Leibgardist	
raven ['reɪvn]	Rabe	
raven master ['reɪvn ˌmɑ:stə]	Herr der Raben	The *raven master* looks after the ravens in the Tower.
careful ['keəfl]	vorsichtig; sorgfältig	
safe [seɪf]	sicher; ungefährlich	*safe* ↔ dangerous
close [kləʊs]	nahe	Don't go too *close* to the ravens.

Describing people, things and actions

I find it **hard** to play tennis.	In tennis, you must hit the ball **hard**.
We're **good** friends.	We know each other **well**.
The bus is **slow**.	It's going **slowly**.
It's a **clear** view.	You can see the hills **clearly**.
The Tower is a **special** sight.	People come **specially** to see the Crown Jewels.
He's a **careful** driver.	He drives **carefully**.
She's a **happy** student.	She always does her homework **happily**.
Don't worry. This place is **safe**.	You can stay here **safely**.
You're so **nervous**.	Why are you jumping back **nervously**?
A library is a **quiet** place.	We have to talk **quietly** there.
It's too **loud** here.	The fans are clapping their hands **loudly**.
Football players are **fast** runners.	They run very **fast**.
These fans are **aggressive**.	They're shouting **aggressively**.

13	**audio tour** ['ɔːdiəʊ ˌtʊə]	Audioführung	! Achtung Aussprache. *Fr.* audio-; *Lat.* audire
	treasure ['treʒə]	Schatz	Just look and you can find real *treasures* in the Thames.
	ghost [gəʊst]	Geist; Gespenst	Sometimes there are stories of *ghosts* in old houses. 
14	to **jump back** [ˌdʒʌmp‿'bæk]	zurückspringen; *hier:* zurückschrecken	My mum *jumps back* when she sees a mouse.
	could [kʊd]	könnte/-n	
15	**one day** [wʌn 'deɪ]	eines Tages	Jay wants to be a famous singer *one day*.

Action UK! A day out in London

	a day out in ... [ə ˌdeɪ‿'aʊt ɪn]	ein Tag in ...	What would you like to do on *a day out in* London?
2	**out and about** [ˌaʊt‿ən‿ə'baʊt]	unterwegs	
3	**adult** ['ædʌlt]	Erwachsene/-r	*adult* ↔ child
	sightseeing ['saɪtsiːɪŋ]	Sightseeing-; Besichtigungs-	
	normal ['nɔːml]	normal	Is it better to take the sightseeing bus or the *normal* one?
4	**choice** [tʃɔɪs]	Wahl; Auswahl	*choice* → to choose *Fr.* choix *(f)*
	location [ləʊ'keɪʃn]	Handlungsort; Lage; Standort	The *location* of the film is a famous street in London. *Lat.* locus *(m)*
	crowd [kraʊd]	Menschenmenge	A lot of people all together in one place.
	view [vjuː]	Aussicht; Sicht; Ausblick; Blick	The house has a fantastic *view* of the Thames.

Out and about in the city

to **take** the bus / the Underground	den Bus / die U-Bahn nehmen
to **go for a walk** in the streets / in a park / along the river	in den Straßen / im Park / am Fluss entlang spazieren gehen
to **sit** in a café / restaurant	in einem Café / Restaurant sitzen
to **have** lunch / dinner	zu Mittag / zu Abend essen
to **go** shopping / to the cinema	einkaufen / ins Kino gehen
to **visit** a sight / a tourist attraction / a museum / a historical building / the zoo	eine Sehenswürdigkeit / eine Touristenattraktion / ein Museum / ein historisches Gebäude / den Zoo besichtigen; besuchen
to **see** famous people / the sights / lots of interesting things	berühmte Leute / die Sehenswürdigkeiten / viele interessante Dinge sehen
to **listen** to street musicians / an audio tour	Straßenmusikern / einer Audioguide-Führung zuhören
to **watch** a football game / a street show	ein Fußballspiel / eine Straßenshow ansehen

What would you like to do in London?

Skills: How to find information on the internet

1	**attraction** [ə'trækʃn]	Attraktion; Sehenswürdigkeit	The London Eye is one of the city's most popular *attractions*.
	basic ['beɪsɪk]	grundlegend; Grund-	In the first two years of English you learn a lot of *basic* words.
	display [dɪ'spleɪ]	Ausstellung	The Natural History Museum has a great *display* with strange animals at the moment.
	news *(sg)* [nju:z]	Nachricht(en); Neuigkeit(en)	! That's good *news*. = Das ist eine gute Nachricht.
2	**life, lives** *(pl)* [laɪf, laɪvz]	Leben	*life* → to live
	earth [ɜ:θ]	Erdboden; Erde; die Erde	
	dinosaur ['daɪnəsɔ:]	Dinosaurier	

Unit task: Our London tour

on foot [ɒn ˈfʊt]	zu Fuß	! by car/train/bus, **but:** *on foot*
distance [ˈdɪstns]	Distanz; Entfernung	What's the *distance* from here to there? *Fr.* distance *(f)*
realistic [ˌrɪəˈlɪstɪk]	realistisch	Are your plans *realistic*?
material [məˈtɪəriəl]	Material	

Story: I'm a mudlark

mudlark [ˈmʌdlɑːk]	*jemand, der im Schlamm nach Sachen sucht, die er dann verkaufen kann*	
high tide [ˈhaɪ ˌtaɪd]	Flut	
low tide [ˈləʊ ˌtaɪd]	Ebbe	The River Thames has two faces – one at high tide, one at *low tide*.
to **flow out** [fləʊ‿ˈaʊt]	hinausfließen	Rivers *flow out* into the sea.
towards [təˈwɔːdz]	in Richtung; auf … zu; darauf zu	Look, that man is coming *towards* us.
central [ˈsentrl]	zentral; Zentral-	*central* → centre ***Lat.*** centrum *(nt)*
heart [hɑːt]	Herz; *hier:* Zentrum	the *heart* of London = the centre of London
metre [ˈmiːtə]	Meter	
muddy [ˈmʌdi]	schlammig	
bank [bæŋk]	Ufer	A river has two *banks*.
wobbly [ˈwɒbli]	wackelig	
bridge [brɪdʒ]	Brücke	A *bridge* goes over a river. 
they were enjoying [ˌðei wər‿ɪnˈdʒɔɪɪŋ]	sie genossen gerade	
silver [ˈsɪlvə]	Silber	
to **try on** [traɪ‿ˈɒn]	anprobieren	That's a nice T-shirt. Why don't you *try* it *on*, Olivia?
quickly [ˈkwɪkli]	schnell	He was scared. He ran away *quickly*.
to **grab** [græb]	greifen; ergreifen; schnappen	Holly *grabbed* her bag and left the house quickly.
wrist [rɪst]	Handgelenk	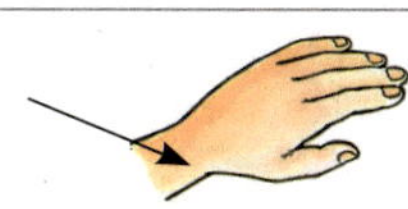
to **drop** [drɒp]	fallen (lassen)	Jay *dropped* Amir's bracelet.
to **roll off** [rəʊl]	hinunterrollen; herunterrollen	The bracelet *rolled* off the bridge.
angrily [ˈæŋgrɪli]	verärgert; zornig; wütend	

It's gone. [ɪts 'gɒn]	Es ist weg.	
down [daʊn]	nach unten; herunter; hinunter	They looked *down* from the bridge.
to **be lucky** [bi‿'lʌki]	Glück haben	*I'm lucky.* = Ich habe Glück. I'm happy. = Ich bin glücklich.
mud [mʌd]	Schlamm	*mud* → muddy → mudlark
shore [ʃɔ:]	Ufer; Küste	*shore* = bank
wet [wet]	nass	
they weren't wearing [ˌðei wɜ:nt 'weərɪŋ]	sie trugen nicht	
bucket ['bʌkɪt]	Eimer	
trowel ['traʊəl]	kleiner Spaten	
a trowel which … [ə ˌtraʊəl 'wɪtʃ]	ein Spaten, der …	
politely [pə'laɪtli]	höflich	
century ['senʃri]	Jahrhundert	We live in the 21st *century*.
anyway ['eniweɪ]	trotzdem; jedenfalls; sowieso	
dirty ['dɜ:ti]	dreckig; schmutzig	I can't wear this T-shirt because it's *dirty*.
dead [ded]	tot	
to **wash up** [ˌwɒʃ‿'ʌp]	angespült werden	Dead animals *washed up* on the river banks.
all the time [ˌɔ:l ðə 'taɪm]	die ganze Zeit	I use my phone almost *all the time*.
human body [ˌhju:mən 'bɒdi]	menschlicher Körper	
clay pipe ['kleɪ paɪp]	Tonpfeife	
at first [ət 'fɜ:st]	zuerst; zunächst	*At first* Luke didn't like Jay very much, but then they became good friends.
to **notice** ['nəʊtɪs]	bemerken; wahrnehmen	Did you *notice* anything strange about the woman?
more easily [mɔ:r‿'i:zɪli]	leichter	
key [ki:]	Schlüssel	
to **scream** [skri:m]	schreien; kreischen	Holly *screamed* because she found something awful.
coconut ['kəʊkənʌt]	Kokosnuss	
to **cut, cut (off)** [kʌt; kʌt (ɒf)]	schneiden; abschneiden	
dramatic [drə'mætɪk]	dramatisch	*dramatic* → drama ***Fr.*** dramatique
hour [aʊə]	Stunde	There are 24 *hours* in a day. ***Lat.*** hora *(f)*
side [saɪd]	Seite	
to **be surprised** [bi sə'praɪzd]	überrascht sein	They *were surprised* about all the 'treasure' in the mud!

	idiot ['ɪdiət]	Idiot/-in	! Achtung Betonung.
2	**modern** ['mɒdn]	modern	Smartphones are *modern* technology. *Fr.* moderne

Water words

sea – river – lake	Meer – Fluss – See
high tide – low tide – wave	Flut – Ebbe – Welle
to flow out – to flow towards ... – to wash up	hinausfließen – in Richtung ... fließen – anspülen
bank – shore	Ufer
bridge	Brücke
mud – muddy – wet	Schlamm – schlammig – nass
ship – boat	Schiff – Boot

Unit 3 Sport is good for you!

Check-in

	experience [ɪk'spɪəriəns]	Erfahrung	What interesting *experiences* can you tell us about?
	things which ... [θɪŋz 'wɪtʃ]	Dinge, die ...	
	health [helθ]	Gesundheit	*health* → healthy
	accident ['æksɪdnt]	Unfall	My sister had a bike *accident*. *Fr.* accident *(m)*
	camel racing ['kæml ˌreɪsɪŋ]	Kamelrennen	Is *camel racing* really a sport?
	marathon ['mærəθn]	Marathon	
1	**radio** ['reɪdiəʊ]	Radio	! Achtung Aussprache. *Fr.* radio *(f)*
	programme ['prəʊgræm]	Programm; Sendung	There's an interesting *programme* about camel racing on TV now. *Fr.* programme *(m)*
	runner ['rʌnə]	Läufer/-in	*runner* → to run
	race [reɪs]	Wettlauf; Rennen	Can we watch the bike *race* on TV, Mum?
	net [net]	Netz	For tennis, you need a *net*. 
	to **lose, lost, lost** [lu:z; lɒst; lɒst]	verlieren	Our team *lost* again!

	match [mætʃ]	Spiel; Match	a game (of football/…)
	racquet ['rækɪt]	Schläger	
	court [kɔ:t]	Spielfeld	! a tennis *court* – a football field
	to **pass** [pɑ:s]	zupassen; zuspielen	
	to **kick** [kɪk]	schießen; treten	'Pass' means to throw or *kick* the ball to another player in the same team.
	stadium ['steɪdiəm]	Stadion	
	score [skɔ:]	Punktestand; Spielstand	At the end of the match the *score* was 2-2.
	point [pɔɪnt]	Punkt	That's right. One *point* for your team.
	to **catch, caught, caught** [kætʃ; kɔ:t; kɔ:t]	fangen	*to catch* a ball ↔ to throw a ball
	pitch [pɪtʃ]	Spielfeld; Platz	You play rugby on a *pitch*.
2	**the … the** [ðə … ðə]	je … desto	*The* quicker you are with your homework, *the* earlier you can meet your friends.
4	**equipment** [ɪ'kwɪpmənt]	Ausstattung; Ausrüstung	*equipment* = things you need for sports activities
	individual [ˌɪndɪ'vɪdʒuəl]	individuell; einzeln	Do you do an *individual* sport or a team sport? *Lat.* individuus/-a/-um

Station 1: Have you ever run in a marathon?

	ever ['evə]	jemals	It was our funniest project *ever*!
	right here [ˌraɪt 'hɪə]	genau hier	The marathon starts *right here*.
	until [ʌn'tɪl]	bis; erst wenn	You can't run in a marathon *until* you're 18.
	11-year-old [ɪˌlevn'jɪərəʊld]	11-Jährige/-r	The mini marathon is for *11-* to *18-year-olds*.
	running ['rʌnɪŋ]	Laufen; Rennen	Gwen loves *running*.
	trial [traɪəl]	Qualifikation	There are *trials* in sports to find the best runners or players.
	Who's in? [hu:z‿'ɪn]	Wer macht mit?; Wer ist dabei?	
	to **be in** [bi‿'ɪn]	dabei sein; mitmachen	Are you going to run? Well, I'*m in*, and I hope you are too!
	run [rʌn]	Rennen; Lauf	*a run* → to run → runner
	to **look out** [ˌlʊk‿'aʊt]	aufpassen	*Look out*, everyone! I'm going to win this race!
1	**area** ['eəriə]	Areal; Gebiet; Fläche	What sports events are there in your *area*?
2	**before** [bɪ'fɔ:]	schon einmal; vorher; zuvor	Have you been here *before*? Or is this your first trip?
4	**arm** [ɑ:m]	Arm	
	leg [leg]	Bein	

Parts of the body

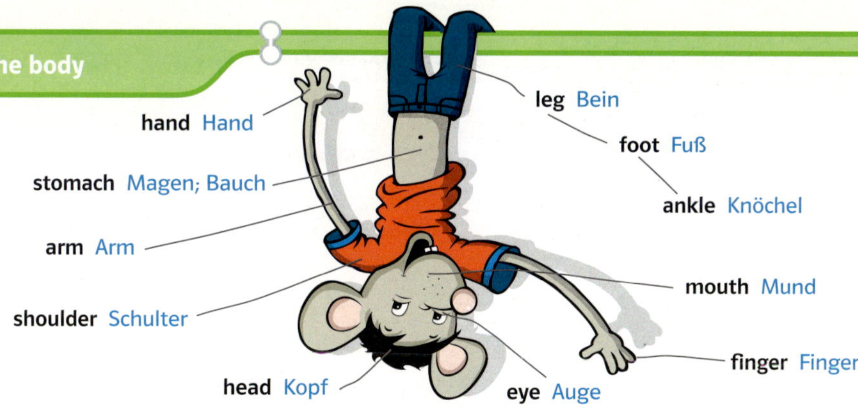

Read the English words to your partner in a different order. Can he/she point to the right part of his/her body?

Station 2: Have you been to the doctor's yet?

	doctor ['dɒktə]	Arzt/Ärztin	! Beachte den Unterschied: Have you seen the *doctor* yet? Have you been to the *doctor's* yet? *doctor's* ist die Abkürzung für *doctor's surgery*. *Fr.* docteur *(m)* 
	yet [jet]	schon; noch	Have you asked your parents about the party *yet*?
	to **leave, left, left** [li:v; left; left]	(los)gehen; abfahren; (ver)lassen	Have you *left* the house yet? – No, I'm still at home.
	not ... yet [nɒt 'jet]	noch nicht	The friends have*n't* left for the marathon *yet*.
	to **train** [treɪn]	trainieren	Luke plays football. He *trains* every day.
	to **hurt, hurt, hurt** [hɜ:t; hɜ:t; hɜ:t]	verletzen; weh tun	I *hurt* my leg last month, and it still *hurts* now.
	to **twist your ankle** [ˌtwɪst jɔ:r‿'æŋkl]	sich den Knöchel verrenken	
	pain [peɪn]	Schmerz	I've got a really bad *pain* in my left foot.
	unfair [ʌn'feə]	unfair	*unfair* ↔ fair
	Bye! [baɪ]	Tschüss!	*bye* ↔ hello
6	**mile** [maɪl]	Meile *(brit. Längenmaß)*	1 *mile* = 1,609 metres
	chant [tʃɑ:nt]	Sprechgesang	*Lat.* cantare
	to **cheer** [tʃɪə]	anfeuern; jubeln; zujubeln	Jay is writing a chant to *cheer* the runners in the marathon.
7	to **fall off, fell off, fallen off** [ˌfɔ:l‿'ɒf; ˌfel‿'ɒf; ˌfɔ:lən‿'ɒf]	herunterfallen; hinunterfallen	I *fell off* my bike and hurt my knee.
8	to **have a look (at)** [ˌhæv‿ə 'lʊk]	anschauen	Let's *have a look* at it. = Let's look at it.
	shouldn't ['ʃʊdnt]	sollte(n) nicht	Olivia *shouldn't* run in the marathon with ankle problems.
	prescription [prɪ'skrɪpʃn]	Rezept *(für Arzneimittel)*	*Lat.* praescribere

ointment [ˈɔɪntmənt]	Salbe	The doctor gave Olivia a prescription for an *ointment*.
shoulder [ˈʃəʊldə]	Schulter	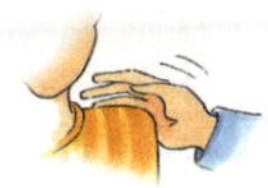
headache *(no pl)* [ˈhedeɪk]	Kopfschmerzen; Kopfweh	! *headache* steht immer im Singular: I've got a bad *headache*. *headache* → head
backache [ˈbækeɪk]	Rückenschmerzen; Rückenweh	
stomachache [ˈstʌməkeɪk]	Bauchschmerzen; Bauchweh	
to **feel sick** [ˌfiːl ˈsɪk]	Übelkeit verspüren; sich schlecht fühlen	I *feel sick*. = Mir ist schlecht/übel.
cold [kəʊld]	Erkältung	
cough [kɒf]	Husten	
fever [ˈfiːvə]	Fieber	People with a cold often have a cough and a *fever*. *Fr.* fièvre *(f)*
pill [pɪl]	Pille; Tablette	The doctor wrote a prescription for some *pills*.
9 **introduction** [ˌɪntrəˈdʌkʃn]	Einführung; Einleitung; Vorstellung	the *introduction* of a report = the first part of a report

Health

to **have an accident**	einen Unfall haben
to **call the emergency service**	den Rettungsdienst rufen
to **hurt your foot / arm / leg / …**	sich den Fuß / Arm / das Bein / … verletzen
to **twist your ankle**	sich den Knöchel verrenken
to **feel a pain in …**	Schmerzen haben in / an …
to **get a prescription**	ein Rezept bekommen
to **put ointment on …**	… einsalben
to **take pills**	Tabletten nehmen
to **have a headache / backache / stomachache**	Kopfweh / Rückenweh / Bauchweh haben
to **feel bad / sick**	sich schlecht / krank fühlen
to **catch a cold / cough / fever**	eine Erkältung / Husten / Fieber bekommen

With a partner, make more doctor dialogues as on p. 73.

Action UK! A picnic in the park

1	**so far** [ˌsəʊ ˈfɑː]	bis jetzt	The players have given the people a great show *so far*.
	attic [ˈætɪk]	Dachboden	
	Korean [kəˈriːən]	koreanisch; Koreanisch; Koreaner/-in	There was *Korean* food at the picnic.
2	to **fake** [feɪk]	vortäuschen; fälschen	
	injury [ˈɪndʒəri]	Verletzung	Who faked an *injury* in the film?
	to **teach somebody a lesson** [ˌtiːtʃ‿ə ˈlesn]	jmdm. eine Lehre/Lektion erteilen	That wasn't a nice thing to do. Let's *teach him a lesson*.
	to **teach, taught, taught** [tiːtʃ; tɔːt; tɔːt]	unterrichten; lehren; beibringen	*to teach* → teacher
	to **deserve** [dɪˈzɜːv]	verdienen	The others are angry with you, but you *deserved* it. You tricked them!
	point of view [ˌpɔɪnt‿əv ˈvjuː]	Standpunkt; Ansicht; Perspektive	Who's right and who's wrong from your *point of view*?
	to **get away with** [ˌget‿əˈweɪ wɪð]	davonkommen mit	Marley didn't *get away with* it.

Skills: How to understand news reports and take notes

1	**rescue** [ˈreskjuː]	Rettung	Here is a report about a *rescue* in the mountains.
	difficult [ˈdɪfɪklt]	schwierig	*difficult* ↔ easy *Fr.* difficil/-e; ***Lat.*** difficilis/-e
	witness [ˈwɪtnəs]	Zeuge/Zeugin	The police is looking for *witnesses* for the accident.
2	**eyewitness** [ˈaɪwɪtnəs]	Augenzeuge/Augenzeugin	The reporter is talking to an *eyewitness* in front of the camera.
	station [ˈsteɪʃn]	Sender	What's your favourite radio *station*?
	listener [ˈlɪsənə]	Zuhörer/-in	*listener* → to listen
	to **receive** [rɪˈsiːv]	empfangen; erhalten; bekommen	A formal word for 'to get'. *Fr.* recevoir; ***Lat.*** recipere
	scene [siːn]	Schauplatz	The reporter tried to get to the *scene* of the accident.
	anyone else [ˌeniwʌn ˈels]	irgendjemand; jemand anderes	Don't tell the story to *anyone else*.
	I couldn't believe my eyes. [aɪ ˌkʊdnt bɪˌliːv maɪ‿ˈaɪz]	Ich traute meinen Augen nicht.	*I couldn't believe my eyes* when I got a dog for my birthday.

Unit task: The aliens have landed!

to **land** [lænd]	landen	Do you believe that aliens have ever *landed* on Earth?
to **record** [rɪˈkɔːd]	aufnehmen; aufzeichnen	Let's *record* the scene with a camera.
assistant [əˈsɪstnt]	Assistent/-in; Verkäufer/-in	! Achtung Schreibung und Aussprache.

hospital ['hɒspɪtl]	Krankenhaus; Hospital	*Fr.* hôpital *(m)*
as [æz; əz]	als	
to **end** [end]	enden; beenden	*to end* ↔ to start *to end* → end
over ['əʊvə]	vorüber; vorbei	School is *over* at 3:15.

Story: Hey, don't call me silly!

almost ['ɔ:lməʊst]	fast; beinahe	It's *almost* 8 o'clock! You're late for school.
to **let go (of)** [ˌlet 'gəʊ (əv)]	loslassen	Don't *let go of* my hand, Gwen!
I'm the one who … [ˌaɪm ðə‿wʌn 'hu:]	ich bin diejenige, die …	
silly ['sɪli]	Dummkopf	
fancy dress ['fænsi dres]	Verkleidung; Kostüm	
to **breathe** [bri:ð]	atmen	
to **keep up, kept, up, kept up (with)** [ˌki:p‿'ʌp; ˌkept‿'ʌp; ˌkept‿'ʌp (wɪð)]	mithalten (mit); Schritt halten (mit)	Can Luke *keep up with* Gwen? = Is Luke fast enough?
to **be worried** [bi 'wʌrid]	beunruhigt sein; besorgt sein	Don't *be worried* = Don't worry
to take sth seriously [ˌteɪk 'sɪəriəsli]	etw. ernst nehmen	If a situation is serious, you must *take it seriously*.
to **get in the way** [ˌget‿ɪn ðə 'weɪ]	stören; im Weg stehen	The people in the costumes shouldn't *get in the way* of the runners.
stomach ['stʌmək]	Magen; Bauch	*Fr.* estomac *(m)* 
glasses *(pl)* ['glɑ:sɪz]	Brille	! *glasses* steht immer im Plural: My *glasses* are broken. I need new ones.
finish line ['fɪnɪʃ ˌlaɪn]	Ziellinie	At the end of a run there's always a *finish line*.
stupid ['stju:pɪd]	dumm; blöd	The *stupid* cat and dog almost ruined the race for Gwen and Luke.
cramp [kræmp]	Krampf	
to **be gone** [bi: 'gɒn]	verschwunden sein; weg sein	Near the end of the race, Gwen's cramp *was gone*.
We did it! [ˌwi: 'dɪd‿ɪt]	Wir haben es geschafft!	*Luke and Gwen did it!*
both [bəʊθ]	beide	Luke and Gwen *both* finished the race.
to **ruin** ['ru:ɪn]	ruinieren; zerstören	Jay and Dave almost *ruined* the race for Luke and Gwen.
official [ə'fɪʃl]	Schiedsrichter/-in	In a race there are always *officials*.

	finally ['faɪnli]	schließlich; endlich; zum Schluss; letztlich	first – then – *finally* ***Lat.*** finis *(m)*
	to **surprise** [sə'praɪz]	überraschen	*to surprise* → surprise
	in secret [ɪn 'si:krət]	heimlich	Jay and Dave trained *in secret*. No one knew about it. *in secret* → a secret
	because of [bɪ'kɒz‿əv]	wegen	My feet really hurt *because of* my new shoes.
	to **forgive, forgave, forgiven** [fə'gɪv; fə'geɪv; fə'gɪvn]	vergeben; verzeihen	Can Gwen *forgive* them?
1	**reason** ['ri:zn]	Grund	Why did you do it? What was the *reason*? ***Fr.*** raison *(f)*
	to **cause** [kɔ:z]	verursachen	What or who *caused* the accident?
	hope [həʊp]	Hoffnung	*hope* → to hope
	fear [fɪə]	Angst; Furcht; Befürchtung	The feeling you have when you are scared.
	relationship [rɪ'leɪʃnʃɪp]	Beziehung	Is the *relationship* between you and your neighbours a good one?
2	**positive** ['pɒzətɪv]	positiv	***Fr.*** positive/positive
	negative ['negətɪv]	negativ; verneint	*negative* ↔ positive
	On the one hand ..., (but) on the other hand ... [ɒn ðə‿'wʌn ˌhænd ... (bʌt) ɒn ði‿'ʌðə ˌhænd ...]	Einerseits ..., (aber) andererseits ...	*On the one hand* he'd like to be a better runner, *but on the other hand* he doesn't want to train very hard.
4	the boy who ... [ðə bɔi 'hu:]	der Junge, der ...	

Positive and negative words

	+	–
What you think of something:	easy, good, great, interesting, useful; amazing, fantastic, perfect	bad, boring, dangerous, difficult; awful, scary
What you think of a person:	creative, cute, fair, friendly, fun, funny, good, polite, popular	aggressive, boring, rude, silly, stupid, unfair, unfriendly
How a person feels:	confident, good, happy, lucky	bad, embarrassed, lonely, sad, shy, unhappy, unlucky

Which of the words are opposites? Write them down together.

Check-out

3	**player** ['pleɪə]	Spieler/-in; Mitspieler/-in	*player* → to play

Across cultures 3 English around the world

1	**member** ['membə]	Mitglied	Dave is a *member* of the Preston family. ***Fr.*** membre *(m)*
	summer camp ['sʌmə kæmp]	Sommerferienlager	I only spoke English when I was at *summer camp* last year.
2	to **mention** ['menʃn]	erwähnen	Did I *mention* that I have a cool new phone? ***Fr.*** mentionner
	statement ['steɪtmənt]	Aussage; Behauptung; Erklärung	to make a *statement* = to say something
	exactly [ɪg'zæktli]	genau	I don't understand. What *exactly* do you mean? ***Lat.*** exactus/-a/-um
	South Korean [ˌsaʊθ kə'riːən]	Südkoreaner/-in; südkoreanisch; Südkoreanisch	
	Romanian [rʊ'meɪniən]	Rumäne/Rumänin; rumänisch; Rumänisch	
3	**first language** [ˌfɜːst 'læŋgwɪdʒ]	Muttersprache	My *first language* is German.
	official language [əˌfɪʃl 'læŋgwɪdʒ]	Amtssprache	In India, English is an *official language*.
	merchant ['mɜːtʃənt]	Kaufmann, Händler	A *merchant* sells and buys things.
	to **cross** [krɒs]	überqueren; kreuzen	You need to *cross* the street to get to the shoe shop.
	colony ['kɒləni]	Kolonie	Many years ago, Germany had *colonies* too. ***Fr.*** colonie *(f)*; ***Lat.*** colonia *(f)*
	for example [fər‿ɪg'zɑːmpl]	zum Beispiel	I speak four languages, *for example* English and French.
	head of state [ˌhed‿əv 'steɪt]	Staatsoberhaupt	The British queen is *head of state* in Australia.
	superpower ['suːpəˌpaʊə]	Supermacht	Will China and India be the next *superpowers*?
	to **influence** ['ɪnfluəns]	beeinflussen	The USA has *influenced* the world in different ways. ! Im Englischen verwendet man für „USA" immer die Einzahl (The USA has …), im Deutschen aber die Mehrzahl (Die USA haben …).
	technology [tek'nɒlədʒi]	Technologie	
	to **communicate** [kə'mjuːnɪkeɪt]	kommunizieren; sich verständigen	An easy way to *communicate* with people is to speak to them. ***Lat.*** communicare
4	**region** ['riːdʒn]	Region; Gegend	What *region* in Germany do you come from? ***Lat.*** regio *(f)*
	expression [ɪk'spreʃn]	Ausdruck; Wendung; Äußerung	We often use English *expressions* in German. ***Lat.*** expressio *(f)*

Unit 4 Stay in touch

Check-in

to **stay in touch (with)** [ˌsteɪ ɪn ˈtʌtʃ (wɪð)]	in Kontakt bleiben (mit)	E-mails are a good way to *stay in touch* with your friends.
media [ˈmiːdiə]	Medien	Radio, TV and the internet are all *media*. ***Fr.*** médias *(f) (pl)*; ***Lat.*** medium *(nt)*
letter [ˈletə]	Brief	 ***Lat.*** littera *(f)*
interest [ˈɪntrəst]	Interesse	*interest* → interesting → be interested
paradise [ˈpærədaɪs]	Paradies	***Fr.*** paradis *(m)*
print [prɪnt]	gedruckt; Druck-	
for [fɔː; fə]	wegen	I buy print magazines *for* the posters.
social network [ˌsəʊʃl ˈnetwɜːk]	soziales Netzwerk	You can chat with all kinds of people in *social networks*.
nasty [ˈnɑːsti]	garstig; gemein	*nasty* ↔ nice
cyber bully [ˌsaɪbə ˈbʊli]	*jemand, der andere in sozialen Netzwerken belästigt oder mobbed*	*Cyber bullies* write nasty comments in social networks.
2 to **change** [tʃeɪndʒ]	wechseln; (sich) ändern	***Fr.*** changer
to **post** [pəʊst]	online stellen; posten	Have you *posted* the photos of the class trip?

Media collocations

to check	checken, überprüfen	my e-mails / my profile / my friend's profile	meine E-Mails / mein Profil / das Profil meines Freundes
to change	ändern	my profile	mein Profil
to post to share	posten; hochladen teilen	photos / information about …	Fotos / Informationen über …
to read / to write / to reply to	lesen / schreiben / antworten auf	texts / text messages / e-mails	SMS-Nachrichten / E-Mails
to send / to receive	senden / empfangen	texts / text messages / e-mails / photos / information	SMS-Nachrichten / E-Mails / Fotos / Informationen
to chat with to text to stay in touch with	chatten mit eine SMS schreiben in Kontakt bleiben mit	a friend	einem Freund
to join to take part in	beitreten teilnehmen an	a discussion / a social network / a forum	einer Diskussion / einem sozialen Netzwerk / einem Forum
to have to take part in	führen teilnehmen an	a discussion / a video chat	eine Diskussion / einen Videochat einer Diskussion / einem Videochat
to play	spielen	video games	Computerspiele

	to **take part (in)** [ˌteɪk ˈpɑːt (ɪn)]	teilnehmen (an)	Let's *take part in* the new Drama Club at school.
	to **text** [tekst]	eine SMS schicken	*to text* → text message
	discussion [dɪˈskʌʃn]	Diskussion	*discussion* → to discuss
3	**practical** [ˈpræktɪkl]	praktisch	Smartphones are *practical* to stay in touch with friends. ***Fr.*** pratique
	mobile [ˈməʊbaɪl]	Handy; Mobiltelefon	*mobile* = phone

Station 1: Dear Ruby

	agony aunt [ˈæɡəniˌɑːnt]	Kummerkastentante	Lauren didn't want to talk about her problem with her friends or her family. So she wrote a letter to her favourite magazine's *agony aunt*.
	teen [tiːn]	Jugend-	*teen* → teenager
	... what to do. [ˈwɒt tə duː]	... was ich tun soll.	I don't know *what to do*.
	fight [faɪt]	Kampf; Streit	
	to **spend, spent, spent** [spend; spent; spent]	verbringen *(Zeit)*	 She *spends* all her free time with her dog.
	the two of them [ðə ˈtuːˌəv ðəm]	beide	My brothers sent me a photo of *the two of them*.
	site [saɪt]	Webseite	
	to **act like** [ˈækt laɪk]	tun als ob	My sister often *acts like* a baby.
	whenever [wenˈevə]	wann immer; jedes Mal, wenn; so oft	*Whenever* I ask my brother for something, he says "no".
	upset [ʌpˈset]	aufgebracht; bestürzt	Why are you so *upset*? – My brother lost my phone!
	to **share** [ʃeə]	teilen	Can I have half of your sandwich? Can we *share* it?
	self-critical [ˈselfˌkrɪtɪkl]	selbstkritisch	The agony aunt's advice is to be *self-critical*. I think she's right.
	to **overreact** [ˌəʊvəriˈækt]	überreagieren	I know you're angry with him, but don't *overreact* and say bad things about him, OK?
	as soon as [əz ˈsuːnˌəz]	sobald	Things usually get better *as soon as* you talk to the person you're fighting with.
	to **make somebody do something** [meɪk]	jmdn. dazu bringen, etw. zu tun	My friend's texts *make* me *feel bad*.
1	**opinion** [əˈpɪnjən]	Meinung	In my *opinion* ... = I think ... ***Lat.*** opinio *(f)*
2	**face-to-face** [ˌfeɪstəˈfeɪs]	*hier:* persönlich; von Angesicht zu Angesicht	It's fun to meet people *face-to-face* and not just in social networks. 
	to **block** [blɒk]	blockieren; abblocken	You can *block* messages from people you don't like.

	forever [fə'revə]	für immer; ewig	When you post photos on the internet, they never go away. They can stay there *forever*.
	to **care (about)** ['keər‿əˌbaʊt]	wichtig nehmen; sich kümmern (um); sich interessieren (für)	If you *care about* something then it's important to you.
	attention [ə'tenʃn]	Aufmerksamkeit; Beachtung	***Fr.*** attention *(f)*; ***Lat.*** attentio *(f)*
	myself [maɪ'self]	ich/mir/mich (selbst); selber	*myself* → yourself → himself
4	**understanding** [ˌʌndə'stændɪŋ]	Verständnis	What can you say to show *understanding*?
	compromise ['kɒmprəmaɪz]	Kompromiss	It isn't always easy to find a *compromise*. ***Fr.*** compromis *(m)*
	to **worry** ['wʌri]	sich Sorgen machen	Don't *worry* about your friend. Everything is OK now.
5	to **mediate** ['mi:dieɪt]	vermitteln	to *mediate* → mediation
6	**friendship** ['frendʃɪp]	Freundschaft	I've got lots of friends. I think *friendship* is very important.

Station 2: Forum? What forum?

to **go over to** [ˌgəʊ 'əʊvə tə]	hinübergehen zu; zu jmdm. nach Hause gehen	Come on, let's *go over* to your house.
What on earth ...? [ˌwɒt‿ɒn‿'ɜ:θ]	Was um alles in der Welt ...?	*What on earth* is this?
pipe [paɪp]	Rohr; Rohrleitung	He broke a *pipe* and now there's water everywhere!
to **fix** [fɪks]	reparieren; befestigen	My bike is broken. Can you *fix* it?
to **go crazy** [ˌgəʊ 'kreɪzi]	ausflippen; durchdrehen; verrückt werden	I think I'm *going crazy*: I don't understand the Maths homework at all!
to **take, took, taken** [teɪk; tʊk; 'teɪkn]	dauern; (Zeit) brauchen	It *takes* two hours to get to London by train.
washing machine ['wɒʃɪŋ məˌʃi:n]	Waschmaschine	*washing machine* → to wash 
to **have to** ['hæv tə]	müssen	Our washing machine is broken. We *have to* repair it.
to **waste** [weɪst]	verschwenden	You're *wasting* your time, Dad!
cannot ['kænɒt]	kann nicht; können nicht	*cannot* = can't
step-by-step [ˌstepbaɪ'step]	Schritt-für-Schritt-	On the internet, there's *step-by-step* advice for everything.
no such thing as [ˌnəʊ sʌtʃ θɪŋ‿'æs]	nicht so etwas wie	When I was young, there weren't any mobile phones. There was *no such thing*.
still [stɪl]	dennoch	I don't have any money, but I'm *still* going to go to London.
I've done this a million times before. [ˌaɪv dʌn ðɪs ə ˌmɪljən taɪmz bɪ'fɔ:]	Ich habe das schon eine Million Mal gemacht.	
knob [nɒb]	Griff	Cupboard doors often have *knobs*.
to **reach** [ri:tʃ]	erreichen; dran kommen	My mum put the chocolate on top of the cupboard so my little sister can't *reach* it.
to **work** [wɜ:k]	*hier:* funktionieren	Is the washing machine *working* again?

	genius ['dʒi:niəs]	Genie	*Fr.* génie *(m)*
	With a very big head! [ˌwɪð ə ˌveri bɪg 'hed]	Und ein Angeber!	
	may [meɪ]	(vielleicht) können; dürfen	! Wenn du auf Englisch nach etwas fragst oder um etwas bittest, beginne deine Frage mit *may*: *May* I take another piece of cake, please?
8	**mess** [mes]	Unordnung, Durcheinander	What a *mess*! Please tidy your room.
10	to **carry** ['kæri]	tragen	Can you *carry* this box for me, please?
11	**flower** [flaʊə]	Blume	
12	**mad** [mæd]	verrückt	My parents think that I'm media *mad*.
	result [rɪ'zʌlt]	Ergebnis; Resultat	Have we got the test *results* yet? Who got the most points? *Fr.* résultat *(m)*
	to **(e-)mail** ['i:meɪl]	mailen; per E-Mail schicken	Could you *e-mail* me your part of the class project? I can *mail* you my part too.
	friends and family who … [frendz‿ən‿ˌfæməli 'hu:]	Freunde und Familienmitglieder, die …	
	to **download** [ˌdaʊn'ləʊd]	herunterladen *(aus dem Internet)*	
	to **comment (on)** ['kɒment‿(ɒn)]	kommentieren	Please don't *comment* on my test results; I didn't do very well at all! *to comment* → a comment
	to **stay away from** [ˌsteɪ‿ə'weɪ frəm]	fernbleiben von; meiden	*Stay away from* too much chocolate. It isn't good for your health.
	clever ['klevə]	schlau; klug	What a *clever* idea!
	in other ways [ɪn‿'ʌðə weɪz]	auf andere Weise	I don't need my phone all the time. I can have fun *in other ways* too.

Skills: How to write a letter and a reply

1	**camping** ['kæmpɪŋ]	Camping; Zelten	We go *camping* every year!
	to **miss** [mɪs]	verpassen; versäumen	Hey, you *missed* a great party! Where were you?
	Yours … [jɔ:z]	Viele Grüße … *(am Ende von Briefen und Mails)*	! You can end a letter or e-mail like this.
	to **begin, began, begun** [bɪ'gɪn; bɪ'gæn; bɪ'gʌn]	beginnen; anfangen	How do you *begin* a letter or e-mail?
	beach [bi:tʃ]	Strand	
2	**weird** [wɪəd]	merkwürdig; seltsam; sonderbar	*weird* = strange

Unit task: Advice letters and replies: Our collection

chance [tʃɑːns]	Chance; Gelegenheit; Möglichkeit	Give me another *chance*, please!
weekday ['wiːkdeɪ]	Wochentag	On *weekday* mornings I usually go to school.
to **do about** ['duː‿əˌbaʊt]	unternehmen wegen	What can I *do about* my teacher? I don't think she likes me.
freely ['friːli]	frei	

Story: It's a disaster!

disaster [dɪ'zɑːstə]	Desaster; Katastrophe; Unglück	Frank's day was a *disaster*. *Fr.* désastre *(m)*
to **rain** [reɪn]	regnen	It's *raining*! 
it was raining [ˌɪt‿wəz 'reɪnɪŋ]	es regnete gerade	
he wasn't able to … [ˌhi wɒznt 'eɪbl‿tə]	er konnte nicht …	
he was able to … [ˌhi wɒz 'eɪbl‿tə]	er konnte …	
light [laɪt]	Licht; Lampe	At night you need *light*.
to **be on** [bi‿'ɒn]	an sein; laufen	The race *is on*.
thunder *(no pl)* ['θʌndə]	Donner	In a storm there's usually *thunder* and lightning.
lightning *(no pl)* ['laɪtnɪŋ]	Blitz	
to **get out of** [get ˌaʊt‿əv]	aussteigen	He *got out of* the car quickly and ran to the house.
front door [ˌfrʌnt 'dɔː]	Haustür	Every house has a *front door*.
nearly ['nɪəli]	fast; annähernd	*nearly* = almost
upstairs [ʌp'steəz]	nach oben; im Obergeschoss; oben	
headphones *(pl)* ['hedfəʊnz]	Kopfhörer	 Take my *headphones* and listen to this!
downstairs [ˌdaʊn'steəz]	nach unten; im Untergeschoss; unten	*downstairs* ↔ upstairs
to **tap** [tæp]	antippen	Jay *tapped* Olivia's shoulder.
I was thinking … [ˌaɪ wəz 'θɪŋkɪŋ]	ich dachte gerade …	
to **cry** [kraɪ]	schreien; rufen	*to cry* = to shout *Fr.* crier

to **fight, fought, fought** [faɪt, fɔ:t, fɔ:t]	kämpfen; (sich) streiten	*to fight* → fight
to **joke** [dʒəʊk]	scherzen	Don't worry, I'm only *joking*! *to joke* → a joke ***Lat.*** iocus *(m)*
to **push** [pʊʃ]	stoßen; schieben; schubsen	He *pushed* me – and I fell over. That wasn't nice!
to **press** [pres]	drücken; pressen	***Fr.*** presser
he was pressing [hi wəz 'presɪŋ]	er drückte gerade	
to **go black** [ˌgəʊ 'blæk]	schwarz werden	After the bang everything *went black*.
to **crash** [kræʃ]	abstürzen	Has your computer ever *crashed*?
to **calm down** [ˌkɑ:m 'daʊn]	sich beruhigen	! Das „l" in *calm* wird nicht ausgesprochen.
power cut ['paʊə ˌkʌt]	Stromausfall	
round [raʊnd]	um … herum	Five minutes later they all sat *round* the table.
candlelight *(no pl)* ['kændlaɪt]	Kerzenlicht	
only ['əʊnli]	einzige/-r/-s	I'm the *only* girl in my tutor group without glasses.
right now [ˌraɪt 'naʊ]	jetzt gleich; sofort; gerade	*Right now* I don't have any problems.
to **cook** [kʊk]	kochen	Have you ever *cooked* an Indian curry?
to **be impressed** [bi ɪm'prest]	beeindruckt sein	The friends *were impressed* with Jay's dancing and singing.
he wasn't speaking [hi ˌwəznt 'spi:kɪŋ]	er sprach gerade nicht	
to **show off** [ʃəʊ‿'ɒf]	angeben	My brother always *shows off* with his expensive smartphone.
to **borrow** ['bɒrəʊ]	(sich) ausleihen	Can I *borrow* this T-shirt? – OK, but please remember to give it back.
mine [maɪn]	mein/-er/-e/-es	Is this my pizza? = Is it *mine*?
1 to **feel left out** [ˌfi:l left‿'aʊt]	sich ausgeschlossen fühlen	Did Frank *feel left out*?
2 to **link** [lɪŋk]	verbinden	
dangerously ['deɪndʒrəsli]	gefährlich	
more quickly [mɔ: 'kwɪkli]	schneller	

Unit 5 Goodbye Greenwich

Check-in

journey ['dʒɜ:ni]	Reise; Fahrt	On our *journey* through England we met a lot of nice people.
future ['fju:tʃə]	Zukunft	What will the *future* be like?

	to **report** [rɪ'pɔ:t]	berichten; melden	*to report* → report
	medieval [ˌmedi'i:vl]	mittelalterlich	Is every castle *medieval*? – No, of course not. *Fr.* médiéval/-e
	living history show [ˌlɪvɪŋ 'hɪstəri ˌʃəʊ]	*Show, in der historischer Alltag nachgespielt wird*	
	pony trekking ['pəʊni ˌtrekɪŋ]	Ponyreiten im Gelände	You go *pony trekking* in the country.
	Scottish ['skɒtɪʃ]	schottisch	Edinburgh is the *Scottish* capital.
1	to **include** [ɪn'klu:d]	einschließen; beinhalten	The trip will be expensive, but the price *includes* all our meals. *Lat.* includere
2	places that … [ˌpleɪsɪz 'ðæt]	Orte, die …	
	landscape ['lændskeɪp]	Landschaft	
3	**sandy** ['sændi]	sandig; Sand-	
	rocky ['rɒki]	felsig; steinig	Not every beach is sandy. Many are *rocky*.
	wide [waɪd]	breit; weit; ausgedehnt	This table is too *wide*, we can't get it through the door.
	deep [di:p]	tief	You mustn't go into *deep* water if you can't swim.
	island ['aɪlənd]	Insel	The British Isles are a group of *islands*.
	harbour ['hɑ:bə]	Hafen	The weather is bad, so the boats are staying in the *harbour*.
	hiking ['haɪkɪŋ]	Wandern	Wales is great for *hiking*.
	mountain biking ['maʊntɪn ˌbaɪkɪŋ]	Mountainbikefahren	
	(wind)surfing ['(wɪnd)sɜ:fɪŋ]	(Wind-)Surfen	! Beachte: Surfen und Windsurfen sind verschiedene Sportarten.
	palm tree ['pɑ:m ˌtri:]	Palme	
	to **grow, grew, grown** [grəʊ; gru:; grəʊn]	wachsen	All kinds of flowers *grow* in our garden.

Parts of the British Isles

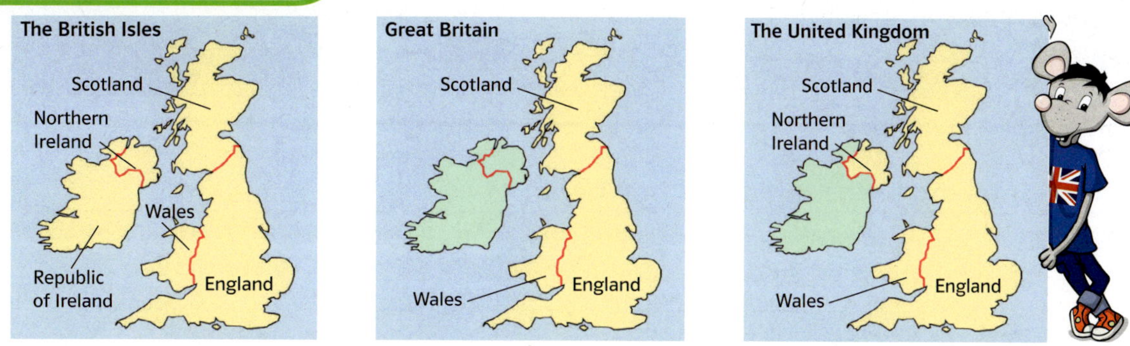

Places and what you can do there

Places		Activities	
in a city / town	in einer Stadt	to visit a museum / castle to go to a festival	ein Museum / Schloss besichtigen ein Festival besuchen
in the fields in the forest	auf den Wiesen und Feldern im Wald	to go hiking / mountain biking / pony trekking to go for a walk	wandern / Mountainbike fahren / wanderreiten gehen spazieren gehen
in the mountains	in den Bergen	to go climbing / hiking / mountain biking / pony trekking to go for a walk to climb a mountain	klettern / … spazieren gehen einen Berg besteigen
on an island at the seaside, by the sea, on the coast on the beach, on the shore on the river bank, on the shore	auf einer Insel am Meer, an der Küste am Strand, am Meeresufer am Flussufer	to go climbing / hiking / mountain biking / pony trekking to go for a walk to climb a mountain to go fishing	klettern/ … angeln gehen
in the sea in a river in a lake	im Meer in einem Fluss in einem See	to go swimming / surfing / windsurfing	schwimmen / surfen / windsurfen gehen

Station 1: Moving to the middle of nowhere

to **move (house)** [muːv (haʊs)]	umziehen	When you *move house*, you leave your old home and go to live in a new one. *Lat.* movēre
nowhere ['nəʊweə]	nirgendwo; nirgendwohin	*nowhere* → somewhere → everywhere
beautiful ['bjuːtɪfl]	schön; hübsch; wunderbar	
Cornish ['kɔːnɪʃ]	aus/in Cornwall; kornisch; Kornisch	Dave and his parents are going to move to a *Cornish* town.
countryside ['kʌntrisaɪd]	Land	in the *countryside* = auf dem Land
to **miss** [mɪs]	vermissen	I *miss* you. = Du fehlst mir.

	won't she …? [wəʊnt‿'ʃi:]	nicht wahr? stimmts?	
	to **stay** [steɪ]	übernachten	We *stayed* at a really nice hotel.
	won't be able to … [ˌwəʊnt bi‿'eɪbl‿tə]	wirst nicht … können	
	(not) any longer [nɒt‿eni 'lɒŋgə]	(nicht) mehr; (nicht) länger	I don't like it here; I don't want to stay here *any longer*.
	to **make friends** [ˌmeɪk 'frendz]	Freundschaft schließen	I *made* lots of *friends* at my new school.
	to **hate** [heɪt]	hassen; nicht mögen	*to hate* ↔ to love
	all of us ['ɔ:l‿əv ˌʌs]	wir alle	
	wonderful ['wʌndəfl]	wunderbar	*wonderful* = great = fantastic
1	**transport** ['trænspɔ:t]	Verkehrsmittel; Transport	*Transport* can be expensive. ***Lat.*** transportare
3	**travel agent's** ['trævl‿eɪdʒnts]	Reisebüro	You can buy holidays at the *travel agent's*.
	ticket ['tɪkɪt]	Fahrschein	***Fr.*** ticket *(m)*
	to **depend (on)** [dɪ'pend‿(ɒn)]	abhängen von	The price of the ticket *depends on* the date. ***Fr.*** dépendre (de)
	per [pɜ:; pə]	pro	The price for the tickets is £5 *per* person.
	to **promise** ['prɒmɪs]	versprechen	Can his parents *promise* that Dave will like Cornwall?
	with a person who … [wɪð‿ə ˌpɜ:sn 'hu:]	mit einer Person, die …	
5	to **book** [bʊk]	buchen; reservieren	You can *book* a ticket for a journey, a holiday, a table at a restaurant.
	to **return** [rɪ'tɜ:n]	zurückkehren; zurückfahren	*to return* = to go or come back ***Fr.*** retourner
	form [fɔ:m]	Formular	You often have to fill in *forms* on the internet.
	to **click on** ['klɪk‿ɒn]	anklicken	*Click on* 'SEND' to send your e-mail. 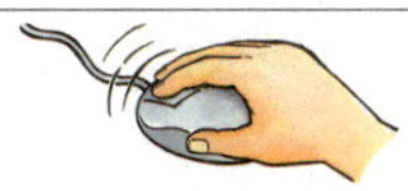
	connection [kə'nekʃn]	Verbindung	What *connections* are there from Greenwich to St Agnes today?
	one-way ticket ['wʌnweɪ ˌtɪkɪt]	einfache Fahrkarte	
	single ticket [ˌsɪŋgl ˌtɪkɪt]	einfache Fahrkarte	*single ticket* = one-way ticket
	return ticket [rɪ'tɜ:n ˌtɪkɪt]	Hin- und Rückfahrkarte	*return ticket* ↔ one-way ticket
	fee [fi:]	Gebühr	Is there an extra *fee* on the ticket?
	to **depart** [dɪ'pɑ:t]	abfahren	When does the train *depart*?
	to **arrive** [ə'raɪv]	ankommen	And when does the next train *arrive*? ***Fr.*** arriver
	outward ['aʊtwəd]	abfahrend	*Outward* trains leave the station.
	inward ['ɪnwəd]	ankommend	*Inward* trains arrive at the station.

fare [feə]	Fahrpreis	Is there a special fare for groups?
platform ['plætfɔːm]	Plattform; Bahnsteig	
to **get on (the bus)** [ˌget‿'ɒn]	einsteigen (in den Bus)	*to get on* ↔ to get off
starting place ['stɑːtɪŋ pleɪs]	Startpunkt	

Travel words

to travel	reisen
travel agent's	Reisebüro
to take a journey / trip	eine Reise machen
transport	Transport
by train / coach / car / Underground	mit dem Zug / Bus / Auto / mit der-U-Bahn
station	Bahnhof, Station
airport	Flughafen
on the road	auf der Straße; unterwegs
one way; single / return	einfach / hin und zurück
outward / inward journey	Hinfahrt / Rückfahrt
to depart / arrive	abfahren / ankommen
to change	umsteigen

Tell your partner about a trip you took last summer / last year / …

6 **weather forecast** ['weðə ˌfɔːkɑːst]	Wettervorhersage	It tells you what the weather will be like.

Weather words

It's / The weather is	cold warm cloudy sunny	kalt warm wolkig; bewölkt sonnig
There is / are	clouds sun rain wind storm thunder lightning	Wolken Sonne Regen Wind Sturm Donner Blitz
It's raining. The sun is shining.		Es regnet. Die Sonne scheint.

Say what the weather is like today and what it will be like tomorrow.

Skills: How to get information

1	**tourist board** ['tʊərɪst bɔ:d]	Touristeninformation	At a *tourist board* you can get information about a country or region.
2	**contact** ['kɒntækt]	Kontakt	! Achtung Aussprache.
	Dear Sir or Madam [dɪə ˌsɜ:r‿ɔ: 'mædəm]	Sehr geehrte Dame, sehr geehrter Herr	You begin a formal letter like this.
	grammar school ['græmə ˌsku:l]	Gymnasium	A *grammar school* is similar to the German 'Gymnasium'.
	Best wishes [ˌbest 'wɪʃɪz]	Viele Grüße; Herzliche Grüße	You can finish a formal letter like this.
	to **send off** [send‿'ɒf]	abschicken	Before you *send off* your e-mail, read it again.
	yourselves [jɔ:'selvz]	selber; ihr/euch/Sie/sich (selbst)	Did you enjoy *yourselves*? – Oh yes, the party was really great.

Station 2: Dave says he can't wait for us to go there

	sunny ['sʌni]	sonnig	The weather is really nice today. It's *sunny*.
	hot [hɒt]	heiß	It's very *hot* today.
	coastline ['kəʊstlaɪn]	Küste; Küstenverlauf	Cornwall's *coastline* is almost 300 miles long.
	It feels so different from … [ˌɪt fi:lz səʊ 'dɪfrnt frɒm]	Es ist so anders hier im Vergleich zu …	
	wild [waɪld]	wild	pets – farm animals – *wild* animals
	ancient history [ˌeɪnʃnt 'hɪstri]	antike Geschichte; Frühgeschichte	I love everything Celtic. I'm into *ancient history*.
	prehistoric [ˌpri:hɪ'stɒrɪk]	vorgeschichtlich	
	monument ['mɒnjəmənt]	Monument; Denkmal	In Cornwall you can visit lots of prehistoric *monuments*. ***Lat.*** monumentum *(nt)*
	tin [tɪn]	Zinn	
	mine [maɪn]	Mine	There's an old tin *mine* near Dave's house.
	to **get bored** [get 'bɔ:d]	sich langweilen	This is boring. I*'m getting bored*.
	to **be sure** [bi: 'ʃʊə]	sicher sein	I*'m sure* that this is the right way.
	definitely ['defɪnətli]	bestimmt; definitiv; eindeutig	Are you really sure? – *Definitely*!
	Me neither. [mi: 'naɪðə]	Ich auch nicht.	I don't like it. – *Me neither*!
10	**besides** [bɪ'saɪdz]	neben	Do you speak any languages *besides* German?
	local ['ləʊkl]	örtlich; lokal	The schools in your area are your *local* schools.
	dialect ['daɪəlekt]	Dialekt	Do people speak a *dialect* where you live?
	accent ['æksnt]	Akzent	My granny has a German accent when she speaks English.
11	**announcement** [ə'naʊnsmənt]	Ankündigung; Durchsage	I never understand the *announcements* at the station. ***Lat.*** annuntiare
12	a father who … [ə ˌfɑ:ðə 'hu:]	ein Vater, der …	
	wife, wives *(pl)* [waɪf, waɪvz]	Ehefrau	Mr and Mrs Preston are husband and *wife*.

	couple ['kʌpl]	Paar	 *Fr.* couple *(m)*
	customer ['kʌstəmə]	Kunde/Kundin	A *customer* buys things in a shop. *customer* ↔ assistant
13	to **supply** [sə'plaɪ]	versorgen	Shops *supply* people with the things they need.
	to **rule** [ru:l]	herrschen; regieren	Elizabeth II *rules* the UK.

Action UK! The caves

	cave [keɪv]	Höhle	*Fr.* caverne *(f)*
1	to **feed, fed, fed** [fi:d; fed; fed]	füttern; ernähren	Did you *feed* the dog this morning? People must work to *feed* their families.
	to **milk** [mɪlk]	melken	
	cow [kaʊ]	Kuh	
	geocaching ['dʒi:əʊkæʃɪŋ]	Geocaching	
2	**love** [lʌv]	Liebe	*love* → to love
3	elements that … [ˌelɪməntz 'ðæt]	Elemente, die …	
	to **get lost** [ˌget 'lɒst]	verloren gehen; sich verirren	In a big city, it's easy to *get lost*.
	darkness ['dɑ:knəs]	Dunkelheit	*darkness* → dark
4	**sequel** ['si:kwl]	Fortsetzung; Folge	

Story: Things will get better

to **get, got, got** [get; gɒt; gɒt]	werden	If you learn more words, your English will *get* better.
to **come in** [ˌkʌm‿'ɪn]	hereinkommen	Mrs Preston invites the friends to *come in*.
hall [hɔ:l]	Flur; Diele; Korridor	
electricity [ˌelɪk'trɪsəti]	Elektrizität; Strom	If there's no *electricity*, you can't make tea. *Fr.* électricité *(f)*
What's the matter? [ˌwɒts ðə 'mætə]	Was ist los?; Was hast du?	
Oh dear! [ˌəʊ 'dɪə]	Oje!	I've hurt my leg. – *Oh dear!*
to **go out** [ˌgəʊ‿'aʊt]	ausgehen; hinausgehen	Let's *go out*!
up [ʌp]	hinauf; nach oben	She looked *up* and down the street.
coastal path [ˌkəʊstl 'pɑ:θ]	Küstenweg	

plumber ['plʌmə]	Installateur/-in; Klempner/-in	A *plumber* can fix your water pipes. 
hill [hɪl]	Berg; Hügel	Our house is on a *hill* and we've got a fantastic view.
by [baɪ]	bei; neben; an	*by* = next to
chimney ['tʃɪmni]	Kamin; Schornstein	
strong [strɒŋ]	stark	
roof [ru:f]	Dach	a *roof* with a chimney 
cloud [klaʊd]	Wolke	
to **go right back to** [ˌgəʊ raɪt 'bæk tə]	zurückgehen auf	Cornwall's mining history *goes right back to* Celtic times.
to **solve** [sɒlv]	lösen	Dave and his friends want to *solve* the puzzle. ***Lat.*** solvere
to **boom** [bu:m]	dröhnen	A loud voice *booms*.
to **keep away from** [ˌki:p‿ə'weɪ frəm]	(sich) fernhalten von	*Keep away from* my chocolate!
to **turn (a)round** [ˌtɜ:n‿(ə)'raʊnd]	(sich) umdrehen; wenden	When they heard a voice behind them, they *turned (a)round.*
skirt [skɜ:t]	Rock	
trousers *(pl)* ['traʊzəz]	Hose	! *trousers* steht immer im Plural: You've got cool *trousers*.
spear [spɪə]	Speer	The *spear* is broken. 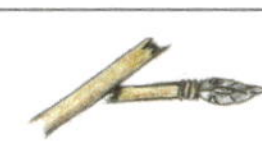
to **steal, stole, stolen** [sti:l; stəʊl; stəʊln]	stehlen	The treasure is gone. I think somebody *has stolen* it.
yours [jɔ:z]	dein/-er/-e/-es; eure/-r/-s; Ihr/-e	*yours* ↔ mine
sun [sʌn]	Sonne	
to **move in/into** [ˌmu:v‿'ɪn/'ɪntə]	einziehen in	Dave and his parents *moved into* a new house in Cornwall.
warrior ['wɒriə]	Krieger	
society [sə'saɪəti]	Verein; Gesellschaft	Bob is a member of a local history *society.* ***Fr.*** société *(f)*
twin [twɪn]	Zwilling; Zwillings-	
tool [tu:l]	Werkzeug; Gerät	A plumber needs special *tools.*

electrician [ˌelɪk'trɪʃn]	Elektriker/-in	*electrician* → electricity
plumbing ['plʌmɪŋ]	Sanitärarbeit	*plumbing* → plumber
electrics [ɪ'lektrɪks]	Elektrik	An electrician can fix the *electrics* in your house.
change [tʃeɪndʒ]	Änderung; Veränderung; Wechsel	*change* → to change
to **turn to** ['tɜːn tə]	sich wenden an; sich zuwenden	I *turned to* him to say something but he wasn't there any more.

More jobs

Who?		What and where?
mechanic	Mechaniker/-in	to fix, car, tools
plumber	Klempner/-in, Sanitärinstallateur/-in	to fix, plumbing, tools
electrician	Elektriker/-in	to fix, electrics, electricity

3	**diary entry** ['daɪəri entri]	Tagebucheintrag	A *diary entry* is a personal text in which you write about what happened and what you felt.
	nobody else ['nəʊbədi els]	niemand anderes	Only you and *nobody else* should read your diary entries.
	postcard ['pəʊstkɑːd]	Postkarte	I love it when I get a real *postcard* and not just photos in an e-mail!
	sailboat ['seɪlbəʊt]	Segelboot	
	to **camp** [kæmp]	campen; zelten	*to camp* → camping

Across cultures 4 British stories and legends

	legend ['ledʒənd]	Legende; Sage	An old story – maybe true in parts.
2	**ingredient** [ɪn'griːdiənt]	Zutat	Something is missing in this cake; hm, what *ingredient* did I forget?
	completely [kəm'pliːtli]	völlig	What you're saying isn't *completely* true! Some of it is wrong, sorry.
	cruel ['kruːəl]	grausam	People are sometimes *cruel* to each other. *Fr.* cruel/-le
	magical ['mædʒɪkəl]	magisch; Zauber-	The world of Harry Potter is a *magical* world.

wizard ['wɪzəd]	Zauberer	
hero, heroes *(pl)* ['hɪərəʊ, 'hɪərəʊz]	Held	The most important character in a book or film, usually good and brave.
heroine ['herəʊɪn]	Heldin	Who is your favourite *heroine*?
villain ['vɪlən]	Bösewicht	*villain* ↔ hero
knight [naɪt]	Ritter	
criminal ['krɪmɪnəl]	Kriminelle/-r; Verbrecher/-in	*criminal* = villain ***Lat.*** criminalis
powerful ['paʊəfl]	stark; mächtig	Who's the most *powerful* person in the world?
power [paʊə]	Kraft; Macht; Stärke	*power* → powerful
private detective [ˌpraɪvət dɪ'tektɪv]	Privatdetektiv/-in	There are lots of books and films about Sherlock Holmes, the famous *private detective*.
mysterious [mɪ'stɪəriəs]	mysteriös; geheimnisvoll	
crime [kraɪm]	Verbrechen; Kriminalität	*crime* → criminal ***Lat.*** crimen *(nt)*
robber ['rɒbə]	Räuber/-in	A *robber* is a criminal.
outlaw ['aʊtlɔː]	Geächtete/-r; Gesetzlose/-r	Robin Hood was a famous *outlaw*.
to **hide, hid, hidden** [haɪd; hɪd; 'hɪdn]	(sich) verstecken	My sister sometimes *hides* my things. She thinks it's funny.
3 **the Round Table** [ðə ˌraʊnd 'teɪbl]	die Tafelrunde	King Arthur and his knights met at the *Round Table*.
the rich [ðə rɪtʃ]	die Reichen	Robin Hood was famous because he stole money from *the rich*.
the poor [ðə pʊə]	die Armen	*the poor* ↔ the rich
4 **prop** [prɒp]	Requisite	You need lots of *props* for a film.
set [set]	Umgebung; Rahmen	A film's *set* shows where the people live, work, etc.

Dictionary

In dieser alphabetischen Wortliste findest du das gesamte Vokabular von *Green Line* 1 und 2.
Namen stehen in einer extra Liste am Ende des ***Dictionary***.
Einträge, die aus mehreren Wörtern bestehen, kannst du meist unter verschiedenen Stichwörtern nachschlagen. So ist z.B. *after all* unter *after* und unter *all* eingetragen.
Die Fundstellen stehen immer hinter dem jeweiligen Wort und zeigen dir an, wo es zum ersten Mal vorkommt, z. B.:
advice [əd'vaɪs] Rat; Ratschlag **II AC1**, 11 kommt zum ersten Mal vor in Band 2, Across cultures 1, Seite 11
adult ['ædʌlt] Erwachsene/-r **II U2**, 44 kommt zum ersten Mal vor in Band 2, Unit 2, Seite 44
U = Unit, AC = Across cultures
Die mit * gekennzeichneten Verben sind unregelmäßig.
Die mit ° gekennzeichneten Vokabeln sind rezeptiv.

A

a [ə] ein/-e **I**
a bit [ə 'bɪt] ein bisschen; ein wenig **II U1**, 22
a couple of [ə 'kʌpl‿əv] ein paar **I**
a few [ə 'fju:] ein paar; wenige; einige **I**
a girl from Germany [ə ˌgɜ:l frəm 'dʒɜ:məni] ein Mädchen aus Deutschland **I**
a group of three [ə ˌgru:p‿əv 'θri:] eine Dreiergruppe **I**
a little [ə 'lɪtl] ein wenig; etwas **I**
a lot [ə 'lɒt] viel **I**
a lot of [ə 'lɒt‿əv] viel/-e; eine Menge **I**
a lot to learn [ə ˌlɒt tə 'lɜ:n] viel zu lernen **I**
a.m. [ˌeɪ'em] vormittags *(Uhrzeit)* **I**
he was **able** to … [ˌhi wəz 'eɪbl‿tə] er konnte … °**II U4**, 86
he wasn't **able** to … [ˌhi wɒznt 'eɪbl‿tə] er konnte nicht … °**II U4**, 86
won't be **able** to … [ˌwəʊnt bi‿'eɪbl‿tə] wirst nicht … können °**II U5**, 94
aboard [ə'bɔ:d] an Bord **I**
about [ə'baʊt] ungefähr; circa; etwa **I**
about [ə'baʊt] über; von **I**
out and **about** [ˌaʊt‿ən‿ə'baʊt] unterwegs **II U2**, 44
What **about** …? ['wɒt‿əbaʊt] Wie wär's mit …?; Was ist mit …? **I**
What is … **about**? [ˌwɒt‿ɪz …‿ə'baʊt] Worum geht es in/im …? **I**
above [ə'bʌv] oben °**II U2**, 39
accent ['æksnt] Akzent **II U5**, 99
accident ['æksɪdnt] Unfall **II U3**, 55
across [ə'krɒs] auf der anderen Seite von; über; hinüber; herüber; quer durch **I**
Across cultures [əˌkrɒs 'kʌltʃəz] Interkulturelles **I**
to **act** [ækt] spielen *(Theater)* **I**
to **act** like ['ækt laɪk] tun als ob **II U4**, 76
to **act** out [ækt 'aʊt] nachspielen °**II AC3**, 72
acting a scene [ˌæktɪŋ‿ə 'si:n] eine Theaterszene spielen **I**
acting ['æktɪŋ] Schauspielen °**II U5**, 101
action ['ækʃn] Handlung; Action; Aktion **I**
activity [æk'tɪvəti] Aktivität **I**
an **activity** that … [ən‿ækˌtɪvəti 'ðæt] eine Aktivität, die … °**II U1**, 16
actor ['æktə] Schauspieler **II AC1**, 11
to **add** [æd] hinzufügen; ergänzen **II AC1**, 11
additional [ə'dɪʃnl] zusätzlich **II AC1**, 8
address [ə'dres] Adresse **I**
adjective ['ædʒɪktɪv] Adjektiv; Eigenschaftswort °**II U1**, 20
adult ['ædʌlt] Erwachsene/-r **II U2**, 44
adventure [əd'ventʃə] Abenteuer **II U1**, 20
advice [əd'vaɪs] Rat; Ratschlag **II AC1**, 11
after ['ɑ:ftə] nach *(zeitlich)* **I**
after all [ˌɑ:ftər‿'ɔ:l] doch; schließlich; immerhin **I**
after that [ˌɑ:ftə 'ðæt] danach **I**
afternoon [ˌɑ:ftə'nu:n] Nachmittag **I**
this **afternoon** [ðɪs 'ɑ:ftənu:n] heute Nachmittag **II U2**, 38
again [ə'gen] wieder; noch einmal; noch mal **I**
against [ə'genst] gegen **II U1**, 23
travel **agent's** ['trævl‿ˌeɪdʒnts] Reisebüro **II U5**, 95
aggressive [ə'gresɪv] aggressiv **II U1**, 28
ago [ə'gəʊ] vor *(zeitlich)* **II U1**, 14
agony aunt ['ægəni‿ˌɑ:nt] Kummerkastentante **II U4**, 76
to **agree** (on) [ə'gri:] sich einigen (auf) °**II U5**, 102
to **agree** (with) [ə'gri:] einer Meinung sein (mit); zustimmen °**II U4**, 81
airport ['eəpɔ:t] Flughafen **II AC2**, 34
alien ['eɪliən] Außerirdische/-r; außerirdisches Wesen **I**
all [ɔ:l] alle/-s; ganz **I**
after **all** [ˌɑ:ftər‿'ɔ:l] doch; schließlich; immerhin **I**
all day [ˌɔ:l 'deɪ] den ganzen Tag **II U1**, 18
all night [ˌɔ:l 'naɪt] die ganze Nacht **I**
all over [ˌɔ:l‿'əʊvə] überall (in) **I**
all the time [ˌɔ:l ðə 'taɪm] die ganze Zeit **II U2**, 48
all of them ['ɔ:l‿əv ˌðem] alle **I**
all of us ['ɔ:l‿əv ˌʌs] wir alle **II U5**, 94
at **all** [ət‿'ɔ:l] überhaupt **I**
bowling **alley** ['bəʊlɪŋ‿ˌæli] Bowlingbahn **I**
almost ['ɔ:lməʊst] fast; beinahe **II U3**, 64
alone [ə'ləʊn] allein; ohne fremde Hilfe **I**
along [ə'lɒŋ] entlang **I**
alphabet ['ælfəbet] Alphabet **I**
alphabetical [ˌælfə'betɪkl] alphabetisch °**II U1**, 25
already [ɔ:l'redi] schon; bereits **I**
also ['ɔ:lsəʊ] auch **II U1**, 14
always ['ɔ:lweɪz] immer; ständig **I**
amazing [ə'meɪzɪŋ] unglaublich; toll; erstaunlich **II U1**, 22
American [ə'merɪkən] Amerikanisch; amerikanisch; aus Amerika; Amerikaner/-in **II U1**, 13
an [ən] ein/-e **I**
ancient history [ˌeɪnʃnt 'hɪstri] antike Geschichte; Frühgeschichte **II U5**, 98
and [ænd; ənd] und **I**
angrily ['æŋgrɪli] verärgert; zornig; wütend °**II U2**, 48
angry ['æŋgri] wütend; zornig; verärgert; böse **I**
animal ['ænɪməl] Tier **I**
ankle ['æŋkl] Fußgelenk; Fußknöchel **II U3**, 58
to twist your **ankle** [ˌtwɪst jɔ:r‿'æŋkl] sich den Knöchel verrenken **II U3**, 58
announcement [ə'naʊnsmənt] Ankündigung; Durchsage **II U5**, 99
anonymous [ən'ɒnɪməs] anonym **II U1**, 17
another [ə'nʌðə] ein/-e andere/-r/-s; noch ein/-e; ein/-e andere/-r/-s **I**
answer ['ɑ:nsə] Antwort **I**
short **answer** [ˌʃɔ:t‿'ɑ:nsə] Kurzantwort **I**
to **answer** ['ɑ:nsə] antworten; beantworten **I**
to **answer** the phone [ˌɑ:nsə ðə 'fəʊn] einen Anruf entgegennehmen **I**
answering machine ['ɑ:nsrɪŋ məˌʃi:n] Anrufbeantworter **I**
any ['eni] irgendein/-e/-er; irgendwelche **I**
not **any** more [ˌnɒt‿eni 'mɔ:] nicht mehr **I**
not … **any** [nɒt … eni] kein/-e/-en **I**

anyone else [ˌeniwʌn 'els] irgendjemand; jemand anderes **II U3**, 61
Anything else? [ˌeniθɪŋ‿'els] Sonst noch etwas? **I**
not … **anything** [ˌnɒt 'eniθɪŋ] nichts **I**
anyway ['eniweɪ] trotzdem; jedenfalls; sowieso **II U2**, 48
anywhere ['eniweə] irgendwo; überall (egal, wo) **II U2**, 40
app [æp] App **II U4**, 81
apple ['æpl] Apfel **I**
April ['eɪprəl] April **I**
area ['eəriə] Areal; Gebiet; Fläche **II U3**, 56
arm [ɑːm] Arm **II U3**, 57
around [ə'raʊnd] um … herum; umher **I**
to turn **around** [ˌtɜːn‿(ə)'raʊnd] (sich) umdrehen; wenden **II U5**, 104
to **arrest** [ə'rest] festnehmen; verhaften **II U1**, 17
to **arrive** [ə'raɪv] ankommen **II U5**, 96
Art [ɑːt] Kunstunterricht **I**
art [ɑːt] Kunst **II AC1**, 9
as [æz; əz] als **II U3**, 63
as … **as** [əz … əz] so … wie **I**
as [æz; əz] während; indem **I**; wie **II AC1**, 11
as soon **as** [əz 'suːn‿əz] sobald **II U4**, 76
to **ask** [ɑːsk] fragen; bitten **I**
Ask about … ['ɑːsk‿əˌbaʊt] Frage/Fragt nach … **I**
to **ask** for ['ɑːsk fə] fragen nach; bitten um **I**
*to be **asleep** [ˌbi ə'sliːp] schlafen **II U1**, 23
*to fall **asleep** [ˌfɔːl‿ə'sliːp] einschlafen **I**
assembly [ə'sembli] Versammlung; Morgenappell **II AC1**, 8
assistant [ə'sɪstnt] Assistent/-in; Verkäufer/-in **II U3**, 62
at [æt; ət] in; auf; bei; an; um *(bei Uhrzeitangaben)* **I**
at 7:30 [ət ˌsevn‿'θɜːti] um halb acht **I**
at all [ət‿'ɔːl] überhaupt **I**
at first [ət 'fɜːst] zuerst; zunächst **II U2**, 49
at home [ət 'həʊm] zu Hause **I**
at last [ət 'lɑːst] endlich; schließlich **I**
at least [ət 'liːst] mindestens; wenigstens °**II U2**, 50
at the back of [ət ðə 'bæk‿əv] hinten; am Ende; im hinteren Teil °**II U2**, 36
at the moment [ət ðə 'məʊmənt] im Moment; gerade **I**
at the same time [ət ðə ˌseɪm 'taɪm] zur selben Zeit; gleichzeitig **I**
at the weekend [ət ðə ˌwiːk'end] am Wochenende **I**
atlas ['ætləs] Atlas **II AC3**, 72
atmosphere ['ætməsfɪə] Atmosphäre; Stimmung °**II U2**, 44
attention [ə'tenʃn] Aufmerksamkeit; Beachtung **II U4**, 77
attic ['ætɪk] Dachboden **II U3**, 60
attraction [ə'trækʃn] Attraktion; Sehenswürdigkeit **II U2**, 45
audio ['ɔːdiəʊ] Audio-; Hör- **I**
audio tour ['ɔːdiəʊ ˌtʊə] Audioführung **II U2**, 42
audio-visual effect [ˌɔːdiəʊvɪʒuəl ɪ'fekt] audiovisueller Effekt °**II U1**, 28
August ['ɔːgəst] August **I**
aunt [ɑːnt] Tante **I**
agony **aunt** ['ægəni‿ˌɑːnt] Kummerkastentante **II U4**, 76
away [ə'weɪ] weg **I**
right **away** [ˌraɪt‿ə'weɪ] sofort; gleich **I**
*to run **away** [ˌrʌn‿ə'weɪ] wegrennen **I**
*to throw **away** [ˌθrəʊ‿ə'weɪ] wegwerfen **I**
awful ['ɔːfl] schrecklich; furchtbar **I**

B

baby ['beɪbi] Baby; Säugling **I**
back [bæk] Rückseite; Rücken °**II U5**, 102
at the **back** of [ət ðə 'bæk‿əv] hinten; am Ende; im hinteren Teil °**II U2**, 36
back to **back** [ˌbæk tʊ 'bæk] Rücken an Rücken **I**
back [bæk] zurück **I**
*to go right **back** to [ˌgəʊ raɪt 'bæk tə] zurückgehen auf **II U5**, 104
backache ['bækeɪk] Rückenschmerzen; Rückenweh **II U3**, 59
background ['bækgraʊnd] Hintergrund **I**
bacon ['beɪkn] Schinkenspeck; Speck **I**
bad [bæd] schlecht; böse; schlimm *(ugs.)* **I**
Too **bad**! [ˌtuː 'bæd] Zu dumm!; Schade! **I**
badminton ['bædmɪntən] Badminton **I**
bag [bæg] Tasche; Tüte **I**
baked beans *(pl)* [ˌbeɪkt 'biːnz] weiße Bohnen in Tomatensoße **I**
ball [bɔːl] Ball **I**
banana [bə'nɑːnə] Banane **I**
Bang! [bæŋ] Peng! **II U4**, 86
bank [bæŋk] Ufer **II U2**, 48
snack **bar** ['snæk ˌbɑː] Café; Imbissstube **I**
bargain ['bɑːgɪn] Schnäppchen **I**
to **bark** [bɑːk] bellen **I**
basic ['beɪsɪk] grundlegend; Grund- **II U2**, 45
basketball ['bɑːskɪtbɔːl] Basketball **I**
bath [bɑːθ] Bad; Badewanne **I**
bathroom ['bɑːθrʊm] Bad; Badezimmer **I**
battery ['bætri] Batterie; Akku **II U1**, 23
*to **be** [biː] sein **I**
*to **be** about [biː‿ə'baʊt] sich handeln um **I**
*to **be** asleep [ˌbi ə'sliːp] schlafen **II U1**, 23
*to **be** gone [biː 'gɒn] verschwunden sein; weg sein **II U3**, 65
*to **be** good at [biː 'gʊd‿ət] gut sein in **I**
*to **be** impressed [bi ɪm'prest] beeindruckt sein **II U4**, 87
*to **be** in [bi‿'ɪn] dabei sein; mitmachen **II U3**, 56
*to **be** in the way [biː‿ɪn ðə 'weɪ] im Weg sein/stehen **I**
*to **be** interested in [bi‿'ɪntrəstɪd‿ɪn] interessiert sein an; sich interessieren für **II U2**, 36
*to **be** into [biː‿'ɪntə] mögen; stehen auf **I**
*to **be** jealous (of) [biː 'dʒeləs] eifersüchtig sein (auf); neidisch sein (auf) **I**
*to **be** late [biː 'leɪt] zu spät dran sein; zu spät kommen **I**
*to **be** lucky [bi‿'lʌki] Glück haben **II U2**, 48
*to **be** on [bi‿'ɒn] an sein; laufen **II U4**, 86
*to **be** right [bi 'raɪt] recht haben **I**
*to **be** scared (of) [biː 'skeəd‿əv] Angst haben (vor) **I**
*to **be** sorry [biː 'sɒri] leid tun **I**
*to **be** sure [bi 'ʃʊə] sicher sein **II U5**, 98
*to **be** surprised [bi sə'praɪzd] überrascht sein **II U2**, 49
*to **be** unlucky [biː‿ʌn'lʌki] Pech haben **I**
*to **be** up to [bi‿'ʌp tə] vorhaben °**II U1**, 28
*to **be** worried [bi 'wʌrid] beunruhigt sein; besorgt sein **II U3**, 64
*to **be** worth [biː 'wɜːθ] wert sein **I**
*to **be** wrong [biː 'rɒŋ] unrecht haben; sich irren **I**
Be careful! [biː 'keəfl] Vorsicht!; Pass/Passt auf! **I**
Be polite. [biː pə'laɪt] Sei/Seid höflich. **I**
Here you **are**. [ˌhɪə ju‿'ɑː] Bitte schön. **I**
How much **is**/**are** …? [ˌhaʊ 'mʌtʃ‿ɪz/ɑː] Wie viel (kostet/kosten) …? **I**
I'**m** from … [ˌaɪm frɒm] Ich bin aus … **I**
Is this how you (do) …? [ɪz 'ðɪs haʊ jʊ ˌduː] Machst du so …? **I**
beach [biːtʃ] Strand **II U4**, 83
baked **beans** *(pl)* [ˌbeɪkt 'biːnz] weiße Bohnen in Tomatensoße **I**
bear [beə] Bär **II U2**, 42
*to **beat** [biːt] schlagen; besiegen **II U2**, 40
beautiful ['bjuːtɪfl] schön; hübsch; wunderbar **II U5**, 94
because [bɪ'kɒz] weil; da **I**
because of [bɪ'kɒz‿əv] wegen **II U3**, 65
*to **become** [bɪ'kʌm] werden **II U2**, 42
bed [bed] Bett **I**
*to go to **bed** [ˌgəʊ tə 'bed] ins Bett gehen **I**
bedroom ['bedrʊm] Schlafzimmer **I**
Beefeater ['biːfˌiːtə] königlicher Leibgardist **II U2**, 42
before [bɪ'fɔː] vor *(zeitlich)*; bevor **I**; schon einmal; vorher; zuvor **II U3**, 57
*to **begin** [bɪ'gɪn] beginnen; anfangen **II U4**, 83
beginning [bɪ'gɪnɪŋ] Anfang; Beginn **II U1**, 27
behind [bɪ'haɪnd] hinter **I**
to **believe** [bɪ'liːv] glauben **I**
I couldn't **believe** my eyes. [ai ˌkʊdnt bɪˌliːv maɪ‿'aɪz] Ich traute meinen Augen nicht. **II U3**, 61
bell [bel] Glocke **II AC2**, 34
to **belong** (to) [bɪ'lɒŋ (tə)] gehören (zu) **II AC1**, 9

below [bɪ'ləʊ] unterhalb; unten **I**
besides [bɪ'saɪdz] neben **II U5**, 99
(the) **best** [best] (der/die/das) Beste **II U1**, 14
best [best] beste/-r/-s; am besten **I**
Best wishes [ˌbest 'wɪʃɪz] Viele Grüße; Herzliche Grüße **II U5**, 97
I **bet** [aɪ 'bet] ich wette **II U2**, 40
better ['betə] besser; lieber **I**
between [bɪ'twiːn] zwischen **I**
big [bɪg] groß **I**
bike [baɪk] Fahrrad **I**
mountain **biking** ['maʊntɪn ˌbaɪkɪŋ] Mountainbikefahren **II U5**, 93
bilingual [baɪ'lɪŋgwl] zweisprachig °**II U1**, 25
bird [bɜːd] Vogel **II AC1**, 8
birdwatching ['bɜːdˌwɒtʃɪŋ] Vogelbeobachtung **II AC1**, 8
birthday ['bɜːθdeɪ] Geburtstag **I**
Happy **Birthday**! [ˌhæpi 'bɜːθdeɪ] Alles Gute zum Geburtstag!; Herzlichen Glückwunsch zum Geburtstag! **I**
biscuit ['bɪskɪt] Keks **I**
a **bit** [ə 'bɪt] ein bisschen; ein wenig **II U1**, 22
*to **bite** [baɪt] beißen **II U2**, 42
black [blæk] schwarz **I**
*to go **black** [ˌgəʊ 'blæk] schwarz werden **II U4**, 86
building **block** ['bɪldɪŋ blɒk] Baustein °**II U4**, 77
to **block** [blɒk] blockieren; abblocken **II U4**, 77
*to **blow** out [ˌbləʊ‿'aʊt] ausblasen; auspusten **I**
blue [bluː] blau **I**
BMX [ˌbiːem'eks] BMX **II U3**, 54
tourist **board** ['tʊərɪst bɔːd] Touristeninformation **II U5**, 97
boat [bəʊt] Boot **I**
boating lake ['bəʊtɪŋ ˌleɪk] See zum Rudern **I**
human **body** [ˌhjuːmən 'bɒdi] menschlicher Körper **II U2**, 48
bonfire ['bɒnfaɪə] Lagerfeuer; Freudenfeuer **I**
book [bʊk] Buch **I**
exercise **book** ['eksəsaɪz ˌbʊk] Übungsheft **I**
to **book** [bʊk] buchen; reservieren **II U5**, 96
to **boom** [buːm] dröhnen **II U5**, 104
bored [bɔːd] gelangweilt **I**
*to get **bored** [get‿'bɔːd] sich langweilen **II U5**, 98
boring ['bɔːrɪŋ] langweilig **I**
to **borrow** ['bɒrəʊ] (sich) ausleihen **II U4**, 87
both [bəʊθ] beide **II U3**, 65
bottle ['bɒtl] Flasche **I**
bowl [bəʊl] Schale; Schälchen; Schüssel **I**
bowling alley ['bəʊlɪŋ‿ˌæli] Bowlingbahn **I**
box [bɒks] Box; Kasten; Schachtel; Kiste **I**
boxing ['bɒksɪŋ] Boxen **II U1**, 12
round of **boxing** [ˌraʊnd‿əv 'bɒksɪŋ] Boxrunde **II U1**, 12
boy [bɔɪ] Junge **I**
cabin **boy** ['kæbɪn ˌbɔɪ] Schiffsjunge **I**
the **boy** who … [ðə bɔi 'huː] der Junge, der … °**II U3**, 66
bracelet ['breɪslət] Armband **I**
brave [breɪv] mutig; tapfer **I**
bread [bred] Brot **I**
break [breɪk] Pause **II AC1**, 10
half-term **break** [ˌhɑːftɜːm 'breɪk] Halbjahresferien **I**
lunch **break** ['lʌnʃbreɪk] Mittagspause **I**
*to **break** [breɪk] brechen; zerbrechen **I**
broken ['brəʊkn] gebrochen; kaputt **I**
breakfast ['brekfəst] Frühstück **I**
*to have **breakfast** [ˌhæv 'brekfəst] frühstücken **I**
Take a deep **breath**. [ˌteɪk‿ə ˌdiːp 'breθ] Atme(t) tief ein. **II AC1**, 11
to **breathe** [briːð] atmen **II U3**, 64
bridge [brɪdʒ] Brücke **II U2**, 48
*to **bring** [brɪŋ] bringen; mitbringen **I**
British ['brɪtɪʃ] britisch; Brite/Britin **I**
brochure ['brəʊʃə] Broschüre; Prospekt **I**
broken ['brəʊkn] gebrochen; kaputt **I**
brother ['brʌðə] Bruder **I**
brown [braʊn] braun **I**
bucket ['bʌkɪt] Eimer **II U2**, 48
*to **build** [bɪld] bauen **II U2**, 42
building ['bɪldɪŋ] Gebäude **I**
building block ['bɪldɪŋ blɒk] Baustein °**II U4**, 77
cyber **bully** [ˌsaɪbə 'bʊli] *jemand, der andere in sozialen Netzwerken belästigt oder mobbed* **II U4**, 75
*to give the **bumps** [ˌgɪv ðə 'bʌmps] hochleben lassen **I**
burger ['bɜːgə] Hamburger **I**
bus [bʌs] Bus **I**
bus station ['bʌs ˌsteɪʃn] Busbahnhof **I**
busy ['bɪzi] belebt; beschäftigt **I**
but [bʌt] aber **I**
*to **buy** [baɪ] kaufen **I**
buyer ['baɪə] Käufer/-in **I**
by [baɪ] bei; neben; an **II U5**, 104
by *(bike)* [baɪ] mit *(dem Fahrrad)* **I**
Bye! [baɪ] Tschüss! **II U3**, 58

C

cabin boy ['kæbɪn ˌbɔɪ] Schiffsjunge **I**
cache [kæʃ] Cache **II U5**, 104
café ['kæfeɪ] Café **I**
cafeteria [ˌkæfə'tɪəriə] Cafeteria **I**
cake [keɪk] Kuchen; Torte **I**
(phone) **call** ['fəʊn ˌkɔːl] Anruf; Telefonanruf **I**
to **call** [kɔːl] nennen; anrufen; rufen **I**
caller ['kɔːlə] Anrufer/-in **I**
to **calm** down [ˌkɑːm 'daʊn] sich beruhigen **II U4**, 87
camel racing ['kæml ˌreɪsɪŋ] Kamelrennen **II U3**, 54
camera ['kæmrə] Fotoapparat; Kamera **II U1**, 12
caught on **camera** [ˌkɔːt‿ɒn 'kæmrə] ertappt; mit der Kamera festgehalten **II U1**, 12
summer **camp** ['sʌmə kæmp] Sommerferienlager **II AC3**, 72
to **camp** [kæmp] campen; zelten **II U5**, 106
camping ['kæmpɪŋ] Camping; Zelten **II U4**, 83
can [kæn] Dose; Büchse **I**
can [kæn; kən] können; dürfen **I**
can't [kɑːnt] kann nicht; können nicht **I**
Can you name …? ['kæn jʊ ˌneɪm] Kannst du … nennen? **I**
candle ['kændl] Kerze **I**
candlelight *(no pl)* ['kændlaɪt] Kerzenlicht **II U4**, 87
cannot ['kænɒt] kann nicht; können nicht **II U4**, 79
capital ['kæpɪtl] Hauptstadt **II AC2**, 34
capital letter [ˌkæpɪtl 'letə] Großbuchstabe **I**
captain ['kæptɪn] Kapitän/-in; Mannschaftsführer/-in **I**
car [kɑː] Auto **I**
card [kɑːd] Karte; Spielkarte **I**
to **care** (about) ['keər‿əˌbaʊt] wichtig nehmen; sich kümmern (um); sich interessieren (für) **II U4**, 77
careful ['keəfl] vorsichtig; sorgfältig **II U2**, 42
Be **careful**! [biː 'keəfl] Vorsicht!; Pass/Passt auf! **I**
carnival ['kɑːnɪvl] Karneval **II AC2**, 34
carrot ['kærət] Karotte; Möhre **I**
to **carry** ['kæri] tragen **II U4**, 80
castle ['kɑːsl] Schloss; Burg **II U2**, 42
cat [kæt] Katze **I**
*to **catch** [kætʃ] fangen **II U3**, 54
category ['kætəgri] Kategorie; Klasse °**II AC3**, 73
caught on camera [ˌkɔːt‿ɒn 'kæmrə] ertappt; mit der Kamera festgehalten **II U1**, 12
to **cause** [kɔːz] verursachen **II U3**, 66
cave [keɪv] Höhle **II U5**, 101
to **celebrate** ['seləbreɪt] feiern **I**
Celtic ['keltɪk; 'seltɪk] keltisch **II U1**, 20
cent [sent] Cent *(Währung)* **I**
central ['sentrl] zentral; Zentral- **II U2**, 48
centre ['sentə] Zentrum; Center **I**
community **centre** [kə'mjuːnəti ˌsentə] Gemeindezentrum **I**
leisure **centre** ['leʒə ˌsentə] Freizeitzentrum **I**
tourist information **centre** [ˌtʊərɪst ɪnfə'meɪʃn ˌsentə] Touristeninformation **I**
century ['senʃri] Jahrhundert **II U2**, 48
cereal *(no pl)* ['sɪəriəl] Frühstückszerealie; Getreideprodukt *(z. B. Cornflakes oder Müsli)* **I**
chair [tʃeə] Stuhl; Sessel **I**

challenge ['tʃælɪndʒ] Herausforderung **II U1**, 20
chance [tʃɑ:ns] Chance; Gelegenheit; Möglichkeit **II U4**, 84
change [tʃeɪndʒ] Änderung; Veränderung; Wechsel **II U5**, 105
to **change** [tʃeɪndʒ] wechseln; (sich) ändern **II U4**, 74
to **change** (onto) [tʃeɪndʒ ('ɒntʊ)] umsteigen (in) **II U2**, 39
chant [tʃɑ:nt] Sprechgesang **II U3**, 58
character ['kærəktə] Charakter; Figur **I**
charity ['tʃærɪti] Wohltätigkeitsverein; wohltätige Zwecke; Wohlfahrt **I**
charity shop ['tʃærɪti ʃɒp] Second-Hand-Laden **I**
lucky **charm** [ˌlʌki 'tʃɑ:m] Glücksbringer; Talisman **I**
to **chase** [tʃeɪs] jagen; nachjagen **I**
chat room ['tʃæt rʊm] Chatroom **II AC3**, 72
video **chat** ['vɪdiəʊ ˌtʃæt] Videochat **II U2**, 36
to **chat** [tʃæt] plaudern; chatten *(sich online unterhalten)* **I**
cheap [tʃi:p] billig; preiswert **I**
to **check** [tʃek] überprüfen; prüfen; kontrollieren **I**
Check-in ['tʃekɪn] Einchecken **I**
checklist ['tʃeklɪst] Checkliste °**II U3**, 58
Check-out ['tʃekaʊt] Auschecken **I**
to **cheer** [tʃɪə] anfeuern; jubeln; zujubeln **II U3**, 58
cheese [tʃi:z] Käse **I**
chess [tʃes] Schach **II AC1**, 8
chicken ['tʃɪkɪn] Huhn; Hähnchen **I**
chicken tikka masala [ˌtʃɪkɪn ˌtɪkə mə'sɑ:lə] *indisches Hühnchengericht* **I**
child [tʃaɪld], **children** ['tʃɪldrən] *(pl)* Kind **I**
only **child** ['əʊnli ˌtʃaɪld] Einzelkind **I**
chimney ['tʃɪmni] Kamin; Schornstein **II U5**, 104
chips *(pl) (BE)* [tʃɪps] Pommes frites **I**
chocolate ['tʃɒklət] Schokolade **I**
choice [tʃɔɪs] Wahl; Auswahl **II U2**, 44
to **choose** [tʃu:z] auswählen; wählen **I**
Christmas ['krɪsməs] Weihnachten **I**
church [tʃɜ:tʃ] Kirche **I**
cinema ['sɪnəmə] Kino **I**
circle ['sɜ:kl] Kreis; Ring **I**
city ['sɪti] Stadt; Großstadt **I**
to **clap** [klæp] klatschen **I**
Clap your hands. [ˌklæp jɔ: 'hændz] Klatsch/Klatscht in die Hände. **I**
class [klɑ:s] Klasse; Schulklasse **I**; *hier:* Unterricht **II AC1**, 8
class display ['klɑ:s dɪˌspleɪ] Ausstellung in der Klasse **I**
class poster ['klɑ:s ˌpəʊstə] Klassenposter **I**
classmate ['klɑ:smeɪt] Klassenkamerad/-in; Mitschüler/-in **I**
classroom ['klɑ:srʊm] Klassenzimmer **I**
clay pipe ['kleɪ paɪp] Tonpfeife **II U2**, 49
to **clean** [kli:n] säubern; reinigen **I**
to **clear** out [ˌklɪər‿'aʊt] ausräumen; entrümpeln **I**
clear [klɪə] klar; deutlich **I**
clever ['klevə] schlau; klug **II U4**, 81
click [klɪk] Klicken; Klick **II U4**, 87
to **click** on ['klɪk‿ɒn] anklicken **II U5**, 96
to **climb** [klaɪm] klettern; besteigen; steigen **I**
climbing ['klaɪmɪŋ] Klettern **II U1**, 20
clock [klɒk] Uhr **I**
o'**clock** [ə'klɒk] Uhr *(Zeitangabe bei vollen Stunden)* **I**
to **close** [kləʊz] schließen; zumachen **I**
close [kləʊs] eng; knapp **I**; nahe **II U2**, 42
Look **closely** … [ˌlʊk 'kləʊsli] Schau(t) genau … °**II U3**, 62
That was **close**! [ˌðæt wəz 'kləʊs] Das war knapp! **I**
close-up ['kləʊsʌp] Nahaufnahme °**II U4**, 82
clothes *(pl)* [kləʊðz] Kleider; Kleidung **I**
cloud [klaʊd] Wolke **II U5**, 104
word **cloud** ['wɜ:d ˌklaʊd] Wörterwolke °**II U3**, 54
cloudy ['klaʊdi] bedeckt; bewölkt **II U1**, 23
clown [klaʊn] Clown **II U3**, 64
club [klʌb] Klub; Verein; AG **I**
Cooking **Club** ['kʊkɪŋ ˌklʌb] Koch-AG **I**
clue [klu:] Hinweis; Spur **II U1**, 17
coach [kəʊtʃ] Trainer/-in **I**; Reisebus **II U1**, 17
coastal path [ˌkəʊstl 'pɑ:θ] Küstenweg **II U5**, 104
coastline ['kəʊstlaɪn] Küste; Küstenverlauf **II U5**, 98
coconut ['kəʊkənʌt] Kokosnuss **II U2**, 49
coffee ['kɒfi] Kaffee **I**
coin [kɔɪn] Münze **I**
coke ['kəʊk] Cola **I**
cold [kəʊld] Erkältung **II U3**, 59
cold [kəʊld] kalt **II U1**, 22
to **collect** [kə'lekt] sammeln **I**
collection [kə'lekʃn] Kollektion; Sammlung **II U1**, 14
collocation [ˌkɒlə'keɪʃn] Wortverbindung °**II U4**, 74
colony ['kɒləni] Kolonie **II AC3**, 73
colour ['kʌlə] Farbe **I**
What **colour** is …? [ˌwɒt 'kʌlər‿ɪz] Welche Farbe hat …? **I**
colourful ['kʌləfl] farbenfroh; bunt **I**
*to **come** [kʌm] kommen **I**
*to **come** down [ˌkʌm 'daʊn] herunterkommen **I**
*to **come** in [ˌkʌm‿'ɪn] hereinkommen **II U5**, 104
Come on! [ˌkʌm‿'ɒn] Komm schon!; Komm jetzt! **I**
comedian [kə'mi:diən] Komiker/-in; Comedian **II U1**, 14
comedy show ['kɒmədi ˌʃəʊ] Comedy Show **II U1**, 14
comic ['kɒmɪk] Comicheft **II U3**, 66
comment ['kɒment] Kommentar **II U1**, 16
to **comment** (on) ['kɒment‿(ɒn)] kommentieren **II U4**, 81
to **communicate** [kə'mju:nɪkeɪt] kommunizieren; sich verständigen **II AC3**, 73
communication [kəˌmju:nɪ'keɪʃn] Kommunikation °**II U4**, 75
community centre [kə'mju:nəti ˌsentə] Gemeindezentrum **I**
comparative [kəm'pærətɪv] Komparativ °**II U1**, 20
to **compare** (with/to) [kəm'peə] vergleichen (mit) **I**
comparison [kəm'pærɪsn] Vergleich °**II U2**, 41
competition [ˌkɒmpə'tɪʃn] Wettbewerb; Turnier **II AC1**, 9
Complete … [kəm'pli:t] Vervollständige/Vervollständigt … **I**
completely [kəm'pli:tli] völlig **II AC4**, 112
compound word ['kɒmpaʊnd wɜ:d] Kompositum *(zusammengesetztes Wort)* °**II U2**, 41
compromise ['kɒmprəmaɪz] Kompromiss **II U4**, 77
computer [ˌkəm'pju:tə] Computer **I**
con [kɒn] Argument dagegen **II U2**, 41
confident ['kɒnfɪdnt] selbstsicher; selbstbewusst **II AC1**, 11
connection [kə'nekʃn] Verbindung **II U5**, 96
contact ['kɒntækt] Kontakt **II U5**, 97
contest ['kɒntest] Wettkampf; Wettbewerb **I**
conversation [ˌkɒnvə'seɪʃn] Konversation; Gespräch; Unterhaltung **I**
to **cook** [kʊk] kochen **II U4**, 87
cooker ['kʊkə] Herd **I**
cooking ['kʊkɪŋ] Kochen **I**
Cooking Club ['kʊkɪŋ ˌklʌb] Koch-AG **I**
*to leave it to **cool** [ˌli:v‿ɪt tə 'ku:l] kalt stellen **I**
cool [ku:l] cool; super **I**
to **copy** ['kɒpi] abschreiben; kopieren **I**
corner ['kɔ:nə] Ecke **II U2**, 40
Cornish ['kɔ:nɪʃ] aus/in Cornwall; kornisch; Kornisch **II U5**, 94
Correct … [kə'rekt] Korrigiere/Korrigiert … **I**
correct [kə'rekt] richtig; korrekt **I**
*to **cost** [kɒst] kosten **I**
costume ['kɒstju:m] Kostüm **I**
cough [kɒf] Husten **II U3**, 59
could [kʊd] könnte/-n **II U2**, 43
to **count** (on) ['kaʊnt‿ɒn] zählen (auf) **I**
country ['kʌntri], **countries** ['kʌntriz] *(pl)* Land **I**
countryside ['kʌntrisaɪd] Land **II U5**, 94
couple ['kʌpl] Paar **II U5**, 100
a **couple** of [ə 'kʌpl‿əv] ein paar **I**
course [kɔ:s] Kurs **II U1**, 20
of **course** [əv 'kɔ:s] natürlich; selbstverständlich **I**
court [kɔ:t] Spielfeld **II U3**, 54

cousin ['kʌzn] Cousin/Cousine **I**
cow [kaʊ] Kuh **II U5**, 101
cramp [kræmp] Krampf **II U3**, 65
to **crash** [kræʃ] abstürzen **II U4**, 87
crazy ['kreɪzi] verrückt **I**
*to go **crazy** [ˌgəʊ 'kreɪzi] ausflippen; durchdrehen; verrückt werden **II U4**, 79
cream [kri:m] Creme; Sahne **I**
ice **cream** [ˌaɪs 'kri:m] Eis; Eiscreme **I**
to **create** [kri'eɪt] schaffen; erschaffen; erfinden **I**
creative [kri'eɪtɪv] kreativ **I**
credit ['kredɪt] Guthaben **II U2**, 38
cricket ['krɪkɪt] Cricket **II U3**, 55
crime [kraɪm] Verbrechen; Kriminalität **II AC4**, 112
criminal ['krɪmɪnəl] Kriminelle/-r; Verbrecher/-in **II AC4**, 112
crisp *(BE)* [krɪsp] Kartoffelchip **I**
to **cross** [krɒs] überqueren; kreuzen **II AC3**, 73
*to keep your fingers **crossed** [ˌki:p jɔ: ˌfɪŋgəz 'krɒst] die Daumen drücken **I**
crowd [kraʊd] Menschenmenge **II U2**, 44
crown jewels [ˌkraʊn 'dʒu:əlz] Kronjuwelen **II U2**, 42
cruel ['kru:əl] grausam **II AC4**, 112
to **cry** [kraɪ] schreien; rufen **II U4**, 86
CU *(= See you)* ['si: ju] Bis dann!; Bis … **I**
culture ['kʌltʃə] Kultur **I**
Across **cultures** [əˌkrɒs 'kʌltʃəz] Interkulturelles **I**
cupboard ['kʌbəd] Küchenschrank; Schrank **I**
curry ['kʌri] Curry *(Gewürz oder Gericht)* **I**
custard ['kʌstəd] Vanillesoße; Vanillepudding **I**
customer ['kʌstəmə] Kunde/Kundin **II U5**, 100
*to **cut** (off) [kʌt (ɒf)] schneiden; abschneiden **II U2**, 49
cute [kju:t] niedlich; süß **I**
cyber bully [ˌsaɪbə 'bʊli] *jemand, der andere in sozialen Netzwerken belästigt oder mobbed* **II U4**, 75
cycling ['saɪklɪŋ] Radfahren **I**

D

dad [dæd] Papa **I**
dance *(no pl)* [dɑ:ns] Tanz; Tanzveranstaltung **II AC1**, 8
to **dance** [dɑ:ns] tanzen **I**
I like singing and **dancing**. [ˌaɪ laɪk ˌsɪŋɪŋ‿ənd 'dɑ:nsɪŋ] Ich singe und tanze gern. **I**
dangerous ['deɪndʒrəs] gefährlich **I**
dangerously ['deɪndzrəsli] gefährlich °**II U4**, 88
the **dark** [ðə 'dɑ:k] Dunkelheit **II U1**, 22
dark [dɑ:k] dunkel **II U1**, 22
darkness ['dɑ:knəs] Dunkelheit **II U5**, 101
date [deɪt] Datum **I**
day [deɪ] Tag **I**
all **day** [ˌɔ:l 'deɪ] den ganzen Tag **II U1**, 18
one **day** [ˌwʌn 'deɪ] eines Tages **II U2**, 43
a **day** out in … [ə ˌdeɪ‿'aʊt ɪn] ein Tag in … **II U2**, 44
the next **day** [ðə ˌnekst 'deɪ] am nächsten Tag **II U1**, 15
dead [ded] tot **II U2**, 48
*to **deal** (with) [di:l] sich befassen mit; umgehen mit **II U2**, 40
Oh **dear**! [ˌəʊ 'dɪə] Oje! **II U5**, 104
Dear … [dɪə] Lieber …; Liebe … *(Anrede in Briefen)* **I**
Dear Sir or Madam [dɪə ˌsɜ:r‿ɔ: 'mædəm] Sehr geehrte Dame, sehr geehrter Herr **II U5**, 97
December [dɪ'sembə] Dezember **I**
to **decide** [dɪ'saɪd] (sich) entscheiden **I**
decision [dɪ'sɪʒn] Entscheidung °**II U5**, 95
*to make a **decision** [ˌmeɪk‿ə dɪ'sɪʒn] eine Entscheidung treffen °**II U2**, 47
deck [dek] Deck **I**
to **decorate** ['dekəreɪt] dekorieren; verzieren; schmücken **I**
decorations *(pl)* [ˌdekə'reɪʃnz] Dekoration; Schmuck **I**
deep [di:p] tief **II U5**, 93
definitely ['defɪnətli] bestimmt; definitiv; eindeutig **II U5**, 98
definition [ˌdefɪ'nɪʃn] Definition °**II U5**, 96
to **depart** [dɪ'pɑ:t] abfahren **II U5**, 96
to **depend** (on) [dɪ'pend‿(ɒn)] abhängen von **II U5**, 95
to **describe** [dɪ'skraɪb] beschreiben **I**
description [dɪ'skrɪpʃn] Beschreibung °**II U2**, 44
to **deserve** [dɪ'zɜ:v] verdienen **II U3**, 60
to **design** [dɪ'zaɪn] entwerfen; gestalten **II AC1**, 11
detail ['di:teɪl] Detail; Einzelheit °**II U2**, 45
private **detective** [ˌpraɪvət dɪ'tektɪv] Privatdetektiv/-in **II AC4**, 112
diagram ['daɪəgræm] Diagramm **I**
dialect ['daɪəlekt] Dialekt **II U5**, 99
dialogue ['daɪəlɒg] Dialog; Gespräch **I**
diary ['daɪəri] Tagebuch **II U5**, 106
diary entry ['daɪəri entri] Tagebucheintrag **II U5**, 106
dice [daɪs] Würfel °**II U1**, 16
Roll two **dice**. [ˌrəʊl ˌtu: 'daɪs] Würfle/Würfelt mit zwei Würfeln. **I**
dictionary ['dɪkʃnri] Wörterbuch **I**
difference ['dɪfrəns] Unterschied **I**
make a **difference** [ˌmeɪk‿ə‿'dɪfrns] etw. verändern **II AC1**, 11
different ['dɪfrnt] anders; unterschiedlich; verschieden **I**
It feels so **different** from … [ˌɪt‿fi:lz səʊ 'dɪfrnt frɒm] Es ist so anders hier im Vergleich zu … **II U5**, 98
difficult ['dɪfɪklt] schwierig **II U3**, 61
dinner ['dɪnə] Abendessen **I**
dinosaur ['daɪnəsɔ:] Dinosaurier **II U2**, 45
direct speech [dɪˌrekt 'spi:tʃ] direkte Rede °**II U5**, 99
direction [dɪ'rekʃn] Richtung **I**
dirty ['dɜ:ti] dreckig; schmutzig **II U2**, 48
disappointed [ˌdɪsə'pɔɪntɪd] enttäuscht **I**
disaster [dɪ'zɑ:stə] Desaster; Katastrophe; Unglück **II U4**, 86
to **discover** [dɪ'skʌvə] entdecken **II AC1**, 8
to **discuss** [dɪ'skʌs] diskutieren **I**
discussion [dɪ'skʌʃn] Diskussion **II U4**, 74
display [dɪ'spleɪ] Ausstellung **II U2**, 45
class **display** ['klɑ:s dɪˌspleɪ] Ausstellung in der Klasse **I**
distance ['dɪstns] Distanz; Entfernung **II U2**, 46
*to **do** [du:] machen; tun **I**
*to **do** about ['du:‿əˌbaʊt] unternehmen wegen **II U4**, 84
*to **do** our hair [ˌdu:‿aʊə 'heə] uns frisieren; unsere Haare machen **I**
Don't translate … [ˌdəʊnt trænz'leɪt] Übersetze/Übersetzt nicht … **I**
Don't worry! [ˌdəʊnt 'wʌri] Keine Sorge! **I**
We **did** it! [ˌwi: 'dɪd‿ɪt] Wir haben es geschafft! **II U3**, 65
doctor ['dɒktə] Arzt/Ärztin **II U3**, 58
dog [dɒg] Hund **I**
to walk the **dog** [ˌwɔ:k ðə 'dɒg] den Hund ausführen; mit dem Hund spazieren gehen **I**
I'm **dog-tired**. [ˌaɪm ˌdɒg'taɪəd] Ich bin hundemüde. **I**
door [dɔ:] Tür **I**
front **door** [ˌfrʌnt 'dɔ:] Haustür **II U4**, 86
down [daʊn] nach unten; herunter; hinunter **II U2**, 48
*to come **down** [ˌkʌm 'daʊn] herunterkommen **I**
*to go **down** [ˌgəʊ 'daʊn] hinuntergehen; nach unten gehen; entlanggehen **I**
to note **down** [ˌnəʊt 'daʊn] notieren; aufschreiben °**II U3**, 61
*to sit **down** [ˌsɪt 'daʊn] sich hinsetzen; sich setzen **I**
*to write **down** [ˌraɪt 'daʊn] aufschreiben **I**
to **download** [daʊn'ləʊd] herunterladen *(aus dem Internet)* **II U4**, 81
downstairs [ˌdaʊn'steəz] nach unten; im Untergeschoss; unten **II U4**, 86
draft [drɑ:ft] Entwurf; Konzept **I**
drama ['drɑ:mə] Theater; Drama **II AC1**, 8
dramatic [drə'mætɪk] dramatisch **II U2**, 49
*to **draw** [drɔ:] zeichnen **I**; ziehen °**II U5**, 103
drawing ['drɔ:ɪŋ] Zeichnung **I**
dream [dri:m] Traum **II U1**, 19
fancy **dress** ['fænsi dres] Verkleidung; Kostüm **II U3**, 64
drink [drɪŋk] Getränk **I**
*to **drink** [drɪŋk] trinken **I**
driver ['draɪvə] Fahrer/-in **II U1**, 17
to **drop** [drɒp] fallen (lassen) **II U2**, 48

during *(+ noun)* ['djʊərɪŋ] während *(+ Nomen)* **II U1**, 13
DVD [ˌdi:vi:'di:] DVD **I**

E

e.g. *(= for example)* [ˌi:'dʒi:] z.B. *(= zum Beispiel)* **I**
each [i:tʃ] jede/-r/-s **I**
each other [ˌi:tʃ‿'ʌðə] einander; sich; sich gegenseitig **I**
each [i:tʃ] pro Person; pro Stück **I**
early ['3:li] früh **I**
to **earn** [3:n] verdienen **I**
earth [3:θ] Erdboden; Erde; die Erde **II U2**, 45
What on **earth** ...? [ˌwɒt:ˌɒn‿'3:θ] Was um alles in der Welt ...? **II U4**, 79
more **easily** [mɔ:r‿'i:zɪli] leichter °**II U2**, 49
east [i:st] Osten; Ost- **I**
Easter ['i:stə] Ostern **I**
easy ['i:zi] einfach; leicht **I**
*to **eat** [i:t] essen; fressen **I**
Eco ['i:kəʊ] Öko- **II AC1**, 11
audio-visual **effect** [ˌɔ:diəʊvɪʒuəl ɪ'fekt] audiovisueller Effekt °**II U1**, 28
egg [eg] Ei **I**
eight [eɪt] acht **I**
electrician [ˌelɪk'trɪʃn] Elektriker/-in **II U5**, 105
electricity [ˌelɪk'trɪsəti] Elektrizität; Strom **II U5**, 104
electrics [ɪ'lektrɪks] Elektrik **II U5**, 105
electronic [ˌelek'trɒnɪk] elektronisch **II U1**, 25
element ['elɪmənt] Element °**II U5**, 101
elements that ... [ˌelɪməntz 'ðæt] Elemente, die ... °**II U5**, 101
eleven [ɪ'levn] elf **I**
nobody **else** ['nəʊbədi els] niemand anderes **II U5**, 106
what **else** [ˌwɒt‿'els] was sonst; was noch **I**
e-mail ['i:meɪl] E-Mail **I**
to **e-mail** ['i:meɪl] mailen; per E-Mail schicken **II U4**, 81
embarrassed [ɪm'bærəst] verlegen **II U1**, 13
embarrassing [ɪm'bærəsɪŋ] peinlich **II U1**, 12
end [end] Ende; Schluss **I**
in the **end** [ˌɪn ði‿'end] schließlich; zum Schluss **II U1**, 14
to **end** [end] enden; beenden **II U3**, 63
to **end** up [ˌend‿'ʌp] enden; landen **II U1**, 12
ending ['endɪŋ] Ende; Schluss *(einer Geschichte)* **I**
energy ['enədʒi] Energie; Kraft **II AC1**, 11
English ['ɪŋglɪʃ] englisch; Englisch; aus England; Engländer/-in **I**
English-speaking ['ɪŋglɪʃˌspi:kɪŋ] englischsprachig **I**
I'm **English**. [aɪm‿'ɪŋglɪʃ] Ich bin Engländer/-in. **I**
to **enjoy** [ɪn'dʒɔɪ] genießen; sich freuen an **II U1**, 16
they were **enjoying** [ˌðeɪ wər‿ɪn'dʒɔɪɪŋ] sie genossen gerade °**II U2**, 48
enough [ɪ'nʌf] genug; genügend **I**
diary **entry** ['daɪəri entri] Tagebucheintrag **II U5**, 106
equipment [ɪ'kwɪpmənt] Ausstattung; Ausrüstung **II U3**, 55
er [3:] äh **I**
escalator ['eskəleɪtə] Rolltreppe **I**
etc. *(= et cetera)* [ɪt'setrə] usw. *(= und so weiter)* °**II U4**, 85
euro ['jʊərəʊ] Euro *(Währung)* **I**
even ['i:vn] sogar; selbst **I**
evening ['i:vnɪŋ] Abend **I**
in the **evenings** [ɪn ði‿'i:vnɪŋz] abends **I**
event [ɪ'vent] Ereignis; Veranstaltung **I**
ever ['evə] jemals **II U3**, 56
every ['evri] jede/-r/-s **I**
everybody ['evribɒdi] jeder; alle **II U2**, 40
everyone ['evriwʌn] jeder; alle **I**
everything ['evriθɪŋ] alles **I**
everywhere ['evriweə] überall **I**
exactly [ɪg'zæktli] genau **II AC3**, 72
exam [ɪg'zæm] Examen; Prüfung **II AC1**, 8
example [ɪg'zɑ:mpl] Beispiel **I**
for **example** [fər‿ɪg'zɑ:mpl] zum Beispiel **II AC3**, 73
to **exchange** [ɪks'tʃeɪndʒ] austauschen °**II AC1**, 11
excited [ɪk'saɪtɪd] aufgeregt; begeistert **I**
exciting [ɪk'saɪtɪŋ] spannend; aufregend **I**
Excuse me ... [ɪk'skju:z mi] Entschuldigung!; Entschuldigen Sie! **I**
exercise ['eksəsaɪz] Übung; Aufgabe **I**
exercise book ['eksəsaɪz ˌbʊk] Übungsheft **I**
expensive [ɪk'spensɪv] teuer **I**
experience [ɪk'spɪəriəns] Erfahrung **II U3**, 55
expert ['eksp3:t] Experte/Expertin °**II U3**, 63
to **explain** [ɪk'spleɪn] erklären **I**
to **explore** [ɪk'splɔ:] auf Entdeckungsreise gehen; sich umschauen; erkunden; erforschen **I**
to **express** [ɪk'spres] ausdrücken °**II U3**, 66
expression [ɪk'spreʃn] Ausdruck; Wendung; Äußerung **II AC3**, 73
extra ['ekstrə] extra; zusätzlich **I**
eye [aɪ] Auge **II U1**, 13
I couldn't believe my **eyes**. [ai ˌkʊdnt bɪˌli:v maɪ‿'aɪz] Ich traute meinen Augen nicht. **II U3**, 61
eyewitness ['aɪwɪtnəs] Augenzeuge/Augenzeugin **II U3**, 61

F

face [feɪs] Gesicht **I**
Put ... **face** down. [pʊt ˌfeɪs 'daʊn] Lege/Legt ... umgedreht hin. **I**
face-to-face [ˌfeɪstə'feɪs] *hier:* persönlich; von Angesicht zu Angesicht **II U4**, 77
fact [fækt] Fakt; Tatsache **II AC2**, 34
fair [feə] gerecht; fair **I**
to **fake** [feɪk] vortäuschen; fälschen **II U3**, 60
*to **fall** [fɔ:l] fallen; hinfallen **I**
*to **fall** asleep [ˌfɔ:l‿ə'sli:p] einschlafen **I**
*to **fall** off [ˌfɔ:l‿'ɒf] herunterfallen; hinunterfallen **II U3**, 59
*to **fall** over [ˌfɔ:l‿'əʊvə] hinfallen; umkippen **I**
family ['fæmli] Familie **I**
family tree ['fæmli ˌtri:] Stammbaum **I**
famous ['feɪməs] berühmt **I**
fancy dress ['fænsi dres] Verkleidung; Kostüm **II U3**, 64
fantastic [fæn'tæstɪk] fantastisch; großartig **II AC1**, 9
fantasy ['fæntəsi] Fantasie; Traum- **I**
far [fɑ:] weit **II U2**, 41
so **far** [ˌsəʊ 'fɑ:] bis jetzt **II U3**, 60
fare [feə] Fahrpreis **II U5**, 96
farm [fɑ:m] Farm; Bauernhof **I**
farmer ['fɑ:mə] Farmer/-in; Landwirt/-in **II U1**, 17
fashion ['fæʃn] Mode **II AC1**, 8
fast [fɑ:st] schnell **I**
father ['fɑ:ðə] Vater **I**
a **father** who ... [ə ˌfɑ:ðə 'hu:] ein Vater, der ... °**II U5**, 100
favourite ['feɪvrɪt] Lieblings- **I**
My **favourite** ... [maɪ 'feɪvrɪt] Mein/e Lieblings ... **I**
What's your **favourite** ...? ['wɒts jə ˌfeɪvrɪt] Was ist dein/-e Lieblings...? **I**
fear [fɪə] Angst; Furcht; Befürchtung **II U3**, 66
February ['februri] Februar **I**
fee [fi:] Gebühr **II U5**, 96
*to **feed** [fi:d] füttern; ernähren **II U5**, 101
*to **feel** [fi:l] fühlen; sich fühlen **I**
*to **feel** left out [ˌfi:l left‿'aʊt] sich ausgeschlossen fühlen **II U4**, 88
*to **feel** sick [ˌfi:l 'sɪk] Übelkeit verspüren; sich schlecht fühlen **II U3**, 59
It **feels** so different from ... [ˌɪt‿fi:lz səʊ 'dɪfrnt frɒm] Es ist so anders hier im Vergleich zu ... **II U5**, 98
feeling ['fi:lɪŋ] Gefühl **II U1**, 13
festival ['festɪvl] Festival; Fest **I**
fever ['fi:və] Fieber **II U3**, 59
few [fju:] wenige **II U1**, 22
a **few** [ə 'fju:] ein paar; wenige; einige **I**
science **fiction** [ˌsaɪəns 'fɪkʃn] Science-Fiction *(Zukunftsdichtung)* **II U1**, 26
field [fi:ld] Feld; Spielfeld; Wiese; Weide; Acker **II U1**, 22
fifteen [ˌfɪf'ti:n] fünfzehn **I**
fight [faɪt] Kampf; Streit **II U4**, 76
*to **fight** [faɪt] kämpfen; (sich) streiten **II U4**, 86
figure ['fɪgə] Figur; Gestalt **II U2**, 37
wax **figure** ['wæks ˌfɪgə] Wachsfigur **II U2**, 37
to **fill** in [ˌfɪl‿'ɪn] ausfüllen °**II U4**, 80

film [fɪlm] Film **I**

to **film** [fɪlm] filmen; drehen °**II U5**, 101

filmmaker ['fɪlm,meɪkə] Filmemacher/-in **II U1**, 28

final ['faɪnl] endgültig °**II U3**, 63

finally ['faɪnli] schließlich; endlich; zum Schluss; letztlich **II U3**, 65

*to **find** [faɪnd] finden; herausfinden **I**

*to **find** out [ˌfaɪnd‿'aʊt] herausfinden **I**

fine [faɪn] gut; in Ordnung; schön **I**

I'm **fine**. [ˌaɪm 'faɪn] Mir geht's gut. **I**

finger ['fɪŋgə] Finger **I**

*to keep your **fingers** crossed [ˌki:p jɔ: ˌfɪŋgəz 'krɒst] die Daumen drücken **I**

finish line ['fɪnɪʃ ˌlaɪn] Ziellinie **II U3**, 65

to **finish** ['fɪnɪʃ] beenden; enden; fertigstellen; aufhören **I**

finished ['fɪnɪʃt] fertig °**II U4**, 83

fireworks *(pl)* ['faɪəwɜ:ks] Feuerwerk **I**

first [fɜ:st] zuerst; als Erstes; erste/-r/-s **I**

at **first** [ət 'fɜ:st] zuerst; zunächst **II U2**, 49

first language [ˌfɜ:st 'læŋgwɪdʒ] Muttersprache **II AC3**, 73

fish [fɪʃ], **fish** [fɪʃ] *(pl)* Fisch **I**

to **fit** [fɪt] passen °**II U4**, 85

*to get **fit** [ˌget 'fɪt] in Form kommen; fit werden **I**

five [faɪv] fünf **I**

to **fix** [fɪks] reparieren; befestigen **II U4**, 79

flair [fleə] Flair; Atmosphäre **II U2**, 37

flat [flæt] Wohnung **I**

flea market ['fli: ˌmɑ:kɪt] Flohmarkt **I**

floor [flɔ:] Fußboden **I**

to **flow** out [fləʊ‿'aʊt] hinausfließen **II U2**, 48

flower ['flaʊə] Blume **II U4**, 80

flyer ['flaɪə] Flyer **I**

folder ['fəʊldə] Ordner; Mappe **I**

to **follow** ['fɒləʊ] folgen; hinterhergehen; befolgen **II U2**, 40

the **following** [ðə 'fɒləʊɪŋ] folgende/-r/-s °**II U5**, 93

food [fu:d] Essen; Lebensmittel **I**

foot [fʊt], **feet** [fi:t] *(pl)* Fuß **I**

on **foot** [ɒn 'fʊt] zu Fuß **II U2**, 46

football ['fʊtbɔ:l] Fußball **I**

for [fɔ:; fə] wegen **II U4**, 75

for example [fər‿ɪg'zɑ:mpl] zum Beispiel **II AC3**, 73

for … [fɔ:; fə] … lang **II U1**, 16

weather **forecast** ['weðə ˌfɔ:kɑ:st] Wettervorhersage **II U5**, 96

forest ['fɒrɪst] Wald **II U1**, 20

forever [fə'revə] für immer; ewig **II U4**, 77

*to **forget** [fə'get] vergessen **I**

*to **forgive** [fə'gɪv] vergeben; verzeihen **II U3**, 65

form [fɔ:m] Form **I**; Formular **II U5**, 96

negative **form** ['negətɪv ˌfɔ:m] verneinte Form **I**

past **form** ['pɑ:st fɔ:m] Vergangenheitsform °**II U1**, 14

possessive **form** [pəˌzesɪv 'fɔ:m] Possessivform **I**

short **form** ['ʃɔ:t fɔ:m] Kurzform **I**

to **form** [fɔ:m] formen; bilden °**II U3**, 63

formal ['fɔ:ml] formal; formell; förmlich °**II U3**, 61

forum ['fɔ:rəm] Forum **II U4**, 74

four [fɔ:] vier **I**

Four and six is ten. [ˌfɔ:r‿ənd ˌsɪks‿ɪz 'ten] Vier plus sechs ist zehn. **I**

free [fri:] frei; kostenlos **I**

free time [ˌfri: 'taɪm] Freizeit **I**

freely ['fri:li] frei ⟨**II U4**, 85⟩

French [frenʃ] französisch; Französisch **II AC1**, 10

frequently asked [ˌfri:kwəntli‿'ɑ:skt] häufig gefragt **I**

fresh [freʃ] frisch **I**

Friday ['fraɪdeɪ] Freitag **I**

fridge [frɪdʒ] Kühlschrank **I**

friend [frend] Freund/-in **I**

*to make **friends** [ˌmeɪk 'frendz] Freundschaft schließen **II U5**, 94

friends and family who … [frendz‿ən‿ˌfæməli 'hu:] Freunde und Familienmitglieder, die … °**II U4**, 81

That's what **friends** are for. [ˌðæts wɒt 'frendz‿ɑ: ˌfɔ:] Dafür sind Freunde da. **I**

friendly ['frendli] freundlich; nett **II U1**, 18

friendship ['frendʃɪp] Freundschaft **II U4**, 78

from [frɒm; frəm] aus; von **I**

from … to [frəm … tə] von … bis **I**

Where … **from**? [ˌweə … 'frɒm] Woher …? **I**

front [frʌnt] Vorderseite; Front-; Vorder- °**II U5**, 102

front door [ˌfrʌnt 'dɔ:] Haustür **II U4**, 86

in **front** of [ɪn 'frʌnt‿əv] vor **I**

fruit [fru:t] Frucht; Obst **I**

full (of) [fʊl‿əv] voll (von) **I**

fun [fʌn] Freude; Spaß **I**

*to have **fun** [ˌhæv 'fʌn] Spaß haben; sich amüsieren **I**

It's **fun**. [ɪts 'fʌn] Es macht Spaß. **I**

fun [fʌn] lustig; witzig; fröhlich **I**

funny ['fʌni] lustig; witzig **I**

future ['fju:tʃə] Zukunft **II U5**, 93

G

gallery walk ['gæləri ˌwɔ:k] Museumsrundgang; Vernissage **I**

game [geɪm] Spiel **I**

guessing **game** ['gesɪŋ ˌgeɪm] Ratespiel °**II U1**, 17

gap [gæp] Lücke; Spalt; Abstand **I**

garage ['gærɑ:ʒ] Garage **I**

garden ['gɑ:dn] Garten **I**

genius ['dʒi:niəs] Genie **II U4**, 79

geocaching ['dʒi:əʊkæʃɪŋ] Geocaching **II U5**, 101

Geography [dʒi'ɒgrəfi] Geografie; Erdkunde **II AC1**, 10

German ['dʒɜ:mən] deutsch; Deutsch; aus Deutschland; Deutsche/-r **I**

*to **get** [get] holen; bringen; bekommen; besorgen; kaufen **I**; werden **II U5**, 104

*to **get** around [ˌget‿ə'raʊnd] *hier:* sich fortbewegen **II U2**, 37

*to **get** away with [ˌget‿ə'weɪ wɪð] davonkommen mit **II U3**, 60

*to **get** bored [get‿'bɔ:d] sich langweilen **II U5**, 98

*to **get** fit [ˌget 'fɪt] in Form kommen; fit werden **I**

*to **get** in the way [ˌget‿ɪn ðə 'weɪ] stören; im Weg stehen **II U3**, 64

*to **get** into [ˌget‿'ɪntə] einsteigen; hineingelangen **I**

*to **get** lost [ˌget 'lɒst] verloren gehen; sich verirren **II U5**, 101

*to **get** off (a bus/train) [ˌget‿'ɒf] aussteigen (aus einem Bus/Zug) **II U2**, 39

*to **get** on (the bus) [ˌget‿'ɒn] einsteigen (in den Bus) **II U5**, 96

*to **get** on people's nerves [ˌget‿ɒn sʌmbɒdiz 'nɜ:vz] jemandem auf die Nerven gehen **I**

*to **get** organised [get 'ɔ:gənaɪzd] sich organisieren °**II U5**, 102

*to **get** out of [get ˌaʊt‿əv] aussteigen; herauskommen aus **II U4**, 86

*to **get** right [get 'raɪt] richtig beantworten °**II U5**, 103

*to **get** there ['get ðeə] hinkommen **I**

*to **get** to ['get tə] kommen zu; kommen nach; erreichen **I**

*to **get** up [ˌget‿'ʌp] aufstehen *(aus dem Bett)* **I**

Time to **get** up! [ˌtaɪm tə ˌget‿'ʌp] Es ist Zeit aufzustehen! **I**

ghost [gəʊst] Geist; Gespenst **II U2**, 42

girl [gɜ:l] Mädchen **I**

a **girl** from Germany [ə ˌgɜ:l frəm 'dʒɜ:məni] ein Mädchen aus Deutschland **I**

girlfriend ['gɜ:lfrend] Freundin *(in einer Paarbeziehung)* **II U2**, 40

gist [dʒɪst] das Wesentliche °**II U2**, 42

*to **give** [gɪv] geben; schenken **I**

*to **give** the bumps [ˌgɪv ðə 'bʌmps] hochleben lassen **I**

glass [glɑ:s] Glas **I**

glasses *(pl)* ['glɑ:sɪz] Brille **II U3**, 64

glove [glʌv] Handschuh **I**

*to **go** [gəʊ] gehen; fahren **I**

*to **go** black [ˌgəʊ 'blæk] schwarz werden **II U4**, 86

*to **go** crazy [ˌgəʊ 'kreɪzi] ausflippen; durchdrehen; verrückt werden **II U4**, 79

*to **go** down [ˌgəʊ 'daʊn] hinuntergehen; nach unten gehen; entlanggehen **I**

*to **go** for a walk [ˌgəʊ fər‿ə 'wɔ:k] spazieren gehen **II U1**, 22
*to **go** on [ˌgəʊ‿'ɒn] weitergehen; weitermachen; weiterführen; fortfahren **I**
*to **go** out [ˌgəʊ‿'aʊt] ausgehen; hinausgehen **II U5**, 104
*to **go** over to [ˌgəʊ 'əʊvə tə] hinübergehen zu; zu jmdm. nach Hause gehen **II U4**, 79
*to **go** right back to [ˌgəʊ raɪt 'bæk tə] zurückgehen auf **II U5**, 104
*to **go** shopping [ˌgəʊ 'ʃɒpɪŋ] einkaufen gehen **I**
*to **go** swimming [ˌgəʊ 'swɪmɪŋ] Schwimmen gehen **I**
*to **go** to bed [ˌgəʊ tə 'bed] ins Bett gehen **I**
*to **go** together [ˌgəʊ tə'geðə] zueinander passen; zueinander gehören **I**
*to **go** with ['gəʊ wɪð] passen zu; gehören zu **I**
*to **go** wrong [ˌgəʊ 'rɒŋ] schiefgehen **I**
*to let **go** (of) [ˌlet 'gəʊ (əv)] loslassen **II U3**, 64
It's **gone**. [ɪts 'gɒn] Es ist weg. **II U2**, 48
*to be **gone** [bi: 'gɒn] verschwunden sein; weg sein **II U3**, 65
goal [gəʊl] Tor; Ziel **I**
good [gʊd] gut **I**
*to be **good** at [bi: 'gʊd‿ət] gut sein in **I**
good for someone who … [ˌgʊd‿fə ˌsʌmwʌn 'hu:] gut für jemanden, der … °**II U2**, 41
Good morning. [ˌgʊd 'mɔ:nɪŋ] Guten Morgen. **I**
goodbye [gʊd'baɪ] auf Wiedersehen **I**
gorge scrambling ['gɔ:dʒ ˌskræmblɪŋ] Schluchtenklettern **II U1**, 20
to **grab** [græb] greifen; ergreifen; schnappen **II U2**, 48
grammar school ['græmə ˌsku:l] Gymnasium **II U5**, 97
grandad ['grændæd] Opa **I**
grandma ['grænmɑ:] Oma **I**
grandparents *(pl)* ['grænˌpeərənts] Großeltern **I**
granny ['græni] Oma **I**
great [greɪt] großartig; toll; super **I**
It's **great** for … [ɪts 'greɪt fə] Es ist super zum/für … **I**
green [gri:n] grün **I**
Greenwich Mean Time *(= GMT)* [ˌgrenɪdʒ 'mi:n ˌtaɪm] westeuropäische Zeit **I**
greeting ['gri:tɪŋ] Gruß **I**
grey [greɪ] grau **I**
grid [grɪd] Gitter; Tabelle; Raster **I**
group [gru:p] Gruppe; Klasse **I**
a **group** of three [ə ˌgru:p‿əv 'θri:] eine Dreiergruppe **I**
tutor **group** ['tju:tə ˌgru:p] Klasse *(in einer englischen Schule)* **I**
*to **grow** [grəʊ] wachsen **II U5**, 93
guard [gɑ:d] Wache; Wächter/-in **II AC2**, 35
to **guess** [ges] raten; erraten; vermuten **I**
guessing game ['gesɪŋ ˌgeɪm] Ratespiel °**II U1**, 17
guide [gaɪd] Führer/-in; Reiseführer **II U2**, 42
guinea pig ['gɪni: ˌpɪg] Meerschweinchen **I**
guy [gaɪ] Typ; Kerl; *(Pl.)* Leute **II U1**, 13

H

*to do our **hair** [ˌdu:‿aʊə 'heə] uns frisieren; unsere Haare machen **I**
half [hɑ:f], **halves** [hɑ:vz] *(pl)* (of) die Hälfte **I**
half [hɑ:f] halb **I**
half past [ˌhɑ:f 'pɑ:st] halb *(bei Uhrzeitangaben)* **I**
half-sister ['hɑ:fˌsɪstə] Halbschwester **I**
half-term break [ˌhɑ:ftɜ:m 'breɪk] Halbjahresferien **I**
hall [hɔ:l] Halle; Saal **II AC1**, 9; Flur; Diele; Korridor **II U5**, 104
hand [hænd] Hand **I**
Clap your **hands**. [ˌklæp jɔ: 'hændz] Klatsch/Klatscht in die Hände. **I**
On the one **hand** …, (but) on the other **hand** … [ɒn ðə‿'wʌn ˌhænd … (bʌt) ɒn ði‿'ʌðə ˌhænd …] Einerseits …, (aber) andererseits … **II U3**, 66
to **happen** ['hæpn] geschehen; passieren **I**
happy ['hæpi] glücklich; froh; fröhlich **I**
Happy Birthday! [ˌhæpi 'bɜ:θdeɪ] Alles Gute zum Geburtstag!; Herzlichen Glückwunsch zum Geburtstag! **I**
harbour ['hɑ:bə] Hafen **II U5**, 93
hard [hɑ:d] hart; schwer; schwierig **II U1**, 16
hat [hæt] Hut **I**
to **hate** [heɪt] hassen; nicht mögen **II U5**, 94
*to **have** [hæv] haben **I**
*to **have** a look (at) [ˌhæv‿ə 'lʊk] anschauen **II U3**, 59
*to **have** breakfast [ˌhæv 'brekfəst] frühstücken **I**
*to **have** fun [ˌhæv 'fʌn] Spaß haben; sich amüsieren **I**
*to **have** got [hæv 'gɒt] besitzen; haben **I**
*to **have** to ['hæv tə] müssen **II U4**, 79
*to **have** *(a sweet)* [hæv] *(ein Bonbon)* nehmen; *(ein Bonbon)* essen **I**
he [hi:] er **I**
head [hed] Kopf **I**
head of state [ˌhed‿əv 'steɪt] Staatsoberhaupt **II AC3**, 73
With a very big **head**! [ˌwɪð ə ˌveri bɪg 'hed] Und ein Angeber! **II U4**, 79
headache *(no pl)* ['hedeɪk] Kopfschmerzen; Kopfweh **II U3**, 59
heading ['hedɪŋ] Überschrift; Titel **I**
headphones *(pl)* ['hedfəʊnz] Kopfhörer **II U4**, 86
health [helθ] Gesundheit **II U3**, 55
healthy ['helθi] gesund **I**
*to **hear** [hɪə] hören **I**
I **hear** … [aɪ 'hɪə] Ich habe gehört, dass … **I**
heart [hɑ:t] Herz; *hier:* Zentrum **II U2**, 48
*to learn … by **heart** [ˌlɜ:n baɪ 'hɑ:t] auswendig lernen **I**
Hello. [hel'əʊ] Hallo. **I**
*to say **hello** (to) [ˌseɪ hel'əʊ tə] grüßen; Grüße ausrichten (an) **I**
help [help] Hilfe **I**
to **help** [help] helfen **I**
helpful ['helpfl] hilfsbereit; hilfreich **I**
helpless ['helpləs] hilflos **I**
her [hɜ:] ihr/-e; sie **I**
here [hɪə] hier **I**
right **here** [ˌraɪt 'hɪə] genau hier **II U3**, 56
Here you are. [ˌhɪə ju‿'ɑ:] Bitte schön. **I**
hero ['hɪərəʊ], **heroes** ['hɪərəʊz] *(pl)* Held **II AC4**, 112
heroine ['herəʊɪn] Heldin **II AC4**, 112
Hey! [heɪ] Hi.; He!; Hallo. **I**
Hi. [haɪ] Hi.; Hallo. **I**
*to **hide** [haɪd] (sich) verstecken **II AC4**, 112
high [haɪ] hoch; groß **II U1**, 21
high tide ['haɪ ˌtaɪd] Flut **II U2**, 48
highlight ['haɪlaɪt] Highlight; Höhepunkt **II U1**, 13
hiking ['haɪkɪŋ] Wandern **II U5**, 93
hill [hɪl] Berg; Hügel **II U5**, 104
him [hɪm] ihn; ihm **I**
himself [hɪm'self] er/sich (selbst); selber **II U1**, 12
his [hɪz] sein/-e **I**
historical [hɪ'stɒrɪkl] historisch; geschichtlich **I**
History ['hɪstri] Geschichte **II AC1**, 10
ancient **history** [ˌeɪnʃnt 'hɪstri] antike Geschichte; Frühgeschichte **II U5**, 98
living **history** show [ˌlɪvɪŋ 'hɪstəri ˌʃəʊ] *Show, in der historischer Alltag nachgespielt wird* **II U5**, 92
*to **hit** [hɪt] schlagen; treffen **I**
hobby ['hɒbi], **hobbies** ['hɒbiz] *(pl)* Hobby **I**
hockey [hɒki] Hockey **II U3**, 55
*to **hold** [həʊld] halten; festhalten **I**
holiday ['hɒlədeɪ] Urlaub; Feiertag **I**
holidays *(pl)* ['hɒlədeɪz] Ferien **I**
home [həʊm] Zuhause; Heim **I**
at **home** [ət 'həʊm] zu Hause **I**
home [həʊm] nach Hause **I**
homepage ['həʊmpeɪdʒ] Homepage **I**
homework ['həʊmwɜ:k] Hausaufgabe(n) **I**
hope [həʊp] Hoffnung **II U3**, 66
to **hope** [həʊp] hoffen **I**
hopeful ['həʊpfl] hoffnungsvoll **I**
horrified ['hɒrɪfaɪd] entsetzt **I**
horse [hɔ:s] Pferd **I**
hospital ['hɒspɪtl] Krankenhaus; Hospital **II U3**, 62
hot [hɒt] heiß **II U5**, 98
hour [aʊə] Stunde **II U2**, 49
house [haʊs] Haus **I**

to move (**house**) [muːv (haʊs)] umziehen **II U5**, 94
how [haʊ] wie **I**
How many …? [ˌhaʊ 'meni] Wie viele …? **I**
How are you? [ˌhaʊ‿'ɑː jə] Wie geht es dir/euch/Ihnen?; Wie geht es euch?; Wie geht es Ihnen? **I**
How much (is/are) …? [ˌhaʊ 'mʌtʃ‿ɪz/ɑː] Wie viel (kostet/kosten) …? **I**
How old are you? [haʊ‿'əʊld‿ə ˌjuː] Wie alt bist du?; Wie alt sind Sie? **I**
How to … ['haʊ tə] Wie man … **I**
Is this **how** you (do) …? [ɪz 'ðɪs haʊ jʊ ˌduː] Machst du so …? **I**
that's **how** [ðæts 'haʊ] so **II U1**, 14
to hug [hʌg] umarmen **I**
huge [hjuːdʒ] riesig; riesengroß; gewaltig **II AC2**, 34
human body [ˌhjuːmən 'bɒdi] menschlicher Körper **II U2**, 48
Humanities *(pl)* [hjuː'mænətiz] Sozialwissenschaften **II AC1**, 10
hungry ['hʌŋgri] hungrig **I**
to hurry ['hʌri] eilen; sich beeilen **I**
*to hurt [hɜːt] verletzen; weh tun **II U3**, 58
hurt [hɜːt] verletzt **II U1**, 28

I

I [aɪ] ich **I**
I don't know! [ˌaɪ ˌdəʊnt 'nəʊ] Ich weiß (es) nicht! **I**
I don't like … [aɪ 'dəʊnt laɪk] Ich mag … nicht.; Ich mache … nicht gern. **I**
I hear … [aɪ 'hɪə] Ich habe gehört, dass … **I**
I like … [aɪ 'laɪk] Mir gefällt …; Ich mag … **I**
I love you. [aɪ 'lʌv ju] Ich liebe dich.; Ich mag dich. **I**
I love … [aɪ 'lʌv] Ich liebe …; Ich mag … total gern. **I**
I'd like to … *(= I would like to)* [aɪd 'laɪk tə] Ich möchte …; Ich würde gern … **I**
I'm (not) scared of … [ˌaɪm (nɒt) 'skeəd‿əv] Ich habe (keine) Angst vor … **I**
I'm dog-tired. [ˌaɪm ˌdɒg'taɪəd] Ich bin hundemüde. **I**
I'm English. [aɪm‿'ɪŋglɪʃ] Ich bin Engländer/-in. **I**
I'm fine. [ˌaɪm 'faɪn] Mir geht's gut. **I**
I'm from … [ˌaɪm frɒm] Ich bin aus … **I**
I'm sorry! [ˌaɪm 'sɒri] Tut mir leid! **I**
I'm the one who … [ˌaɪm ðə‿wʌn 'huː] ich bin diejenige, die … °**II U3**, 64
ice [aɪs] Eis **I**
ice cream [ˌaɪs 'kriːm] Eis; Eiscreme **I**
ice rink ['aɪs ˌrɪŋk] Eisbahn; Schlittschuhbahn **I**
idea [aɪ'dɪə] Idee; Einfall **I**
no **idea** [ˌnəʊ‿aɪ'dɪə] keine Ahnung **II U1**, 23
identity [aɪ'dentəti] Identität **II AC2**, 35
idiot ['ɪdiət] Idiot/-in **II U2**, 49
if [ɪf] wenn; falls; ob **I**
to imagine [ɪ'mædʒɪn] sich (etwas) vorstellen **I**
important [ɪm'pɔːtnt] wichtig **I**
*to be impressed [bi ɪm'prest] beeindruckt sein **II U4**, 87
to improve [ɪm'pruːv] sich verbessern; verbessern **I**
in [ɪn] in; im; rein; herein **I**
in front of [ɪn 'frʌnt‿əv] vor **I**
in need [ɪn 'niːd] bedürftig; in Not **II U1**, 14
in secret [ɪn 'siːkrət] heimlich **II U3**, 65
in the end [ˌɪn ði‿'end] schließlich; zum Schluss **II U1**, 14
in the evenings [ɪn ði‿'iːvnɪŋz] abends **I**
in the mornings [ˌɪn ðə 'mɔːnɪŋz] morgens; vormittags **I**
in the photo(s) [ˌɪn ðə 'fəʊtəʊ(z)] auf dem Foto/den Fotos **I**
in the street [ˌɪn ðə 'striːt] in der Straße; auf der Straße **I**
to include [ɪn'kluːd] einschließen; beinhalten **II U5**, 92
Indian ['ɪndiən] Inder/-in; indisch **I**
indirect speech [ˌɪndɪrekt 'spiːtʃ] indirekte Rede °**II U5**, 99
individual [ˌɪndɪ'vɪdʒuəl] individuell; einzeln **II U3**, 55
infinitive [ɪn'fɪnətɪv] Infinitiv **I**
to influence ['ɪnfluəns] beeinflussen **II AC3**, 73
information *(no pl)* [ˌɪnfə'meɪʃn] Information; Informationen **I**
ingredient [ɪn'griːdiənt] Zutat **II AC4**, 112
injury ['ɪndʒəri] Verletzung **II U3**, 60
inline skating ['ɪnlaɪn ˌskeɪtɪŋ] Inlineskatefahren **I**
inside [ˌɪn'saɪd] innen; im Innern; hinein; nach drinnen; in; drin **I**
instruction [ɪn'strʌkʃn] Instruktion; Anweisung **I**
instructor [ɪn'strʌktə] Lehrer/-in; Betreuer/-in **II U1**, 22
interest ['ɪntrəst] Interesse **II U4**, 74
*to be interested in [bi‿'ɪntrəstɪd‿ɪn] interessiert sein an; sich interessieren für **II U2**, 36
interesting ['ɪntrəstɪŋ] interessant **I**
international [ˌɪntə'næʃnl] international **I**
internet ['ɪntənet] Internet **I**
interview ['ɪntəvjuː] Interview; Befragung **I**
to interview ['ɪntəvjuː] interviewen; befragen **I**
into ['ɪntə] in; in … hinein **I**
*to be **into** [biː‿'ɪntə] mögen; stehen auf **I**
Introduce … [ˌɪntrə'djuːs] Stelle/Stellt … vor. **I**
introduction [ˌɪntrə'dʌkʃn] Einführung; Einleitung; Vorstellung **II U3**, 59
invitation [ˌɪnvɪ'teɪʃn] Einladung **I**
to invite [ɪn'vaɪt] einladen **I**
inward ['ɪnwəd] ankommend **II U5**, 96
irregular [ɪ'regjələ] unregelmäßig **I**
Is this how you (do) …? [ɪz 'ðɪs haʊ jʊ ˌduː] Machst du so …? **I**
island ['aɪlənd] Insel **II U5**, 93
it [ɪt] es **I**
It's fun. [ɪts 'fʌn] Es macht Spaß. **I**
It's great for … [ɪts 'greɪt fə] Es ist super zum/für … **I**
It's your turn. [ˌɪts 'jɔː tɜːn] Du bist dran. **I**
It's …/They're … [ɪts/ðeə] Es kostet …/Sie kosten … **I**
its [ɪts] sein/-e; ihr/-e **I**

J

January ['dʒænjuri] Januar **I**
*to be jealous (of) [biː 'dʒeləs] eifersüchtig sein (auf); neidisch sein (auf) **I**
jelly ['dʒeli] Tortenguss; Götterspeise; Wackelpudding; Gelee **I**
crown jewels [ˌkraʊn 'dʒuːəlz] Kronjuwelen **II U2**, 42
jewellery ['dʒuːəlri] Schmuck **I**
job [dʒɒb] Arbeit; Aufgabe; Job **I**
mouth jogging ['maʊθ ˌdʒɒgɪŋ] Training für den Mund **I**
to join [dʒɔɪn] beitreten; sich anschließen; verbinden **II AC1**, 11
joke [dʒəʊk] Witz **I**
to joke [dʒəʊk] scherzen **II U4**, 86
journey ['dʒɜːni] Reise; Fahrt **II U5**, 93
juice [dʒuːs] Saft **I**
July [dʒʊ'laɪ] Juli **I**
to jump [dʒʌmp] springen **I**
to **jump** back [ˌdʒʌmp‿'bæk] zurückspringen; *hier:* zurückschrecken **II U2**, 43
to **jump** the queue [ˌdʒʌmp ðə 'kjuː] sich vordrängeln **I**
June [dʒuːn] Juni **I**
just [dʒʌst] gerade; nur; einfach **I**

K

*to keep [kiːp] behalten; aufbewahren; halten **I**
*to **keep** away from [ˌkiːp‿ə'weɪ frəm] (sich) fernhalten von **II U5**, 104
*to **keep** going [ˌkiːp 'gəʊɪŋ] aufrechterhalten **II U1**, 16
*to **keep** up (with) [ˌkiːp‿'ʌp (wɪð)] mithalten (mit); Schritt halten (mit) **II U3**, 64
*to **keep** your fingers crossed [ˌkiːp jɔː ˌfɪŋgəz 'krɒst] die Daumen drücken **I**
key [kiː] Schlüssel **II U2**, 49
key word ['kiː wɜːd] Stichwort; Schlüsselbegriff **I**
to kick [kɪk] schießen; treten **II U3**, 54
kind [kaɪnd] Art; Sorte **I**
king [kɪŋ] König **I**
kitchen ['kɪtʃɪn] Küche **I**

knight [naɪt] Ritter **II AC4**, 112
knob [nɒb] Griff **II U4**, 79
*to **know** [nəʊ] kennen; wissen **I**
I don't **know**! [ˌaɪ ˌdəʊnt 'nəʊ] Ich weiß (es) nicht! **I**
You **know** how to ... [ju: 'nəʊ ˌhaʊ tə] Du weißt, wie man ...; Ihr wisst, wie man ... **I**
Korean [kə'ri:ən] koreanisch; Koreanisch; Koreaner/-in **II U3**, 60
South **Korean** [ˌsaʊθ kə'ri:ən] Südkoreaner/-in; südkoreanisch; Südkoreanisch **II AC3**, 72

L

lake [leɪk] See **I**
boating **lake** ['bəʊtɪŋ ˌleɪk] See zum Rudern **I**
lamb [læm] Lamm; Lämmchen **I**
land [lænd] Land **I**
to **land** [lænd] landen **II U3**, 62
landscape ['lændskeɪp] Landschaft **II U5**, 92
language ['læŋgwɪdʒ] Sprache **I**
first **language** [ˌfɜ:st 'læŋgwɪdʒ] Muttersprache **II AC3**, 73
official **language** [əˌfɪʃl 'læŋgwɪdʒ] Amtssprache **II AC3**, 73
laptop ['læptɒp] Laptop **II U4**, 81
large [lɑ:dʒ] groß; riesig **II AC2**, 34
lassi ['lʌsi] Lassi **I**
last [lɑ:st] letzte/-r/-s **I**
at **last** [ət 'lɑ:st] endlich; schließlich **I**
late [leɪt] spät; zu spät **I**
*to be **late** [bi: 'leɪt] zu spät dran sein; zu spät kommen **I**
later ['leɪtə] später **I**
to **laugh** [lɑ:f] lachen **I**
*to **learn** [lɜ:n] lernen **I**
*to **learn** ... by heart [ˌlɜ:n baɪ 'hɑ:t] auswendig lernen **I**
a lot to **learn** [ə ˌlɒt tə 'lɜ:n] viel zu lernen **I**
at **least** [ət 'li:st] mindestens; wenigstens °**II U2**, 50
*to **leave** [li:v] losgehen; abfahren; verlassen **II U3**, 58
*to **leave** a message [ˌli:v‿ə 'mesɪdʒ] eine Nachricht hinterlassen **I**
*to **leave** it to cool [ˌli:v‿ɪt tə 'ku:l] kalt stellen **I**
*to **leave** space [li:v 'speɪs] Platz lassen **I**
left [left] linke/-r/-s; links **I**
on the **left** [ɒn ðə 'left] auf der linken Seite; links **I**
left [left] übrig **I**
leg [leg] Bein **II U3**, 57
legend ['ledʒənd] Legende; Sage **II AC4**, 112
leisure ['leʒə] Freizeit; Freizeit- **I**
leisure centre ['leʒə ˌsentə] Freizeitzentrum **I**
lemon ['lemən] Zitrone **II U1**, 28
lemonade [ˌlemə'neɪd] Limonade **I**
lesson ['lesn] Unterrichtsstunde; Schulstunde; Unterricht **I**
*to **let** [let] lassen **I**
*to **let** go (of) [ˌlet 'gəʊ (əv)] loslassen **II U3**, 64
Let's ... [lets] Lass/Lasst uns ... **I**
letter ['letə] Buchstabe **I**; Brief **II U4**, 75
capital **letter** [ˌkæpɪtl 'letə] Großbuchstabe **I**
to **lie** [laɪ] lügen **II U1**, 13
life [laɪf], **lives** [laɪvz] *(pl)* Leben **II U2**, 45
lifeboat ['laɪfbəʊt] Rettungsboot **I**
lifebuoy ['laɪfbɔɪ] Rettungsring **I**
light [laɪt] Licht; Lampe **II U4**, 86
lightning *(no pl)* ['laɪtnɪŋ] Blitz **II U4**, 86
to **like** [laɪk] mögen; gern haben **I**
would **like** [wʊd 'laɪk] würde/-st/-n/-t gern; hätte/-st/-n/-t gern **I**
I don't **like** ... [aɪ 'dəʊnt laɪk] Ich mag ... nicht.; Ich mache ... nicht gern. **I**
I **like** ... [aɪ 'laɪk] Mir gefällt ...; Ich mag ... **I**
I **like** singing and dancing. [ˌaɪ laɪk ˌsɪŋɪŋ‿ənd 'dɑ:nsɪŋ] Ich singe und tanze gern. **I**
I'd **like** to ... *(= I would like to)* [aɪd 'laɪk tə] Ich möchte ...; Ich würde gern ... **I**
Would you **like** ...? [ˌwʊd jʊ 'laɪk] Möchtest du ...?; Möchten Sie ...?; Möchtet ihr ...? °**II U3**, 56
like [laɪk] wie; als ob **I**
like that [laɪk 'ðæt] so **I**
like this [laɪk 'ðɪs] so **I**
line [laɪn] Zeile; Linie **I**
finish **line** ['fɪnɪʃ ˌlaɪn] Ziellinie **II U3**, 65
time **line** ['taɪm ˌlaɪn] Zeitstrahl **I**
link [lɪŋk] Link; Verbindung **II U2**, 45
to **link** [lɪŋk] verbinden **II U4**, 88
linking word ['lɪŋkɪŋ ˌwɜ:d] Bindewort **I**
lion [laɪən] Löwe **II U2**, 42
list [lɪst] Liste **I**
to **listen** (to) ['lɪsn] zuhören; anhören **I**
Listen again. [ˌlɪsn‿ə'gen] Hör/Hört noch einmal zu. **I**
to **listen** for ['lɪsn fə] horchen auf **I**
listener ['lɪsənə] Zuhörer/-in **II U3**, 61
listening ['lɪsnɪŋ] Hören **I**
little ['lɪtl] klein **I**
a **little** [ə 'lɪtl] ein wenig; etwas **I**
to **live** [lɪv] wohnen; leben **I**
living history show [ˌlɪvɪŋ 'hɪstəri ˌʃəʊ] *Show, in der historischer Alltag nachgespielt wird* **II U5**, 92
living room ['lɪvɪŋ rʊm] Wohnzimmer **I**
local ['ləʊkl] örtlich; lokal **II U5**, 99
location [ləʊ'keɪʃn] Handlungsort; Lage; Standort **II U2**, 44
locked [lɒkt] abgeschlossen **II U1**, 23
locker ['lɒkə] Schließfach; Spind **I**
loft [lɒft] Dachboden **I**
LOL (= laughing out loud) [lɒl] LOL **II U1**, 12
Londoner ['lʌndənə] Londoner/-in **I**
lonely ['ləʊnli] einsam **I**
long [lɒŋ] lang **I**
(not) any **longer** [nɒt‿eni 'lɒŋgə] (nicht) mehr; (nicht) länger **II U5**, 94
look [lʊk] Blick **I**
*to have a **look** (at) [ˌhæv‿ə 'lʊk] anschauen **II U3**, 59
to **look** [lʊk] schauen; sehen; aussehen **I**
to **look** after [ˌlʊk‿'ɑ:ftə] aufpassen auf; hüten; sich kümmern um **I**
to **look** at ['lʊk‿ət] anschauen; ansehen **I**
to **look** for ['lʊk fɔ:] suchen nach **I**
to **look** out [ˌlʊk‿'aʊt] aufpassen **II U3**, 56
to **look** up [ˌlʊk‿'ʌp] nachschlagen; nachschauen **I**
Look! [lʊk] Schau/Schaut mal! **I**
Look closely ... [ˌlʊk 'kləʊsli] Schau(t) genau ... °**II U3**, 62
what the man **looked** like [ˌwɒt ðə mæn 'lʊkt laɪk] wie der Mann aussah **II U1**, 17
*to **lose** [lu:z] verlieren **II U3**, 54
*to get **lost** [ˌget 'lɒst] verloren gehen; sich verirren **II U5**, 101
a **lot** [ə 'lɒt] viel **I**
a **lot** of [ə 'lɒt‿əv] viel/-e; eine Menge **I**
lots (of) ['lɒts‿əv] viel/-e; jede Menge **I**
loud [laʊd] laut **I**
love [lʌv] Liebe **II U5**, 101
Love ... [lʌv] Liebe Grüße *(am Briefende)*; Herzliche Grüße *(am Briefende)* **I**
to **love** [lʌv] lieben; gern mögen **I**
would **love** [wʊd 'lʌv] würde/-st/-n/-t sehr gern; hätte/-st-/-n/-t sehr gern **I**
I **love** you. [aɪ 'lʌv ju] Ich liebe dich.; Ich mag dich. **I**
I **love** ... [aɪ 'lʌv] Ich liebe ...; Ich mag ... total gern. **I**
lovebirds *(pl)* ['lʌvˌbɜ:dz] Turteltauben **II U1**, 13
low [ləʊ] niedrig **II U1**, 21
low tide ['ləʊ ˌtaɪd] Ebbe **II U2**, 48
lucky ... ['lʌki] ... der/die Glückliche **I**
*to be **lucky** [bi‿'lʌki] Glück haben **II U2**, 48
lucky charm [ˌlʌki 'tʃɑ:m] Glücksbringer; Talisman **I**
... is/are **lucky**. [ɪz/ɑ: 'lʌki] ... hat/haben Glück. **I**
lunch [lʌnʃ] Mittagessen **I**
lunch break ['lʌnʃbreɪk] Mittagspause **I**

M

machine [mə'ʃi:n] Automat; Maschine; Apparat; Gerät **I**
answering **machine** ['ɑ:nsrɪŋ məˌʃi:n] Anrufbeantworter **I**
washing **machine** ['wɒʃɪŋ məˌʃi:n] Waschmaschine **II U4**, 79
mad [mæd] verrückt **II U4**, 81
Dear Sir or **Madam** [dɪə ˌsɜ:r‿ɔ: 'mædəm] Sehr geehrte Dame, sehr geehrter Herr **II U5**, 97

magazine [ˌmægəˈzi:n] Zeitschrift **I**
magical ['mædʒɪkəl] magisch; Zauber- **II AC4**, 112
to **mail** ['i:meɪl] mailen; per E-Mail schicken **II U4**, 81
main [meɪn] Haupt- **I**
*to **make** [meɪk] machen; tun; bilden; *hier:* ergeben **I**
*to **make** a decision [ˌmeɪk‿ə dɪ'sɪʒn] eine Entscheidung treffen °**II U2**, 47
*to **make** a difference [ˌmeɪk‿ə‿'dɪfrns] etw. verändern **II AC1**, 11
*to **make** a wish [ˌmeɪk‿ə 'wɪʃ] sich etwas wünschen **I**
*to **make** friends [ˌmeɪk 'frendz] Freundschaft schließen **II U5**, 94
*to **make** money [ˌmeɪk 'mʌni] Geld verdienen **I**
*to **make** notes [ˌmeɪk 'nəʊts] Notizen machen **I**
*to **make** somebody do something [meɪk] jmdn. dazu bringen, etw. zu tun **II U4**, 76
*to **make** sure [ˌmeɪk 'ʃɔ:] sich versichern **I**
*to **make** trouble [ˌmeɪk 'trʌbl] Ärger machen; in Schwierigkeiten bringen **I**
man [mæn], **men** [men] *(pl)* Mann **I**
what the **man** looked like [ˌwɒt ðə mæn 'lʊkt laɪk] wie der Mann aussah **II U1**, 17
mango ['mæŋgəʊ] Mango **I**
many ['meni] viele **I**
How **many** ...? [ˌhaʊ 'meni] Wie viele ...? **I**
map [mæp] Stadtplan; Landkarte **I**
mind **map** ['maɪnd mæp] Wörternetz *(eine Art Schaubild)* **I**
marathon ['mærəθn] Marathon **II U3**, 54
March [mɑ:tʃ] März **I**
to **mark** [mɑ:k] markieren; kennzeichnen °**II U5**, 103
market ['mɑ:kɪt] Markt **I**
flea **market** ['fli: ˌmɑ:kɪt] Flohmarkt **I**
raven **master** ['reɪvn ˌmɑ:stə] Herr der Raben **II U2**, 42
match [mætʃ] Spiel; Match **II U3**, 54
to **match** [mætʃ] zuordnen; passen zu; entsprechen **I**
mate [meɪt] Schiffsoffizier; Maat **I**
material [mə'tɪəriəl] Material **II U2**, 47
Maths [mæθs] Mathematik; Mathe **II AC1**, 9
What's the **matter?** [ˌwɒts ðə 'mætə] Was ist los?; Was hast du? **II U5**, 104
May [meɪ] Mai **I**
may [meɪ] (vielleicht) können; dürfen **II U4**, 79
maybe ['meɪbi] vielleicht **I**
me [mi:] ich; mich; mir **I**
meal [mi:l] Mahlzeit; Essen **II U1**, 22
ready **meal** [ˌredi 'mi:l] Fertiggericht **I**
*to **mean** [mi:n] bedeuten; meinen **II U2**, 40
meaning ['mi:nɪŋ] Bedeutung; Sinn **II U1**, 25
mechanic [mə'kænɪk] Mechaniker/-in; Kfz-Mechaniker/-in **II U1**, 17
media ['mi:diə] Medien **II U4**, 75
to **mediate** ['mi:dieɪt] vermitteln **II U4**, 70
mediation [ˌmi:di'eɪʃn] Sprachmittlung **I**
medieval [ˌmedi'i:vl] mittelalterlich **II U5**, 92
*to **meet** [mi:t] treffen; sich treffen **I**
member ['membə] Mitglied **II AC3**, 72
memory ['memri] Erinnerung; Gedächtnis **II U1**, 23
to **mention** ['menʃn] erwähnen **II AC3**, 72
merchant ['mɜ:tʃənt] Kaufmann; Händler **II AC3**, 73
mess [mes] Unordnung; Durcheinander **II U4**, 80
message ['mesɪdʒ] Botschaft; Nachricht **I**
*to leave a **message** [ˌli:v‿ə 'mesɪdʒ] eine Nachricht hinterlassen **I**
*to take a **message** [ˌteɪk‿ə 'mesɪdʒ] eine Nachricht entgegennehmen; jmdm. etw. ausrichten **I**
text **(message)** ['tekst ˌmesɪdʒ] SMS; Kurznachricht **I**
metre ['mi:tə] Meter **II U2**, 48
middle ['mɪdl] Mitte **I**
mile [maɪl] Meile *(brit. Längenmaß)* **II U3**, 58
milk [mɪlk] Milch **I**
to **milk** [mɪlk] melken **II U5**, 101
million ['mɪljən] Million **II AC2**, 34
I've done this a **million** times before. [ˌaɪv dʌn ðɪs ə ˌmɪljən taɪmz bɪ'fɔ:] Ich habe das schon eine Million Mal gemacht. **II U4**, 79
mind map ['maɪnd mæp] Wörternetz *(eine Art Schaubild)* **I**
mine [maɪn] Mine **II U5**, 98
mine [maɪn] mein/-er/-e/-es **II U4**, 87
mini [mɪni] Mini- **II U3**, 56
minute ['mɪnɪt] Minute **I**
to **miss** [mɪs] verpassen; versäumen **II U4**, 83; vermissen **II U5**, 94
missing ['mɪsɪŋ] fehlend; verschwunden **II U1**, 17
What is **missing?** [ˌwɒt‿ɪz 'mɪsɪŋ] Was fehlt? **I**
mistake [mɪ'steɪk] Fehler **I**
mobile ['məʊbaɪl] Handy; Mobiltelefon **II U4**, 75
modal ['məʊdl] Modalverb °**II U4**, 75
model ['mɒdl] Modell; Tonmodell; Model **I**
modern ['mɒdn] modern **II U2**, 50
moment ['məʊmənt] Moment; Augenblick **II AC1**, 11
at the **moment** [ət ðə 'məʊmənt] im Moment; gerade **I**
Monday ['mʌndeɪ] Montag **I**
on **Mondays** [ɒn 'mʌndeɪz] montags **I**
money ['mʌni] Geld **I**
*to make **money** [ˌmeɪk 'mʌni] Geld verdienen **I**
pocket **money** ['pɒkɪt ˌmʌni] Taschengeld **I**
to raise **money** [ˌreɪz 'mʌni] Geld sammeln **II U1**, 14
monster ['mɒnstə] Monster; Ungeheuer **I**
month [mʌnθ] Monat **II U1**, 14
monument ['mɒnjəmənt] Monument; Denkmal **II U5**, 98
mood [mu:d] Stimmung; Laune **II U1**, 28
more [mɔ:] mehr; weitere **I**
more easily [mɔ:r‿'i:zɪli] leichter °**II U2**, 49
more quickly [mɔ: 'kwɪkli] schneller °**II U4**, 88
not any **more** [ˌnɒt‿eni 'mɔ:] nicht mehr **I**
more ... than ['mɔ: ðən] mehr ... als **I**
morning ['mɔ:nɪŋ] Morgen; Vormittag **I**
in the **mornings** [ˌɪn ðə 'mɔ:nɪŋz] morgens; vormittags **I**
Good **morning.** [ˌgʊd 'mɔ:nɪŋ] Guten Morgen. **I**
(the) **most** [ðə 'məʊst] der/die/das meiste; die meisten **I**
mother ['mʌðə] Mutter **I**
to **motivate** ['məʊtɪveɪt] motivieren **I**
mountain ['maʊntɪn] Berg **II U1**, 20
mountain biking ['maʊntɪn ˌbaɪkɪŋ] Mountainbikefahren **II U5**, 93
mouse [maʊs], **mice** [maɪs] *(pl)* Maus/Mäuse **I**
mouth [maʊθ] Mund **I**
mouth jogging ['maʊθ ˌdʒɒgɪŋ] Training für den Mund **I**
move [mu:v] Bewegung **I**
to **move** [mu:v] (sich) bewegen **I**
to **move** (house) [mu:v (haʊs)] umziehen **II U5**, 94
to **move** in/into [ˌmu:v‿'ɪn/'ɪntə] einziehen in **II U5**, 104
Mr ['mɪstə] Herr *(Anrede)* **I**
Mrs ['mɪsɪz] Frau *(Anrede)* **I**
much [mʌtʃ] viel **I**
mud [mʌd] Schlamm **II U2**, 48
muddy ['mʌdi] schlammig **II U2**, 48
mudlark ['mʌdlɑ:k] *jemand, der im Schlamm nach Sachen sucht, die er dann verkaufen kann* **II U2**, 48
multi-ethnic [ˌmʌlti'eθnɪk] Vielvölker-; international **II AC2**, 34
mum [mʌm] Mama **I**
museum [mju:'zi:əm] Museum **I**
music ['mju:zɪk] Musik **I**
musician [mju:'zɪʃn] Musiker/-in **II U2**, 39
must [mʌst] müssen **I**
mustn't ['mʌsnt] nicht dürfen **I**
my [maɪ] mein/-e **I**
My favourite ... [maɪ 'feɪvrɪt] Mein/e Lieblings ... **I**
My name is ... [maɪ 'neɪm‿ɪz] Ich heiße ... **I**
myself [maɪ'self] ich/mir/mich (selbst); selber **II U4**, 77
mysterious [mɪ'stɪəriəs] mysteriös; geheimnisvoll **II AC4**, 112

N

name [neɪm] Name **I**
name day ['neɪm ˌdeɪ] Namenstag **I**
My **name** is … [maɪ 'neɪm‿ɪz] Ich heiße … **I**
What's your **name**? [ˌwɒts jə 'neɪm] Wie heißt du?; Wie heißen Sie? **I**
to **name** [neɪm] nennen; benennen **I**
nasty ['nɑ:sti] garstig; gemein **II U4**, 75
national ['næʃnl] national; landesweit **I**
nature ['neɪtʃə] Natur **II AC1**, 11
near [nɪə] nahe; in der Nähe von **I**
nearly ['nɪəli] fast; annähernd **II U4**, 86
in **need** [ɪn 'ni:d] bedürftig; in Not **II U1**, 14
with special **needs** [wɪð ˌspeʃl 'ni:dz] behindert **II AC1**, 9
to **need** (to) [ni:d] brauchen; benötigen **I**
to **need** (to do) [ni:d] (tun) müssen **I**
needn't ['ni:dnt] nicht brauchen; nicht müssen **I**
negative ['negətɪv] negativ; verneint **II U3**, 66
negative form ['negətɪv ˌfɔ:m] verneinte Form **I**
neighbour *(BE)* ['neɪbə] Nachbar/-in **I**
Me **neither**. [mi: 'naɪðə] Ich auch nicht. **II U5**, 98
*to get on people's **nerves** [ˌget‿ɒn sʌmbɒdiz 'nɜ:vz] jemandem auf die Nerven gehen **I**
nervous ['nɜ:vəs] nervös; aufgeregt **II U1**, 16
net [net] Netz **II U3**, 54
netball ['netbɔ:l] Korbball **I**
social **network** [ˌsəʊʃl 'netwɜ:k] soziales Netzwerk **II U4**, 75
never ['nevə] nie; niemals **I**
new [nju:] neu **I**
news *(sg)* [nju:z] Nachrichten; Neuigkeiten **II U2**, 45
next [nekst] nächste/-r/-s; der/die Nächste(n); als Nächstes **I**
next to ['nekst tə] neben **I**
the **next** day [ðə ˌnekst 'deɪ] am nächsten Tag **II U1**, 15
nice [naɪs] nett; schön; lieb **I**
night [naɪt] Nacht **I**
all **night** [ˌɔ:l 'naɪt] die ganze Nacht **I**
night walk ['naɪt wɔ:k] Nachtwanderung **II U1**, 23
nine [naɪn] neun **I**
2nite *(= tonight)* [tə'naɪt] heute Abend **I**
no [nəʊ] kein/-e **I**
no idea [ˌnəʊ‿aɪ'dɪə] keine Ahnung **II U1**, 23
no such thing as [ˌnəʊ sʌtʃ θɪŋ‿'æz] nicht so etwas wie **II U4**, 79
no [nəʊ] nein **I**
nobody ['nəʊbədi] niemand **II U2**, 40
nobody else ['nəʊbədi els] niemand anderes **II U5**, 106
noise [nɔɪz] Lärm; Geräusch **II U1**, 22
non- [nɒn] nicht- **II U1**, 14
normal ['nɔ:ml] normal **II U2**, 44
north [nɔ:θ] Norden; Nord- **II U2**, 39
nose [nəʊz] Nase **II U1**, 12
not [nɒt] nicht **I**
not any more [ˌnɒt‿eni 'mɔ:] nicht mehr **I**
not … any [nɒt … eni] kein/-e/-en **I**
not … anything [ˌnɒt 'eniθɪŋ] nichts **I**
not … yet [nɒt 'jet] noch nicht **II U3**, 58
note [nəʊt] Notiz; Anmerkung **I**
*to make **notes** [ˌmeɪk 'nəʊts] Notizen machen **I**
*to take **notes** [ˌteɪk 'nəʊts] sich Notizen machen **I**
to **note** down [ˌnəʊt 'daʊn] notieren; aufschreiben °**II U3**, 61
nothing ['nʌθɪŋ] nichts **I**
to **notice** ['nəʊtɪs] bemerken; wahrnehmen **II U2**, 49
noticeboard ['nəʊtɪsbɔ:d] schwarzes Brett **II U1**, 14
noun [naʊn] Nomen; Hauptwort **I**
November [nə'vembə] November **I**
now [naʊ] jetzt; nun **I**
right **now** [ˌraɪt 'naʊ] jetzt gleich; sofort; gerade **II U4**, 87
nowhere ['nəʊweə] nirgendwo; nirgendwohin **II U5**, 94
number ['nʌmbə] Zahl; Nummer **I**
nut [nʌt] Nuss **I**

O

o'clock [ə'klɒk] Uhr *(Zeitangabe bei vollen Stunden)* **I**
October [ɒk'təʊbə] Oktober **I**
of [ɒv; əv] von **I**
of course [əv 'kɔ:s] natürlich; selbstverständlich **I**
*to take **off** [ˌteɪk‿'ɒf] abnehmen; herunternehmen; ausziehen **I**
to turn **off** [ˌtɜ:n‿'ɒf] abschalten; ausschalten **II U1**, 16
special **offer** [ˌspeʃl‿'ɒfə] Sonderangebot **I**
to **offer** ['ɒfə] anbieten **II AC1**, 8
office ['ɒfɪs] Büro **I**
official [ə'fɪʃl] Schiedsrichter/-in **II U3**, 65
official language [əˌfɪʃl 'læŋgwɪdʒ] Amtssprache **II AC3**, 73
offline ['ɒflaɪn] offline **II U4**, 87
often ['ɒfn] oft; häufig **I**
oh [əʊ] null *(bei Telefonnummern und Uhrzeitangaben)* **I**
Oh! [əʊ] O! **I**
Oh dear! [ˌəʊ 'dɪə] Oje! **II U5**, 104
ointment ['ɔɪntmənt] Salbe **II U3**, 59
OK [əʊ'keɪ] o.k.; in Ordnung **I**
old [əʊld] alt **I**
How **old** are you? [haʊ‿'əʊld‿ə ˌju:] Wie alt bist du?; Wie alt sind Sie? **I**
11-year-**old** [ɪˌlevn'jɪərəʊld] 11-Jährige/-r **II U3**, 56
on [ɒn] auf; an; am; in; im **I**
*to be **on** [bi‿'ɒn] an sein; laufen **II U4**, 86
on Mondays [ɒn 'mʌndeɪz] montags **I**
on the left [ɒn ðə 'left] auf der linken Seite; links **I**
on the right [ɒn ðə 'raɪt] auf der rechten Seite; rechts **I**
on top [ɒn 'tɒp] oben; obendrauf **I**
Come **on**! [ˌkʌm‿'ɒn] Komm schon!; Komm jetzt! **I**
once [wʌns] einmal; einst **I**
one [wʌn] eins **I**
one day [wʌn 'deɪ] eines Tages **II U2**, 43
one-way ticket ['wʌnweɪ ˌtɪkɪt] einfache Fahrkarte **II U5**, 96
one [wʌn], **ones** [wʌnz] *(pl)* eine/-r/-s **II U2**, 40
online [ɒn'laɪn] online **II U1**, 25
only ['əʊnli] einzige/-r/-s **II U4**, 87
only ['əʊnli] erst; bloß; nur **I**
only child ['əʊnli ˌtʃaɪld] Einzelkind **I**
Oops! [u:ps] Hoppla!; Huch! **I**
to **open** ['əʊpn] öffnen; aufmachen **I**
open ['əʊpn] offen; geöffnet; aufgeschlagen **I**
opinion [ə'pɪnjən] Meinung **II U4**, 76
opposite ['ɒpəzɪt] gegenüber; auf der anderen Seite von **I**
or [ɔ:] oder **I**
orange ['ɒrɪndʒ] Orange **I**
orange ['ɒrɪndʒ] orange **I**
order ['ɔ:də] Reihenfolge; Ordnung **I**
word **order** ['wɜ:d‿ɔ:də] Wortstellung; Satzstellung **I**
organisation [ˌɔ:gnaɪ'zeɪʃn] Organisation °**II U5**, 97
to **organise** ['ɔ:gənaɪz] organisieren **I**
*to get **organised** [get 'ɔ:gənaɪzd] sich organisieren °**II U5**, 102
originally [ə'rɪdʒnli] ursprünglich **II AC2**, 34
other ['ʌðə] anders; andere/-r/-s; weitere **I**
each **other** [ˌi:tʃ‿'ʌðə] einander; sich; sich gegenseitig **I**
the **others** [ði‿'ʌðəz] die anderen **I**
Ouch! [aʊtʃ] Aua! **II U1**, 12
our [aʊə; ɑ:] unser/-e **I**
out [aʊt] außerhalb; heraus; hinaus; nach draußen **I**
to clear **out** [ˌklɪər‿'aʊt] ausräumen; entrümpeln **I**
out and about [ˌaʊt‿ən‿ə'baʊt] unterwegs **II U2**, 44
a day **out** in … [ə ˌdeɪ‿'aʊt ɪn] ein Tag in … **II U2**, 44
outdoor [ˌaʊt'dɔ:] Freiluft-; Outdoor- **II U1**, 20
outfit ['aʊtfɪt] Outfit; Kleidung **II U1**, 12
outlaw ['aʊtlɔ:] Geächtete/-r; Gesetzlose/-r **II AC4**, 112
outline ['aʊtlaɪn] Skizze; Umriss °**II U5**, 103
outside [aʊt'saɪd] nach draußen; draußen; außerhalb **I**
outward ['aʊtwəd] abfahrend **II U5**, 96

over ['əʊvə] hinüber; über **I**; vorüber; vorbei **II U3**, 63
*to go **over** to [ˌgəʊ 'əʊvə tə] hinübergehen zu; zu jmdm. nach Hause gehen **II U4**, 79
to **overreact** [ˌəʊvəri'ækt] überreagieren **II U4**, 76
own [əʊn] eigene/-r/-s **I**

P

p.m. [ˌpi:'em] nachmittags *(Uhrzeit)*; abends *(Uhrzeit)* **I**
packet ['pækɪt] Päckchen; Paket; Packung **I**
page [peɪdʒ] Seite **I**
pain [peɪn] Schmerz **II U3**, 58
to **paint** [peɪnt] anmalen; malen **I**
painting ['peɪntɪŋ] Malerei; Gemälde **II AC1**, 8
pair [peə] Paar **I**
pair work ['peə wɜ:k] Partnerarbeit °**II U4**, 84
palm tree ['pɑ:m ˌtri:] Palme **II U5**, 93
to **panic** ['pænɪk] panisch werden **II AC1**, 11
paper ['peɪpə] Papier **I**
piece of **paper** [ˌpi:s‿əv 'peɪpə] Stück Papier **I**
paradise ['pærədaɪs] Paradies **II U4**, 74
parcel ['pɑ:sl] Paket; Päckchen **I**
parents *(pl)* ['peərənts] Eltern **I**
park [pɑ:k] Park **I**
part [pɑ:t] Teil; Stadtteil **I**
*to take **part** (in) [ˌteɪk 'pɑ:t (ɪn)] teilnehmen (an) **II U4**, 74
partially sighted [ˌpɑ:ʃəli 'saɪtɪd] sehbehindert **II AC1**, 9
past **participle** [ˌpɑ:st pɑ:'tɪsɪpl] Partizip °**II U3**, 57
partner ['pɑ:tnə] Partner/-in **I**
party ['pɑ:ti] Party; Feier **I**
to **pass** [pɑ:s] zupassen; zuspielen **II U3**, 54
to **pass** (on) [ˌpɑ:s‿'ɒn] weitergeben **I**
past [pɑ:st] Vergangenheit **II U1**, 13
past form ['pɑ:st fɔ:m] Vergangenheitsform °**II U1**, 14
past participle [ˌpɑ:st pɑ:'tɪsɪpl] Partizip °**II U3**, 57
simple **past** [ˌsɪmpl 'pɑ:st] Vergangenheitsform °**II U1**, 13
past [pɑ:st] nach *(bei Uhrzeitangaben)*; vorbei (an); vorüber (an) **I**
half **past** [ˌhɑ:f 'pɑ:st] halb *(bei Uhrzeitangaben)* **I**
quarter **past**/to ['kwɔ:tə pɑ:st/tə] Viertel nach/vor **I**
pasta ['pæstə] Pasta; Nudeln **I**
coastal **path** [ˌkəʊstl 'pɑ:θ] Küstenweg **II U5**, 104
*to **pay (for)** [peɪ] bezahlen **I**
PC *(= Personal Computer)* [pi:'si:] PC **II AC3**, 73
PE *(= Physical Education)* [ˌpi:'i:; ˌfɪzɪkl‿edʒʊ'keɪʃn] Sportunterricht **II AC1**, 10
to **peer-edit** [ˌpɪər‿'edɪt] gegenseitig kontrollieren °**II AC1**, 11
pen [pen] Füller **I**
pencil ['pensl] Bleistift; Buntstift **I**
pencil-case ['pensl ˌkeɪs] Federmäppchen; Mäppchen **I**
penny ['peni], **pence** [pens] *(pl)* Penny *(brit. Währungseinheit)*; Pence *(brit. Währungseinheit)* **I**
people *(pl)* ['pi:pl] Leute; Menschen **I**
per [pɜ:; pə] pro **II U5**, 95
present **perfect** [ˌpreznt 'pɜ:fɪkt] das Perfekt °**II U3**, 55
perfect ['pɜ:fɪkt] perfekt; vollkommen **I**
person ['pɜ:sn], people ['pi:pl] *(pl)* Person; Mensch **I**
with a **person** who ... [wɪð‿ə ˌpɜ:sn 'hu:] mit einer Person, die ... °**II U5**, 95
personal ['pɜ:snl] persönlich **I**
perspective [pə'spektɪv] Perspektive; Blickwinkel °**II U2**, 50
to **persuade** [pə'sweɪd] überreden **II U2**, 38
pet [pet] Haustier **I**
phone [fəʊn] Telefon; Handy **I**
to answer the **phone** [ˌɑ:nsə ðə 'fəʊn] einen Anruf entgegennehmen **I**
phone call ['fəʊn ˌkɔ:l] Anruf; Telefonanruf **I**
photo ['fəʊtəʊ] Foto; Fotografie **I**
in the **photo**(s) [ˌɪn ðə 'fəʊtəʊ(z)] auf dem Foto/den Fotos **I**
photo story ['fəʊtəʊ ˌstɔ:ri] Fotostory; Bildgeschichte **I**
*to take **photos** [ˌteɪk 'fəʊtəʊz] fotografieren; Fotos machen **I**
phrase [freɪz] Redewendung; Ausdruck; Satz **I**
Useful **phrases** [ˌju:sfl 'freɪsɪz] nützliche Ausdrücke **I**
phrases that ... [ˌfreɪzɪz 'ðæt] Redewendungen, die ... °**II U1**, 13
to **pick** [pɪk] auswählen; aussuchen °**II U4**, 85
pick-up ['pɪkʌp] Pick-up; Wiederaufnehmen **I**
picnic ['pɪknɪk] Picknick **I**
picture ['pɪktʃə] Bild; Foto **I**
pie [paɪ] Kuchen; Pastete **I**
piece [pi:s] Stück **I**
piece of paper [ˌpi:s‿əv 'peɪpə] Stück Papier **I**
pier [pɪə] Pier; Hafendamm **I**
pig [pɪg] Schwein **I**
guinea **pig** ['gɪni: ˌpɪg] Meerschweinchen **I**
pill [pɪl] Pille; Tablette **II U3**, 59
pink [pɪŋk] pink; rosa **I**
pipe [paɪp] Pfeife **II U2**, 49; Rohr; Rohrleitung **II U4**, 79
clay **pipe** ['kleɪ paɪp] Tonpfeife **II U2**, 49
pitch [pɪtʃ] Spielfeld; Platz **II U3**, 54
pizza ['pi:tsə] Pizza **I**
place [pleɪs] Ort; Stelle; Platz **I**
starting **place** ['stɑ:tɪŋ pleɪs] Startpunkt **II U5**, 96
*to take **place** [ˌteɪk 'pleɪs] stattfinden **I**
places that ... [ˌpleɪsɪz 'ðæt] Orte, die ... °**II U5**, 92
to **place** [pleɪs] legen °**II U5**, 103
placemat ['pleɪsmæt] Placemat; Platzdeckchen **I**
plan [plæn] Plan; Entwurf **I**
to **plan** [plæn] planen **I**
planet ['plænɪt] Planet **II U1**, 22
planner ['plænə] Handbuch; Kalender **I**
platform ['plætfɔ:m] Plattform; Bahnsteig **II U5**, 96
role **play** ['rəʊl ˌpleɪ] Rollenspiel **I**
to **play** [pleɪ] spielen **I**
to **play** a trick (on) [ˌpleɪ‿ə 'trɪk‿ɒn] einen Streich spielen **I**
player ['pleɪə] Spieler/-in; Mitspieler/-in **II U3**, 67
Please. [pli:z] Bitte. **I**
plumber ['plʌmə] Installateur/-in; Klempner/-in **II U5**, 104
plumbing ['plʌmɪŋ] Sanitärarbeit **II U5**, 105
plural ['plʊərəl] Plural; Mehrzahl **I**
pocket money ['pɒkɪt ˌmʌni] Taschengeld **I**
poem ['pəʊɪm] Gedicht **I**
point [pɔɪnt] Punkt **II U3**, 54; Zeitpunkt °**II U4**, 88
point of view [ˌpɔɪnt‿əv 'vju:] Standpunkt; Ansicht; Perspektive **II U3**, 60
Point. [pɔɪnt] Zeige/Zeigt darauf. **I**
Point to ... ['pɔɪnt tə] Zeige/Zeigt auf ... **I**
police [pə'li:s] Polizei **II U1**, 17
polite [pə'laɪt] höflich **I**
Be **polite.** [bi: pə'laɪt] Sei/Seid höflich. **I**
politely [pə'laɪt] höflich °**II U2**, 48
pollution [pə'lu:ʃn] Verschmutzung **II AC1**, 11
pony ['pəʊni] Pony **I**
pony trekking ['pəʊni ˌtrekɪŋ] Ponyreiten im Gelände **II U5**, 93
the **poor** [ðə pʊə] die Armen **II AC4**, 113
popular ['pɒpjələ] beliebt; populär **I**
positive ['pɒzətɪv] positiv **II U3**, 66
possessive form [pəˌsesɪv 'fɔ:m] Possessivform **I**
possible ['pɒsəbl] möglich **I**
post [pəʊst] Post *(Eintrag im Internet)* **I**
to **post** [pəʊst] online stellen; posten **II U4**, 74
postcard ['pəʊstkɑ:d] Postkarte **II U5**, 106
poster ['pəʊstə] Poster **I**
class **poster** ['klɑ:s ˌpəʊstə] Klassenposter **I**
postman ['pəʊstmən] Briefträger **II U1**, 17
pound (£) [paʊnd] Pfund *(brit. Währungseinheit)* **I**
to **pour** [pɔ:] einschenken; eingießen; schütten **I**

power [paʊə] Kraft; Macht; Stärke **II AC4**, 112
power cut ['paʊə ˌkʌt] Stromausfall **II U4**, 87
Word **power** ['wɜ:d ˌpaʊə] die Kraft der Wörter *(Wortschatzübung)* **I**
powerful ['paʊəfl] stark; mächtig **II AC4**, 112
practical ['præktɪkl] praktisch **II U4**, 75
to **practise** ['præktɪs] üben; trainieren **I**
practising ['præktɪsɪŋ] Üben **I**
prediction [prɪ'dɪkʃn] Vorhersage; Voraussage °**II U5**, 95
prehistoric [ˌpri:hɪ'stɒrɪk] vorgeschichtlich **II U5**, 98
to **prepare** [prɪ'peə] vorbereiten; zubereiten **I**
preposition [ˌprepə'zɪʃn] Präposition **I**
pre-reading [ˌpri:'ri:dɪŋ] vor dem Lesen **I**
prescription [prɪ'skrɪpʃn] Rezept *(für Arzneimittel)* **II U3**, 59
present ['preznt] Geschenk **I**
present ['preznt] Gegenwart; Präsens °**II U1**, 18
present perfect [ˌpreznt 'pɜ:fɪkt] das Perfekt °**II U3**, 55
present progressive [ˌpreznt prə'gresɪv] Verlaufsform des Präsens/der Gegenwart **I**
simple **present** [ˌsɪmpl 'preznt] Gegenwart; Präsens **I**
to **present** [prɪ'zent] präsentieren; vorstellen **I**
presentation [ˌprezn'teɪʃn] Präsentation; Vortrag **I**
presenter [prɪ'zentə] Moderator/-in **I**
to **press** [pres] drücken; pressen **II U4**, 86
he was **pressing** [ˌhi wəz 'presɪŋ] er drückte gerade °**II U4**, 86
price [praɪs] Preis **I**
primary school ['praɪmri ˌsku:l] Grundschule **I**
print [prɪnt] gedruckt; Druck- **II U4**, 75
prison ['prɪzn] Gefängnis **II U2**, 42
private detective [ˌpraɪvət dɪ'tektɪv] Privatdetektiv/-in **II AC4**, 112
prize [praɪz] Preis; Gewinn **I**
pro [prəʊ] Argument dafür **II U2**, 41
probably ['prɒbəbli] möglicherweise; wahrscheinlich **II U2**, 38
problem ['prɒbləm] Problem; Schwierigkeit **I**
profile ['prəʊfaɪl] Profil; Porträt **I**
programme ['prəʊgræm] Programm; Sendung **II U3**, 54
present **progressive** [ˌpreznt prə'gresɪv] Verlaufsform des Präsens/der Gegenwart **I**
project ['prɒdʒekt] Projekt **I**
to **promise** ['prɒmɪs] versprechen **II U5**, 95
pronunciation [prəˌnʌnsi'eɪʃn] Aussprache **I**
prop [prɒp] Requisite **II AC4**, 113
to **protect** [prə'tekt] schützen **II AC1**, 11
proud (of) ['praʊd‿əv] stolz (auf) **II U1**, 13
public ['pʌblɪk] öffentlich **II U2**, 37
public transport *(no pl)* [ˌpʌblɪk 'trænspɔ:t] öffentliche Verkehrsmittel **II U2**, 37
pudding ['pʊdɪŋ] Pudding; Nachtisch **I**
to **pull** [pʊl] ziehen **I**
purple ['pɜ:pl] violett; lila **I**
to **push** [pʊʃ] stoßen; schieben; schubsen **II U4**, 86
*to **put** [pʊt] setzen; stellen; legen **I**
*to **put** through [ˌpʊt‿'θru:] verbinden **I**
Put in … [pʊt‿'ɪn] Setze/Setzt ein … **I**
Put it in … [ˌpʊt‿ɪt‿'ɪn] Lege/Legt es in …; Stelle/Stellt es in … **I**
Put … face down. [pʊt ˌfeɪs 'daʊn] Lege/Legt … umgedreht hin. **I**
puzzle ['pʌzl] Rätsel; Puzzle **I**
pyjamas *(pl)* [pɪ'dʒɑ:məz] Schlafanzug; Pyjama **II U1**, 16

Q

quality ['kwɒləti] Qualität **I**
quarter past/to ['kwɔ:tə pɑ:st/tə] Viertel nach/vor **I**
queen [kwi:n] Königin **II AC2**, 35
question ['kwestʃən] Frage **I**
queue [kju:] Schlange; Warteschlange **I**
to jump the **queue** [ˌdʒʌmp ðə 'kju:] sich vordrängeln **I**
quick [kwɪk] schnell **I**
quickly ['kwɪkli] schnell **II U2**, 48
more **quickly** [mɔ: kwɪkli] schneller °**II U4**, 88
quiet [kwaɪət] still; ruhig; leise **I**
quiz [kwɪz] Quiz; Rätsel **I**
quote [kwəʊt] Zitat °**II AC1**, 9

R

rabbit ['ræbɪt] Kaninchen **I**
race [reɪs] Wettlauf; Rennen **II U3**, 54
camel **racing** ['kæml ˌreɪsɪŋ] Kamelrennen **II U3**, 54
racquet ['rækɪt] Schläger **II U3**, 54
radio ['reɪdiəʊ] Radio **II U3**, 54
raffle ['ræfl] Tombola **I**
to **rain** [reɪn] regnen **II U4**, 86
it was **raining** [ˌɪt‿wəz 'reɪnɪŋ] es regnete °**II U4**, 86
to **raise** money [ˌreɪz 'mʌni] Geld sammeln **II U1**, 14
rap [ræp] Rap **I**
to **rap** [ræp] rappen **I**
rat [ræt] Ratte **I**
raven ['reɪvn] Rabe **II U2**, 42
raven master ['reɪvn ˌmɑ:stə] Herr der Raben **II U2**, 42
RE *(= Religious Education)* [ˌɑ:r'i:; rɪˌlɪdʒəs‿edʒʊ'keɪʃn] Religion *(Schulfach)* **II AC1**, 10
to **reach** [ri:tʃ] erreichen; dran kommen **II U4**, 79
reaction [ri'ækʃn] Reaktion **II AC1**, 9
*to **read** [ri:d] lesen **I**
reader ['ri:də] Leser/-in **I**
reading ['ri:dɪŋ] Lesen **I**
ready meal [ˌredi 'mi:l] Fertiggericht **I**
real [rɪəl] echt; richtig; wirklich **II U1**, 14
realistic [ˌrɪə'lɪstɪk] realistisch **II U2**, 47
really ['rɪəli] wirklich **I**
reason ['ri:zn] Grund **II U3**, 66
to **receive** [rɪ'si:v] empfangen; erhalten; bekommen **II U3**, 61
to **record** [rɪ'kɔ:d] aufnehmen; aufzeichnen **II U3**, 62
recording [rɪ'kɔ:dɪŋ] Aufnahme; Aufzeichnung **I**
recording studio [rɪ'kɔ:dɪŋ ˌstju:diəʊ] Aufnahmestudio; Tonstudio **I**
to **recycle** [ˌri:'saɪkl] recyceln; wiederverwerten **II AC1**, 11
red [red] rot **I**
to **reef** the sails [ˌri:f ðə 'seɪlz] die Segel einholen **I**
region ['ri:dʒn] Region; Gegend **II AC3**, 73
registration [ˌredʒɪs'treɪʃn] Anwesenheitskontrolle **II AC1**, 10
regular ['regjələ] regelmäßig; gleichmäßig **I**
relationship [rɪ'leɪʃnʃɪp] Beziehung **II U3**, 66
to **relax** [rɪ'læks] sich entspannen; sich ausruhen; sich beruhigen **II AC1**, 11
religious [rɪ'lɪdʒəs] religiös; gläubig **I**
to **remember** [rɪ'membə] sich erinnern (an); sich merken; denken an **I**
Remember? [rɪ'membə] Erinnerst du dich?; Erinnert ihr euch? **I**
reply [rɪ'plaɪ] Antwort; Erwiderung; Entgegnung **I**
to **reply** [rɪ'plaɪ] antworten; erwidern; entgegnen **I**
report [rɪ'pɔ:t] Bericht; Meldung **II U1**, 13
travel **report** [ˌtrævl rɪ'pɔ:t] Reisebericht **II U1**, 24
to **report** [rɪ'pɔ:t] berichten; melden **II U5**, 93
reporter [rɪ'pɔ:tə] Reporter/-in **II U3**, 61
rescue ['reskju:] Rettung **II U3**, 61
the **rest** [rest] der Rest **I**
restaurant ['restrɒnt] Restaurant; Gaststätte **I**
result [rɪ'zʌlt] Ergebnis; Resultat **II U4**, 81
*to **retell** [ˌri:'tel] nacherzählen; nochmals erzählen **I**
return ticket [rɪ'tɜ:n ˌtɪkɪt] Hin- und Rückfahrkarte **II U5**, 96
to **return** [rɪ'tɜ:n] zurückkehren; zurückfahren **II U5**, 96
revision [rɪ'vɪʒn] Wiederholung °**II U1**, 19
rhyme [raɪm] Reim **I**
rhythm ['rɪðm] Rhythmus **I**
the **rich** [ðə rɪtʃ] die Reichen **II AC4**, 113
rigging ['rɪgɪŋ] Takelage **I**
right [raɪt] richtig; korrekt; rechts; rechte/-r/-s **I**
*to be **right** [bi 'raɪt] recht haben **I**

*to get **right** [get 'raɪt] richtig beantworten °II U5, 103
on the **right** [ɒn ðə 'raɪt] auf der rechten Seite; rechts I
right away [ˌraɪt‿ə'weɪ] sofort; gleich I
right here [ˌraɪt 'hɪə] genau hier II U3, 56
right now [ˌraɪt 'naʊ] jetzt gleich; sofort; gerade II U4, 87
*to **ring** [rɪŋ] klingeln; läuten I
ice **rink** ['aɪs ˌrɪŋk] Eisbahn; Schlittschuhbahn I
river ['rɪvə] Fluss I
road [rəʊd] Straße II U1, 22
robber ['rɒbə] Räuber/-in II AC4, 112
rock 'n' roll [ˌrɒk‿ən 'rəʊl] Rock 'n' Roll II AC3, 73
rocky ['rɒki] felsig; steinig II U5, 93
role [rəʊl] Rolle I
role play ['rəʊl ˌpleɪ] Rollenspiel I
to swap **roles** [ˌswɒp 'rəʊlz] Rollen tauschen I
rock 'n' **roll** [ˌrɒk‿ən 'rəʊl] Rock 'n' Roll II AC3, 73
to **roll** off [rəʊl] hinunterrollen; herunterrollen II U2, 48
Roll two dice. [ˌrəʊl ˌtu: 'daɪs] Würfle/Würfelt mit zwei Würfeln. I
Roman ['rəʊmən] Römer/-in; römisch II AC2, 34
Romanian [rʊ'meɪniən] Rumäne/Rumänin; rumänisch; Rumänisch II AC3, 72
roof [ru:f] Dach II U5, 104
room [ru:m; rʊm] Zimmer; Raum I
chat **room** ['tʃæt rʊm] Chatroom II AC3, 72
living **room** ['lɪvɪŋ rʊm] Wohnzimmer I
roommate ['ru:mmeɪt] Zimmergenosse/Zimmergenossin I
round [raʊnd] Runde II U1, 12
round of boxing [ˌraʊnd‿əv 'bɒksɪŋ] Boxrunde II U1, 12
the **Round** Table [ðə ˌraʊnd 'teɪbl] die Tafelrunde II AC4, 113
round [raʊnd] um … herum II U4, 87
to turn **round** [tɜ:n‿(ə)'raʊnd] (sich) umdrehen; wenden II U5, 104
route [ru:t] Strecke; Route II U1, 20
royal ['rɔɪəl] königlich I
rubber ['rʌbə] Radiergummi I
rubbish ['rʌbɪʃ] Müll; Gerümpel I
rude [ru:d] unhöflich; unverschämt I
rugby ['rʌgbi] Rugby II U3, 54
to **ruin** ['ru:ɪn] ruinieren; zerstören II U3, 65
rule [ru:l] Regel I
What's the **rule** for …? [ˌwɒts ðə 'ru:l fə] Was ist die Regel für …? I
to **rule** [ru:l] herrschen; regieren II U5, 100
ruler ['ru:lə] Lineal I
run [rʌn] Rennen; Lauf II U3, 56
*to **run** [rʌn] rennen; laufen I
*to **run** away [ˌrʌn‿ə'weɪ] wegrennen I
runner ['rʌnə] Läufer/-in II U3, 54
running ['rʌnɪŋ] Laufen; Rennen II U3, 56

S

sad [sæd] traurig I
safe [seɪf] sicher; ungefährlich II U2, 42
to reef the **sails** [ˌri:f ðə 'seɪlz] die Segel einholen I
sailboat ['seɪlbəʊt] Segelboot II U5, 106
sailor ['seɪlə] Seemann; Matrose I
salad ['sæləd] Salat I
sale [seɪl] Verkauf II U1, 16
the **same** [ðə 'seɪm] der-/die-/dasselbe; der/die/das gleiche I
the **same** way as [ˌðə seɪm 'weɪ æz] genauso wie °II U1, 28
sandwich ['sænwɪdʒ] Sandwich; belegtes Brot I
sandy ['sændi] sandig; Sand- II U5, 93
Saturday ['sætədeɪ] Samstag I
to **save** [seɪv] retten; bergen I; sparen II AC1, 11
sax ['sæks] Saxofon I
saxophone ['sæksəfəʊn] Saxofon I
*to **say** [seɪ] sagen; aufsagen; sprechen I
*to **say** hello (to) [ˌseɪ hel'əʊ tə] grüßen; Grüße ausrichten (an) I
to **scan** [skæn] scannen; nach Details durchsuchen °II U2, 45
*to be **scared** (of) [bi: 'skeəd‿əv] Angst haben (vor) I
I'm (not) **scared** of … [ˌaɪm (nɒt) 'skeəd‿əv] Ich habe (keine) Angst vor … I
scary ['skeəri] unheimlich; gruselig; beängstigend II U1, 28
scene [si:n] Szene I; Schauplatz II U3, 61
acting a **scene** [ˌæktɪŋ‿ə 'si:n] eine Theaterszene spielen I
school [sku:l] Schule I
grammar **school** ['græmə ˌsku:l] Gymnasium II U5, 97
primary **school** ['praɪmri ˌsku:l] Grundschule I
schoolbag ['sku:lbæg] Schultasche I
Science [saɪəns] Naturwissenschaften II AC1, 9
science fiction [ˌsaɪəns 'fɪkʃn] Science-Fiction *(Zukunftsdichtung)* II U1, 26
score [skɔ:] Punktestand; Spielstand II U3, 54
Scottish ['skɒtɪʃ] schottisch II U5, 93
gorge **scrambling** ['gɔ:dʒ ˌskræmblɪŋ] Schluchtenklettern II U1, 20
to **scream** [skri:m] schreien; kreischen II U2, 49
sea [si:] Meer I
search [sɜ:tʃ] Suche; Such- II U1, 25
second ['seknd] zweite/-r/-s I
secret ['si:krət] Geheimnis II U1, 23
in **secret** [ɪn 'si:krət] heimlich II U3, 65
section ['sekʃn] Abschnitt; Paragraf °II U1, 26
*to **see** [si:] sehen I
See you! ['si: jə] Bis dann!; Bis … I
Wait and **see**! [ˌweɪt‿ənd 'si:] Warte ab! I

self-critical ['selfˌkrɪtɪkl] selbstkritisch II U4, 76
self-evaluation [ˌselfɪˌvælju'eɪʃn] Selbsteinschätzung I
selfie ['selfi] Selfie II U3, 65
*to **sell** [sel] verkaufen I
seller ['selə] Verkäufer/-in *(auf einem Flohmarkt)* I
*to **send** [send] schicken; senden I
*to **send** off [send‿'ɒf] abschicken II U5, 97
sentence ['sentəns] Satz I
separate ['seprət] separat; getrennt; verschieden II U1, 20
September [sep'tembə] September I
sequel ['si:kwl] Fortsetzung; Folge II U5, 101
serious ['sɪəriəs] ernsthaft; ernst I
*to take sth **seriously** [ˌteɪk 'sɪəriəsli] etw. ernst nehmen II U3, 64
set [set] Umgebung; Rahmen II AC4, 113
*to **set** up [set‿'ʌp] einrichten; aufbauen I
setting ['setɪŋ] Schauplatz; Rahmen °II U2, 44
seven ['sevn] sieben I
to **share** [ʃeə] teilen II U4, 76
she [ʃi:] sie I
sheep [ʃi:p], **sheep** [ʃi:p] *(pl)* Schaf II U1, 22
ship [ʃɪp] Schiff I
shock [ʃɒk] Schock II U3, 63
shoe [ʃu:] Schuh I
shop [ʃɒp] Geschäft; Laden I
charity **shop** ['tʃærɪti ʃɒp] Second-Hand-Laden I
shopping ['ʃɒpɪŋ] Einkaufen; Einkäufe I
*to go **shopping** [ˌgəʊ 'ʃɒpɪŋ] einkaufen gehen I
shore [ʃɔ:] Ufer; Küste II U2, 48
short [ʃɔ:t] kurz I
short answer [ˌʃɔ:t‿'ɑ:nsə] Kurzantwort I
short form ['ʃɔ:t fɔ:m] Kurzform I
shot [ʃɒt] Einstellung; Kameraeinstellung °II U4, 82
should [ʃʊd] sollte; solltest; sollten; solltet II AC1, 11
shouldn't ['ʃʊdnt] sollte(n) nicht II U3, 59
shoulder ['ʃəʊldə] Schulter II U3, 59
to **shout** [ʃaʊt] schreien; rufen I
show [ʃəʊ] Show; Schau; Aufführung II AC1, 9
comedy **show** ['kɒmədi ˌʃəʊ] Comedy Show II U1, 14
living history **show** [ˌlɪvɪŋ 'hɪstəri ˌʃəʊ] *Show, in der historischer Alltag nachgespielt wird* II U5, 92
talent **show** ['tælənt ˌʃəʊ] Talentwettbewerb I
to **show** [ʃəʊ] zeigen I
to **show** off [ʃəʊ‿'ɒf] angeben II U4, 87
shower ['ʃaʊə] Dusche I
to **shuffle** ['ʃʌfl] mischen °II U5, 93
shy [ʃaɪ] schüchtern II U1, 13
sick [sɪk] krank; unwohl II U3, 59

*to feel **sick** [ˌfiːl 'sɪk] Übelkeit verspüren; sich schlecht fühlen **II U3**, 59
side [saɪd] Seite **II U2**, 49
sight [saɪt] Sehenswürdigkeit; Anblick **II AC2**, 34
sightseeing ['saɪtsiːɪŋ] Sightseeing-; Besichtigungs- **II U2**, 44
sign [saɪn] Zeichen; Schild **II AC1**, 8
signal word ['sɪgnəl ˌwɜːd] Signalwort **I**
silly ['sɪli] Dummkopf **II U3**, 64
silly ['sɪli] dumm; doof; albern **I**
silver ['sɪlvə] Silber **II U2**, 48
similar ['sɪmɪlə] ähnlich °**II AC2**, 35
simple past [ˌsɪmpl 'pɑːst] Vergangenheitsform °**II U1**, 13
simple present [ˌsɪmpl 'preznt] Gegenwart; Präsens **I**
*to **sing** [sɪŋ] singen **I**
I like **singing** and dancing. [ˌaɪ laɪk ˌsɪŋɪŋ‿ənd 'dɑːnsɪŋ] Ich singe und tanze gern. **I**
singer ['sɪŋə] Sänger/-in **II U1**, 19
single ticket ['sɪŋgl ˌtɪkɪt] einfache Fahrkarte **II U5**, 96
Dear **Sir** or Madam [dɪə ˌsɜːr‿ɔː 'mædəm] Sehr geehrte Dame, sehr geehrter Herr **II U5**, 97
sister ['sɪstə] Schwester **I**
half-**sister** ['hɑːfˌsɪstə] Halbschwester **I**
*to **sit** [sɪt] sitzen **I**
Sit! [sɪt] Sitz! *(Befehl für Hunde)*; Platz! *(Befehl für Hunde)* **I**
*to **sit** down [ˌsɪt 'daʊn] sich hinsetzen; sich setzen **I**
*to **sit** face to face [ˌsɪt feɪs tə ˌfeɪs] sich gegenüber sitzen **I**
site [saɪt] Webseite **II U4**, 76
situation [ˌsɪtju'eɪʃn] Situation **I**
six [sɪks] sechs **I**
Four and **six** is ten. [ˌfɔːr‿ənd ˌsɪks‿ɪz 'ten] Vier plus sechs ist zehn. **I**
size [saɪz] Größe; Kleidergröße **I**
to **skate** [skeɪt] Inlineskates fahren; Schlittschuh laufen **I**
skateboard ['skeɪtbɔːd] Skateboard **II U1**, 15
skateboarding ['skeɪtbɔːdɪŋ] Skateboardfahren **I**
skates *(pl)* [skeɪts] Inlineskates; Rollschuhe; Schlittschuhe **I**
(inline) **skating** ['ɪnlaɪn ˌskeɪtɪŋ] Inlineskatefahren **I**
skill [skɪl] Fertigkeit; Geschick **I**
to **skim** [skɪm] überfliegen °**II U2**, 45
skirt [skɜːt] Rock **II U5**, 104
*to **sleep** [sliːp] schlafen **I**
sleepover ['sliːpˌəʊvə] Übernachtung **I**
to **slice** [slaɪs] in Scheiben schneiden **I**
slide [slaɪd] Rutschbahn **I**
water **slide** ['wɔːtə ˌslaɪd] Wasserrutsche **I**
slogan ['sləʊgən] Slogan; Werbespruch **II AC1**, 11
slow [sləʊ] langsam **I**
small [smɔːl] klein **I**
smartcard ['smɑːtkɑːd] Chipkarte **II U2**, 38
smartphone ['smɑːtfəʊn] Smartphone **II U3**, 63
smile [smaɪl] Lächeln **I**
to **smile** [smaɪl] lächeln **I**
snack [snæk] Snack; Imbiss **I**
snack bar ['snæk ˌbɑː] Café; Imbissstube **I**
word **snake** ['wɜːd ˌsneɪk] Wortschlange **I**
to **sneak** around [ˌsniːk‿ə'raʊnd] herumschleichen **II U1**, 28
to **snore** [snɔː] schnarchen **I**
so [səʊ] so; also **I**
so far [ˌsəʊ 'fɑː] bis jetzt **II U3**, 60
social network [ˌsəʊʃl 'netwɜːk] soziales Netzwerk **II U4**, 75
society [sə'saɪəti] Verein; Gesellschaft **II U5**, 105
sofa ['səʊfə] Sofa; Couch **I**
solution [sə'luːʃn] Lösung **II U1**, 17
to **solve** [sɒlv] lösen **II U5**, 104
some [sʌm; səm] einige; ein paar; etwas **I**
somebody ['sʌmbədi] jemand **I**
someone ['sʌmwʌn] jemand **II U1**, 17
something ['sʌmθɪŋ] etwas **I**
sometimes ['sʌmtaɪmz] manchmal **I**
somewhere ['sʌmweə] irgendwo **II U2**, 51
song [sɒŋ] Song; Lied **I**
soon [suːn] bald **II U1**, 22
as **soon** as [əz 'suːn‿əz] sobald **II U4**, 76
Sorry! ['sɒri] Entschuldigung!; Tut mir leid! **I**
*to be **sorry** [biː 'sɒri] leid tun **I**
I'm **sorry**! [ˌaɪm 'sɒri] Tut mir leid! **I**
sound [saʊnd] Ton; Geräusch; Klang **I**
to **sound** [saʊnd] klingen **I**
source [sɔːs] Quelle °**II U5**, 102
south [saʊθ] Süden; Süd- **II U2**, 39
South Korean [ˌsaʊθ kə'riːən] Südkoreaner/-in; südkoreanisch; Südkoreanisch **II AC3**, 72
souvenir [ˌsuːvn'ɪə] Souvenir; Andenken **II U2**, 40
space [speɪs] Raum; Fläche; Platz; Ort **II AC2**, 34
*to leave **space** [liːv 'speɪs] Platz lassen **I**
spaceship ['speɪsʃɪp] Raumschiff **II U1**, 26
*to **speak** [spiːk] sprechen **I**
he wasn't **speaking** [hi ˌwɒznt 'spiːkɪŋ] er sprach nicht °**II U4**, 87
speaker ['spiːkə] Redner/-in; Sprecher/-in **I**
speaking ['spiːkɪŋ] Sprechen **I**
spear [spɪə] Speer **II U5**, 104
special ['speʃl] besonders; speziell **I**
special offer [ˌspeʃl‿'ɒfə] Sonderangebot **I**
with **special** needs [wɪð ˌspeʃl 'niːdz] behindert **II AC1**, 9
direct **speech** [dɪˌrekt 'spiːtʃ] direkte Rede °**II U5**, 99
indirect **speech** [ˌɪndɪrekt 'spiːtʃ] indirekte Rede °**II U5**, 99
speech bubble ['spiːtʃ ˌbʌbl] Sprechblase **I**
*to **spell** [spel] buchstabieren **I**
spelling ['spelɪŋ] Rechtschreibung **I**
*to **spend** [spend] ausgeben *(Geld)* **I**; verbringen *(Zeit)* **II U4**, 76
spoken ['spəʊkn] gesprochen °**II U3**, 66
sponge [spʌndʒ] Rühr-; Biskuit- **I**
spontaneous [spɒn'teɪniəs] spontan °**II U5**, 95
sport [spɔːt] Sport; Sportart **I**
squirrel ['skwɪrəl] Eichhörnchen **I**
stadium ['steɪdiəm] Stadion **II U3**, 54
*to **stand** [stænd] stehen **I**
*to **stand** up [ˌstænd‿'ʌp] aufstehen *(von einer Sitzgelegenheit)* **I**
star [stɑː] Star; Stern **I**
to **stare** [steə] starren; anstarren **I**
to **start** [stɑːt] anfangen; beginnen; starten **I**
starting place ['stɑːtɪŋ pleɪs] Startpunkt **II U5**, 96
head of **state** [ˌhed‿əv 'steɪt] Staatsoberhaupt **II AC3**, 73
statement ['steɪtmənt] Aussage; Behauptung; Erklärung **II AC3**, 72
station ['steɪʃn] Haltestelle; Bahnhof; Station **I**; Sender **II U3**, 61
bus **station** ['bʌs ˌsteɪʃn] Busbahnhof **I**
to **stay** [steɪ] bleiben **I**; übernachten **II U5**, 94
to **stay** away from [ˌsteɪ‿ə'weɪ frəm] fernbleiben von; meiden **II U4**, 81
to **stay** in touch (with) [ˌsteɪ ɪn 'tʌtʃ wɪð] in Kontakt bleiben (mit) **II U4**, 74
to **stay** with ['steɪ wɪð] wohnen bei **II U2**, 38
steak [steɪk] Steak **I**
*to **steal** [stiːl] stehlen **II U5**, 104
step [step] Stufe; Schritt **I**
step-by-**step** [ˌstepbaɪ'step] Schritt-für-Schritt- **II U4**, 79
stepmum ['stepmʌm] Stiefmutter **I**
still [stɪl] Standbild °**II AC1**, 11
still [stɪl] still **I**
still [stɪl] noch; immer noch **I**; dennoch **II U4**, 79
stomach ['stʌmək] Magen; Bauch **II U3**, 64
stomachache ['stʌməkeɪk] Bauchschmerzen; Bauchweh **II U3**, 59
stop [stɒp] Haltestelle; Halt **II U2**, 39
to **stop** [stɒp] aufhören (mit); anhalten; stoppen **I**
Stop and think [ˌstɒp‿ənd 'θɪŋk] Warte/Wartet und denk/denkt nach. **I**
Stop it! ['stɒp‿ɪt] Mach/Macht das aus!; Hör/Hört auf! **I**
storm [stɔːm] Sturm **I**
story ['stɔːri], **stories** ['stɔːriz] *(pl)* Story; Geschichte; Erzählung **I**
photo **story** ['fəʊtəʊ ˌstɔːri] Fotostory; Bildgeschichte **I**
straight on [streɪt‿'ɒn] geradeaus **I**
strange [streɪndʒ] fremd; seltsam; merkwürdig **I**
street [striːt] Straße *(in der Stadt)* **I**

in the **street** [ˌɪn ðə 'stri:t] in der Straße; auf der Straße **I**
strong [strɒŋ] stark **II U5**, 104
student ['stju:dnt] Schüler/-in; Student/-in **I**
studies *(pl)* ['stʌdiz] Studium; Lernen; Arbeit für die Schule **II AC1**, 8
recording **studio** [rɪ'kɔ:dɪŋ ˌstju:diəʊ] Aufnahmestudio; Tonstudio **I**
stuff [stʌf] Zeug **I**
stupid ['stju:pɪd] dumm; blöd **II U3**, 65
subject ['sʌbdʒɪkt] Schulfach **II AC1**, 8
suddenly ['sʌdnli] plötzlich; auf einmal **I**
suggestion [sə'dʒestʃn] Vorschlag; Anregung **I**
summer ['sʌmə] Sommer **II AC3**, 72
summer camp ['sʌmə kæmp] Sommerferienlager **II AC3**, 72
sun [sʌn] Sonne **II U5**, 104
Sunday ['sʌndeɪ] Sonntag **I**
sunny ['sʌni] sonnig **II U5**, 98
superlative [su:'pɜ:lətɪv] Superlativ °**II U1**, 20
supermarket ['su:pəˌmɑ:kɪt] Supermarkt **I**
superpower ['su:pəˌpaʊə] Supermacht **II AC3**, 73
to **supply** [sə'plaɪ] versorgen **II U5**, 100
sure [ʃʊə; ʃɔ:] sicher **I**
*to be **sure** [bi 'ʃʊə] sicher sein **II U5**, 98
*to make **sure** [ˌmeɪk 'ʃɔ:] sich versichern **I**
surfing ['sɜ:fɪŋ] Surfen **II U5**, 93
surgery ['sɜ:dʒəri] Arztpraxis; Praxis; Praxisräume **I**
surprise [sə'praɪz] Überraschung **I**
to **surprise** [sə'praɪz] überraschen **II U3**, 65
*to be **surprised** [bi sə'praɪzd] überrascht sein **II U2**, 49
surprising [sə'praɪzɪŋ] überraschend **II U1**, 28
survey ['sɜ:veɪ] Umfrage; Studie **I**
suspense [sə'spens] Spannung °**II U5**, 101
to **swap** roles [ˌswɒp 'rəʊlz] Rollen tauschen **I**
sweet [swi:t] süß **I**
sweets *(pl)* [swi:ts] Süßigkeiten; Bonbons **I**
*to **swim** [swɪm] schwimmen **I**
swimming ['swɪmɪŋ] Schwimmen **I**
*to go **swimming** [ˌgəʊ 'swɪmɪŋ] Schwimmen gehen **I**
symbol ['sɪmbl] Symbol °**II U2**, 44

T

table ['teɪbl] Tisch **I**
the Round **Table** [ðə ˌraʊnd 'teɪbl] die Tafelrunde **II AC4**, 113
tablet ['tæblət] Tablet **II U4**, 79
tail [teɪl] Schwanz; Schweif **I**
*to **take** [teɪk] nehmen; mitnehmen; wegnehmen; bringen; mitbringen **I**; dauern; (Zeit) brauchen **II U4**, 79
*to **take** a message [ˌteɪk‿ə 'mesɪdʒ] eine Nachricht entgegennehmen; jmdm. etw. ausrichten **I**
*to **take** a test [ˌteɪk‿ə 'test] einen Test machen °**II U4**, 81
*to **take** a vote [ˌteɪk ə 'vəʊt] abstimmen **I**
*to **take** notes [ˌteɪk 'nəʊts] sich Notizen machen **I**
*to **take** off [ˌteɪk‿'ɒf] abnehmen; herunternehmen; ausziehen **I**
*to **take** part (in) [ˌteɪk 'pɑ:t (ɪn)] teilnehmen (an) **II U4**, 74
*to **take** photos [ˌteɪk 'fəʊtəʊz] fotografieren; Fotos machen **I**
*to **take** place [ˌteɪk 'pleɪs] stattfinden **I**
*to **take** sth seriously [ˌteɪk 'sɪəriəsli] etw. ernst nehmen **II U3**, 64
Take a deep breath. [ˌteɪk‿ə ˌdi:p 'breθ] Atme(t) tief ein. **II AC1**, 11
Take turns. [ˌteɪk 'tɜ:nz] Wechselt euch ab. **I**
talent ['tælənt] Talent **I**
talent show ['tælənt ˌʃəʊ] Talentwettbewerb **I**
to **talk** [tɔ:k] sprechen; reden **I**
to **talk** about … ['tɔ:k‿əbaʊt] sprechen über; erzählen von **I**
to **talk** to ['tɔ:k tə] reden mit **I**
talking ['tɔ:kɪŋ] Sprechen **I**
tall [tɔ:l] groß; hoch **II U1**, 21
to **tap** [tæp] antippen **II U4**, 86
task [tɑ:sk] Aufgabe; Auftrag **I**
taxi ['tæksi] Taxi **II U1**, 17
tea [ti:] Tee **I**
*to **teach** [ti:tʃ] unterrichten; lehren; beibringen **II U3**, 60
*to **teach** somebody a lesson [ˌti:tʃ‿ə 'lesn] jmdm. eine Lehre/Lektion erteilen **II U3**, 60
teacher ['ti:tʃə] Lehrer/-in **I**
team [ti:m] Team; Gruppe **II U1**, 12
Technology [tek'nɒlədʒi] Technik; Computerunterricht **II AC1**, 9
technology [tek'nɒlədʒi] Technologie **II AC3**, 73
teen [ti:n] Jugend- **II U4**, 76
teenager ['ti:nˌeɪdʒə] Teenager; Jugendliche/-r **I**
telephone ['telɪfəʊn] Telefon **I**
*to **tell** [tel] erzählen; sagen; mitteilen **I**
Tell me about … ['tel mi:‿əˌbaʊt] Erzähle mir von … **I**
ten [ten] zehn **I**
ten times [ten 'taɪmz] zehnmal **I**
Four and six is **ten**. [ˌfɔ:r‿ənd ˌsɪks‿ɪz 'ten] Vier plus sechs ist zehn. **I**
tennis ['tenɪs] Tennis **I**
tense [tens] Zeit; Zeitform *(grammatisch)* °**II U3**, 57
test [test] Test; Klassenarbeit; Prüfung **I**
*to take a **test** [ˌteɪk‿ə 'test] einen Test machen °**II U4**, 81
to **test** [test] testen; prüfen °**II U5**, 103
text [tekst] Text **I**
text (message) ['tekst ˌmesɪdʒ] SMS; Kurznachricht **I**
to **text** [tekst] eine SMS schicken **II U4**, 74
than [ðæn] als *(bei Vergleichen)* **II U1**, 20
more … **than** ['mɔ: ðən] mehr … als **I**
to **thank** [θæŋk] danken **II AC1**, 11
Thank you. ['θæŋk ju] Danke. **I**
thankful ['θæŋkfl] dankbar **I**
Thanks. [θæŋks] Danke. **I**
that [ðæt; ðət] dass **I**
that [ðæt] das; jenes **I**
after **that** [ˌɑ:ftə 'ðæt] danach **I**
like **that** [laɪk 'ðæt] so **I**
That's … [ðæts] Das macht … **I**
that's how [ðæts 'haʊ] so **II U1**, 14
that's why [ðæts 'waɪ] deshalb **II U1**, 20
That was close! [ˌðæt wɒz 'kləʊs] Das war knapp! **I**
That's what friends are for. [ˌðæts wɒt'frendz‿ɑ: ˌfɔ:] Dafür sind Freunde da. **I**
an activity **that** … [ən‿ækˌtɪvəti 'ðæt] eine Aktivität, die … °**II U1**, 16
elements **that** … [ˌelɪməntz 'ðæt] Elemente, die … °**II U5**, 101
phrases **that** … [ˌfreɪzɪz 'ðæt] Redewendungen, die … °**II U1**, 13
places **that** … [ˌpleɪsɪz 'ðæt] Orte, die … °**II U5**, 92
things **that** … [ˌθɪŋz 'ðæt] Dinge, die … °**II U2**, 37
words **that** … [ˌwɜ:dz 'ðæt] Wörter, die … °**II U1**, 24
the [ðə; ði] der; die *(auch Pl.)*; das **I**
the others [ði‿'ʌðəz] die anderen **I**
the same [ðə 'seɪm] der-/die-/dasselbe; der/die/das gleiche **I**
the … **the** [ðə … ðə] je … desto **II U3**, 54
theatre ['θɪətə] Theater **I**
their [ðeə] ihr/-e *(Pl.)* **I**
them [ðem] sie *(Pl.)*; ihnen **I**
theme [θi:m] Thema; Motto **I**
then [ðen] dann; danach **I**
there [ðeə] da; dort; dahin; dorthin **I**
there is/are [ðər‿'ɪz/'ɑ:] da ist/sind; es gibt **I**
these [ði:z] diese (hier) **I**
they [ðeɪ] sie *(Pl.)* **I**
It's …/**They**'re … [ɪts/ðeə] Es kostet …/ Sie kosten … **I**
thing [θɪŋ] Ding; Sache **I**
things that … [ˌθɪŋz 'ðæt] Dinge, die … °**II U2**, 37
things which … [θɪŋz 'wɪtʃ] Dinge, die … °**II U3**, 55
*to **think** [θɪŋk] denken; nachdenken; glauben **I**
*to **think** of ['θɪŋk‿əv] halten von; denken über **I**; (sich) ausdenken; sich etwas einfallen lassen **II U1**, 16
Stop and **think** [ˌstɒp‿ənd 'θɪŋk] Warte/Wartet und denk/denkt nach. **I**

Think of … ['θɪŋk_əv] Denke/Denkt an … **I**
I was **thinking** [ˌaɪ wəz 'θɪŋkɪŋ] ich dachte gerade °**II U4**, 86
third [θɜ:d] dritte/-r/-s **I**
thirteen [ˌθɜ:'ti:n] dreizehn **I**
this [ðɪs] dies; diese/-r/-s **I**
this afternoon [ðɪs ˌɑ:ftə'nu:n] heute Nachmittag **II U2**, 38
This is … ['ðɪs_ɪz] Das (hier) ist … **I**
those [ðəʊz] diese dort; jene **I**
thought [θɔ:t] Gedanke °**II U3**, 66
thousands of ['θaʊzndz_əv] tausende (von) **I**
three [θri:] drei **I**
through [θru:] durch **I**
*to **throw** (at) [θrəʊ] werfen (nach) **I**
*to **throw** away [ˌθrəʊ_ə'weɪ] wegwerfen **I**
thunder *(no pl)* ['θʌndə] Donner **II U4**, 86
Thursday ['θɜ:zdeɪ] Donnerstag **I**
to **tick** [tɪk] abhaken °**II U2**, 47
ticket ['tɪkɪt] Los; Ticket; Eintrittskarte **I**; Fahrschein **II U5**, 95
one-way **ticket** ['wʌnweɪ ˌtɪkɪt] einfache Fahrkarte **II U5**, 96
return **ticket** [rɪ'tɜ:n ˌtɪkɪt] Hin- und Rückfahrkarte **II U5**, 96
single **ticket** ['sɪŋgl ˌtɪkɪt] einfache Fahrkarte **II U5**, 96
high **tide** ['haɪ ˌtaɪd] Flut **II U2**, 48
low **tide** ['ləʊ ˌtaɪd] Ebbe **II U2**, 48
to **tidy** *(a room)* ['taɪdi] aufräumen; in Ordnung bringen **I**
till [tɪl] bis **I**
time [taɪm] Zeit **I**; Mal **II U1**, 14
all the **time** [ˌɔ:l ðə 'taɪm] die ganze Zeit **II U2**, 48
at the same **time** [ət ðə ˌseɪm 'taɪm] zur selben Zeit; gleichzeitig **I**
free **time** [ˌfri: 'taɪm] Freizeit **I**
ten **times** [ten 'taɪmz] zehnmal **I**
time line ['taɪm ˌlaɪn] Zeitstrahl **I**
I can't wait till next **time**. [aɪ kɑ:nt ˌweɪt tɪl nekst 'taɪm] Ich kann es bis zum nächsten Mal kaum erwarten. **II U1**, 14
Time to get up! [ˌtaɪm tə ˌget_'ʌp] Es ist Zeit aufzustehen! **I**
What **time**? [ˌwɒt 'taɪm] Um wie viel Uhr? **I**
What's the **time**? [ˌwɒts ðə 'taɪm] Wie spät ist es?; Wie viel Uhr ist es? **I**
timetable ['taɪmˌteɪbl] Stundenplan; Fahrplan **I**
tin [tɪn] Zinn **II U5**, 98
tinned [tɪnd] Dosen-; aus der Dose **I**
tip [tɪp] Tipp; Ratschlag **I**
to **tiptoe** ['tɪptəʊ] auf Zehenspitzen gehen **II U1**, 23
tired [taɪəd] müde **I**
title ['taɪtl] Titel; Überschrift °**II U4**, 88
to [tʊ; tə] zu; nach; auf; in; vor *(bei Uhrzeitangaben)* **I**
from … **to** [frəm … tə] von … bis **I**
quarter past/**to** ['kwɔ:tə pɑ:st/tə] Viertel nach/vor **I**
toast [təʊst] Toast **I**
today [tə'deɪ] heute **I**
together [tə'geðə] zusammen; miteinander; gemeinsam **I**
toilet ['tɔɪlət] Toilette **I**
tomato [tə'mɑ:təʊ], **tomatoes** [tə'mɑ:təʊz] *(pl)* Tomate **I**
tomorrow [tə'mɒrəʊ] morgen **I**
too [tu:] auch; zu **I**
Too bad! [ˌtu: 'bæd] Zu dumm!; Schade! **I**
You **too**? [ju: 'tu:] Du auch? **I**
tool [tu:l] Werkzeug; Gerät **II U5**, 105
top [tɒp] Spitze; oberer Teil; oberes Ende **I**
on **top** [ɒn 'tɒp] oben; obendrauf **I**
to **top** up [tɒp_'ʌp] aufladen **II U2**, 38
topic ['tɒpɪk] Thema **II U1**, 26
torch [tɔ:tʃ] Fackel; Taschenlampe **II U1**, 22
to stay in **touch** (with) [ˌsteɪ ɪn 'tʌtʃ wɪð] in Kontakt bleiben (mit) **II U4**, 74
tour [tʊə] Tour; Fahrt; Rundgang **II U2**, 42
audio **tour** ['ɔ:diəʊ ˌtʊə] Audioführung **II U2**, 42
tourist ['tʊərɪst] Tourist/-in **I**
tourist board ['tʊərɪst bɔ:d] Touristeninformation **II U5**, 97
tourist information centre [ˌtʊərɪst ɪnfə'meɪʃn ˌsentə] Touristeninformation **I**
towards [tə'wɔ:dz] in Richtung; auf … zu; darauf zu **II U2**, 48
town [taʊn] Stadt **I**
toy [tɔɪ] Spielzeug **I**
to **trace** [treɪs] verfolgen; nachspüren **I**
to **trade** [treɪd] austauschen °**II U3**, 63
tradition [trə'dɪʃn] Tradition **I**
train [treɪn] Zug **I**
to **train** [treɪn] trainieren **II U3**, 58
training ['treɪnɪŋ] Training **II U3**, 64
to **translate** [trænz'leɪt] übersetzen **I**
Don't **translate** … [ˌdəʊnt trænz'leɪt] Übersetze/Übersetzt nicht … **I**
translation [trænz'leɪʃn] Übersetzung **I**
transport ['trænspɔ:t] Verkehrsmittel; Transport **II U5**, 94
public **transport** *(no pl)* [ˌpʌblɪk 'trænspɔ:t] öffentliche Verkehrsmittel **II U2**, 37
travel ['trævl] (das) Reisen; Reise **II U1**, 24
travel agent's ['trævl_ˌeɪdʒnts] Reisebüro **II U5**, 95
travel report [ˌtrævl rɪ'pɔ:t] Reisebericht **II U1**, 24
to **travel** ['trævl] fahren; reisen **II U2**, 38
treasure ['treʒə] Schatz **II U2**, 42
tree [tri:] Baum **I**
family **tree** ['fæmli ˌtri:] Stammbaum **I**
palm **tree** ['pɑ:m ˌtri:] Palme **II U5**, 93
pony **trekking** ['pəʊni ˌtrekɪŋ] Ponyreiten im Gelände **II U5**, 93
trial [traɪəl] Qualifikation **II U3**, 56
trick [trɪk] Trick; Streich **I**
to play a **trick** (on) [ˌpleɪ_ə 'trɪk_ɒn] einen Streich spielen **I**
trifle ['traɪfl] Trifle *(englischer Nachtisch)* **I**
trip [trɪp] Trip; Reise; Ausflug; Fahrt **II U1**, 13
trouble ['trʌbl] Ärger; Probleme; Schwierigkeiten **II U1**, 23
*to make **trouble** [ˌmeɪk 'trʌbl] Ärger machen; in Schwierigkeiten bringen **I**
trousers *(pl)* ['traʊzəz] Hose **II U5**, 104
trowel ['traʊəl] kleiner Spaten **II U2**, 48
a **trowel** which … [ə 'traʊəl wɪtʃ] ein Spaten, der … °**II U2**, 48
true [tru:] wahr °**II U1**, 18
to **try** [traɪ] versuchen; probieren **I**
to **try** on [ˌtraɪ_'ɒn] anprobieren **II U2**, 48
Try … [traɪ] Versuch es mal mit …; Probier mal … **I**
T-shirt ['ti:ʃɜ:t] T-Shirt **I**
the **Tube** [ðə 'tju:b] die Londoner U-Bahn **II AC2**, 34
Tuesday ['tju:zdeɪ] Dienstag **I**
tunnel ['tʌnl] Tunnel **I**
It's your **turn**. [ˌɪts 'jɔ: tɜ:n] Du bist dran. **I**
Take **turns**. [ˌteɪk 'tɜ:nz] Wechselt euch ab. **I**
Your **turn**. ['jɔ: tɜ:n] Du bist dran. **I**
to **turn** [tɜ:n] einbiegen; abbiegen **I**
to **turn** (a)round [ˌtɜ:n_(ə)'raʊnd] (sich) umdrehen; wenden **II U5**, 104
to **turn** off [ˌtɜ:n_'ɒf] abschalten; ausschalten **II U1**, 16
to **turn** to ['tɜ:n tə] sich wenden an; sich zuwenden **II U5**, 105
tutor ['tju:tə] Klassenlehrer/-in **I**
tutor group ['tju:tə ˌgru:p] Klasse *(in einer englischen Schule)* **I**
TV (= television) [ˌti:'vi: ('telɪvɪʒn)] Fernsehen; Fernseher **I**
to watch **TV** [ˌwɒtʃ ti:'vi:] fernsehen **I**
twelve [twelv] zwölf **I**
twin [twɪn] Zwilling; Zwillings- **II U5**, 105
to **twist** your ankle [ˌtwɪst jɔ:r_'æŋkl] sich den Knöchel verrenken **II U3**, 58
two [tu:] zwei **I**
the **two** of them [ðə 'tu:_əv ðəm] beide **II U4**, 76
two of which ['tu:_əv wɪtʃ] zwei von ihnen °**II U5**, 102
typical ['tɪpɪkl] typisch **I**

U

u *(= you)* [ju:; jə] du; Sie; ihr **I**
UFO [ˌju:ef'əʊ] UFO **II U3**, 62
uncle ['ʌŋkl] Onkel **I**
under ['ʌndə] unter **I**
underground ['ʌndəgraʊnd] U-Bahn **II AC2**, 34
*to **understand** [ˌʌndə'stænd] verstehen **I**
understanding [ˌʌndə'stændɪŋ] Verständnis **II U4**, 77
unfair [ʌn'feə] unfair **II U3**, 58

unfriendly [ʌn'frendli] unfreundlich **II U1**, 28
uniform ['ju:nɪfɔ:m] Uniform **I**
unit ['ju:nɪt] Lektion; Kapitel; Einheit **I**
*to be **unlucky** [bi: ʌn'lʌki] Pech haben **I**
until [ʌn'tɪl] bis; erst wenn **II U3**, 56
to **unwrap** [ʌn'ræp] auswickeln; auspacken **I**
up [ʌp] hinauf; (nach) oben **II U5**, 104
to end **up** [ˌend‿'ʌp] enden; landen **II U1**, 12
*to get **up** [ˌget‿'ʌp] aufstehen *(aus dem Bett)* **I**
to look **up** [ˌlʊk‿'ʌp] nachschlagen; nachschauen **I**
upset [ʌp'set] aufgebracht; bestürzt **II U4**, 76
upstairs [ʌp'steəz] nach oben; im Obergeschoss; oben **II U4**, 86
us [ʌs] uns **I**
to **use** [ju:z] benutzen; verwenden; gebrauchen **I**
useful ['ju:sfl] nützlich; hilfreich **I**
Useful phrases [ˌju:sfl 'freɪsɪz] nützliche Ausdrücke **I**
usually ['ju:ʒli] normalerweise; gewöhnlich; meistens **I**

V

verb [vɜ:b] Verb **I**
very ['veri] sehr **I**
very much [ˌveri 'mʌtʃ] sehr **I**
vet [vet] Tierarzt/Tierärztin **I**
video ['vɪdiəʊ] Video **II U4**, 75
video chat ['vɪdiəʊ ˌtʃæt] Videochat **II U2**, 36
view [vju:] Aussicht; Sicht; Ausblick; Blick **II U2**, 44
point of **view** [ˌpɔɪnt‿əv 'vju:] Standpunkt; Ansicht; Perspektive **II U3**, 60
viewer ['vju:ə] Zuschauer/-in °**II U2**, 44
viewing ['vju:ɪŋ] Hör-/Sehverstehen **I**
village ['vɪlɪdʒ] Dorf **I**
villain ['vɪlən] Bösewicht **II AC4**, 112
visit ['vɪzɪt] Besuch **I**
to **visit** ['vɪzɪt] besichtigen; besuchen **I**
visitor ['vɪzɪtə] Besucher/-in **I**
vocabulary [və'kæbjələri] Vokabular; Wortschatz **I**
voice [vɔɪs] Stimme **I**
volleyball ['vɒlibɔ:l] Volleyball **I**
*to take a **vote** [ˌteɪk‿ə 'vəʊt] abstimmen **I**
to **vote** [vəʊt] abstimmen; wählen **I**

W

to **wait** (for) [weɪt] warten (auf) **I**
I can't **wait** till next time. [aɪ kɑ:nt ˌweɪt tɪl nekst 'taɪm] Ich kann es bis zum nächsten Mal kaum erwarten. **II U1**, 14
Wait and see! [ˌweɪt‿ənd 'si:] Warte ab! **I**
gallery **walk** ['gælri ˌwɔ:k] Museumsrundgang; Vernissage **I**
*to go for a **walk** [ˌgəʊ fər‿ə 'wɔ:k] spazieren gehen **II U1**, 22
night **walk** ['naɪt wɔ:k] Nachtwanderung **II U1**, 23
to **walk** [wɔ:k] gehen; laufen **I**
to **walk** the dog [ˌwɔ:k ðə 'dɒg] den Hund ausführen; mit dem Hund spazieren gehen **I**
walking ['wɔ:kɪŋ] Wandern **II U1**, 20
wall [wɔ:l] Wand; Mauer **I**
to **want** (to) ['wɒnt tə] wollen; mögen **I**
wardrobe ['wɔ:drəʊb] Kleiderschrank **I**
to **warm** up [ˌwɔ:m‿'ʌp] aufwärmen; sich aufwärmen **I**
warm-up ['wɔ:m‿ʌp] Aufwärmübung **I**
warrior ['wɒriə] Krieger **II U5**, 105
to **wash** [wɒʃ] waschen; sich waschen **I**
to **wash** up [ˌwɒʃ‿'ʌp] angespült werden **II U2**, 48
washing machine ['wɒʃɪŋ məˌʃi:n] Waschmaschine **II U4**, 79
to **waste** [weɪst] verschwenden **II U4**, 79
to **watch** [wɒtʃ] beobachten; (sich) ansehen; zuschauen **I**
to **watch** TV [ˌwɒtʃ ti:'vi:] fernsehen **I**
water ['wɔ:tə] Wasser **I**
water slide ['wɔ:tə ˌslaɪd] Wasserrutsche **I**
wave [weɪv] Welle **I**
wax [wæks] Wachs **II U2**, 37
wax figure ['wæks ˌfɪgə] Wachsfigur **II U2**, 37
way [weɪ] Weg; Art und Weise **I**
*to be in the **way** [bi:‿ɪn ðə 'weɪ] im Weg sein/stehen **I**
*to get in the **way** [ˌget‿ɪn ðə 'weɪ] stören; im Weg stehen **II U3**, 64
in other **ways** [ɪn‿'ʌðə weɪz] auf andere Weise **II U4**, 81
the same **way** as [ˌðə seɪm 'weɪ æz] genauso wie °**II U1**, 28
we [wi:; wi] wir **I**
We're from … ['wɪə frəm] Wir sind aus … **I**
*to **wear** [weə] anhaben; tragen *(Kleidung)* **I**
they weren't **wearing** [ˌðeɪ wɜ:nt 'weərɪŋ] sie trugen nicht °**II U2**, 48
weather ['weðə] Wetter **I**
weather forecast ['weðə ˌfɔ:kɑ:st] Wettervorhersage **II U5**, 96
website ['websaɪt] Website; Internetauftritt **I**
wedding ['wedɪŋ] Hochzeit **I**
Wednesday ['wenzdeɪ] Mittwoch **I**
week [wi:k] Woche **I**
weekday ['wi:kdeɪ] Wochentag **II U4**, 84
weekend [ˌwi:k'end] Wochenende **I**
at the **weekend** [ət ðə ˌwi:k'end] am Wochenende **I**
weird [wɪəd] merkwürdig; seltsam; sonderbar **II U4**, 83
Welcome! ['welkəm] Willkommen! **II U1**, 22
to **welcome** ['welkəm] willkommen heißen **II AC1**, 11
You're **welcome**. [jɔ: 'welkəm] Bitte schön.; Nichts zu danken.; Gern geschehen. **I**
well [wel] tja; nun **I**
Welsh [welʃ] walisisch; Walisisch; Waliser/-in **II U1**, 20
west [west] Westen; West- **I**
wet [wet] nass **II U2**, 48
what [wɒt] was; welche/-r/-s; was für ein **I**
What about … ? ['wɒt‿əbaʊt] Wie wär's mit …?; Was ist mit …? **I**
What are …? ['wɒt‿ɑ:] Welche … sind es? **I**
What colour is …? [ˌwɒt 'kʌlər‿ɪz] Welche Farbe hat …? **I**
what else [ˌwɒt‿'els] was sonst; was noch **I**
What is missing? [ˌwɒt‿ɪz 'mɪsɪŋ] Was fehlt? **I**
What is … about? [ˌwɒt‿ɪz …‿ə'baʊt] Worum geht es in/im …? **I**
What on earth …? [ˌwɒt‿ɒn‿'ɜ:θ] Was um alles in der Welt …? **II U4**, 79
What time? [ˌwɒt 'taɪm] Um wie viel Uhr? **I**
what to … ['wɒt tə] was man … **I**
What's that? [wɒts 'ðæt] Was ist das? **I**
What's the matter? [ˌwɒts ðə 'mætə] Was ist los?; Was hast du? **II U5**, 104
What's the rule for …? [ˌwɒts ðə 'ru:l fə] Was ist die Regel für …? **I**
What's the time? [ˌwɒts ðə 'taɪm] Wie spät ist es?; Wie viel Uhr ist es? **I**
What's your favourite …? ['wɒts jə ˌfeɪvrɪt] Was ist dein/-e Lieblings…? **I**
What's your name? [ˌwɒts jə 'neɪm] Wie heißt du?; Wie heißen Sie? **I**
… **what** to do. ['wɒt tə du:] … was ich tun soll. **II U4**, 76
what the man looked like [ˌwɒt ðə mæn 'lʊkt laɪk] wie der Mann aussah **II U1**, 17
wheel [wi:l] Rad; Steuerrad; Steuer **I**
wheelchair ['wi:ltʃeə] Rollstuhl **II U2**, 39
when [wen] wenn; wann; als **I**
whenever [wen'evə] wann immer; jedes Mal, wenn; so oft **II U4**, 76
where [weə] wo; wohin **I**
Where … from? [ˌweə … 'frɒm] Woher …? **I**
… **where** to go. [ˌweə tə 'gəʊ] … wohin ich gehen kann. **II U2**, 40
which [wɪtʃ] welche/-r/-s **I**
a trowel **which** … [ə 'traʊəl wɪtʃ] ein Spaten, der … °**II U2**, 48
things **which** … [θɪŋz 'wɪtʃ] Dinge, die … °**II U3**, 55
a **while** [ə 'waɪl] eine Weile **II U2**, 40
while [waɪl] während **I**
to **whip** [wɪp] schlagen **I**
to **whisper** ['wɪspə] flüstern **I**
white [waɪt] weiß **I**
who [hu:] wer; wem; wen **I**
Who … for? [ˌhu: 'fɔ:] Für wen …? **I**

Who is it? [ˌhu:‿ˈɪz‿ɪt] Wer ist es? **I**
Who's in? [hu:z‿ˈɪn] Wer macht mit?; Wer ist dabei? **II U3**, 56
a father **who** … [ə ˌfɑ:ðə ˈhu:] ein Vater, der … **°II U5**, 100
friends and family **who** … [frendz‿ən‿ˌfæməli ˈhu:] Freunde und Familienmitglieder, die … **°II U4**, 81
good for someone **who** … [ˌgʊd‿fə ˌsʌmwʌn ˈhu:] gut für jemanden, der … **°II U2**, 41
I'm the one **who** … [ˌaɪm ðə‿wʌn ˈhu:] ich bin diejenige, die … **°II U3**, 64
the boy **who** … [ðə bɔi ˈhu:] der Junge, der … **°II U3**, 66
with a person **who** … [wɪð‿ə ˌpɜ:sn ˈhu:] mit einer Person, die … **°II U5**, 95
whole [həʊl] ganz **I**
whoosh [wʊʃ] wusch **I**
why [waɪ] warum **I**
that's **why** [ðæts ˈwaɪ] deshalb **II U1**, 20
wide [waɪd] breit; weit; ausgedehnt **II U5**, 93
wife [waɪf], **wives** [waɪvz] *(pl)* Ehefrau **II U5**, 100
wild [waɪld] wild **II U5**, 98
wildlife [ˈwaɪldlaɪf] Tierwelt *(in freier Wildbahn)* **II AC1**, 11
*to **win** [wɪn] gewinnen; siegen **I**
wind [wɪnd] Wind **II U5**, 104
window [ˈwɪndəʊ] Fenster **I**
windsurfing [ˈwɪndsɜ:fɪŋ] Windsurfen **II U5**, 93
wine [waɪn] Wein **I**
winner [ˈwɪnə] Gewinner/-in; Sieger/-in **I**
wish [wɪʃ] Wunsch **I**
*to make a **wish** [ˌmeɪk‿ə ˈwɪʃ] sich etwas wünschen **I**
Best **wishes** [ˌbest ˈwɪʃɪz] Viele Grüße; Herzliche Grüße **II U5**, 97
with [wɪð] mit; bei **I**
without [wɪˈðaʊt] ohne **I**
witness [ˈwɪtnəs] Zeuge/Zeugin **II U3**, 61
wizard [ˈwɪzəd] Zauberer **II AC4**, 112
wobbly [ˈwɒbli] wackelig **II U2**, 48
woman [ˈwʊmən], **women** [ˈwɪmɪn] *(pl)* Frau **I**
won't she [wəʊnt‿ˈʃi:] nicht wahr?; stimmts? **°II U5**, 94
wonderful [ˈwʌndəfl] wunderbar **II U5**, 94
Woof! [wʊf] Wau! **I**
word [wɜ:d] Wort **I**
compound **word** [ˈkɒmpaʊnd wɜ:d] Kompositum *(zusammengesetztes Wort)* **°II U2**, 41
key **word** [ˈki: wɜ:d] Stichwort; Schlüsselbegriff **I**
linking **word** [ˈlɪŋkɪŋ ˌwɜ:d] Bindewort **I**
signal **word** [ˈsɪgnəl ˌwɜ:d] Signalwort **I**
word cloud [ˈwɜ:d ˌklaʊd] Wörterwolke **°II U3**, 54
word order [ˈwɜ:d‿ˌɔ:də] Wortstellung; Satzstellung **I**
Word power [ˈwɜ:d ˌpaʊə] die Kraft der Wörter *(Wortschatzübung)* **I**
word snake [ˈwɜ:d ˌsneɪk] Wortschlange **I**
word-building [ˈwɜ:dˌbɪldɪŋ] Wortbildung **°II U2**, 37
words that … [ˌwɜ:dz ˈðæt] Wörter, die … **°II U1**, 24
work [wɜ:k] Arbeit **I**
pair **work** [ˈpeə wɜ:k] Partnerarbeit **°II U4**, 84
to **work** [wɜ:k] arbeiten **I**; funktionieren **II U4**, 79
to **work** out [ˌwɜ:k‿ˈaʊt] herausfinden; ausarbeiten **°II U2**, 47
workshop [ˈwɜ:kʃɒp] Workshop **I**
world [wɜ:ld] Erde; Welt **I**
worm [wɜ:m] Wurm **I**
*to be **worried** [bi ˈwʌrid] beunruhigt sein; besorgt sein **II U3**, 64
to **worry** [ˈwʌri] sich Sorgen machen **II U4**, 77
Don't **worry**! [ˌdəʊnt ˈwʌri] Keine Sorge! **I**
the **worst** [ðə ˈwɜ:st] der/die/das schlimmste; der/die/das schlechteste **II U1**, 20
*to be **worth** [bi: ˈwɜ:θ] wert sein **I**
would like [wʊd ˈlaɪk] würde/-st/-n/-t gern; hätte/-st/-n/-t gern **I**
would love [wʊd ˈlʌv] würde/-st/-n/-t sehr gern; hätte/-st-/-n/-t sehr gern **I**
Would you like …? [ˌwʊd jʊ ˈlaɪk] Möchtest du …?; Möchten Sie …?; Möchtet ihr …? **°II U3**, 56
Wow! [waʊ] Wow! **I**
to **wrap** [ræp] einwickeln; einpacken **I**
wrapping [ˈræpɪŋ] Verpackung; Hülle **I**
wrist [rɪst] Handgelenk **II U2**, 48
*to **write** [raɪt] schreiben **I**
*to **write** down [ˌraɪt ˈdaʊn] aufschreiben **I**
writing [ˈraɪtɪŋ] Schreiben **I**
wrong [rɒŋ] falsch **I**
*to be **wrong** [bi: ˈrɒŋ] unrecht haben; sich irren **I**
*to go **wrong** [ˌgəʊ ˈrɒŋ] schiefgehen **I**

X

XOXO [ˌhʌgz‿ən ˈkɪsɪz] Umarmungen und Küsse *(am Ende von E-Mails und SMS)* **I**

Y

yeah *(infml)* [jeə] ja **I**
year [jɪə] Jahr; Schuljahr **I**
11-**year**-old [ɪˌlevnˈjɪərəʊld] 11-Jährige/-r **II U3**, 56
18-**year**-old [ˌeɪti:n ˈjɪər‿əʊld] 18-jährig **II U2**, 38
yearbook [ˈjɪəbʊk] Jahrbuch **II U1**, 12
yellow [ˈjeləʊ] gelb **I**
yes [jes] ja **I**
yesterday [ˈjestədeɪ] gestern **II U1**, 15
yet [jet] schon; noch **II U3**, 58
not … **yet** [nɒt ˈjet] noch nicht **II U3**, 58
yoghurt [ˈjɒgət] Joghurt **I**
you [ju:; jə] du; ihr; Sie **I**
You know how to … [ju: ˈnəʊ ˌhaʊ tə] Du weißt, wie man …; Ihr wisst, wie man … **I**
You too? [ju: ˈtu:] Du auch? **I**
You're into … [ˈjɔ:r‿ɪntə] Du magst …; Du stehst auf … **I**
You're welcome. [ˌjɔ: ˈwelkəm] Bitte schön.; Nichts zu danken.; Gern geschehen. **I**
young [jʌŋ] jung **I**
your [jɔ:; jə] dein/-e; euer/eure; Ihr/-e **I**
What's **your** name? [ˌwɒts jə ˈneɪm] Wie heißt du?; Wie heißen Sie? **I**
Your turn. [ˈjɔ: tɜ:n] Du bist dran. **I**
yours [jɔ:z] dein/-er/-e/-es; eure/-r/-s; Ihr/-e **II U5**, 104
Yours … [jɔ:z] Viele Grüße … *(am Ende von Briefen und Mails)* **II U4**, 83
yourself [jɔ:ˈself] du/dir/dich/Sie/sich (selbst); selber **I**
yourselves [jɔ:ˈselvz] selber; ihr/euch/Sie/sich (selbst) **II U5**, 97

Z

zero [ˈzɪərəʊ] null **I**
zoo [zu:] Zoo; Tierpark **II U2**, 39

Boys' names

Amir [ˌɑ:'mi:r] **II U2**, 36
Ben [ben] **I**
Bob [bɒb] **I**
Damian ['deɪmiən] **I**
Dave [deɪv] **I**
David ['deɪvɪd] **I**
Desmond ['dezmənd] **I**
Filip ['fɪlɪp] **I**
Frank [fræŋk] **II U4**, 86
Henry ['henri] **I**
Jack [dʒæk] **I**
Jago ['dʒeɪgəʊ] **II U5**, 105
Jahangir [dʒə'hʌŋgɪə] **I**
Jamie ['dʒeɪmi] **I**
Jay [dʒeɪ] **I**
Jinsoo ['dʒɪnzu:] **II U2**, 44
John [dʒɒn] **II U1**, 17
Jon [dʒɒn] **II U4**, 74
Luke [lu:k] **I**
Marley ['mɑ:li] **II U2**, 44
Mick [mɪk] **II U4**, 84
Mike [maɪk] **II U2**, 48
Nathan ['neɪθn] **II U4**, 82
Nick [nɪk] **II U2**, 44
Peter ['pi:tə] **II U1**, 17
Shahid [ʃɑ:'hi:d] **I**
Steve [sti:v] **I**
Tony ['təʊni] **I**
Tyler ['taɪlə] **I**
Will [wɪl] **II U1**, 22

Girls' names

Alicia [ə'lɪsiə; ə'lɪʃə] **I**
Amber ['æmbə] **I**
Anna ['ænə] **I**
Anne [æn] **I**
Beata [bi'ɑ:tə] **I**
Carol ['kærəl] **I**
Ceri ['keri] **II U1**, 22
Claire ['kleə] **I**
Emily ['emɪli] **I**
Frances ['frɑ:nsɪs] **I**
Gwen [gwen] **II AC1**, 9
Helen ['helɪn] **II U5**, 105
Holly ['hɒli] **I**
Irina [ɪ'ri:nə] **I**
Judith ['dʒu:dɪθ] **II U5**, 100
Julie ['dʒu:li] **I**
Laura ['lɔ:rə] **I**
Lauren ['lɔ:rən] **II U4**, 76
Lou [lu:] **I**
Lucy ['lu:si] **I**
Maisie ['meɪzi] **II U4**, 82
Megan ['megən] **II U5**, 106
Mila ['mi:lə] **I**
Mina ['mi:nə] **II U2**, 44
Olivia [ɒl'ɪviə] **I**
Pia ['pi:ə] **I**
Polly ['pɒli] **II AC1**, 11
Rose [rəʊz] **I**
Ruby ['ru:bi] **II U4**, 76
Sally ['sæli] **I**
[illegible] **I**
Tamara [tə'mɑ:rə] **II U5**, 105
Vivien ['vɪvjən] **II AC4**, 113

Surnames

Azad [ə'zɑ:d] **I**
Elliot ['eliət] **I**
Fraser ['freɪzə] **I**
Green [gri:n] **I**
Nicholls ['nɪkəlz] **II U5**, 100
Parker ['pɑ:kə] **II U3**, 65
Preston ['prestən] **I**
Richardson ['rɪtʃədsn] **I**
Swindon ['swɪndən] **I**
Thompson ['tɒmsən] **II U3**, 60
Walker ['wɔ:kə] **I**
Zajac ['zeɪdʒæk] **I**

Place names

Baker Street ['beɪkə ˌstri:t] **II AC4**, 113
Begbie Road [ˌbegbi 'rəʊd] **II U4**, 86
Bradford ['brædfəd] **II U2**, 36
Brick Lane [ˌbrɪk 'leɪn] **II U2**, 37
Brook Lane [ˌbrʊk 'leɪn] **I**
Caerphilly [keə'fɪli] *walisische Stadt* **II U5**, 92
Camden Market ['kæmdən ˌmɑ:kɪt] **II U2**, 44
College Way [ˌkɒlɪdʒ 'weɪ] **I**
Cologne [kə'ləʊn] Köln **I**
Covent Garden [ˌkɒvnt 'gɑ:dn] **II U2**, 37
Cracow ['krækɒv; 'krɑ:kaʊ] Krakau **I**
Edinburgh ['edɪnbrə] **II U5**, 93
Enfield [en'fi:ld] **I**
Greenwich Park [ˌgrenɪdʒ 'pɑ:k] **I**
Greenwich Pier [ˌgrenɪdʒ 'pɪə] **I**
Hollywood ['hɒliwʊd] **II AC3**, 73
Hyde Park [ˌhaɪd 'pɑ:k] **II AC2**, 34
Isle of Man [ˌaɪl‿əv 'mæn] **II U5**, 99
Kidbrooke Gardens [ˌkɪdbrʊk 'gɑ:dnz] **I**
King William Walk [ˌkɪŋ 'wɪljəm ˌwɔ:k] **I**
London ['lʌndən] **I**
Nelson Road [ˌnelsn 'rəʊd] **I**
Nottingham ['nɒtɪŋəm] **II AC4**, 113
Oxford Street ['ɒksfəd ˌstri:t] **II AC2**, 34
Paddington ['pædɪŋtən] **II U5**, 95
South Street ['saʊθ ˌstri:t] **I**
Southend [saʊθ'end] **II U1**, 29
St Agnes [ˌseɪnt 'ægnəs] **II U5**, 94
Tintagel [tɪn'tædʒl] **II AC4**, 113
Tower Hill [ˌtaʊə 'hɪl] **II U2**, 39
Ty'n y Berth [ti:n‿ə 'bɜ:θ] **II U1**, 20
Victoria Park [ˌvɪktɔ:riə 'pɑ:k] **I**
Village Way ['vɪlɪdʒ ˌweɪ] **I**
Wimbledon ['wɪmbldən] **I**

Geographical names

America [ə'merɪkə] **II AC3**, 73
Australia [ɒs'treɪliə] Australien **II AC3**, 73
Austria ['ɔ:strɪə] Österreich **II U3**, 57
Bodmin Moor [ˌbɒdmɪn 'mɔ:] *Hochmoorlandschaft im nordöstlichen Cornwall* **II U5**, 98
Britain ['brɪtn] Großbritannien **I**
British Empire [ˌbrɪtɪʃ‿'empaɪə] britisches Königreich **II AC3**, 73
British Isles [ˌbrɪtɪʃ‿'aɪlz] Britische Inseln **II U5**, 93
Canada ['kænədə] Kanada **I**
China ['tʃaɪnə] China **I**
Cornwall ['kɔ:nwɔ:l] **II U5**, 92
England ['ɪŋglənd] England **I**
Europe ['jʊərəp] Europa **II AC2**, 34
France [frɑ:ns] Frankreich **II U2**, 42
Germany ['dʒɜ:məni] Deutschland **I**
Great Britain (GB) [ˌgreɪt 'brɪtn] Großbritannien **II U5**, 92
India ['ɪndiə] Indien **II AC3**, 72
Isle of Dogs [ˌaɪl‿əv 'dɒgz] **I**
Kent [kent] *Grafschaft im Südosten Englands* **II U3**, 60
Normandy ['nɔ:məndi] die Normandie **II U2**, 42
North Sea [ˌnɔ:θ 'si:] Nordsee **II U5**, 93
Northern Ireland [ˌnɔ:ðn‿'aɪələnd] Nordirland **II U5**, 92
Pakistan [ˌpɑ:kɪ'stɑ:n] **I**
Poland ['pəʊlənd] Polen **I**
Republic of Ireland [rɪˌpʌblɪk‿əv‿'aɪələnd] Republik Irland **II U5**, 92
Riviera [rɪv'jeɪrə] *Landschaft in Italien* **II U5**, 93
Scotland ['skɒtlənd] Schottland **II U5**, 97
Sherwood Forest [ˌʃɜ:wʊd 'fɒrɪst] **II AC4**, 113
Snowdonia National Park [snəʊˌdəʊniə ˌnæʃnl 'pɑ:k] **II U1**, 20
South Africa [ˌsaʊθ‿'æfrɪkə] Südafrika **II AC3**, 73
Spain [speɪn] Spanien **II U4**, 83
Thames [temz] **I**
United Kingdom (UK) [ju:ˌnaɪtɪd 'kɪŋdəm (ju:'keɪ)] Vereinigtes Königreich von Großbritannien und Nordirland **I**
USA (United States of America) [ˌju:es'eɪ (ju:ˌnaɪtɪd ˌsteɪts‿əv‿ə'merɪkə)] USA (Vereinigte Staaten von Amerika) **II AC3**, 73
Wales [weɪlz] **II U1**, 20

Other names

Big Ben [ˌbɪg 'ben] **II AC2**, 34
British Museum [ˌbrɪtɪʃ mju:'zi:əm] **II U2**, 36
Buckingham Palace [ˌbʌkɪŋəm 'pælɪs] **II AC2**, 34
Changing of the Guards [ˌtʃeɪndʒɪŋ əv ðə 'gɑ:dz] *Wachwechsel vor dem Buckingham Palace* **II AC2**, 35

Comic Relief [ˌkɒmɪk rɪ'liːf] *wohltätige Organisation* **II U1**, 14
Croeso i Gymru [ˌkrɔɪsəʊ‿iː 'gʌmri] **II U1**, 22
Crossharbour ['krɒsˌhɑːbə] **II U2**, 39
Cutty Sark [ˌkʌti 'sɑːk] **I**
Diwali [dɪ'wɑːli] **I**
Docklands Light Railway *(DLR)* [ˌdɒklændz ˌlaɪt 'reɪlweɪ] *Regionalbahn im Osten Londons* **I**
Eid [iːd] **I**
Elephant & Castle ['elɪfənt ənd kɑːsl] **II U2**, 39
Excalibur [ek'skælɪbə] **II AC4**, 113
For he's a jolly good fellow [fə ˌhiːz‿ə ˌdʒɒli gʊd 'feləʊ] *Volkslied* **I**
Greenwich Foot Tunnel [ˌgrenɪdʒ 'fʊt ˌtʌnl] **I**
Guy Fawkes Night ['gaɪ fɔːks ˌnaɪt] **I**
Halloween [ˌhæləʊ'iːn] *Tag vor Allerheiligen* **I**
Hanukkah ['hɑːnəkə] **I**
the **Houses of Parliament** [ðə ˌhaʊzɪz‿əv 'pɑːləmənt] *britisches Parlamentsgebäude* **II U2**, 36
London Eye [ˌlʌndən‿'aɪ] **II AC2**, 34
London Wall [ˌlʌndən 'wɔːl] **II U2**, 36
London Zoo [ˌlʌndən 'zuː] **II U2**, 39
Madame Tussauds [ˌmædəm tʊ'sɔːdz] **II U2**, 37
Meridian Line [məˌrɪdiən 'laɪn] Nullmeridian **I**
Mickey Mouse [ˌmɪki 'maʊs] **I**
Millennium Footbridge [mɪˌleniəm 'fʊtbrɪdʒ] **II U2**, 48
Mother's Day ['mʌðəz ˌdeɪ] **I**
Mousebook ['maʊsbʊk] **II U4**, 74
Mudchute Farm [ˌmʌdʃuːt 'fɑːm] **I**
Natural History Museum [ˌnætʃrl 'hɪstri mjuːˌziːəm] **II U2**, 45
Notting Hill Carnival [ˌnɒtɪŋ hɪl 'kɑːnɪvl] **I**
Oyster card ['ɔɪstə ˌkɑːd] **II U2**, 38
Red Nose Day [ˌred nəʊz 'deɪ] **II U1**, 12
Rocky ['rɒki] **II U2**, 42
Royal Observatory [ˌrɔɪəl‿əb'zɜːvətri] **I**
Sherlock ['ʃɜːlɒk] **I**
Shrove Tuesday [ˌʃrəʊv 'tjuːzdeɪ] Fastnachtsdienstag **I**
Sid [sɪd] **I**
Tandoori [tæn'dʊəri] **I**
Thomas Tallis School *(= TTS)* [ˌtɒməs 'tælɪs ˌskuːl] **I**
the **Tower of London** [ðə ˌtaʊər‿əv 'lʌndən] **II AC2**, 35
Transport Museum [ˌtrænspɔːt mjuː'ziːəm] **II U2**, 39
TTS planner [ˌtiːtiːˌes 'plænə] Handbuch für TTS-Schülerinnen und -Schüler **I**
Valentine's Day ['væləntaɪnz ˌdeɪ] **I**
Victoria [vɪk'tɔːriə] **II U2**, 39
Whitehall ['waɪthɔːl] *Straße in London* **II U2**, 37
World War II [ˌwɜːld ˌwɔː 'tuː] Zweiter Weltkrieg **II AC3**, 73

Famous names

Agatha Christie [ˌægəθə 'krɪsti] **II AC4**, 113
Boudicca ['buːdɪkə] **II AC4**, 113
Daniel Craig [ˌdænjəl 'kreɪg] **II U1**, 19
Dr Watson [ˌdɒktə 'wɒtsən] **II AC4**, 113
James Bond [ˌdʒeɪmz 'bɒnd] **II U1**, 19
King Arthur [ˌkɪŋ‿'ɑːθə] König Artus **II AC4**, 113
Lenny Harry [ˌleni 'hæri] *britischer Comedian* **II U1**, 14
Maid Marian [ˌmeɪd 'mæriən] **II AC4**, 113
Miss Marple [mɪs 'mɑːpl] **II AC4**, 113
Prince Albert [ˌprɪns 'ælbət] **II AC2**, 35
Queen Victoria [ˌkwiːn vɪk'tɔːriə] **II AC2**, 35
Robin Hood [ˌrɒbɪn 'hʊd] **II AC4**, 113
Sherlock Holmes [ˌʃɜːlɒk 'həʊmz] **II AC4**, 112
William the Conqueror [ˌwɪljəm ðə 'kɒŋkrə] **II U2**, 42;

A

abbiegen to turn **I**
abblocken to block **II U4**, 77
Abend evening **I**
  heute **Abend** 2nite *(= tonight)* **I**
Abendessen dinner **I**
abends in the evenings **I**
abends *(Uhrzeit)* p.m. **I**
Abenteuer adventure **II U1**, 20
aber but **I**
abfahren *to leave **II U3**, 58; to depart **II U5**, 96
abfahrend outward **II U5**, 96
abgeschlossen locked **II U1**, 23
abhängen von to depend (on) **II U5**, 95
abnehmen *to take off **I**
abschalten to turn off **I**
  Schalt/Schaltet es ab! Turn it off! **I**
abschicken *to send off **II U5**, 97
abschneiden *to cut (off) **II U2**, 49
abschreiben to copy **I**
Abstand gap **I**
abstimmen *to take a vote; to vote **I**
abstürzen to crash **II U4**, 87
acht eight **I**
Acker field **II U1**, 22
Action action **I**
Adresse address **I**
AG club **I**
aggressiv aggressive **II U1**, 28
äh er **I**
keine **Ahnung** no idea **II U1**, 23
Akku battery **II U1**, 23
Aktion action **I**
Aktivität activity **I**
Akzent accent **II U5**, 99
albern silly **I**
alle all of them; everyone **I**; everybody **II U2**, 40
  wir **alle** all of us **II U5**, 94
alle/-s all **I**
allein alone **I**
alles everything **I**
Alphabet alphabet **I**
als as **II U3**, 63
  als ob like **I**
als *(bei Vergleichen)* than **II U1**, 20
als when **I**
also so **I**
alt old **I**
  Wie **alt** bist du? How old are you? **I**
  Wie **alt** sind Sie? How old are you? **I**
am on **I**
  am besten best **I**
  am Wochenende at the weekend **I**
aus **Amerika** American **II U1**, 13
Amerikaner/-in American **II U1**, 13
amerikanisch American **II U1**, 13
Amtssprache official language **II AC3**, 73
sich **amüsieren** *to have fun **I**
an on; at **I**; by **II U5**, 104
  an Bord aboard **I**
  an sein *to be on **II U4**, 86
anbieten to offer **II AC1**, 8
Anblick sight **II AC2**, 34
Andenken souvenir **II U2**, 40
andere/-r/-s other **I**
  die **anderen** the others **I**
  ein/-e **andere**/-r/-s another **I**
Einerseits …, (aber) **andererseits** … On the one hand …, (but) on the other hand … **II U3**, 66
(sich) **ändern** to change **II U4**, 74
anders different; other **I**
Änderung change **II U5**, 105
Anfang beginning **II U1**, 27
anfangen to start **I**; *to begin **II U4**, 83
anfeuern to cheer **II U3**, 58
angeben to show off **II U4**, 87
Und ein **Angeber**! With a very big head! **II U4**, 79
von **Angesicht** zu **Angesicht** face-to-face **II U4**, 77
angespült werden to wash up **II U2**, 48
Angst fear **II U3**, 66
  Angst haben (vor) *to be scared (of) **I**
  Ich habe (keine) **Angst** vor … I'm (not) scared of … **I**
anhaben *to wear **I**
anhalten to stop **I**
anhören to listen (to) **I**
anklicken to click on **II U5**, 96
ankommen to arrive **II U5**, 96
ankommend inward **II U5**, 96
Ankündigung announcement **II U5**, 99
anmalen to paint **I**
Anmerkung note **I**
annähernd nearly **II U4**, 86
anonym anonymous **II U1**, 17
anprobieren to try on **II U2**, 48
Anregung suggestion **I**
Anruf phone call **I**
  einen **Anruf** entgegennehmen to answer the phone **I**
Anrufbeantworter answering machine **I**
anrufen to call **I**
Anrufer/-in caller **I**
anschauen to look at **I**; *to have a look (at) **II U3**, 59
sich **anschließen** to join **II AC1**, 11
ansehen to look at **I**
(sich) **ansehen** to watch **I**
Ansicht point of view **II U3**, 60
anstarren to stare **I**
antike Geschichte ancient history **II U5**, 98
antippen to tap **II U4**, 86
Antwort answer; reply **I**
antworten to answer; to reply **I**
Anweisung instruction **I**
Anwesenheitskontrolle registration **II AC1**, 10
Apfel apple **I**
App app **II U4**, 81
Apparat machine **I**
April April **I**
Arbeit job; work **I**
Arbeit für die Schule studies *(pl)* **II AC1**, 8
arbeiten to work **I**
Areal area **II U3**, 56
Ärger trouble **II U1**, 23
  Ärger machen *to make trouble **I**
Argument dafür pro **II U2**, 41
  Argument dagegen con **II U2**, 41
Arm arm **II U3**, 57
die **Armen** the poor **II AC4**, 113
Art kind **I**
  Art und Weise way **I**
Arzt/Ärztin doctor **II U3**, 58
Arztpraxis surgery **I**
Assistent/-in assistant **II U3**, 62
Atlas atlas **II AC3**, 72
atmen to breathe **II U3**, 64
  Atme(t) tief ein. Take a deep breath. **II AC1**, 11
Atmosphäre flair **II U2**, 37
Attraktion attraction **II U2**, 45
Aua! Ouch! **II U1**, 12
auch too **I**; also **II U1**, 14
  Du **auch**? You too? **I**
Audio- audio **I**
Audioführung audio tour **II U2**, 42
auf on; at; to **I**
  auf dem Foto/den Fotos in the photo(s) **I**
  auf der anderen Seite von across; opposite **I**
  auf der Straße in the street **I**
  auf einmal suddenly **I**
  auf Wiedersehen goodbye **I**
  auf … zu towards **II U2**, 48
aufbauen *to set up **I**
aufbewahren *to keep **I**
Aufführung show **II AC1**, 9
Aufgabe task; exercise; job **I**
aufgebracht upset **II U4**, 76
aufgeregt excited **I**; nervous **II U1**, 16
aufgeschlagen open **I**
aufhören to finish **I**
  Hör/Hört auf! Stop it! **I**
aufhören (mit) to stop **I**
aufladen to top up **II U2**, 38
aufmachen to open **I**
Aufmerksamkeit attention **II U4**, 77
Aufnahme recording **I**
Aufnahmestudio recording studio **I**
aufnehmen to record **II U3**, 62
aufpassen to look out **II U3**, 56
  aufpassen auf to look after **I**
  Pass/Passt auf! Be careful! **I**
aufräumen to tidy *(a room)* **I**
aufrechterhalten *to keep going **II U1**, 16
aufregend exciting **I**
aufsagen *to say **I**
aufschreiben *to write down **I**
aufstehen *(aus dem Bett)* *to get up **I**
  Es ist Zeit **aufzustehen**! Time to get up! **I**

aufstehen *(von einer Sitzgelegenheit)* *to stand up **I**
Auftrag task **I**
aufwärmen to warm up **I**
sich **aufwärmen** to warm up **I**
Aufwärmübung warm-up **I**
aufzeichnen to record **II U3**, 62
Aufzeichnung recording **I**
Auge eye **II U1**, 13
Ich traute meinen **Augen** nicht. I couldn't believe my eyes. **II U3**, 61
Augenblick moment **II AC1**, 11
Augenzeuge/**Augenzeugin** eyewitness **II U3**, 61
August August **I**
aus from **I**
aus Cornwall Cornish **II U5**, 94
ausblasen *to blow out **I**
Ausblick view **II U2**, 44
Auschecken Check-out **I**
(sich) **ausdenken** *to think of **II U1**, 16
Ausdruck phrase **I**; expression **II AC3**, 73
nützliche **Ausdrücke** Useful phrases **I**
ausflippen *to go crazy **II U4**, 79
Ausflug trip **II U1**, 13
den Hund **ausführen** to walk the dog **I**
ausgeben *(Geld)* *to spend **I**
ausgedehnt wide **II U5**, 93
ausgehen *to go out **II U5**, 104
sich **ausgeschlossen** fühlen *to feel left out **II U4**, 88
(sich) **ausleihen** to borrow **II U4**, 87
auspacken to unwrap **I**
auspusten *to blow out **I**
ausräumen to clear out **I**
jmdm. etw. **ausrichten** *to take a message **I**
sich **ausruhen** to relax **II AC1**, 11
Ausrüstung equipment **II U3**, 55
Aussage statement **II AC3**, 72
ausschalten to turn off **I**
Schalt/Schaltet es aus! Turn it off! **I**
aussehen to look **I**
wie der Mann **aussah** what the man looked like **II U1**, 17
außerhalb outside; out **I**
Außerirdische/-r alien **I**
Äußerung expression **II AC3**, 73
Aussicht view **II U2**, 44
Aussprache pronunciation **I**
Ausstattung equipment **II U3**, 55
aussteigen *to get out of **II U4**, 86
aussteigen (aus einem Bus/Zug) *to get off (a bus/train) **II U2**, 39
Ausstellung display **II U2**, 45
Ausstellung in der Klasse class display **I**
Auswahl choice **II U2**, 44
auswendig lernen *to learn … by heart **I**
auswickeln to unwrap **I**
ausziehen *to take off **I**
Auto car **I**
Automat machine **I**

B

Baby baby **I**
Bad bath **I**
Badewanne bath **I**
Badezimmer bathroom **I**
Badminton badminton **I**
Bahnhof station **I**
Bahnsteig platform **II U5**, 96
bald soon **II U1**, 22
Ball ball **I**
Banane banana **I**
Bär bear **II U2**, 42
Basketball basketball **I**
Batterie battery **II U1**, 23
Bauch stomach **II U3**, 64
Bauchschmerzen stomachache **II U3**, 59
Bauchweh stomachache **II U3**, 59
bauen *to build **II U2**, 42
Bauernhof farm **I**
Baum tree **I**
Beachtung attention **II U4**, 77
beängstigend scary **II U1**, 28
beantworten to answer **I**
bedeckt cloudy **II U1**, 23
bedeuten *to mean **II U2**, 40
Bedeutung meaning **II U1**, 25
bedürftig in need **II U1**, 14
sich **beeilen** to hurry **I**
beeindruckt sein *to be impressed **II U4**, 87
beeinflussen to influence **II AC3**, 73
beenden to finish **I**; to end **II U3**, 63
sich **befassen** mit *to deal (with) **II U2**, 40
befestigen to fix **II U4**, 79
befolgen to follow **II U2**, 40
befragen to interview **I**
Befragung interview **I**
Befürchtung fear **II U3**, 66
begeistert excited **I**
Beginn beginning **II U1**, 27
beginnen to start **I**; *to begin **II U4**, 83
behalten *to keep **I**
Behauptung statement **II AC3**, 72
behindert with special needs **II AC1**, 9
bei with; at **I**; by **II U5**, 104
beibringen *to teach **II U3**, 60
beide both **II U3**, 65
beide the two of them **II U4**, 76
Bein leg **II U3**, 57
beinahe almost **II U3**, 64
beinhalten to include **II U5**, 92
Beispiel example **I**
zum **Beispiel** for example **II AC3**, 73
beißen *to bite **II U2**, 42
beitreten to join **II AC1**, 11
bekommen *to get **I**; to receive **II U3**, 61
belebt busy **I**
beliebt popular **I**
bellen to bark **I**
bemerken to notice **II U2**, 49
benötigen to need (to) **I**
benutzen to use **I**
beobachten to watch **I**
bereits already **I**
Berg mountain **II U1**, 20; hill **II U5**, 104
bergen to save **I**
Bericht report **II U1**, 13
berichten to report **II U5**, 93
sich **beruhigen** to relax **II AC1**, 11; to calm down **II U4**, 87
berühmt famous **I**
beschäftigt busy **I**
beschreiben to describe **I**
besichtigen to visit **I**
Besichtigungs- sightseeing **II U2**, 44
besiegen *to beat **II U2**, 40
besitzen *to have got **I**
besonders special **I**
besorgen *to get **I**
besorgt sein *to be worried **II U3**, 64
besser better **I**
(der/die/das) **Beste** (the) best **II U1**, 14
besteigen to climb **I**
beste/-r/-s best **I**
am **besten** best **I**
bestimmt definitely **II U5**, 98
bestürzt upset **II U4**, 76
Besuch visit **I**
besuchen to visit **I**
Besucher/-in visitor **I**
Betreuer/-in instructor **II U1**, 22
Bett bed **I**
ins **Bett** gehen *to go to bed **I**
beunruhigt sein *to be worried **II U3**, 64
bevor before **I**
(sich) **bewegen** to move **I**
Bewegung move **I**
bewölkt cloudy **II U1**, 23
bezahlen *to pay (for) **I**
Beziehung relationship **II U3**, 66
bieten to offer **II AC1**, 8
Bild picture **I**
bilden *to make **I**
Bildgeschichte photo story **I**
billig cheap **I**
Bindewort linking word **I**
bis till **I**; until **II U3**, 56
Bis … CU *(= See you)*; See you! **I**
Bis dann! CU *(= See you)*; See you! **I**
bis jetzt so far **II U3**, 60
von … **bis** from … to **I**
Biskuit- sponge **I**
ein **bisschen** a bit **II U1**, 22
Bitte. Please. **I**
Bitte schön. Here you are.; You're welcome. **I**
bitten to ask **I**
bitten um to ask for **I**
blau blue **I**
bleiben to stay **I**
Bleistift pencil **I**
Blick look **I**; view **II U2**, 44
Blitz lightning *(no pl)* **II U4**, 86
blockieren to block **II U4**, 77

blöd stupid II U3, 65
bloß only I
Blume flower II U4, 80
BMX BMX II U3, 54
weiße Bohnen in Tomatensoße baked beans *(pl)* I
Bonbons sweets *(pl)* I
Boot boat I
an Bord aboard I
böse angry; bad I
Bösewicht villain II AC4, 112
Botschaft message I
Bowlingbahn bowling alley I
Box box I
Boxen boxing II U1, 12
Boxrunde round of boxing II U1, 12
brauchen to need (to) I
  nicht **brauchen** needn't I
  (Zeit) **brauchen** *to take II U4, 79
braun brown I
brechen *to break I
breit wide II U5, 93
schwarzes Brett noticeboard II U1, 14
Brief letter II U4, 75
Briefträger postman II U1, 17
Brille glasses *(pl)* II U3, 64
bringen *to bring; *to get; *to take I
  in Schwierigkeiten **bringen** *to make trouble I
  jmdn. dazu **bringen**, etw. zu tun *to make somebody do something II U4, 76
Brite/Britin British I
britisch British I
Broschüre brochure I
Brot bread I
  belegtes **Brot** sandwich I
Brücke bridge II U2, 48
Bruder brother I
Buch book I
buchen to book II U5, 96
Büchse can I
Buchstabe letter I
buchstabieren *to spell I
bunt colourful I
Buntstift pencil I
Burg castle II U2, 42
Büro office I
Bus bus I
Busbahnhof bus station I

C

Cache cache II U5, 104
Café café; snack bar I
Cafeteria cafeteria I
campen to camp II U5, 106
Camping camping II U4, 83
Cent *(Währung)* cent I
Center centre I
Chance chance II U4, 84
Charakter character I
Chatroom chat room II AC3, 72
chatten *(sich online unterhalten)* to chat I
Chipkarte smartcard II U2, 38
circa about I
Clown clown II U3, 64
Cola coke I
Comedian comedian II U1, 14
Comedy Show comedy show II U1, 14
Comic comic II U3, 66
Comicheft comic II U3, 66
Computer computer I
Computerunterricht Technology II AC1, 9
cool cool I
aus Cornwall Cornish II U5, 94
Couch sofa I
Cousin/Cousine cousin I
Creme cream I
Cricket cricket II U3, 55
Curry *(Gewürz oder Gericht)* curry I

D

da because I
da there I
  da ist/sind there is/are I
dabei sein *to be in II U3, 56
Dach roof II U5, 104
Dachboden loft I; attic II U3, 60
dahin there I
Sehr geehrte Dame, sehr geehrter Herr Dear Sir or Madam II U5, 97
danach then; after that I
dankbar thankful I
Danke. Thank you.; Thanks. I
danken to thank II AC1, 11
  Nichts zu **danken**. You're welcome. I
dann then I
darauf zu towards II U2, 48
das the I
das that I
  Das (hier) ist … This is … I
  Das macht … That's … I
  Das war knapp! That was close! I
dass that I
Datum date I
dauern *to take II U4, 79
die Daumen drücken *to keep your fingers crossed I
davonkommen mit *to get away with II U3, 60
Deck deck I
definitiv definitely II U5, 98
dein/-e your I
dein/-er/-e/-es yours II U5, 104
Dekoration decorations *(pl)* I
dekorieren to decorate I
denken *to think I
  Denke/Denkt an … Think of … I
  denken an to remember I
  denken über *to think of I
Denkmal monument II U5, 98
dennoch still II U4, 79
der the I
der-/die-/dasselbe the same I
Desaster disaster II U4, 86
deshalb that's why II U1, 20
deutlich clear I
Deutsch German I
deutsch German I
Deutsche/-r German I
aus Deutschland German I
Dezember December I
Diagramm diagram I
Dialekt dialect II U5, 99
Dialog dialogue I
die *(auch Pl.)* the I
Diele hall II U5, 104
Dienstag Tuesday I
dies this I
diese (hier) these I
  diese dort those I
diese/-r/-s this I
Ding thing I
Dinosaurier dinosaur II U2, 45
Diskussion discussion II U4, 74
diskutieren to discuss I
Distanz distance II U2, 46
doch after all I
Donner thunder *(no pl)* II U4, 86
Donnerstag Thursday I
doof silly I
Dorf village I
dort there I
dorthin there I
Dose can I
  aus der **Dose** tinned I
Dosen- tinned I
Drama drama II AC1, 8
dramatisch dramatic II U2, 49
dran kommen to reach II U4, 79
Du bist dran. Your turn.; It's your turn. I
draußen outside I
  nach **draußen** out I
dreckig dirty II U2, 48
drei three I
eine Dreiergruppe a group of three I
dreizehn thirteen I
drin inside I
dritte/-r/-s third I
dröhnen to boom II U5, 104
Druck- print II U4, 75
drücken to press II U4, 86
  die Daumen **drücken** *to keep your fingers crossed I
du you; u *(= you)* I
  Du auch? You too? I
  Du bist dran. Your turn.; It's your turn. I
  Du bist … You're … I
  Du weißt, wie man … You know how to … I
du/dir/dich/Sie/sich (selbst) yourself I
dumm silly I; stupid II U3, 65
  Zu **dumm**! Too bad! I
Dummkopf silly II U3, 64
dunkel dark II U1, 22

Dunkelheit the dark **II U1**, 22; darkness **II U5**, 101
durch through **I**
durchdrehen *to go crazy **II U4**, 79
Durcheinander mess **II U4**, 80
Durchsage announcement **II U5**, 99
dürfen can **I**; may **II U4**, 79
nicht **dürfen** mustn't **I**
Dusche shower **I**
DVD DVD **I**

E

Ebbe low tide **II U2**, 48
echt real **II U1**, 14
Ecke corner **II U2**, 40
Ehefrau wife, wives *(pl)* **II U5**, 100
Ei egg **I**
Eichhörnchen squirrel **I**
eifersüchtig sein (auf) *to be jealous (of) **I**
eigene/-r/-s own **I**
eilen to hurry **I**
Eimer bucket **II U2**, 48
ein/-e a; an **I**
ein paar a couple of **I**
ein wenig a little **I**
ein/-e andere/-r/-s another **I**
noch **ein**/-e another **I**
einander each other **I**
einbiegen to turn **I**
Einchecken Check-in **I**
eindeutig definitely **II U5**, 98
eine/-r/-s one, ones *(pl)* **II U2**, 40
Einerseits ..., (aber) andererseits ... On the one hand ..., (but) on the other hand ... **II U3**, 66
einfach easy **I**
einfache Fahrkarte one-way ticket; single ticket **II U5**, 96
einfach just **I**
Einfall idea **I**
sich etwas **einfallen** lassen *to think of **II U1**, 16
Einführung introduction **II U3**, 59
eingießen to pour **I**
Einheit unit **I**
die Segel **einholen** to reef the sails **I**
einige some; a few **I**
Einkäufe shopping **I**
Einkaufen shopping **I**
einkaufen gehen *to go shopping **I**
einladen to invite **I**
Einladung invitation **I**
Einleitung introduction **II U3**, 59
einmal once **I**
einpacken to wrap **I**
einrichten *to set up **I**
eins one **I**
einsam lonely **I**
einschenken to pour **I**
einschlafen *to fall asleep **I**
einschließen to include **II U5**, 92
einst once **I**
einsteigen *to get into **I**
einsteigen (in den Bus) *to get on (the bus) **II U5**, 96
Eintrittskarte ticket **I**
einwickeln to wrap **I**
Einzelkind only child **I**
einzeln individual **II U3**, 55
einziehen in to move in/into **II U5**, 104
einzige/-r/-s only **II U4**, 87
Eis ice; ice cream **I**
Eisbahn ice rink **I**
Eiscreme ice cream **I**
Elektrik electrics **II U5**, 105
Elektriker/-in electrician **II U5**, 105
Elektrizität electricity **II U5**, 104
elektronisch electronic **II U1**, 25
elf eleven **I**
Eltern parents *(pl)* **I**
E-Mail e-mail **I**
per **E-Mail** schicken to mail **II U4**, 81
empfangen to receive **II U3**, 61
Ende ending; end **I**
enden to finish **I**; to end up **II U1**, 12; to end **II U3**, 63
endlich at last **I**; finally **II U3**, 65
Energie energy **II AC1**, 11
eng close **I**
aus **England** English **I**
Engländer/-in English **I**
Ich bin **Engländer**/-in. I'm English. **I**
Englisch English **I**
englisch English **I**
englischsprachig English-speaking **I**
entdecken to discover **II AC1**, 8
auf **Entdeckungsreise** gehen to explore **I**
Entfernung distance **II U2**, 46
eine Nachricht **entgegennehmen** *to take a message **I**
einen Anruf **entgegennehmen** to answer the phone **I**
entgegnen to reply **I**
Entgegnung reply **I**
entlang along **I**
entlanggehen *to go down **I**
entrümpeln to clear out **I**
(sich) **entscheiden** to decide **I**
Entschuldigen Sie! Excuse me ... **I**
Entschuldigung! Sorry!; Excuse me ... **I**
entsetzt horrified **I**
sich **entspannen** to relax **II AC1**, 11
entsprechen to match **I**
enttäuscht disappointed **I**
entwerfen to design **II AC1**, 11
Entwurf plan; draft **I**
er he **I**
Erdboden earth **II U2**, 45
Erde world **I**; earth **II U2**, 45
die **Erde** earth **II U2**, 45
Erdkunde Geography **II AC1**, 10
Ereignis event **I**
Erfahrung experience **II U3**, 55
erfinden to create **I**
erforschen to explore **I**
ergänzen to add **I**
Ergebnis result **II U4**, 81
ergreifen to grab **II U2**, 48
erhalten to receive **II U3**, 61
sich **erinnern** (an) to remember **I**
Erinnerst du dich? Remember? **I**
Erinnert ihr euch? Remember? **I**
Erinnerung memory **II U1**, 23
Erkältung cold **II U3**, 59
erklären to explain **I**
Erklärung statement **II AC3**, 72
erkunden to explore **I**
ernähren *to feed **II U5**, 101
ernst serious **I**
etw. **ernst** nehmen *to take sth seriously **II U3**, 64
ernsthaft serious **I**
erraten to guess **I**
erreichen *to get to **I**; to reach **II U4**, 79
erschaffen to create **I**
erst only **I**
erst wenn until **II U3**, 56
erstaunlich amazing **II U1**, 22
erste/-r/-s first **I**
als **Erstes** first **I**
ertappt caught on camera **II U1**, 12
Erwachsene/-r adult **II U2**, 44
erwähnen to mention **II AC3**, 72
erwidern to reply **I**
Erwiderung reply **I**
erzählen *to tell **I**
erzählen von to talk about ... **I**
nochmals **erzählen** *to retell **I**
Erzähle mir von ... Tell me about ... **I**
Erzählung story, stories *(pl)* **I**
es it **I**
Es ist super zum/für ... It's great for ... **I**
Essen food **I**; meal **II U1**, 22
essen *to eat **I**
(ein Bonbon) **essen** *to have *(a sweet)* **I**
etwa about **I**
etwas some; something; a little **I**
euer/**eure** your **I**
eure/-r/-s yours **II U5**, 104
Euro *(Währung)* euro **I**
ewig forever **II U4**, 77
Examen exam **II AC1**, 8
extra extra **I**

F

Fackel torch **II U1**, 22
fahren *to go **I**; to travel **II U2**, 38
Fahrer/-in driver **II U1**, 17
einfache **Fahrkarte** one-way ticket; single ticket **II U5**, 96
Fahrplan timetable **I**
Fahrpreis fare **II U5**, 96
Fahrrad bike **I**
Fahrschein ticket **II U5**, 95

Fahrt trip II U1, 13; tour II U2, 42; journey II U5, 93
fair fair I
Fakt fact II AC2, 34
fallen *to fall I
 fallen (lassen) to drop II U2, 48
falls if I
falsch wrong I
fälschen to fake II U3, 60
Familie family I
fangen *to catch II U3, 54
Fantasie fantasy I
fantastisch fantastic II AC1, 9
Farbe colour I
 Welche **Farbe** hat …? What colour is …? I
farbenfroh colourful I
Farm farm I
Farmer/-in farmer II U1, 17
fast almost II U3, 64; nearly II U4, 86
Fastnachtsdienstag Shrove Tuesday I
Februar February I
Federmäppchen pencil-case I
Was **fehlt**? What is missing? I
fehlend missing II U1, 17
Fehler mistake I
Feier party I
feiern to celebrate I
Feiertag holiday I
Feld field II U1, 22
felsig rocky II U5, 93
Fenster window I
Ferien holidays *(pl)* I
fernbleiben von to stay away from II U4, 81
(sich) **fernhalten** von *to keep away from II U5, 104
Fernsehen TV (= television) I
fernsehen to watch TV I
Fernseher TV (= television) I
Fertiggericht ready meal I
Fertigkeit skill I
fertigstellen to finish I
Fest festival I
fest(e) hard II U2, 42
festhalten *to hold I
Festival festival I
festnehmen to arrest II U1, 17
Feuerwerk fireworks *(pl)* I
Fieber fever II U3, 59
Figur character I; figure II U2, 37
Film film I
Filmemacher/-in filmmaker II U1, 28
finden *to find I
Finger finger I
Fisch fish, fish *(pl)* I
fit werden *to get fit I
Fläche space II AC2, 34; area II U3, 56
Flair flair II U2, 37
Flasche bottle I
Flohmarkt flea market I
Flughafen airport II AC2, 34
Flur hall II U5, 104
Fluss river I
flüstern to whisper I
Flut high tide II U2, 48
Flyer flyer I
Folge sequel II U5, 101
folgen to follow II U2, 40
Form form I
 in **Form** kommen *to get fit I
 verneinte **Form** negative form I
Formular form II U5, 96
hier: sich **fortbewegen** *to get around II U2, 37
fortfahren *to go on I
Fortsetzung sequel II U5, 101
Forum forum II U4, 74
Foto photo; picture I
 auf dem **Foto**/den **Fotos** in the photo(s) I
 Fotos machen *to take photos I
Fotoapparat camera II U1, 12
Fotografie photo I
fotografieren *to take photos I
Fotostory photo story I
Frage question I
fragen to ask I
 Frage/Fragt nach … Ask about … I
 fragen nach to ask for I
Französisch French II AC1, 10
französisch French II AC1, 10
Frau woman, women (pl) I
Frau *(Anrede)* Mrs I
frei free I
frei freely ⟨II U4, 85⟩
Freiluft- outdoor II U1, 20
Freitag Friday I
Freizeit free time; leisure I
Freizeitzentrum leisure centre I
fremd strange I
fressen *to eat I
Freude fun I
Freudenfeuer bonfire I
sich **freuen** an to enjoy II U1, 16
Freund/-in friend I
 Dafür sind **Freunde** da. That's what friends are for. I
Freundin *(in einer Paarbeziehung)* girlfriend II U2, 40
freundlich friendly II U1, 18
Freundschaft friendship II U4, 78
 Freundschaft schließen *to make friends II U5, 94
frisch fresh I
uns **frisieren** *to do our hair I
froh happy I
fröhlich happy; fun I
Frucht fruit I
früh early I
Frühgeschichte ancient history II U5, 98
Frühstück breakfast I
frühstücken *to have breakfast I
Frühstückszerealie cereal *(no pl)* I
fühlen *to feel I
 sich **fühlen** *to feel I
 sich ausgeschlossen **fühlen** *to feel left out II U4, 88
 sich schlecht **fühlen** *to feel sick II U3, 59
Führer/-in guide II U2, 42
Füller pen I
fünf five I
fünfzehn fifteen I
funktionieren to work II U4, 79
Für wen …? Who … for? I
Furcht fear II U3, 66
furchtbar awful I
Fuß foot, feet *(pl)* I
 zu **Fuß** on foot II U2, 46
Fußball football I
Fußboden floor I
Fußgelenk ankle II U3, 58
Fußknöchel ankle II U3, 58
füttern *to feed II U5, 101

G

ganz all I; whole I
 den **ganzen** Tag all day II U1, 18
Garage garage I
garstig nasty II U4, 75
Garten garden I
Gaststätte restaurant I
Geächtete/-r outlaw II AC4, 112
Gebäude building I
geben *to give I
 es **gibt** there is/are I
Gebiet area II U3, 56
gebrauchen to use I
gebrochen broken I
Gebühr fee II U5, 96
Geburtstag birthday I
 Alles Gute zum **Geburtstag**! Happy Birthday! I
 Herzlichen Glückwunsch zum **Geburtstag**! Happy Birthday! I
Gedächtnis memory II U1, 23
Gedicht poem I
gedruckt print II U4, 75
Sehr **geehrte** Dame, sehr **geehrter** Herr Dear Sir or Madam II U5, 97
gefährlich dangerous I
Mir **gefällt** … I like … I
Gefängnis prison II U2, 42
Gefühl feeling II U1, 13
gegen against II U1, 23
Gegend region II AC3, 73
sich **gegenseitig** each other I
gegenüber opposite I
Geheimnis secret II U1, 23
geheimnisvoll mysterious II AC4, 112
gehen *to go; to walk I; *to leave II U3, 58
 ins Bett **gehen** *to go to bed I
 nach unten **gehen** *to go down I
 zu jmdm. nach Hause **gehen** *to go over to II U4, 79
 Wie **geht** es dir/euch/Ihnen? How are you? I

gehören (zu) to belong (to) II AC1, 9
gehören zu *to go with I
zueinander **gehören** *to go together I
Geist ghost II U2, 42
gelangweilt bored I
gelb yellow I
Geld money I
Geld sammeln to raise money II U1, 14
Geld verdienen *to make money I
Gelee jelly I
Gelegenheit chance II U4, 84
Gemälde painting II AC1, 8
gemein nasty II U4, 75
Gemeindezentrum community centre I
gemeinsam together I
genau exactly II AC3, 72
genau hier right here II U3, 56
Genie genius II U4, 79
genießen to enjoy II U1, 16
genug enough I
genügend enough I
Geocaching geocaching II U5, 101
geöffnet open I
Geografie Geography II AC1, 10
gerade just; at the moment I; right now II U4, 87
geradeaus straight on I
Gerät machine I; tool II U5, 105
Geräusch sound I; noise II U1, 22
gerecht fair I
Gern geschehen. You're welcome. I
gern haben to like I
gern mögen to love I
hätte/-st/-n/-t **gern** would like I
hätte/-st-/-n/-t sehr **gern** would love I
würde/-st/-n/-t **gern** would like I
würde/-st/-n/-t sehr **gern** would love I
Gerümpel rubbish I
Geschäft shop I
geschehen to happen I
Geschenk present I
Geschichte story, stories *(pl)* I; History II AC1, 10
antike **Geschichte** ancient history II U5, 98
geschichtlich historical I
Geschick skill I
Gesellschaft society II U5, 105
Gesetzlose/-r outlaw II AC4, 112
Gesicht face I
Gespenst ghost II U2, 42
Gespräch dialogue; conversation I
Gestalt figure II U2, 37
gestalten to design II AC1, 11
gestern yesterday II U1, 15
gesund healthy I
Gesundheit health II U3, 55
Getränk drink I
getrennt separate II U1, 20
gewaltig huge II AC2, 34
Gewinn prize I
gewinnen *to win I
Gewinner/-in winner I
gewöhnlich usually I
Gitter grid I
Glas glass I
glauben *to think; to believe I
gläubig religious I
der/die/das gleiche the same I
gleich right away I
jetzt **gleich** right now II U4, 87
gleichmäßig regular I
gleichzeitig at the same time I
Glocke bell II AC2, 34
Glück haben *to be lucky II U2, 48
… hat/haben **Glück**. … is/are lucky. I
glücklich happy I
Glücksbringer lucky charm I
Götterspeise jelly I
grau grey I
grausam cruel II AC4, 112
greifen to grab II U2, 48
Griff knob II U4, 79
groß big I; tall; high II U1, 21; large II AC2, 34
großartig great I; fantastic II AC1, 9
Großbuchstabe capital letter I
Größe size I
Großeltern grandparents *(pl)* I
Großstadt city I
grün green I
Grund reason II U3, 66
Grund- basic II U2, 45
grundlegend basic II U2, 45
Grundschule primary school I
Gruppe group I; team II U1, 12
gruselig scary II U1, 28
Gruß greeting I
Grüße ausrichten (an) *to say hello (to) I
Herzliche **Grüße** Best wishes II U5, 97
Herzliche **Grüße** *(am Briefende)* Love … I
Liebe **Grüße** *(am Briefende)* Love … I
Viele **Grüße** Best wishes II U5, 97
Viele **Grüße** … *(am Ende von Briefen und Mails)* Yours … II U4, 83
grüßen *to say hello (to) I
gut good; fine I
gut sein in *to be good at I
Guten Morgen. Good morning. I
Mir geht's **gut**. I'm fine. I
Guthaben credit II U2, 38
Gymnasium grammar school II U5, 97

H

unsere Haare machen *to do our hair I
haben *to have got; *to have I
hätte/-st/-n/-t gern would like I
hätte/-st-/-n/-t sehr gern would love I
Hafen harbour II U5, 93
Hafendamm pier I
Hähnchen chicken I
halb *(bei Uhrzeitangaben)* half past I
halb half I
Halbjahresferien half-term break I
Halbschwester half-sister I
die Hälfte half, halves *(pl)* (of) I
Halle hall II AC1, 9
Hallo. Hello.; Hi.; Hey! I
Halt stop II U2, 39
halten *to hold; *to keep I
halten von *to think of I
Haltestelle station I; stop II U2, 39
Hamburger burger I
Hand hand I
Klatsch/Klatscht in die **Hände**. Clap your hands. I
Handbuch planner I
Handbuch für TTS-Schülerinnen und -Schüler TTS planner I
sich handeln um *to be about I
Handgelenk wrist II U2, 48
Händler merchant II AC3, 73
Handlung action I
Handlungsort location II U2, 44
Handschuh glove I
Handy phone I; mobile II U4, 75
hart hard II U1, 16
hassen to hate II U5, 94
häufig often I
häufig gefragt frequently asked I
Haupt- main I
Hauptstadt capital II AC2, 34
Hauptwort noun I
Haus house I
nach **Hause** home I
zu **Hause** at home I
zu jmdm. nach **Hause** gehen *to go over to II U4, 79
Hausaufgabe(n) homework I
Haustier pet I
Haustür front door II U4, 86
He! Hey! I
Heim home I
heimlich in secret II U3, 65
heiß hot II U5, 98
Ich heiße … My name is … I
Wie **heißen** Sie? What's your name? I
Wie **heißt** du? What's your name? I
Held hero, heroes *(pl)* II AC4, 112
Heldin heroine II AC4, 112
helfen to help I
heraus out I
herausfinden *to find; *to find out I
Herausforderung challenge II U1, 20
herauskommen aus *to get out of II U4, 86
Herd cooker I
herein in I
hereinkommen *to come in II U5, 104
Herr *(Anrede)* Mr I
Herr der Raben raven master II U2, 42
Sehr geehrte Dame, sehr geehrter **Herr** Dear Sir or Madam II U5, 97
herrschen to rule II U5, 100
um … herum around I
herumschleichen to sneak around II U1, 28
herunter down II U2, 48
herunterfallen *to fall off II U3, 59

herunterkommen *to come down **I**
herunterladen *(aus dem Internet)* to download **II U4**, 81
herunternehmen *to take off **I**
herunterrollen to roll off **II U2**, 48
Herz heart **II U2**, 48
Herzliche Grüße Best wishes **II U5**, 97
Herzliche Grüße *(am Briefende)* Love … **I**
heute today **I**
heute Abend 2nite *(= tonight)* **I**
heute Nachmittag this afternoon **II U2**, 38
Hi. Hi.; Hey! **I**
hier here **I**
genau **hier** right here **II U3**, 56
Hier ist … Here's … **I**
Highlight highlight **II U1**, 13
Hilfe help **I**
ohne fremde **Hilfe** alone **I**
hilflos helpless **I**
hilfreich useful; helpful **I**
hilfsbereit helpful **I**
hinauf up **II U5**, 104
hinaus out **I**
hinausfließen to flow out **II U2**, 48
hinausgehen *to go out **II U5**, 104
hinein inside **I**
hineingelangen *to get into **I**
Hin- und Rückfahrkarte return ticket **II U5**, 96
hinfallen *to fall over; *to fall **I**
hinkommen *to get there **I**
sich **hinsetzen** *to sit down **I**
hinter behind **I**
Hintergrund background **I**
hinterhergehen to follow **II U2**, 40
hinüber over; across **I**
hinübergehen zu *to go over to **II U4**, 79
hinunter down **II U2**, 48
hinunterfallen *to fall off **II U3**, 59
hinuntergehen *to go down **I**
hinunterrollen to roll off **II U2**, 48
Hinweis clue **II U1**, 17
hinzufügen to add **I**
historisch historical **I**
Hobby hobby, hobbies *(pl)* **I**
hoch tall; high **II U1**, 21
hochleben lassen *to give the bumps **I**
Hochzeit wedding **I**
Hockey hockey **II U3**, 55
hoffen to hope **I**
Hoffnung hope **II U3**, 66
hoffnungsvoll hopeful **I**
höflich polite **I**
Sei/Seid **höflich**. Be polite. **I**
Höhepunkt highlight **II U1**, 13
Höhle cave **II U5**, 101
holen *to get **I**
Homepage homepage **I**
Hoppla! Oops! **I**
Hör- audio **I**
horchen auf to listen for **I**
Hören listening **I**
hören *to hear **I**
Ich habe **gehört**, dass … I hear … **I**
Hör-/Sehverstehen viewing **I**
Hose trousers *(pl)* **II U5**, 104
Hospital hospital **II U3**, 62
hübsch beautiful **II U5**, 94
Huch! Oops! **I**
Hügel hill **II U5**, 104
Huhn chicken **I**
Hülle wrapping **I**
Hund dog **I**
den **Hund** ausführen to walk the dog **I**
mit dem **Hund** spazieren gehen to walk the dog **I**
Ich bin **hundemüde**. I'm dog-tired. **I**
hungrig hungry **I**
Husten cough **II U3**, 59
Hut hat **I**
hüten to look after **I**

I

ich I; me **I**
Ich bin aus … I'm from … **I**
Ich bin Engländer/-in. I'm English. **I**
Ich bin … I'm … **I**
Ich heiße … My name is … **I**
Ich mache … nicht gern. I don't like … **I**
Ich mag … nicht. I don't like … **I**
Ich möchte … I'd like to … *(= I would like to)* **I**
Ich weiß (es) nicht! I don't know! **I**
Ich würde gern … I'd like to … *(= I would like to)* **I**
Idee idea **I**
Identität identity **II AC2**, 35
Idiot/-in idiot **II U2**, 49
ihm him **I**
ihn him **I**
ihnen them **I**
ihr you; u *(= you)* **I**
Ihr/-e your **I**; yours **II U5**, 104
ihr/-e her; its **I**
ihr/-e *(Pl.)* their **I**
Ihr wisst, wie man … You know how to … **I**
im in; on **I**
im Innern inside **I**
im Moment at the moment **I**
im Weg sein/stehen *to be in the way **I**
Imbiss snack **I**
Imbissstube snack bar **I**
immer always **I**
für **immer** forever **II U4**, 77
immer noch still **I**
immerhin after all **I**
in in; on; at; to; into; inside **I**
in Cornwall Cornish **II U5**, 94
in der Nähe von near **I**
in der Straße in the street **I**
in Not in need **II U1**, 14
in … hinein into **I**
in Ordnung OK; fine **I**
indem as **I**
Inder/-in Indian **I**
indisch Indian **I**
individuell individual **II U3**, 55
Infinitiv infinitive **I**
Information information *(no pl)* **I**
Informationen information *(no pl)* **I**
Inlineskates fahren to skate **I**
Inlineskatefahren inline skating **I**
Inlineskates skates *(pl)* **I**
innen inside **I**
Insel island **II U5**, 93
Installateur/-in plumber **II U5**, 104
Instruktion instruction **I**
interessant interesting **I**
Interesse interest **II U4**, 74
sich **interessieren** (für) to care (about) **II U4**, 77
sich **interessieren** für *to be interested in **II U2**, 36
interessiert sein an *to be interested in **II U2**, 36
Interkulturelles Across cultures **I**
international international **I**; multi-ethnic **II AC2**, 34
Internet internet **I**
Internetauftritt website **I**
Interview interview **I**
interviewen to interview **I**
irgendein/-e/-er any **I**
irgendjemand anyone else **II U3**, 61
irgendwelche any **I**
irgendwo anywhere **II U2**, 40; somewhere **II U2**, 51
sich **irren** *to be wrong **I**

J

ja yes; yeah *(infml)* **I**
jagen to chase **I**
Jahr year **I**
Jahrbuch yearbook **II U1**, 12
Jahrhundert century **II U2**, 48
18-jährig 18-year-old **II U2**, 38
11-Jährige/-r 11-year-old **II U3**, 56
Januar January **I**
je … desto the … the **II U3**, 54
jedenfalls anyway **II U2**, 48
jede/-r/-s every; each **I**
jede Menge lots (of) **I**
jedes Mal, wenn whenever **II U4**, 76
jeder everyone **I**; everybody **II U2**, 40
jemals ever **II U3**, 56
jemand somebody **I**; someone **II U1**, 17
jemand anderes anyone else **II U3**, 61
jene those **I**
jenes that **I**
jetzt now **I**
jetzt gleich right now **II U4**, 87
Job job **I**
Joghurt yoghurt **I**

jubeln to cheer II U3, 58
Jugend- teen II U4, 76
Jugendliche/-r teenager I
Juli July I
jung young I
Junge boy I
Juni June I

K

Kaffee coffee I
Kalender planner I
kalt cold II U1, 22
  kalt stellen *to leave it to cool I
Kamelrennen camel racing II U3, 54
Kamera camera II U1, 12
  mit der **Kamera** festgehalten caught on camera II U1, 12
Kamin chimney II U5, 104
Kampf fight II U4, 76
kämpfen *to fight II U4, 86
Kaninchen rabbit I
Kapitän/-in captain I
Kapitel unit I
kaputt broken I
Karneval carnival II AC2, 34
Karotte carrot I
Karte card I
Kartoffelchip crisp *(BE)* I
Käse cheese I
Kasten box I
Katastrophe disaster II U4, 86
Katze cat I
kaufen *to buy; *to get I
Käufer/-in buyer I
Kaufmann merchant II AC3, 73
keine Ahnung no idea II U1, 23
Keine Sorge! Don't worry! I
kein/-e no I
kein/-e/-en not … any I
Keks biscuit I
keltisch Celtic II U1, 20
kennen *to know I
Kerl guy II U1, 13
Kerze candle I
Kerzenlicht candlelight *(no pl)* II U4, 87
Kfz-Mechaniker/-in mechanic II U1, 17
Kind child, children *(pl)* I
Kino cinema I
Kirche church I
Kiste box I
Klang sound I
klar clear I
Klasse group; class I
  Ausstellung in der **Klasse** class display I
Klasse *(in einer englischen Schule)* tutor group I
Klassenarbeit test I
Klassenkamerad/-in classmate I
Klassenlehrer/-in tutor I
Klassenposter class poster I
Klassenzimmer classroom I
klatschen to clap I
  Klatsch/Klatscht in die Hände. Clap your hands. I
Kleider clothes *(pl)* I
Kleidergröße size I
Kleiderschrank wardrobe I
Kleidung clothes *(pl)* I; outfit II U1, 12
klein small; little I
Klempner/-in plumber II U5, 104
Klettern climbing II U1, 20
klettern to climb I
Klick click II U4, 87
Klicken click II U4, 87
klingeln *to ring I
klingen to sound I
Klub club I
klug clever II U4, 81
knapp close I
  Das war **knapp**! That was close! I
sich den **Knöchel** verrenken to twist your ankle II U3, 58
Koch-AG Cooking Club I
Kochen cooking I
kochen to cook II U4, 87
Kokosnuss coconut II U2, 49
Kollektion collection II U1, 14
Kolonie colony II AC3, 73
Komiker/-in comedian II U1, 14
kommen *to come I
  kommen nach *to get to I
  kommen zu *to get to I
  Komm jetzt! Come on! I
  Komm schon! Come on! I
Kommentar comment II U1, 16
kommentieren to comment (on) II U4, 81
kommunizieren to communicate II AC3, 73
Kompromiss compromise II U4, 77
König king I
Königin queen II AC2, 35
königlich royal I
  königlicher Leibgardist Beefeater II U2, 42
können can I
  kann nicht can't I; cannot II U4, 79
  können nicht can't I; cannot II U4, 79
  (vielleicht) **können** may II U4, 79
  Kannst du … nennen? Can you name …? I
könnte/-n could II U2, 43
Kontakt contact II U5, 97
  in **Kontakt** bleiben (mit) to stay in touch (with) II U4, 74
kontrollieren to check I
Konversation conversation I
Konzept draft I
Kopf head I
Kopfhörer headphones *(pl)* II U4, 86
Kopfschmerzen headache *(no pl)* II U3, 59
Kopfweh headache *(no pl)* II U3, 59
kopieren to copy I
Korbball netball I
Koreaner/-in Korean II U3, 60
Koreanisch Korean II U3, 60
koreanisch Korean II U3, 60
menschlicher **Körper** human body II U2, 48
korrekt correct; right I
Korridor hall II U5, 104
Korrigiere/Korrigiert … Correct … I
kosten *to cost I
  Es **kostet** …/Sie **kosten** … It's …/They're … I
  Wie viel **kostet/kosten** …? How much is/are …? I
kostenlos free I
Kostüm costume I; fancy dress II U3, 64
Kraft energy II AC1, 11; power II AC4, 112
  die **Kraft** der Wörter *(Wortschatzübung)* Word power I
kräftig hard II U2, 42
Krampf cramp II U3, 65
krank sick II U3, 59
Krankenhaus hospital II U3, 62
kreativ creative I
Kreis circle I
kreischen to scream II U2, 49
kreuzen to cross II AC3, 73
Krieger warrior II U5, 105
Kriminalität crime II AC4, 112
Kriminelle/-r criminal II AC4, 112
Kronjuwelen crown jewels II U2, 42
Küche kitchen I
Kuchen cake; pie I
Küchenschrank cupboard I
Kuh cow II U5, 101
Kühlschrank fridge I
Kultur culture I
Kummerkastentante agony aunt II U4, 76
sich **kümmern** (um) to care (about) II U4, 77
  sich **kümmern** um to look after I
Kunde/Kundin customer II U5, 100
Kunst art II AC1, 9
Kunstunterricht Art I
Kurs course II U1, 20
kurz short I
Kurzantwort short answer I
Kurzform short form I
Kurznachricht text (message) I
Küste shore II U2, 48; coastline II U5, 98
Küstenverlauf coastline II U5, 98
Küstenweg coastal path II U5, 104

L

Lächeln smile I
lächeln to smile I
lachen to laugh I
Laden shop I
Lage location II U2, 44
Lagerfeuer bonfire I
Lamm lamb I
Lämmchen lamb I
Lampe light II U4, 86
Land country, countries *(pl)*; land I; countryside II U5, 94
landen to end up II U1, 12; to land II U3, 62

landesweit national **I**
Landkarte map **I**
Landschaft landscape **II U5**, 92
Landwirt/-in farmer **II U1**, 17
lang long **I**
(nicht) **länger** (not) any longer **II U5**, 94
... **lang** for ... **II U1**, 16
langsam slow **I**
sich **langweilen** *to get bored **II U5**, 98
langweilig boring **I**
Laptop laptop **II U4**, 81
Lärm noise **II U1**, 22
lassen *to let **I**; *to leave **II U3**, 58
Lass/Lasst uns ... Let's ... **I**
Lassi lassi **I**
Lauf run **II U3**, 56
Laufen running **II U3**, 56
laufen *to run; to walk **I**; *to be on **II U4**, 86
Läufer/-in runner **II U3**, 54
Laune mood **II U1**, 28
laut loud **I**
läuten *to ring **I**
Leben life, lives *(pl)* **II U2**, 45
leben to live **I**
Lebensmittel food **I**
legen *to put **I**
Lege/Legt es in ... Put it in ... **I**
Legende legend **II AC4**, 112
jmdm. eine **Lehre**/Lektion erteilen *to teach somebody a lesson **II U3**, 60
lehren *to teach **II U3**, 60
Lehrer/-in teacher **I**; instructor **II U1**, 22
königlicher **Leibgardist** Beefeater **II U2**, 42
leicht easy **I**
leid tun *to be sorry **I**
Tut mir **leid**! Sorry!; I'm sorry! **I**
leise quiet **I**
Lektion unit **I**
jmdm. eine Lehre/**Lektion** erteilen *to teach somebody a lesson **II U3**, 60
Lernen studies *(pl)* **II AC1**, 8
lernen *to learn **I**
viel zu **lernen** a lot to learn **I**
auswendig **lernen** *to learn ... by heart **I**
Lesen reading **I**
vor dem **Lesen** pre-reading **I**
lesen *to read **I**
Leser/-in reader **I**
letzte/-r/-s last **I**
letztlich finally **II U3**, 65
Leute people *(pl)* **I**
(Pl.) **Leute** guy **II U1**, 13
Licht light **II U4**, 86
lieb nice **I**
Lieber ... Dear ... **I**
Liebe ... *(Anrede in Briefen)* Dear ... **I**
Liebe Grüße *(am Briefende)* Love ... **I**
Liebe love **II U5**, 101
lieben to love **I**
Ich **liebe** dich. I love you. **I**
Ich **liebe** ... I love ... **I**
lieber better **I**
Lieblings- favourite **I**
Mein/e **Lieblings** ... My favourite ... **I**
Was ist dein/-e **Lieblings**...? What's your favourite ...? **I**
Lied song **I**
lila purple **I**
Limonade lemonade **I**
Lineal ruler **I**
Linie line **I**
Link link **II U2**, 45
linke/-r/-s left **I**
links on the left; left **I**
auf der **linken** Seite on the left **I**
Liste list **I**
lokal local **II U5**, 99
LOL LOL (= laughing out loud) **II U1**, 12
Londoner/-in Londoner **I**
Los ticket **I**
lösen to solve **II U5**, 104
losgehen *to leave **II U3**, 58
loslassen *to let go (of) **II U3**, 64
Lösung solution **II U1**, 17
Löwe lion **II U2**, 42
Lücke gap **I**
lügen to lie **II U1**, 13
lustig funny; fun **I**

M

Maat mate **I**
machen *to do; *to make **I**
Fotos **machen** *to take photos **I**
sich Notizen **machen** *to take notes **I**
Machst du so ...? Is this how you (do) ...? **I**
Macht power **II AC4**, 112
mächtig powerful **II AC4**, 112
Mädchen girl **I**
ein **Mädchen** aus Deutschland a girl from Germany **I**
Magen stomach **II U3**, 64
magisch magical **II AC4**, 112
Mahlzeit meal **II U1**, 22
Mai May **I**
mailen to mail **II U4**, 81
Mal time **II U1**, 14
malen to paint **I**
Malerei painting **II AC1**, 8
Mama mum **I**
manchmal sometimes **I**
Mango mango **I**
Mann man, men *(pl)* **I**
wie der **Mann** aussah what the man looked like **II U1**, 17
Mannschaftsführer/-in captain **I**
Mäppchen pencil-case **I**
Mappe folder **I**
Marathon marathon **II U3**, 54
Markt market **I**
März March **I**
Maschine machine **I**
Match match **II U3**, 54
Material material **II U2**, 47
Mathe Maths **II AC1**, 9
Mathematik Maths **II AC1**, 9
Matrose sailor **I**
Mauer wall **I**
Maus/Mäuse mouse, mice *(pl)* **I**
Mechaniker/-in mechanic **II U1**, 17
Medien media **II U4**, 75
Meer sea **I**
Meerschweinchen guinea pig **I**
mehr more **I**
(nicht) **mehr** (not) any longer **II U5**, 94
mehr ... als more ... than **I**
Mehrzahl plural **I**
meiden to stay away from **II U4**, 81
Meile *(brit. Längenmaß)* mile **II U3**, 58
mein/-e my **I**
Mein/e Lieblings... My favourite ... **I**
mein/-er/-e/-es mine **II U4**, 87
meinen *to mean **II U2**, 40
Meinung opinion **II U4**, 76
die **meisten** (the) most **I**
der/die/das **meiste** (the) most **I**
meistens usually **I**
melden to report **II U5**, 93
Meldung report **II U1**, 13
melken to milk **II U5**, 101
eine **Menge** a lot of **I**
jede **Menge** lots (of) **I**
Mensch person, people *(pl)* **I**
Menschen people *(pl)* **I**
Menschenmenge crowd **II U2**, 44
menschlicher Körper human body **II U2**, 48
sich **merken** to remember **I**
merkwürdig strange **I**; weird **II U4**, 83
Meter metre **II U2**, 48
mich me **I**
Milch milk **I**
Million million **II AC2**, 34
Mine mine **II U5**, 98
Mini- mini **II U3**, 56
Minute minute **I**
mir me **I**
Mir geht's gut. I'm fine. **I**
mit with **I**
mit *(dem Fahrrad)* by *(bike)* **I**
mitbringen *to bring; *to take **I**
miteinander together **I**
Mitglied member **II AC3**, 72
mithalten (mit) *to keep up (with) **II U3**, 64
mitmachen *to be in **II U3**, 56
mitnehmen *to take **I**
Mitschüler/-in classmate **I**
Mitspieler/-in player **II U3**, 67
Mittagessen lunch **I**
Mittagspause lunch break **I**
Mitte middle **I**
mitteilen *to tell **I**
mittelalterlich medieval **II U5**, 92
Mittwoch Wednesday **I**
Mobiltelefon mobile **II U4**, 75
Mode fashion **II AC1**, 8

Model model I
Modell model I
Moderator/-in presenter I
modern modern II U2, 50
mögen to like; *to be into; to want (to) I
gern **mögen** to love I
nicht **mögen** to hate II U5, 94
Du **magst** … You're into … I
Ich **mag** dich. I love you. I
Ich **mag** … I like … I
Ich **mag** … nicht. I don't like … I
Ich **mag** … total gern. I love … I
Ich **möchte** … I'd like to … *(= I would like to)* I
möglich possible I
möglicherweise probably II U2, 38
Möglichkeit chance II U4, 84
Möhre carrot I
Moment moment II AC1, 11
im **Moment** at the moment I
Monat month II U1, 14
Monster monster I
Montag Monday I
montags on Mondays I
Monument monument II U5, 98
Morgen morning I
Guten **Morgen**. Good morning. I
morgen tomorrow I
morgens in the mornings I
motivieren to motivate I
Motto theme I
Mountainbikefahren mountain biking II U5, 93
müde tired I
Müll rubbish I
Mund mouth I
Münze coin I
Museum museum I
Museumsrundgang gallery walk I
Musik music I
Musiker/-in musician II U2, 39
müssen must I; *to have to II U4, 79
(tun) **müssen** to need (to do) I
nicht **müssen** needn't I
mutig brave I
Mutter mother I
Muttersprache first language II AC3, 73
mysteriös mysterious II AC4, 112

N

nach to I
nach draußen outside; out I
nach drinnen inside I
nach Hause home I
nach unten downstairs II U4, 86
nach oben upstairs II U4, 86
(**nach**) oben up II U5, 104
nach unten down II U2, 48
nach *(bei Uhrzeitangaben)* past I
nach *(zeitlich)* after I
Nachbar/-in neighbour *(BE)* I
nachdenken *to think I
Warte/Wartet und **denk/denkt nach**. Stop and think I
nacherzählen *to retell I
nachjagen to chase I
Nachmittag afternoon I
heute **Nachmittag** this afternoon II U2, 38
nachmittags *(Uhrzeit)* p.m. I
Nachricht message I
eine **Nachricht** entgegennehmen *to take a message I
eine **Nachricht** hinterlassen *to leave a message I
Nachrichten news *(sg)* II U2, 45
nachschauen to look up I
nachschlagen to look up I
nachspüren to trace I
nächste/-r/-s next I
der/die **Nächste(n)** next I
als **Nächstes** next I
am **nächsten** Tag the next day II U1, 15
Nacht night I
die ganze **Nacht** all night I
Nachtisch pudding I
Nachtwanderung night walk II U1, 23
in der Nähe von near I
nahe near I; close II U2, 42
Name name I
Namenstag name day I
Nase nose II U1, 12
nass wet II U2, 48
national national I
Natur nature II AC1, 11
natürlich of course I
Naturwissenschaften Science II AC1, 9
neben next to I; besides II U5, 99; by II U5, 104
negativ negative II U5, 92
nehmen *to take I
(ein Bonbon) **nehmen** *to have *(a sweet)* I
etw. ernst **nehmen** *to take sth seriously II U3, 64
neidisch sein (auf) *to be jealous (of) I
nein no I
nennen to name; to call I
jemandem auf die Nerven gehen *to get on people's nerves I
nervös nervous II U1, 16
nett nice I; friendly II U1, 18
Netz net II U3, 54
soziales Netzwerk social network II U4, 75
neu new I
Neuigkeiten news *(sg)* II U2, 45
neun nine I
nicht not I
nicht mehr not any more I
nicht mögen to hate II U5, 94
noch **nicht** not … yet II U3, 58
Ich auch **nicht**. Me neither. II U5, 98
nicht- non- II U1, 14
nichts nothing; not … anything I
Nichts zu danken. You're welcome. I
nie never I
niedlich cute I
niedrig low II U1, 21
niemals never I
niemand nobody II U2, 40
niemand anderes nobody else II U5, 106
nirgendwo nowhere II U5, 94
nirgendwohin nowhere II U5, 94
noch still I; yet II U3, 58
noch ein/-e another I
noch einmal again I
noch mal again I
noch nicht not … yet II U3, 58
Nomen noun I
Nord- north II U2, 39
Norden north II U2, 39
normal normal II U2, 44
normalerweise usually I
in Not in need II U1, 14
Notiz note I
Notizen machen *to make notes I
sich **Notizen** machen *to take notes I
November November I
Nudeln pasta I
null zero I
null *(bei Telefonnummern und Uhrzeitangaben)* oh I
Nullmeridian Meridian Line I
Nummer number I
nun now I
nun well I
nur only; just I
Nuss nut I
nützlich useful I
nützliche Ausdrücke Useful phrases I

O

O! Oh! I
o.k. OK I
ob if I
oben on top I; upstairs II U4, 86
(nach) **oben** up II U5, 104
obendrauf on top I
oberer Teil top I
oberes Ende top I
im Obergeschoss upstairs II U4, 86
Obst fruit I
oder or I
offen open I
öffentlich public II U2, 37
offline offline II U4, 87
öffnen to open I
oft often I
so **oft** whenever II U4, 76
ohne without I
ohne fremde Hilfe alone I
Oje! Oh dear! II U5, 104
Öko- Eco II AC1, 11
Oktober October I
Oma grandma; granny I
Onkel uncle I

online stellen to post **II U4**, 74
online online **II U1**, 25
Opa grandad **I**
Orange orange **I**
orange orange **I**
Ordner folder **I**
Ordnung order **I**
in **Ordnung** fine **I**
in **Ordnung** bringen to tidy *(a room)* **I**
organisieren to organise **I**
Ort place **I**; space **II AC2**, 34
örtlich local **II U5**, 99
Ost- east **I**
Osten east **I**
Ostern Easter **I**
Outdoor- outdoor **II U1**, 20
Outfit outfit **II U1**, 12

P

Paar pair **I**; couple **II U5**, 100
ein paar some; a few; a couple of **I**
Päckchen packet; parcel **I**
Packung packet **I**
Paket packet; parcel **I**
Palme palm tree **II U5**, 93
panisch werden to panic **II AC1**, 11
Papa dad **I**
Papier paper **I**
Stück **Papier** piece of paper **I**
Paradies paradise **II U4**, 74
Park park **I**
Partner/-in partner **I**
Party party **I**
passen zu *to go with; to match **I**
zueinander **passen** *to go together **I**
passieren to happen **I**
Pasta pasta **I**
Pastete pie **I**
Pause break **II AC1**, 10
PC PC *(= Personal Computer)* **II AC3**, 73
Pech haben *to be unlucky **I**
peinlich embarrassing **II U1**, 12
Pence *(brit. Währungseinheit)* penny, pence *(pl)* **I**
Peng! Bang! **II U4**, 86
Penny *(brit. Währungseinheit)* penny, pence *(pl)* **I**
perfekt perfect **I**
Person person, people *(pl)* **I**
pro **Person** each **I**
hier: persönlich face-to-face **II U4**, 77
persönlich personal **I**
Perspektive point of view **II U3**, 60
Pfeife pipe **II U2**, 49
Pferd horse **I**
Pfund *(brit. Währungseinheit)* pound (£) **I**
Picknick picnic **I**
Pick-up pick-up **I**
Pier pier **I**
Pille pill **II U3**, 59
pink pink **I**
Pizza pizza **I**
Placemat placemat **I**
Platzdeckchen placemat **I**
Plan plan **I**
planen to plan **I**
Planet planet **II U1**, 22
Plattform platform **II U5**, 96
Platz place **I**; space **II AC2**, 34; pitch **II U3**, 54
Platz! *(Befehl für Hunde)* Sit! **I**
plaudern to chat **I**
plötzlich suddenly **I**
Plural plural **I**
Polen Poland **I**
Polizei police **II U1**, 17
Pommes frites chips *(pl) (BE)* **I**
Pony pony **I**
Ponyreiten im Gelände pony trekking **II U5**, 93
populär popular **I**
Porträt profile **I**
Possessivform possessive form **I**
Post *(Eintrag im Internet)* post **I**
Poster poster **I**
Postkarte postcard **II U5**, 106
praktisch practical **II U4**, 75
Präposition preposition **I**
Präsentation presentation **I**
präsentieren to present **I**
Praxis surgery **I**
Praxisräume surgery **I**
Preis price; prize **I**
preiswert cheap **I**
pressen to press **II U4**, 86
Privatdetektiv/-in private detective **II AC4**, 112
pro per **II U5**, 95
pro Person each **I**
pro Stück each **I**
probieren to try **I**
Probier mal … Try … **I**
Problem problem **I**
Probleme trouble **II U1**, 23
Profil profile **I**
Programm programme **II U3**, 54
Projekt project **I**
Prospekt brochure **I**
prüfen to check **I**
Prüfung test **I**; exam **II AC1**, 8
Pudding pudding **I**
Punkt point **II U3**, 54
Punktestand score **II U3**, 54
Puzzle puzzle **I**
Pyjama pyjamas *(pl)* **II U1**, 16

Q

Qualifikation trial **II U3**, 56
Qualität quality **I**
quer durch across **I**
Quiz quiz **I**

R

Rabe raven **II U2**, 42
Herr der **Raben** raven master **II U2**, 42
Rad wheel **I**
Radfahren cycling **I**
Radiergummi rubber **I**
Radio radio **II U3**, 54
Rahmen set **II AC4**, 113
Rap rap **I**
rappen to rap **I**
Raster grid **I**
Rat advice **II AC1**, 11
raten to guess **I**
Ratschlag tip **I**; advice **II AC1**, 11
Rätsel puzzle; quiz **I**
Ratte rat **I**
Räuber/-in robber **II AC4**, 112
Raum room **I**; space **II AC2**, 34
Raumschiff spaceship **II U1**, 26
Reaktion reaction **II AC1**, 9
realistisch realistic **II U2**, 47
recht haben *to be right **I**
rechte/-r/-s right **I**
rechts on the right; right **I**
auf der **rechten** Seite on the right **I**
Rechtschreibung spelling **I**
recyceln to recycle **II AC1**, 11
reden to talk **I**
reden mit to talk to **I**
Redewendung phrase **I**
Redner/-in speaker **I**
Regel rule **I**
Was ist die **Regel** für …? What's the rule for …? **I**
regelmäßig regular **I**
regieren to rule **II U5**, 100
Region region **II AC3**, 73
regnen to rain **II U4**, 86
die Reichen the rich **II AC4**, 113
Reihenfolge order **I**
Reim rhyme **I**
rein in **I**
reinigen to clean **I**
Reise trip **II U1**, 13; travel **II U1**, 24; journey **II U5**, 93
Reisebericht travel report **II U1**, 24
Reisebüro travel agent's **II U5**, 95
Reisebus coach **II U1**, 17
Reiseführer guide **II U2**, 42
(das) Reisen travel **II U1**, 24
reisen to travel **II U2**, 38
Religion *(Schulfach)* RE *(= Religious Education)* **II AC1**, 10
religiös religious **I**
Rennen race **II U3**, 54; running; run **II U3**, 56
rennen *to run **I**
reparieren to fix **II U4**, 79
Reporter/-in reporter **II U3**, 61
Requisite prop **II AC4**, 113
reservieren to book **II U5**, 96
der Rest the rest **I**

Restaurant restaurant **I**
Resultat result **II U4**, 81
retten to save **I**
Rettung rescue **II U3**, 61
Rettungsboot lifeboat **I**
Rettungsring lifebuoy **I**
Rezept *(für Arzneimittel)* prescription **II U3**, 59
Rhythmus rhythm **I**
richtig correct; right **I**; real **II U1**, 14
Richtung direction **I**
in **Richtung** towards **II U2**, 48
riesengroß huge **II AC2**, 34
riesig huge; large **II AC2**, 34
Ring circle **I**
Ritter knight **II AC4**, 112
Rock skirt **II U5**, 104
Rock 'n' Roll rock 'n' roll **II AC3**, 73
Rohr pipe **II U4**, 79
Rohrleitung pipe **II U4**, 79
Rolle role **I**
Rollen tauschen to swap roles **I**
Rollenspiel role play **I**
Rollschuhe skates *(pl)* **I**
Rollstuhl wheelchair **II U2**, 39
Rolltreppe escalator **I**
Römer/-in Roman **II AC2**, 34
römisch Roman **II AC2**, 34
rosa pink **I**
rot red **I**
Route route **II U1**, 20
Rücken an **Rücken** back to back **I**
Rückenschmerzen backache **II U3**, 59
Rückenweh backache **II U3**, 59
Hin- und **Rückfahrkarte** return ticket **II U5**, 96
rufen to shout; to call **I**; to cry **II U4**, 86
Rugby rugby **II U3**, 54
ruhig quiet **I**
Rühr- sponge **I**
ruinieren to ruin **II U3**, 65
Rumäne/**Rumänin** Romanian **II AC3**, 72
Rumänisch Romanian **II AC3**, 72
rumänisch Romanian **II AC3**, 72
Runde round **II U1**, 12
Rundgang tour **II U2**, 42
Rutschbahn slide **I**

S

Saal hall **II AC1**, 9
Sache thing **I**
Saft juice **I**
Sage legend **II AC4**, 112
sagen *to say; *to tell **I**
Sahne cream **I**
Salat salad **I**
Salbe ointment **II U3**, 59
sammeln to collect **I**
Geld **sammeln** to raise money **II U1**, 14
Sammlung collection **II U1**, 14
Samstag Saturday **I**
Sand- sandy **II U5**, 93
sandig sandy **II U5**, 93
Sandwich sandwich **I**
Sänger/-in singer **II U1**, 19
Sanitärarbeit plumbing **II U5**, 105
Satz phrase; sentence **I**
Satzstellung word order **I**
säubern to clean **I**
Säugling baby **I**
Saxofon saxophone; sax **I**
Schach chess **II AC1**, 8
Schachtel box **I**
Schade! Too bad! **I**
Schaf sheep, sheep *(pl)* **II U1**, 22
schaffen to create **I**
Wir haben es **geschafft**! We did it! **II U3**, 65
Schälchen bowl **I**
Schale bowl **I**
Schatz treasure **II U2**, 42
Schau show **II AC1**, 9
schauen to look **I**
Schau/**Schaut** mal! Look! **I**
Schauplatz scene **II U3**, 61
in **Scheiben** schneiden to slice **I**
schenken *to give **I**
scherzen to joke **II U4**, 86
schicken *to send **I**
schieben to push **II U4**, 86
Schiedsrichter/-in official **II U3**, 65
schiefgehen *to go wrong **I**
schießen to kick **II U3**, 54
Schiff ship **I**
Schiffsjunge cabin boy **I**
Schiffsoffizier mate **I**
Schild sign **II U1**, 22
Schinkenspeck bacon **I**
Schlafanzug pyjamas *(pl)* **II U1**, 16
schlafen *to sleep **I**; *to be asleep **II U1**, 23
Schlafzimmer bedroom **I**
schlagen *to hit; to whip **I**; *to beat **II U2**, 40
Schläger racquet **II U3**, 54
Schlamm mud **II U2**, 48
schlammig muddy **II U2**, 48
Schlange queue **I**
schlau clever **II U4**, 81
schlecht bad **I**
der/die/das **schlechteste** the worst **II U1**, 20
sich **schlecht** fühlen *to feel sick **II U3**, 59
schließen to close **I**
Schließfach locker **I**
schließlich at last; after all **I**; in the end **II U1**, 14; finally **II U3**, 65
schlimm *(ugs.)* bad **I**
der/die/das **schlimmste** the worst **II U1**, 20
Schlittschuh laufen to skate **I**
Schlittschuhbahn ice rink **I**
Schlittschuhe skates *(pl)* **I**
Schloss castle **II U2**, 42
Schluchtenklettern gorge scrambling **II U1**, 20
Schluss end **I**
zum **Schluss** in the end **II U1**, 14; finally **II U3**, 65
Schluss *(einer Geschichte)* ending **I**
Schlüssel key **II U2**, 49
Schlüsselbegriff key word **I**
Schmerz pain **II U3**, 58
Schmuck jewellery; decorations *(pl)* **I**
schmücken to decorate **I**
schmutzig dirty **II U2**, 48
Schnäppchen bargain **I**
schnappen to grab **II U2**, 48
schnarchen to snore **I**
schneiden *to cut (off) **II U2**, 49
in Scheiben **schneiden** to slice **I**
schnell fast; quick **I**
schnell quickly **II U2**, 48
Schock shock **II U3**, 63
Schokolade chocolate **I**
schön nice; fine **I**; beautiful **II U5**, 94
schon already **I**; yet **II U3**, 58
schon einmal before **II U3**, 57
Schornstein chimney **II U5**, 104
schottisch Scottish **II U5**, 93
Schrank cupboard **I**
schrecklich awful **I**
Schreiben writing **I**
schreiben *to write **I**
schreien to shout **I**; to scream **II U2**, 49; to cry **II U4**, 86
Schritt step **I**
Schritt halten (mit) *to keep up (with) **II U3**, 64
Schritt-für-**Schritt**- step-by-step **II U4**, 79
schubsen to push **II U4**, 86
schüchtern shy **II U1**, 13
Schuh shoe **I**
Schule school **I**
Schüler/-in student **I**
Schulfach subject **II AC1**, 8
Schuljahr year **I**
Schulklasse class **I**
Schulstunde lesson **I**
Schultasche schoolbag **I**
Schulter shoulder **II U3**, 59
Schüssel bowl **I**
schütten to pour **I**
schützen to protect **II AC1**, 11
Schwanz tail **I**
schwarz black **I**
schwarz werden *to go black **II U4**, 86
schwarzes Brett noticeboard **II U1**, 14
Schweif tail **I**
Schwein pig **I**
schwer hard **II U1**, 16
Schwester sister **I**
schwierig hard **II U1**, 16; difficult **II U3**, 61
Schwierigkeit problem **I**
Schwierigkeiten trouble **II U1**, 23

in **Schwierigkeiten** bringen *to make trouble **I**
Schwimmen swimming **I**
Schwimmen gehen *to go swimming **I**
schwimmen *to swim **I**
Science-Fiction *(Zukunftsdichtung)* science fiction **II U1**, 26
sechs six **I**
Vier plus **sechs** ist zehn. Four and six is ten. **I**
Second-Hand-Laden charity shop **I**
See lake **I**
See zum Rudern boating lake **I**
Seemann sailor **I**
die Segel einholen to reef the sails **I**
Segelboot sailboat **II U5**, 106
sehbehindert partially sighted **II AC1**, 9
sehen *to see; to look **I**
Sehenswürdigkeit sight **II AC2**, 34; attraction **II U2**, 45
sehr very; very much **I**
Sehr geehrte Dame, sehr geehrter Herr Dear Sir or Madam **II U5**, 97
Hör-/Sehverstehen viewing **I**
sein *to be **I**
beeindruckt **sein** *to be impressed **II U4**, 87
Sei/**Seid** höflich. Be polite. **I**
sein/-e his; its **I**
Seite page **I**; side **II U2**, 49
auf der anderen **Seite** von across; opposite **I**
selber yourself **I**; himself **II U1**, 12; myself **II U4**, 77; yourselves **II U5**, 97
selbst even **I**
du/dir/dich/Sie/sich (selbst) yourself **I**
ihr/euch/Sie/sich (**selbst**) yourselves **II U5**, 97
er/sich (**selbst**) himself **II U1**, 12
ich/mir/mich (**selbst**) myself **II U4**, 77
selbstbewusst confident **II U1**, 20
Selbsteinschätzung self-evaluation **I**
selbstkritisch self-critical **II U4**, 76
selbstsicher confident **II U1**, 20
selbstverständlich of course **I**
Selfie selfie **II U3**, 65
seltsam strange **I**; weird **II U4**, 83
senden *to send **I**
Sender station **II U3**, 61
Sendung programme **II U3**, 54
separat separate **II U1**, 20
September September **I**
Sessel chair **I**
setzen *to put **I**
sich **setzen** *to sit down **I**
Show show **II AC1**, 9
Comedy **Show** comedy show **II U1**, 14
sich each other **I**
sicher sure **I**; safe **II U2**, 42
sicher sein *to be sure **II U5**, 98
Sicht view **II U2**, 44
Sie you; u *(= you)* **I**
Sie sind … You're … **I**
sie her; she **I**
sie *(Pl.)* them **I**; they **I**
sieben seven **I**
siegen *to win **I**
Sieger/-in winner **I**
Sightseeing- sightseeing **II U2**, 44
Signalwort signal word **I**
Silber silver **II U2**, 48
singen *to sing **I**
Ich **singe** und tanze gern. I like singing and dancing. **I**
Sinn meaning **II U1**, 25
Situation situation **I**
sitzen *to sit **I**
Sitz! *(Befehl für Hunde)* Sit! **I**
sich gegenüber **sitzen** *to sit face to face **I**
Skateboard skateboard **II U1**, 15
Skateboardfahren skateboarding **I**
Slogan slogan **II AC1**, 11
Smartphone smartphone **II U3**, 63
SMS text (message) **I**
eine **SMS** schicken to text **II U4**, 74
Snack snack **I**
so like this; so; like that **I**; that's how **II U1**, 14
so oft whenever **II U4**, 76
so … wie as … as **I**
sobald as soon as **II U4**, 76
Sofa sofa **I**
sofort right away **I**; right now **II U4**, 87
sogar even **I**
sollte should **II AC1**, 11
sollte(n) nicht shouldn't **II U3**, 59
Sommer summer **II AC3**, 72
Sommerferienlager summer camp **II AC3**, 72
Sonderangebot special offer **I**
sonderbar weird **II U4**, 83
Song song **I**
Sonne sun **II U5**, 104
sonnig sunny **II U5**, 98
Sonntag Sunday **I**
Sonst noch etwas? Anything else? **I**
Keine Sorge! Don't worry! **I**
sich **Sorgen** machen to worry **II U4**, 77
sorgfältig careful **II U2**, 42
Sorte kind **I**
Souvenir souvenir **II U2**, 40
sowieso anyway **II U2**, 48
soziales Netzwerk social network **II U4**, 75
Sozialwissenschaften Humanities *(pl)* **II AC1**, 10
Spalt gap **I**
Spanien Spain **II U4**, 83
spannend exciting **I**
sparen to save **II AC1**, 11
Spaß fun **I**
Spaß haben *to have fun **I**
Es macht **Spaß**. It's fun. **I**
spät late **I**
zu **spät** late **I**
zu **spät** kommen *to be late **I**
Wie **spät** ist es? What's the time? **I**
zu **spät** dran sein *to be late **I**
kleiner Spaten trowel **II U2**, 48
später later **I**
spazieren gehen *to go for a walk **II U1**, 22
mit dem Hund **spazieren** gehen to walk the dog **I**
Speck bacon **I**
Speer spear **II U5**, 104
speziell special **I**
Spiel game **I**; match **II U3**, 54
spielen to play **I**
einen Streich **spielen** to play a trick (on) **I**
spielen *(Theater)* to act **I**
eine Theaterszene **spielen** acting a scene **I**
Spieler/-in player **II U3**, 67
Spielfeld field **II U1**, 22; court; pitch **II U3**, 54
Spielkarte card **I**
Spielstand score **II U3**, 54
Spielzeug toy **I**
Spind locker **I**
Spitze top **I**
Sport sport **I**
… ist ein toller **Sport**. … is a great sport. **I**
Sportart sport **I**
Sportunterricht PE *(= Physical Education)* **II AC1**, 10
Sprache language **I**
Sprachmittlung mediation **I**
Sprechblase speech bubble **I**
Sprechen speaking; talking **I**
sprechen *to say; to talk; *to speak **I**
sprechen über to talk about … **I**
Sprecher/-in speaker **I**
Sprechgesang chant **II U3**, 58
springen to jump **I**
Spur clue **II U1**, 17
Staatsoberhaupt head of state **II AC3**, 73
Stadion stadium **II U3**, 54
Stadt city; town **I**
Stadtplan map **I**
Stadtteil part **I**
Stammbaum family tree **I**
ständig always **I**
Standort location **II U2**, 44
Standpunkt point of view **II U3**, 60
Star star **I**
stark strong **II U5**, 104; powerful **II AC4**, 112
Stärke power **II AC4**, 112
starren to stare **I**
starten to start **I**
Startpunkt starting place **II U5**, 96
Station station **I**
stattfinden *to take place **I**
Steak steak **I**
stehen *to stand **I**
stehen auf *to be into **I**
Du **stehst** auf … You're into … **I**
stehlen *to steal **II U5**, 104
steigen to climb **I**
steinig rocky **II U5**, 93
Stelle place **I**

stellen *to put I
online stellen to post II U4, 74
Stelle/Stellt es in … Put it in … I
Stern star I
Steuer wheel I
Steuerrad wheel I
Stichwort key word I
Stiefmutter stepmum I
still quiet; still I
Stimme voice I
Stimmung mood II U1, 28
stolz (auf) proud (of) II U1, 13
stoppen to stop I
stören *to get in the way II U3, 64
Story story, stories (pl) I
stoßen to push II U4, 86
Strand beach II U4, 83
Straße road II U1, 22
Straße (in der Stadt) street I
auf der Straße in the street I
in der Straße in the street I
Strecke route II U1, 20
Streich trick I
einen Streich spielen to play a trick (on) I
Streit fight II U4, 76
(sich) streiten *to fight II U4, 86
Strom electricity II U5, 104
Stromausfall power cut II U4, 87
Stück piece I
pro Stück each I
Stück Papier piece of paper I
Student/-in student I
Studie survey I
Studium studies (pl) II AC1, 8
Stufe step I
Stuhl chair I
Stunde hour II U2, 49
Stundenplan timetable I
Sturm storm I
Such- search II U1, 25
Suche search II U1, 25
suchen nach to look for I
Süd- south II U2, 39
Südafrika South Africa II AC3, 73
Süden south II U2, 39
Südkoreaner/-in South Korean II AC3, 72
Südkoreanisch South Korean II AC3, 72
südkoreanisch South Korean II AC3, 72
super great; cool I
Es ist super zum/für … It's great for … I
Supermacht superpower II AC3, 73
Supermarkt supermarket I
Surfen surfing II U5, 93
süß cute; sweet I
Süßigkeiten sweets (pl) I
Szene scene I

T

Tabelle grid I
Tablet tablet II U4, 79
Tablette pill II U3, 59
die Tafelrunde the Round Table II AC4, 113
Tag day I
am nächsten Tag the next day II U1, 15
den ganzen Tag all day II U1, 18
ein Tag in … a day out in … II U2, 44
eines Tages one day II U2, 43
Tagebuch diary II U5, 106
Tagebucheintrag diary entry II U5, 106
Takelage rigging I
Talent talent I
Talentwettbewerb talent show I
Talisman lucky charm I
Tante aunt I
Tanz dance (no pl) II AC1, 8
tanzen to dance I
Ich singe und tanze gern. I like singing and dancing. I
Tanzveranstaltung dance (no pl) II AC1, 8
tapfer brave I
Tasche bag I
Taschengeld pocket money I
Taschenlampe torch II U1, 22
Tatsache fact II AC2, 34
Rollen tauschen to swap roles I
tausende (von) thousands of I
Taxi taxi II U1, 17
Team team II U1, 12
Technik Technology II AC1, 9
Technologie technology II AC3, 73
Tee tea I
Teenager teenager I
Teil part I
teilen to share II U4, 76
teilnehmen (an) *to take part (in) II U4, 74
Telefon phone; telephone I
Telefonanruf phone call I
Tennis tennis I
Test test I
teuer expensive I
Text text I
Theater theatre I; drama II AC1, 8
eine Theaterszene spielen acting a scene I
Thema theme I; topic II U1, 26
Ticket ticket I
tief deep II U5, 93
Tier animal I
Tierarzt/Tierärztin vet I
Tierpark zoo II U2, 39
Tierwelt (in freier Wildbahn) wildlife II AC1, 11
Tipp tip I
Tisch table I
Titel heading I
tja well I
Toast toast I
Toilette toilet I
toll great I; amazing II U1, 22
… ist ein toller Sport. … is a great sport. I
Tomate tomato, tomatoes (pl) I
Tombola raffle I
Ton sound I
Tonmodell model I
Tonpfeife clay pipe II U2, 49
Tonstudio recording studio I
Tor goal I
Torte cake I
Tortenguss jelly I
tot dead II U2, 48
Tour tour II U2, 42
Tourist/-in tourist I
Touristeninformation tourist information centre I; tourist board II U5, 97
Tradition tradition I
tragen to carry II U4, 80
tragen (Kleidung) *to wear I
Trainer/-in coach I
trainieren to practise I; to train II U3, 58
Training training II U3, 64
Training für den Mund mouth jogging I
Transport transport II U5, 94
Ich traute meinen Augen nicht. I couldn't believe my eyes. II U3, 61
Traum dream II U1, 19
Traum- fantasy I
traurig sad I
treffen *to meet; *to hit I
sich treffen *to meet I
treten to kick II U3, 54
Trick trick I
Trifle (englischer Nachtisch) trifle I
trinken *to drink I
Trip trip II U1, 13
trotzdem anyway II U2, 48
Tschüss! Bye! II U3, 58
T-Shirt T-shirt I
tun *to do; *to make I
tun als ob to act like II U4, 76
Tunnel tunnel I
Tür door I
Turnier competition II AC1, 9
Turteltauben lovebirds (pl) II U1, 13
Tüte bag I
Typ guy II U1, 13
typisch typical I

U

U-Bahn underground II AC2, 34
die Londoner U-Bahn the Tube II AC2, 34
Übelkeit verspüren *to feel sick II U3, 59
Üben practising I
üben to practise I
über about; over; across I
überall everywhere I
überall (in) all over I
überall (egal, wo) anywhere II U2, 40
überhaupt at all I
übernachten to stay II U5, 94
Übernachtung sleepover I
überprüfen to check I
überqueren to cross II AC3, 73
überraschen to surprise II U3, 65
überraschend surprising II U1, 28
überrascht sein *to be surprised II U2, 49

Überraschung surprise I
überreagieren to overreact II U4, 76
überreden to persuade II U2, 38
Überschrift heading I
übersetzen to translate I
Übersetze/Übersetzt nicht … Don't translate … I
Übersetzung translation I
übrig left I
Übung exercise I
Übungsheft exercise book I
Ufer bank; shore II U2, 48
UFO UFO II U3, 62
Uhr clock I
Um wie viel Uhr? What time? I
Wie viel Uhr ist es? What's the time? I
Uhr *(Zeitangabe bei vollen Stunden)* o'clock I
um *(bei Uhrzeitangaben)* at I
um halb acht at 7:30 I
um … herum around I; round II U4, 87
Um wie viel Uhr? What time? I
umarmen to hug I
(sich) umdrehen to turn round II U5, 104
Umfrage survey I
Umgebung set II AC4, 113
Lege/Legt … umgedreht hin. Put … face down. I
umgehen mit *to deal (with) II U2, 40
umher around I
umkippen *to fall over I
sich umschauen to explore I
umsteigen (in) to change (onto) II U2, 39
umziehen to move (house) II U5, 94
und and I
unfair unfair II U3, 58
Unfall accident II U3, 55
unfreundlich unfriendly II U1, 28
ungefähr about I
ungefährlich safe II U2, 42
Ungeheuer monster I
unglaublich amazing II U1, 22
Unglück disaster II U4, 86
unheimlich scary II U1, 28
unhöflich rude I
Uniform uniform I
Unordnung mess II U4, 80
unrecht haben *to be wrong I
unregelmäßig irregular I
uns us I
unser/-e our I
unten downstairs II U4, 86
nach unten down II U2, 48
nach unten gehen *to go down I
unten below I
unter under I
im Untergeschoss downstairs II U4, 86
unterhalb below I
Unterhaltung conversation I
unternehmen wegen *to do about II U4, 84
hier: Unterricht class II AC1, 8
Unterricht lesson I
unterrichten *to teach II U3, 60
Unterrichtsstunde lesson I
Unterschied difference I
unterschiedlich different I
unterwegs out and about II U2, 44
unverschämt rude I
unwohl sick II U3, 59
Urlaub holiday I
Seid ihr im Urlaub? Are you on holiday? I
Sind Sie im Urlaub? Are you on holiday? I
ursprünglich originally II AC2, 34

V

Vanillepudding custard I
Vanillesoße custard I
Vater father I
etw. verändern make a difference II AC1, 11
Veränderung change II U5, 105
Veranstaltung event I
verärgert angry I
Verb verb I
verbessern to improve I
sich verbessern to improve I
verbinden *to put through I; to join II AC1, 11; to link II U4, 88
Verbindung link II U2, 45; connection II U5, 96
Verbrechen crime II AC4, 112
Verbrecher/-in criminal II AC4, 112
verbringen *(Zeit)* *to spend II U4, 76
verdienen to earn I; to deserve II U3, 60
Geld verdienen *to make money I
Verein club I; society II U5, 105
verfolgen to trace I
Vergangenheit past II U1, 13
vergeben *to forgive II U3, 65
vergessen *to forget I
vergleichen (mit) to compare (with/to) I
verhaften to arrest II U1, 17
sich verirren *to get lost II U5, 101
Verkauf sale II U1, 16
verkaufen *to sell I
Verkäufer/-in assistant II U3, 62
Verkäufer/-in *(auf einem Flohmarkt)* seller I
Verkehrsmittel transport II U5, 94
öffentliche Verkehrsmittel public transport *(no pl)* II U2, 37
Verkleidung fancy dress II U3, 64
verlassen *to leave II U3, 58
verlegen embarrassed II U1, 13
verletzen *to hurt II U3, 58
verletzt hurt II U1, 28
Verletzung injury II U3, 60
verlieren *to lose II U3, 54
verloren gehen *to get lost II U5, 101
vermissen to miss II U5, 94
vermitteln to mediate II U4, 78
vermuten to guess I
verneint negative II U5, 92
verneinte Form negative form I
Vernissage gallery walk I
Verpackung wrapping I
verpassen to miss II U4, 83
sich den Knöchel verrenken to twist your ankle II U3, 58
verrückt crazy I; mad II U4, 81
verrückt werden *to go crazy II U4, 79
Versammlung assembly II AC1, 8
versäumen to miss II U4, 83
verschieden different I; separate II U1, 20
Verschmutzung pollution II AC1, 11
verschwenden to waste II U4, 79
verschwunden missing II U1, 17
verschwunden sein *to be gone II U3, 65
sich versichern *to make sure I
versorgen to supply II U5, 100
versprechen to promise II U5, 95
sich verständigen to communicate II AC3, 73
Verständnis understanding II U4, 77
(sich) verstecken *to hide II AC4, 112
verstehen *to understand I
versuchen to try I
Versuch es mal mit … Try … I
verursachen to cause II U3, 66
Vervollständige/Vervollständigt … Complete … I
verwenden to use I
verzeihen *to forgive II U3, 65
verzieren to decorate I
Video video II U4, 75
Videochat video chat II U2, 36
viel much I; a lot I; lots (of); a lot of I
viel zu lernen a lot to learn I
Viele Grüße Best wishes II U5, 97
viele many I
vielleicht maybe I
Vielvölker- multi-ethnic II AC2, 34
vier four I
Vier plus sechs ist zehn. Four and six is ten. I
Viertel nach/vor quarter past/to I
violett purple I
Vogel bird II AC1, 8
Vogelbeobachtung birdwatching II AC1, 8
Vokabular vocabulary I
voll (von) full (of) I
Volleyball volleyball I
völlig completely II AC4, 112
vollkommen perfect I
von from; about; of I
von … bis from … to I
vor in front of I
vor *(bei Uhrzeitangaben)* to I
vor *(zeitlich)* before I; ago II U1, 14
vor dem Lesen pre-reading I
vorbei over II U3, 63
vorbei (an) past I
vorbereiten to prepare I
sich vordrängeln to jump the queue I
vorgeschichtlich prehistoric II U5, 98
vorher before II U3, 57
Vormittag morning I
vormittags in the mornings I

vormittags *(Uhrzeit)* a.m. **I**
Vorschlag suggestion **I**
Vorsicht! Be careful! **I**
vorsichtig careful **II U2**, 42
vorstellen to present **I**
sich (etwas) **vorstellen** to imagine **I**
Stelle/Stellt … **vor**. Introduce … **I**
Vorstellung introduction **II U3**, 59
vortäuschen to fake **II U3**, 60
Vortrag presentation **I**
vorüber over **II U3**, 63
vorüber (an) past **I**

W

Wache guard **II AC2**, 35
Wachs wax **II U2**, 37
wachsen *to grow **II U5**, 93
Wachsfigur wax figure **II U2**, 37
Wächter/-in guard **II AC2**, 35
wackelig wobbly **II U2**, 48
Wackelpudding jelly **I**
Wahl choice **II U2**, 44
wählen to vote **I**
während *(+ Nomen)* during *(+ noun)* **II U1**, 13
während while; as **I**
wahrnehmen to notice **II U2**, 49
wahrscheinlich probably **II U2**, 38
Wald forest **II U1**, 20
Waliser/-in Welsh **II U1**, 20
Walisisch Welsh **II U1**, 20
walisisch Welsh **II U1**, 20
Wand wall **I**
Wandern walking **II U1**, 20; hiking **II U5**, 93
wann when **I**
wann immer whenever **II U4**, 76
warten (auf) to wait (for) **I**
Warte/Wartet und denk/denkt nach. Stop and think **I**
Warte ab! Wait and see! **I**
Warteschlange queue **I**
warum why **I**
was what **I**
was für ein what **I**
Was fehlt? What is missing? **I**
Was hast du? What's the matter? **II U5**, 104
Was ist das? What's that? **I**
Was ist dein/-e Lieblings…? What's your favourite …? **I**
Was ist die Regel für …? What's the rule for …? **I**
Was ist los? What's the matter? **II U5**, 104
Was ist mit …? What about …? **I**
was man … what to … **I**
was noch what else **I**
was sonst what else **I**
Was um alles in der Welt …? What on earth …? **II U4**, 79
… **was** ich tun soll. … what to do. **II U4**, 76
waschen to wash **I**
sich **waschen** to wash **I**
Waschmaschine washing machine **II U4**, 79
Wasser water **I**
Wasserrutsche water slide **I**
Wau! Woof! **I**
Webseite site **II U4**, 76
Website website **I**
Wechsel change **II U5**, 105
wechseln to change **II U4**, 74
Wechselt euch ab. Take turns. **I**
Weg way **I**
im **Weg** sein/stehen *to be in the way **I**
im **Weg** stehen *to get in the way **II U3**, 64
weg away **I**
weg sein *to be gone **II U3**, 65
Es ist **weg**. It's gone. **II U2**, 48
wegen because of **II U3**, 65; for **II U4**, 75
wegnehmen *to take **I**
wegrennen *to run away **I**
wegwerfen *to throw away **I**
weh tun *to hurt **II U3**, 58
Weide field **II U1**, 22
Weihnachten Christmas **I**
weil because **I**
eine Weile a while **II U2**, 40
Wein wine **I**
auf andere Weise in other ways **II U4**, 81
weiß white **I**
weit far **II U2**, 41; wide **II U5**, 93
weitere more; other **I**
weiterführen *to go on **I**
weitergeben to pass (on) **I**
weitergehen *to go on **I**
weitermachen *to go on **I**
welche/-r/-s what; which **I**
Welche Farbe hat …? What colour is …? **I**
Welche … sind es? What are …? **I**
Welle wave **I**
Welt world **I**
Was um alles in der **Welt** …? What on earth …? **II U4**, 79
wem who **I**
wen who **I**
Für **wen** …? Who … for? **I**
wenden to turn round **II U5**, 104
sich **wenden** an to turn to **II U5**, 105
Wendung expression **II AC3**, 73
ein wenig a little **I**; a bit **II U1**, 22
wenige a few **I**; few **II U1**, 22
wenn when; if **I**
wer who **I**
Wer ist dabei? Who's in? **II U3**, 56
Wer ist es? Who is it? **I**
Wer macht mit? Who's in? **II U3**, 56
Werbespruch slogan **II AC1**, 11
werden *to become **II U2**, 42; *to get **II U5**, 104
werfen (nach) *to throw (at) **I**
Werkzeug tool **II U5**, 105
wert sein *to be worth **I**
West- west **I**
Westen west **I**
westeuropäische Zeit Greenwich Mean Time *(= GMT)* **I**
Wettbewerb contest **I**; competition **II AC1**, 9
ich wette I bet **II U2**, 40
Wetter weather **I**
Wettervorhersage weather forecast **II U5**, 96
Wettkampf contest **I**
Wettlauf race **II U3**, 54
wichtig important **I**
wichtig nehmen to care (about) **II U4**, 77
wie like **I**
wie as **II AC1**, 11
wie how **I**
Wie viele …? How many …? **I**
Wie alt bist du? How old are you? **I**
Wie alt sind Sie? How old are you? **I**
wie der Mann aussah what the man looked like **II U1**, 17
Wie geht es dir/euch/Ihnen? How are you? **I**
Wie heißen Sie? What's your name? **I**
Wie heißt du? What's your name? **I**
Wie man … How to … **I**
Wie spät ist es? What's the time? **I**
Wie viel (kostet/kosten) …? How much is/are …? **I**
Wie viel Uhr ist es? What's the time? **I**
Wie wär's mit …? What about …? **I**
wieder again **I**
Wiederaufnehmen pick-up **I**
auf Wiedersehen goodbye **I**
wiederverwerten to recycle **II AC1**, 11
Wiese field **II U1**, 22
wild wild **II U5**, 98
Willkommen! Welcome! **II U1**, 22
willkommen heißen to welcome **II AC1**, 11
Wind wind **II U5**, 104
Windsurfen windsurfing **II U5**, 93
wir we **I**
Wir sind aus … We're from … **I**
wirklich real **II U1**, 14
wirklich really **I**
wissen *to know **I**
Du **weißt**, wie man … You know how to … **I**
Ich **weiß** (es) nicht! I don't know! **I**
Ihr **wisst**, wie man … You know how to … **I**
Witz joke **I**
witzig funny; fun **I**
wo where **I**
Woche week **I**
Wochenende weekend **I**
am **Wochenende** at the weekend **I**
Wochentag weekday **II U4**, 84
Woher …? Where … from? **I**
wohin where **I**
… **wohin** ich gehen kann. … where to go. **II U2**, 40
Wohlfahrt charity **I**
wohltätige Zwecke charity **I**

Wohltätigkeitsverein charity **I**
wohnen to live **I**
  wohnen bei to stay with **II U2**, 38
Wohnung flat **I**
Wohnzimmer living room **I**
Wolke cloud **II U5**, 104
wollen to want (to) **I**
Workshop workshop **I**
Wort word **I**
  die Kraft der **Wörter** *(Wortschatzübung)* Word power **I**
Wörterbuch dictionary **I**
Wörternetz *(eine Art Schaubild)* mind map **I**
Wortschatz vocabulary **I**
Wortschlange word snake **I**
Wortstellung word order **I**
Worum geht es in/im …? What is … about? **I**
Wow! Wow! **I**
wunderbar beautiful; wonderful **II U5**, 94
Wunsch wish **I**
sich etwas **wünschen** *to make a wish **I**
würde/-st/-n/-t gern would like **I**
  würde/-st/-n/-t sehr gern would love **I**
  Ich **würde** gern … I'd like to … *(= I would like to)* **I**
Würfle/Würfelt mit zwei Würfeln. Roll two dice. **I**
Wurm worm **I**
wusch whoosh **I**
wütend angry **I**

Z

z.B. *(= zum Beispiel)* e.g. *(= for example)* **I**
Zahl number **I**
zählen (auf) to count (on) **I**
Zauber- magical **II AC4**, 112
Zauberer wizard **II AC4**, 112
auf **Zehenspitzen** gehen to tiptoe **II U1**, 23
zehn ten **I**
  Vier plus sechs ist **zehn**. Four and six is ten. **I**
zehnmal ten times **I**
Zeichen sign **II U1**, 22
zeichnen *to draw **I**
Zeichnung drawing **I**
zeigen to show **I**
  Zeige/Zeigt auf … Point to … **I**
  Zeige/Zeigt darauf. Point. **I**
Zeile line **I**
Zeit time **I**
  (**Zeit**) brauchen *to take **II U4**, 79
  zur selben **Zeit** at the same time **I**
  die ganze **Zeit** all the time **II U2**, 48
  Es ist **Zeit** aufzustehen! Time to get up! **I**
Zeitschrift magazine **I**
Zeitstrahl time line **I**
Zelten camping **II U4**, 83
zelten to camp **II U5**, 106
zentral central **II U2**, 48
Zentral- central **II U2**, 48
hier: **Zentrum** heart **II U2**, 48
Zentrum centre **I**
zerbrechen *to break **I**
zerstören to ruin **II U3**, 65
Zeug stuff **I**
Zeuge/Zeugin witness **II U3**, 61
ziehen to pull **I**
Ziel goal **I**
Ziellinie finish line **II U3**, 65
Zimmer room **I**
Zimmergenosse/Zimmergenossin roommate **I**
Zinn tin **II U5**, 98
Zitrone lemon **II U1**, 28
Zoo zoo **II U2**, 39
zornig angry **I**
zu too **I**
  Zu dumm! Too bad! **I**
zu to **I**
  zu Hause at home **I**
zubereiten to prepare **I**
zuerst first **I**; at first **II U2**, 49
Zug train **I**
Zuhause home **I**
zuhören to listen (to) **I**
  Hör/Hört noch einmal **zu**. Listen again. **I**
Zuhörer/-in listener **II U3**, 61
zujubeln to cheer **II U3**, 58
Zukunft future **II U5**, 93
zum Beispiel for example **II AC3**, 73
zumachen to close **I**
zunächst at first **II U2**, 49
zuordnen to match **I**
zupassen to pass **II U3**, 54
zurück back **I**
zurückfahren to return **II U5**, 96
zurückgehen auf *to go right back to **II U5**, 104
zurückkehren to return **II U5**, 96
hier: **zurückschrecken** to jump back **II U2**, 43
zurückspringen to jump back **II U2**, 43
zusammen together **I**
zusätzlich extra **I**; additional **II AC1**, 8
zuschauen to watch **I**
zuspielen to pass **II U3**, 54
Zutat ingredient **II AC4**, 112
zuvor before **II U3**, 57
sich **zuwenden** to turn to **II U5**, 105
zwei two **I**
zweite/-r/-s second **I**
Zwilling twin **II U5**, 105
Zwillings- twin **II U5**, 105
zwischen between **I**
zwölf twelve **I**;

In the classroom

Asking for help and information

Can you help me, please?	Kannst du / Können Sie mir bitte helfen?
How do you do this exercise?	Wie macht man diese Übung?
How do you spell …, please?	Wie schreibt man …, bitte?
Is this right? I'm not sure.	Ist das richtig? Ich bin mir nicht sicher.
Is it OK to …?	Ist es in Ordnung, wenn ich / wir …?
Is it true or false?	Ist das richtig oder falsch?
Sorry, I don't know. Ask …	Tut mir leid, das weiß ich nicht. Frag …
Sorry. Can you say that again, please?	Wie bitte? Können Sie das bitte wiederholen?
What does that mean?	Was bedeutet das?
What's for homework?	Was haben wir als Hausaufgabe auf?
What's that in English / German?	Was heißt das auf Englisch / Deutsch?

Vocabulary for instructions and activities

Act (out) one of the scenes. / Act (out) the dialogues.	Spiele eine der Szenen. / Spiele die Dialoge.
Add more words / ideas.	Füge weitere Wörter / Ideen hinzu.
Ask your partner questions.	Stelle deinem Partner / deiner Partnerin Fragen.
Answer your partner's questions.	Beantworte die Fragen deines Partners / deiner Partnerin.
Check your partner's text.	Überprüfe den Text deines Partners / deiner Partnerin.
Collect ideas.	Sammle Ideen.
Compare English and German.	Vergleiche das Englische und Deutsche.
Complete the answers.	Vervollständige die Antworten.
Copy the grid / the mind map.	Schreibe die Tabelle / das Wörternetz ab.
Correct the wrong sentences.	Korrigiere die falschen Sätze.
Describe your room.	Beschreibe dein Zimmer.

Decide who writes which part.	Entscheidet, wer welchen Teil schreibt.
Discuss different ideas.	Diskutiert verschiedene Ideen.
Draw a picture.	Zeichne ein Bild.
Exchange your flyers / questions.	Tauscht eure Flyer / Fragen untereinander aus.
Explain your answer. / Explain why.	Erkläre deine Antwort. / Erkläre warum.
Fill in your grid / the form.	Fülle deine Tabelle / das Formular aus.
Find somebody who …	Finde jemanden, der …
Find the rule / the right word order.	Finde die Regel / die richtige Wortstellung.
Finish your brochure.	Stelle deine Broschüre fertig.
Form expert groups.	Bildet Expertengruppen.
Get organised.	Organisiert euch.
Go back to your home group.	Gehe zurück zu deiner ersten Gruppe.
Guess the new words.	Errate die neuen Wörter.
Imagine you're one of the people in the story.	Stelle dir vor, du bist eine der Personen in der Geschichte.
Improve your text / part of the report.	Verbessere deinen Text / Teil des Berichts.
Learn your text by heart.	Lerne deinen Text auswendig.
Listen to the sentences / the dialogue.	Höre dir die Sätze / den Dialog an.
Look at the picture / the examples.	Schau dir das Bild / die Beispiele an.
Look up the words.	Schlage die Wörter nach.
Make a poster / a grid / a mind map.	Fertige ein Poster / eine Tabelle / ein Wörternetz an.
Match the sentence parts.	Ordne die Satzteile einander zu.
Name more sports.	Nenne mehr Sportarten.
Note down what is missing.	Notiere, was fehlt.
Peer-edit each other's work.	Kontrolliert eure Arbeiten gegenseitig.
Plan the scenes.	Plane die Szenen.
Record your final report / dialogue.	Nehmt euren fertigen Bericht / Dialog auf.
Scan the text for details.	Suche den Text nach Details ab.
Share the information with your partner.	Teile die Informationen mit deinem Partner / deiner Partnerin.
Skim the text for the gist.	Überfliege den Text und finde die wichtigsten Aussagen.
Sum up what happens in the story.	Fasse zusammen, was in der Geschichte passiert.
Practise your scenes / the dialogues.	Übe deine Szenen / die Dialoge.
Present the information from your text.	Präsentiere die Informationen aus deinem Text.
Put in the correct forms.	Setze die richtigen Formen ein.
Read your text aloud.	Lies deinen Text laut vor.
Repeat the sentences / the dialogues.	Wiederhole die Sätze / die Dialoge.
Say the words / the sounds.	Sage die Wörter / die Laute.
Show your brochure.	Zeige deine Broschüre.
Swap roles.	Tauscht die Rollen.
Take a card.	Nimm eine Karte.

Take notes.	Mache dir Notizen.
Take turns.	Wechselt euch ab.
Talk with your partner.	Sprich mit deinem Partner / deiner Partnerin.
Tell your partner about your hobby.	Erzähle deinem Partner / deiner Partnerin von deinem Hobby.
Think of ideas for …	Überlege dir Ideen für …
Trade your part with somebody else.	Tausche deinen Teil mit jemandem.
Translate the words / sentences.	Übersetze die Wörter / Sätze.
Use the ideas / the vocabulary.	Verwende die Ideen / die Vokabeln.
Work with a partner or in a group.	Arbeite mit einem Partner / einer Partnerin oder in einer Gruppe.
Write dialogues / a short text / a reply.	Schreibe Dialoge / einen kurzen Text / eine Antwort.
Write about your friends.	Schreibe über deine Freunde.
Write down school words.	Schreibe Wörter zum Thema „Schule" auf.

Useful words

- activity – Aktivität
- answer – Antwort
- class display – Ausstellung in der Klasse
- collocation – Wortverbindung
- description – Beschreibung
- dialogue – Dialog
- dice – Würfel
- draft – Entwurf; Konzept
- drawing – Zeichnung
- example – Beispiel
- fact – Tatsache; Fakt
- folder – Ordner; Mappe
- game – Spiel
- grid – Gitter; Tabelle; Raster
- heading – Überschrift
- information – Information(en)
- key word – Schlüsselwort
- list – Liste
- mind map – Wörternetz
- order – Reihenfolge
- perspective – Perspektive
- phrase – Redewendung; Ausdruck
- picture story – Bildergeschichte
- point of view – Standpunkt; Ansicht
- presentation – Präsentation; Vortrag
- prompt card – Rollenkarte
- puzzle – Rätsel; Puzzle
- pros and cons – Vor- und Nachteile
- question – Frage
- quiz – Quiz; Rätsel
- quote – Zitat
- report – Bericht
- revision – Wiederholung
- rhyme – Reim
- role play – Rollenspiel
- rule – Regel
- scene – Szene
- signal word – Signalwort
- slogan – Slogan; Werbespruch
- speech bubble – Sprechblase
- story – Geschichte; Erzählung
- task – Aufgabe
- theme – Thema
- title – Titel; Überschrift
- unit – Lektion; Kapitel
- useful phrases – nützliche Ausdrücke
- vocabulary – Vokabular; Wortschatz
- word cloud – Wörterwolke

Irregular verbs

■■■ Grundform, *simple past* und *past participle* sind identisch
■●● Grundform unterscheidet sich vom *simple past* und *past participle*
■●■ Grundform und *past participle* sind identisch, nur das *simple past* hat eine andere Form
■●▲ Grundform, *simple past* und *past participle* haben alle eine andere Form

■ Grundform	■ simple past	■ past participle	Deutsch
cost [kɒst]	cost [kɒst]	cost [kɒst]	kosten
cut [kʌt]	cut [kʌt]	cut [kʌt]	schneiden
hit [hɪt]	hit [hɪt]	hit [hɪt]	schlagen, treffen
hurt [hɜːt]	hurt [hɜːt]	hurt [hɜːt]	verletzen, sich weh tun
let [let]	let [let]	let [let]	lassen
put [pʊt]	put [pʊt]	put [pʊt]	legen, setzen, stellen
set up ['set ˌʌp]	set up ['set ˌʌp]	set up ['set ˌʌp]	erbauen, errichten

■ Grundform	● simple past	● past participle	Deutsch
bring [brɪŋ]	brought [brɔːt]	brought [brɔːt]	(mit)bringen
build [bɪld]	built [bɪlt]	built [bɪlt]	bauen
buy [baɪ]	bought [bɔːt]	bought [bɔːt]	kaufen
feel [fiːl]	felt [felt]	felt [felt]	fühlen
find [faɪnd]	found [faʊnd]	found [faʊnd]	finden
get [get]	got [gɒt]	got [gɒt]	bekommen, erhalten
have [hæv]	had [hæd]	had [hæd]	haben
hear [hɪə]	heard [hɜːd]	heard [hɜːd]	hören
hold [həʊld]	held [held]	held [held]	halten
keep [kiːp]	kept [kept]	kept [kept]	(auf)bewahren, behalten
learn [lɜːn]	learned [lɜːnd] / learnt [lɜːnt]	learned [lɜːnd] / learnt [lɜːnt]	lernen
leave [liːv]	left [left]	left [left]	(ver)lassen
make [meɪk]	made [meɪd]	made [meɪd]	machen, tun
meet [miːt]	met [met]	met [met]	treffen
pay [peɪ]	paid [peɪd]	paid [peɪd]	(be)zahlen
read [riːd]	read [red]	read [red]	lesen
retell [ˌriː'tel]	retold [ˌriː'təʊld]	retold [ˌriː'təʊld]	nacherzählen
say [seɪ]	said [sed]	said [sed]	sagen
sell [sel]	sold [səʊld]	sold [səʊld]	verkaufen
send [send]	sent [sent]	sent [sent]	senden, verschicken
sit [sɪt]	sat [sæt]	sat [sæt]	sitzen
sleep [sliːp]	slept [slept]	slept [slept]	schlafen
spell [spel]	spelt [spelt]	spelt [spelt]	buchstabieren

spend [spend]	spent [spent]	spent [spent]	ausgeben, verbringen
stand (up) [stænd]	stood (up) [stʊd]	stood (up) [stʊd]	(auf)stehen
tell [tel]	told [təʊld]	told [təʊld]	erzählen
think [θɪŋk]	thought [θɔ:t]	thought [θɔ:t]	(nach)denken, glauben
understand [ˌʌndə'stænd]	understood [ˌʌndə'stʊd]	understood [ˌʌndə'stʊd]	verstehen
win [wɪn]	won [wʌn]	won [wʌn]	gewinnen, siegen

■ Grundform	● simple past	■ past participle	Deutsch
become [bɪ'kʌm]	became [bɪ'keɪm]	become [bɪ'kʌm]	werden
come [kʌm]	came [keɪm]	come [kʌm]	kommen
run [rʌn]	ran [ræn]	run [rʌn]	laufen, rennen

■ Grundform	● simple past	▲ past participle	Deutsch
be [bi:]	was / were [wɒz / wɜ:]	been [bi:n]	sein
blow (out) [bləʊ]	blew [blu:]	blown [bləʊn]	(aus)blasen, (aus)pusten
break [breɪk]	broke [brəʊk]	broken ['brəʊkn]	(zer)brechen, kaputt machen
choose [tʃu:z]	chose [tʃəʊz]	chosen [tʃəʊzn]	(aus)wählen
do [du:]	did [dɪd]	done [dʌn]	machen, tun
draw [drɔ:]	drew [dru:]	drawn [drɔ:n]	zeichnen
drink [drɪŋk]	drank [dræŋk]	drunk [drʌŋk]	trinken
eat [i:t]	ate [et]	eaten [i:tn]	essen
fall [fɔ:l]	fell [fel]	fallen ['fɔ:lən]	fallen
fly [flaɪ]	flew [flu:]	flown [fləʊn]	fliegen
forget [fə'get]	forgot [fə'gɒt]	forgotten [fə'gɒtn]	vergessen
give [gɪv]	gave [geɪv]	given['gɪvn]	geben
go [gəʊ]	went [went]	gone [gɒn]	gehen, fahren
know [nəʊ]	knew [nju:]	known [nəʊn]	kennen, wissen
see [si:]	saw [sɔ:]	seen [si:n]	sehen
show [ʃəʊ]	showed [ʃəʊd]	shown [ʃəʊn]	zeigen
sing [sɪŋ]	sang [sæŋ]	sung [sʌŋ]	singen
speak [spi:k]	spoke [spəʊk]	spoken ['spəʊkn]	sprechen
swim [swɪm]	swam [swæm]	swum [swʌm]	schwimmen
take [teɪk]	took [tʊk]	taken ['teɪkn]	nehmen
throw [θrəʊ]	threw [θru:]	thrown [θrəʊn]	werfen
wear [weə]	wore [wɔ:]	worn [wɔ:n]	anhaben, tragen
write [raɪt]	wrote [rəʊt]	written ['rɪtn]	schreiben

Check-out solutions

Unit 1 Page 29

Exercise 1

They talked about the 'dreams' page. / They put the sports pages together. / They looked at Jay's ideas for the music pages. / They collected ideas for the puzzles page. / They took a photo of the yearbook team. / They made a list of jobs for next week.

Exercise 2

1. went
2. was
3. wasn't
4. invited
5. did you go
6. did
7. were
8. was
9. was
10. didn't stay

Exercise 3

1. When did you get up this morning?
2. Where did you go?
3. What did you see?
4. Why did your classmates laugh at you?

Exercise 4

1. Luke's dog Sherlock is **the craziest** animal in England. There's nothing **funnier** than when he chases his tail. It's always **faster** than he is!
2. The **cutest** pets for Holly are her two guinea pigs. Mr Fluff likes to explore. He thinks a trip in a bag is **more interesting** than a game on the floor! Honey isn't **as brave as** Mr Fluff.
3. Cats are **the most popular** pets in the class. Dave's cat Sid brings presents for the family. Some presents are **better** than others. The **worst** thing for Dave is a mouse in his bed!

Unit 2 Page 51

Exercise 1

1. The Frasers are going to have a picnic. / The Frasers are going to go on a picnic.
2. Luke and Sherlock are going to play ball in the park. / Luke and Sherlock are going to play in the park.
3. Mr and Mrs Azad are going to visit / see / go to the Tower of London.
4. Holly is going to go (inline) skating. / Holly is going to have fun on her skates.
5. Amir is going to take (lots of) photos / pictures.
6. Shahid is going to meet someone / his girlfriend / a friend (somewhere).

Exercise 2

1. anybody
2. someone
3. everybody
4. something
5. somewhere
6. everything
7. anywhere
8. nothing

Exercise 3

Lösungsvorschlag:

You take the S1 to Filderstadt. You change at Hauptbahnhof and take the U7 to Ostfildern. It's seven stops to Ruhbank. You get off at Ruhbank. / You get off there. From Ruhbank you walk to the Fernsehturm for about 11 minutes.

Unit 3 Page 67

Exercise 1

1 c)
2 e)
3 b)
4 a)
5 f)
6 d)

Exercise 2

1. Luke: Have you found any information on the internet yet?
   Dave: Yes, I have. I've already used some (information) in the report.
2. Luke: Has Jay drawn any mangas for his report (yet)?
   Dave: Yes, he has. He has created great new characters.
3. Dave: Have you seen the two new manga comics yet?
   Luke: Yes, I have. I've already finished one of them.
4. Luke: Have you seen Olivia today?
   Dave: No, I haven't. But I've just sent her a text.
5. Dave: Has Holly written about guinea pigs?
   Luke: I hope not! She's written about guinea pigs many times before.
6. Dave: Have you gone to the park with Sherlock yet?
   Luke: No, I haven't. But Irina has just gone for a walk with him.

Exercise 3

I love football. I think it's the best **game** in the world! I **watch** every **match** of my favourite team, the Wellsey. Do you want to **see** my new poster of the best player ever, Adriano Donaldo? He scores lots of goals with his head because he's very **tall**. He even **got** the **highest** score of three head goals in one match. My dream is to **become** a football star like him.

Unit 4 Page 89

Exercise 1

1 e) When my dad wants to relax, he watches football on TV.
2 d) When I want to know the words of a song I've heard, I look it up on the internet.
3 b) When my mum works away from home, she sends me text messages.
4 a) When I want to tell all my friends how great my holiday is, I post it on my social network profile.
5 c) When my sister wants to know about the coolest new clothes, she reads girls' magazines.

Exercise 2

1. Lösungsvorschlag:
   A: I really hurt my foot. I hope it isn't broken. / I think it could be broken.
   B: Does it really hurt?
   A: Yes, it does.
   B: Well, you should go to the doctor's. / Why don't you go to the doctor's?
   A: Yes, maybe you're right.

2. Lösungsvorschlag:
   A: I can't believe I missed my favourite show last night!
   B: Well, you could watch it on the internet. / Why don't you watch it on the internet?
   A: The internet doesn't always have everything.
   B: Have you tried looking yet?
   A: Well, no.

3. Lösungsvorschlag:
   A: Oh no, something is wrong with my bike!
   B: What's the problem?
   A: I don't know.
   B: Have you tried looking on the internet yet? / Have you asked Mum and Dad / Ben / … for help?

4. Lösungsvorschlag:
   A: I can't believe she posted those photos – they're really embarrassing.
   B: Have you talked to her yet?
   A: Yes, I have. She doesn't think they're embarrassing. And she thinks she looks really good in them.
   B: Well, why don't you tell her to cut you off the photos?
   A: OK, that's a good idea.

5. Lösungsvorschlag:
   A: I can't use my phone for a week because my parents are really angry with me.
   B: Well, maybe you should tell them that you're sorry.
   A: I've already told them, but they still took my phone.
   B: Just use my phone when you need it.

Exercise 3

1. Das Handy meines Bruders ist sehr alt, ich glaube, er muss (sich) ein neues kaufen.
2. Er hat Glück, weil er nicht selbst dafür bezahlen muss – er hat in zwei Monaten Geburtstag.
3. Ich habe noch mehr Glück, weil ich nicht so lange zu warten brauche / nicht so lange warten muss. Ich kann das neue Smartphone meines Vaters haben!
4. Aber ich darf meinem Bruder nichts (davon) erzählen – er kann sehr eifersüchtig sein.

Unit 5 Page 107

Exercise 1

1. will be
2. will be
3. won't be
4. will be
5. will get
6. will be
7. won't rain
8. will be
9. will change
10. will move in
11. will start

Exercise 2

2. I have to work late today. – No problem. We'll cook dinner for you.
3. I didn't do my homework. – Too bad! Mum will say you can't play on your computer.
4. Hurry up! The train leaves in one hour. – Don't worry, it's not far to the station. We won't be late.
5. Let's book the train tickets now. Tomorrow they'll be more expensive.

Exercise 3

1. Jamie says **he knows** about the Celts from the Asterix stories. They're **his** favourite comics.
2. Irina tells me **I** must **take** some Celtic souvenirs! **She loves** everything Celtic.
3. My dad says Sherlock is really missing **me**! He must **come** with **me** next time.
4. Mum says / promises the whole family will go to Cornwall next year. **She's** going to make a list of places to visit when **I'm** back home.

Grammar solutions

Unit 1

G1 Two years ago we raised lots of money.

Dear Olivia,
Thank you for your e-mail and the photos. I like them a lot.
You **wanted** to know about our charity event. Well, last month we **organised** an event in the park and we **planned** lots of activities. First there **were** games for students, parents and teachers. After that we **sold** cakes. In the afternoon the students in Year 7 **did** some really cool tricks. And then it **was** the turn of the students in Year 8. They **created** a comedy show. The girls **wanted** to look funny so they **painted** their faces and **wore** some funny costumes too. In the evening the school band **sang** in the park – lots of people **came** to listen. Michael **was** the real star of their show. He **did** some cool moves!
We **raised** 400 euros in just one day!
Write soon.
Pia

G2 How did they know?

Lösungsvorschlag:
How old was he? – He was about twenty years old.
When did you see him? – I saw him at 10 o'clock.
Where did you see him? – I saw him in front of the sports shop in Trafalgar Road.
Did you see what he took from the shop? – Well, he had two bags full of T-shirts and shoes.
Was he alone? – Yes, he was.

G3 The police didn't know what the man looked like.

Man arrested
Greenwich. On 4th September a young man **broke into** a sports shop in Trafalgar Road. Yesterday the police **arrested** him. They **didn't know** what he **looked** like at first. But then they **got** an anonymous phone call. The caller **didn't give** them much information, but she **gave** them an address in Greenwich. When the police **got to** the house, two women **were** there but the man **wasn't**. So they **waited** till he **came** home and then they **arrested** him – he **didn't try** to run away. The police **found** the sports shoes and the T-shirts in the loft, but they **didn't find** the bike.

G4 An adventure course helps students to be more confident.

a) big – bigger – the biggest
bad – worse – the worst
happy – happier – the happiest
important – more important – the most important

b)
1. Luke is tall. Holly is taller. But Olivia is the tallest of the three.
2. The red car is expensive. The blue car is more expensive. But the black car is the most expensive of the three.
3. Hook Lane is a busy road. King's Street is busier. But London Road is the busiest of the three.
4. Luke has got a good idea. Holly's idea is better. But Dave has got the best idea of the three.

G5 Outdoor activities are as important as lessons in the classroom.

Lösungsvorschlag:
The Rhine is longer than the Spree/Oder.
The Spree is shorter than the Oder/Rhine.
Düsseldorf is as big as Stuttgart.
Cologne is bigger than Düsseldorf/Stuttgart.
The Feldberg is the highest mountain. It is higher than the Brocken/the Großer Arber.
The Großer Arber is about as high as the Feldberg.
The Saarland is the smallest state/region. It is smaller than Hesse/Saxony.
Hesse is bigger than Saxony.

Unit 2

G6 It's going to be fun.

Jay is going to go to Covent Garden. He's going to listen to the buskers there.
Amir is going to send / write a postcard home.
Olivia and Holly aren't going to see / visit Brick Lane with its street art / graffiti.
Shahid is going to go to a café with his girlfriend.
Mrs Azad isn't going to go shopping / to the supermarket.
Mr Azad is going to wash his car.

G7 It's something important.

Amir: Listen, **everybody**. I want to buy a little present for my aunt to say 'thank you'. Is there a good shop **anywhere**?
Olivia: What are you thinking of?
Amir: Well, it must be **something** special, but it mustn't be **anything** expensive.
Jay: **Everything** is expensive in London!
Holly: That's not true! I know a good shop where **nothing** costs more than £10.
Amir: OK. Let's go there and see if we can find **something** for her.

Unit 3

G8 Have you ever run in a marathon?

Lösungsvorschlag:
a)
1. Have you prepared for Sports Day yet?
2. Have you bought new sports shoes yet?
3. Have you already started eating healthy food?
4. Have you ever hurt your foot?
5. Have you found a name for your team yet?

b) 2. Have you bought new sports shoes yet?
   - No, I haven't. I don't need any new shoes. My old ones/ shoes are OK.
   - Yes, I have. I've just bought some new shoes. Look, they are in this bag.

3. Have you already started eating healthy food?
   - Yes, I have. I've already eaten two apples today.
4. Have you ever hurt your foot?
   - Yes, I have. I've hurt my leg twice/two times.
   - No, I haven't.
5. Have you found a name for your team yet?
   - Yes, I have. But I'm not going to tell you.
   - No, I haven't found a nice name yet.

Unit 4

G9 I'm writing to you because I need your advice.

Joe: I like your magazine **because** it's always got the interesting news on my favourite stars in it.
Ginny: I buy *TeenLife* **as soon as/when** I get my pocket money from my parents. I love it!
Michael: The concert photos are fantastic. When I look at them, it's **like** I'm there.
Lisa: **Whenever/When** I read Ruby's advice, I think she really understands our problems.
Sheila: **After** I tried the make-up in last week's magazine, I'm not going to buy *TeenLife* again! It looked awful on my face.

G10 I must fix it before your mum comes home.

You have to arrive early.
You needn't bring your own computer.
You must pay before the course starts.
You needn't / don't have to wear a uniform.
They can do fun things with computers.
Students can't / mustn't eat in computer room.
Students must / have to keep the computer room clean.

G11 You could look at a forum for help.

Lösungsvorschlag:

1. You should say sorry (to her). / You could ask if she needs help. / You should be more careful when you play netball.
2. You should tell Dave. / You could buy him a new book. / You could ask how much the book was and give him the money.
3. You shouldn't pull him out from under the bed. / You could put some food in front of the bed. / You could leave a gap between the bed and the wall. Then it's easier to pick him up.
4. You should say sorry (to her). / You could buy her new flowers for her garden. / Next time if you are not sure, you should ask her first.

Unit 5

G12 I'll miss you so much!

1. Olivia: I hope Dave **will love** his new school.
2. Holly: I'm sure the Prestons **will visit** Granny Rose and Aunt Frances in London soon.
3. Luke: I don't think the new home **will be** a problem for Sid. He **will make** new cat friends quickly. He **won't get bored**!
4. Gwen: I hope Dave **won't forget** us.

G13 He says the landscape in Cornwall is very wild.

Lou says (that) she loves climbing.
Tony tells me (that) his homework is difficult.
They say (that) they're winning that race.
Tony says (that) it's his iPod.

Bildquellennachweis:
U1.1 February Films (Andrew Kemp), London; **U1.2** Corbis (Marco Simoni/Robert Harding World Imagery), Berlin; **2ff** shutterstock.com (suicidecrew), New York, NY **2.1** February Films (Andrew Kemp), London; **2.2** February Films (Andrew Kemp), London; **2.3** February Films (Andrew Kemp), London; **3.1** February Films (Andrew Kemp), London; **3.2** February Films (Andrew Kemp), London; **3.3** February Films (Andrew Kemp), London; **4.1** February Films (Andrew Kemp), London; **4.2** iStockphoto (andrearoad), Calgary, Alberta; **4.3** February Films (Andrew Kemp), London; **5.1** February Films (Andrew Kemp), London; **5.2** Thinkstock (Salah Malkawi), München; **5.3** February Films (Andrew Kemp), London; **6.1** Fotolia.com (visoook), New York; **6.2** iStockphoto (MattStansfield), Calgary, Alberta; **6.3** February Films (Andrew Kemp), London; **7.1** February Films (Andrew Kemp), London; **7.2** Alamy Images (Melissa Gaskell), Abingdon, Oxon; **7.3** Alamy Images (Jeff Morgan 06), Abingdon, Oxon; **8.1** February Films (Elke Bock), London; **8.2** February Films (Andrew Kemp), London; **8.3** February Films (Andrew Kemp), London; **8.4** February Films (Andrew Kemp), London; **8.5** February Films (Andrew Kemp), London; **9.1** February Films (Andrew Kemp), London; **10.1** Thinkstock (Simon Greig), München; **10.2** Fotolia.com (matttilda), New York; **10.4** akg-images, Berlin; **10.5** shutterstock.com (S-BELOV), New York, NY; **11.1** February Films, London; **12.1** February Films (Andrew Kemp), London; **12.2** February Films (Andrew Kemp), London; **13.1** February Films (Andrew Kemp), London; **13.2** February Films (Andrew Kemp), London; **14.2** Getty Images (Stuart Wilson), München; **16.1** shutterstock.com (Studio 37), New York, NY; **20.1** Fotolia.com (Jakub Cejpek), New York; **20.2** Thinkstock (Ammit), München; **20.3** Dream Maker Software (RF), Colorado; **23.1** February Films (Andrew Kemp), London; **24.1** Hath, Jessica Alice, Freiburg; **25.1** shutterstock.com (granata1111), New York, NY; **25.2** February Films (Andrew Kemp), London; **26.1** Fotolia.com (evron.info), New York; **26.2** ddp images GmbH (Newscom/UPI), Hamburg; **26.3** Fotolia.com (toolklickit), New York; **28.1** February Films, London; **33.1** Getty Images (Blend Images), München; **34.1** Getty Images, München; **34.2** shutterstock.com (Bikeworldtravel), New York, NY; **34.3** shutterstock.com (Carsten Medom Madsen), New York, NY; **34.4** shutterstock.com (Francesco Carucci), New York, NY; **34.5** dreamstime.com (Emanuel Corso), Brentwood, TN; **34.6** Fotolia.com (geckospake), New York; **35.1** February Films, London; **36.1** February Films (Andrew Kemp), London; **37.1** iStockphoto (andrearoad), Calgary, Alberta; **37.2** laif (Polaris Images), Köln; **37.3** Corbis (Mike Kemp/In Pictures), Berlin; **37.4** February Films (Andrew Kemp), London; **40.1** February Films (Andrew Kemp), London; **40.2** February Films (Andrew Kemp), London; **40.3** February Films (Andrew Kemp), London; **40.4** February Films (Andrew Kemp), London; **40.5** February Films (Andrew Kemp), London; **40.6** February Films (Andrew Kemp), London; **42.1** Argus (Peter Frischmuth), Hamburg; **42.2** Corbis (Alison Wright), Berlin; **43.1** shutterstock.com (Arvydas Kniuksta), New York, NY; **43.2** shutterstock.com (Jacek Chabraszewski), New York, NY; **43.3** Fotolia.com (kateignatenko), New York; **43.4** BigStockPhoto.com (toxawww), Davis, CA; **43.5** Thinkstock (boggy22), München; **43.6** Thinkstock (Søren Sielemann), München; **44.1** February Films, London; **44.2** February Films, London; **46.1** Google Inc. (Kartendaten © 2014 Google), Mountain View, CA 94043; **48.1** Thinkstock (John Pavel), München; **51.1** shutterstock.com (Four Oaks), New York, NY; **51.2** February Films (Andrew Kemp), London; **51.4** February Films (Andrew Kemp), London; **51.5** dreamstime.com (Woo Bing Siew), Brentwood, TN; **51.6** February Films (Andrew Kemp), London; **54.1** Thinkstock (Salah Malkawi), München; **54.2** shutterstock.com (Bikeworldtravel), New York, NY; **54.3** Klett-Archiv (Thomas Weccard), Stuttgart; **54.4** shutterstock.com (Eoghan McNally), New York, NY; **55.1** Picture-Alliance (Uli Gasper), Frankfurt; **57.1** Hath, Jessica Alice, Freiburg; **58.1** February Films (Andrew Kemp), London; **58.2** February Films (Andrew Kemp), London; **60.1** February Films, London; **61.1** dreamstime.com (A1shutterbug), Brentwood, TN; **66.1** shutterstock.com (Michaelpuche), New York, NY; **67.1** February Films (Andrew Kemp), London; **70.1** Mauritius Images (Alamy), Mittenwald; **71.1** Alamy Images (David Robertson), Abingdon, Oxon; **72.1** February Films, London; **72.2** February Films, London; **73.1** Thinkstock (Ramon Purcell), München; **73.2** Ullstein Bild GmbH (ullstein - iT), Berlin; **74.1** February Films (Andrew Kemp), London; **75.1** Fotolia.com (visoook), New York; **75.2** Getty Images (Photodisc), München; **75.3** Thinkstock (Purestock), München; **75.4** February Films (Andrew Kemp), London; **76.1** iStockphoto (RF/Matt Ramos), Calgary, Alberta; **78.1** Imago, Berlin; **78.2** Picture-Alliance (PhotoAlto), Frankfurt; **82.1** February Films, London; **82.2** February Films, London; **82.3** February Films, London; **84.1** Getty Images (Photodisc), München; **88.1** www.CartoonStock.com (Cook, Gary), Bath; **89.1** Thinkstock (Elena Elisseeva), München; **92.1** Alamy Images (Melissa Gaskell), Abingdon, Oxon; **92.2** Alamy Images (Jeff Morgan 06), Abingdon, Oxon; **93.1** Alamy Images (Peter Horree), Abingdon, Oxon; **93.2** Thinkstock (versevend), München; **94.1** February Films (Andrew Kemp), London; **97.1** Klett-Archiv (Weccard), Stuttgart; **98.1** iStockphoto (MattStansfield), Calgary, Alberta; **99.1** Alamy Images (Kevin Britland), Abingdon, Oxon; **100.1** shutterstock.com (antb), New York, NY; **101.1** February Films, London; **102.1** iStockphoto (Deejpilot), Calgary, Alberta; **104.1** shutterstock.com (Helen Hotson), New York, NY; **106.1** Fotolia.com (acceleratorhams), New York; **107.1** shutterstock.com (Atlaspix), New York, NY; **111.1** Picture-Alliance (dpa/Armin Weigel), Frankfurt; **111.2** shutterstock.com (iurii), New York, NY; **111.3** Getty Images, München; **112.1** February Films, London; **112.2** February Films, London; **112.3** February Films, London; **114.1** dreamstime.com (Oleg Shipov), Brentwood, TN; **115.1** dreamstime.com (Ingrid Hogenbijl), Brentwood, TN; **115.2** Klett-Archiv (Simianer & Blühdorn), Stuttgart; **115.3** shutterstock.com (Michaelpuche), New York, NY; **115.4** shutterstock.com (criben), New York, NY; **121.1** Getty Images (Vetta), München; **122.1** Getty Images (Brand X Pictures), München; **129.1** iStockphoto (alexxx1981), Calgary, Alberta; **129.2** iStockphoto (archives), Calgary, Alberta; **135.1** shutterstock.com (Ferencz Teglas), New York, NY; **140.1** February Films, London; **140.2** February Films, London; **144.1** February Films (Andrew Kemp), London; **147.1** Thinkstock (RTimages), München; **148.1** February Films (Elke Bock), London; **152.1** Corbis (David Batterbury, Eye Ubiquitous), Berlin; **152.2** shutterstock.com (Orion-v),

New York, NY; **152.3** shutterstock.com, New York, NY; **152.4** iStockphoto (Kohlerphoto), Calgary, Alberta; **152.5** shutterstock.com, New York, NY; **152.6** iStockphoto (slobo mitic), Calgary, Alberta; **153.1** February Films (Andrew Kemp), London; **155.1** iStockphoto (Stephen Rees), Calgary, Alberta; **160.1** February Films (Andrew Kemp), London; **162.1** February Films (Andrew Kemp), London; **162.2** February Films (Andrew Kemp), London; **168.1** iStockphoto (craftvision), Calgary, Alberta; **175.1** dreamstime.com (Alenmax), Brentwood, TN; **177.1** shutterstock.com (Willyam Bradberry), New York, NY; **186.1** shutterstock.com (Monkey Business Images), New York, NY; **192.1** Fotolia.com (Jaroslaw Grudzinski), New York; **192.1** Fotolia.com (Jaroslaw Grudzinski), New York; **194.1** iStockphoto (Grafissimo), Calgary, Alberta; **194.2** Fotolia.com (micromonkey), New York; **198.1** Getty Images RF (Cultura/Juice Images), München; **241.1** February Films (Elke Bock), London; **256.1** Pulse Creative Limited - Transport for London, Heaton Mersey, Stockport;

Sollte es in einem Einzelfall nicht gelungen sein, den korrekten Rechteinhaber ausfindig zu machen, so werden berechtigte Ansprüche selbstverständlich im Rahmen der üblichen Regelungen abgegolten.

Text- und Liedquellen:

S. 30 From *Middle School: How I Got Lost in London* by James Patterson. Published by Random House Children's Publishers. Reprinted by permission of the Random House Group Ltd.; **S. 52** Excerpt from *The Copper Treasure* by Melvin Burgess, A & C Black Publishers Ltd, London, 1999/2002 © Melvin Burgess (adapted); **S. 59** Excerpt from the brochure *Erkennen – Bewerten – Handeln: Zur Gesundheit von Kindern und Jugendlichen in Deutschland*, Robert Koch-Institut, Bundeszentrale für gesundheitliche Aufklärung, p. 33, Berlin und Köln, 2008 © Robert Koch-Institut; **S. 68** „The Summer Table" from WONDER by R. J. Palacio, copyright © 2012 by R.J. Palacio. Reprinted by permission of R.J. Palacio and Alfred A. Knopf, an imprint of Random House Childrens's Books, a division of Random House LLC. All rights reserved; **S. 78** „Friends" Text: Armato, Antonina/Dione, Aura marie/James, Tim/Jost, David © Akashic Field Music/Antonina Songs/Good Songs Publishing A/S/ Universal/MCA Music Publishing GmbH, Berlin/Universal Music Publishing GmbH, Berlin/Rolf Budde Musikverlag GmbH, Berlin/Jost Music Publisching David Jost, Berlin; **S. 90** Excerpt from *Ratburger* by David Walliams, HarperCollins Children's Books, a division of HarperCollins Publishers Ltd, London, 2012 © David Walliams 2012 (adapted); **S. 100** From www.poetryarchive.org/poem/romans-britain, © Judith Nicholls; **S. 108** Excerpt from „A Harp on the Water" from *Welsh Legends and Folktales* by Gwyn Jones (ed.), Oxford University Press, 1955 (adapted); **S. 133** Excerpt from *Ratburger* by David Walliams, HarperCollins Children's Books, a division of HarperCollins Publishers Ltd, London, 2012 © David Walliams 2012 (adapted)

LONDON
0km
1km
CAMDEN TOWN
Camden Market
Regent's Park
Outer Circle
Albany Street
Hampstead Road
Park Road
Maida Vale
SHERLOCK HOLMES
Sherlock Holmes Museum
Madame Tussauds
Marylebone Road
Westway A40
Edgware Road
Gloucester Place
Baker Street
Wigmore Street
Oxford Street
Oxford Circus
Regent Street
Marble Arch
Bond Street
Piccadilly Circus
Notting Hill Carnival
NOTTING HILL
Bayswater Road
Hyde Park
Piccadilly
The Serpentine
Rotten Row
Green Park
Kensington Road
Buckingham Palace
National History Museum
Brompton Road
Sloane Street
Victoria Station
Heathrow Airport
Cromwell Road
Brompton Road
Wimbledon
Fulham Road
King's Road
Chelsea Embankment
Grosvenor Road

Highbury
King's Cross Station
St. Pancras Station
City Road
Gray's Inn Road
Old Street
Woburn Place
Farringdon Road
Great Eastern St.
Clerkenwell Road
City of London
Brick Lane
Bloomsbury St.
British Museum
High Holborn
London Wall
Charing Cross Road
Avenue
St. Paul's Cathedral
Covent Garden
Fleet Street
Tower of London
Millennium Bridge
Embankment
Strand
Blackfriars Bridge
Southwark Bridge
Waterloo Bridge
Victoria
Tate Modern
Trafalgar Square
London Eye
Southwark Street
Globe Theatre
The Shard
Tower Bridge
London Dungeon
SOUTHWARK
Borough High Street
Docklands
Horse Guards
Waterloo Station
Waterloo Road
Blackfriars Road
Thames Barrier
Houses of Parliament
Westminster Bridge
Abbey
River Thames
MINSTER
Lambeth Bridge
Millbank
Albert Embankment
Vauxhall Bridge
Mudchute Farm
Trinity Hospital
Thames
Swimming Pool (Arches Leisure Centre)
London
Cutty Sark
Playground
Greenwich
GREENWICH MARKET
Boating Lake
Vanbrugh Castle
Planetarium
Greenwich Station
Fan Museum
Royal Observatory
Deer Park
Tennis Court
Rose Garden
GREENWICH
Thomas Tallis School

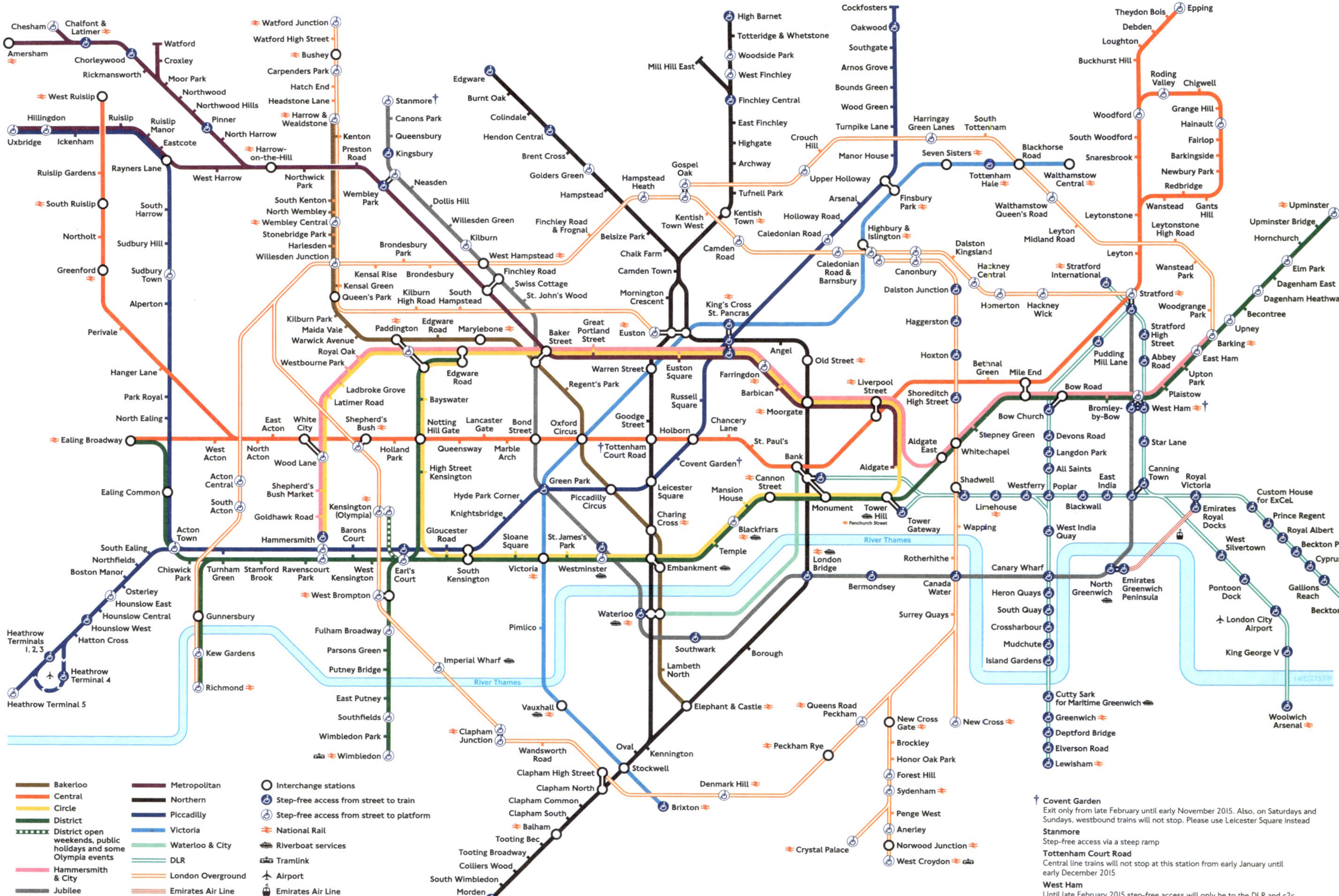

† **Covent Garden**
Exit only from late February until early November 2015. Also, on Saturdays and Sundays, westbound trains will not stop. Please use Leicester Square instead

Stanmore
Step-free access via a steep ramp

Tottenham Court Road
Central line trains will not stop at this station from early January until early December 2015

West Ham
Until late February 2015 step-free access will only be to the DLR and c2c

MAYOR OF LONDON

tfl.gov.uk

24 hour travel information
0343 222 1234*

*Service and network charges may apply. See tfl.gov.uk/terms for details.

Sign up for email updates
tfl.gov.uk/emailupdates

@TfLTravelAlerts

UNDERGROUND

TRANSPORT FOR LONDON
EVERY JOURNEY MATTERS

Reg. user No. 14/E/2757/P

Improvement works may affect your journey, please check before you travel

Version A TfL 12. 2014

Correct at time of going to print

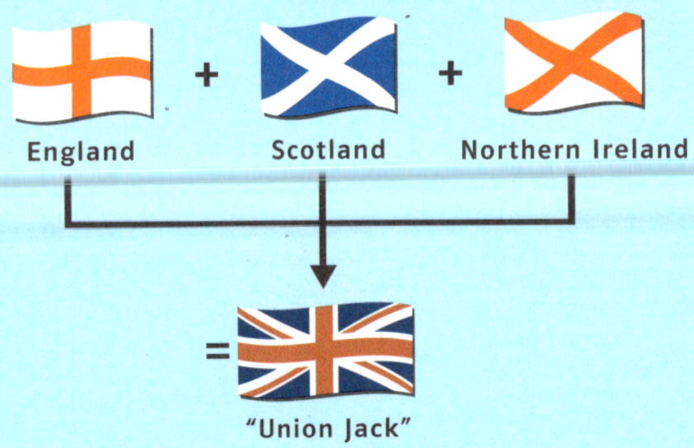
England
Scotland
Northern Ireland
"Union Jack"

Atlantic Ocean
Galway
REPUBLIC OF IRELAND
Cork